Politicians Don't Pander

Studies in Communication,

Media, and Public Opinion

A series edited by Susan Herbst

and Benjamin I. Page

Lawrence R. Jacobs and Robert Y. Shapiro

Politicians Don't Pander

Political Manipulation

and the Loss of

Democratic

Responsiveness

THE UNIVERSITY OF CHICAGO PRESS
CHICAGO AND LONDON

The University of Chicago Press, Chicago 60637
The University of Chicago Press, Ltd., London
© 2000 by The University of Chicago
All rights reserved. Published 2000
Printed in the United States of America
09 08 07 06 05 04 03 02   2 3 4 5

ISBN: 0-226-38982-0 (cloth)
ISBN: 0-226-38983-9 (paper)

Library of Congress Cataloging-in-Publication Data

Jacobs, Lawrence R.
    Politicians don't pander : political manipulation and the loss of democratic
responsiveness / Lawrence R. Jacobs, Robert Y. Shapiro.
        p.   cm.—(Studies in communication, media, and public opinion)
    Includes bibliographical references and index.
    ISBN 0-226-38982-0 (cloth : alk. paper)—ISBN 0-226-38983-9 (pbk : alk. paper)
    1. Political planning—United States. 2. Public opinion—United States.
3. Representative government and representation—United States. 4. Political
leadership—United States. 5. Politicians—United States. I. Shapiro, Robert Y.,
1953– II. Title. III. Series.

JK468.P64J36   2000
324'.0973—dc21

                                                                    99-086011

We dedicate this book to our inspirations:

Henry and Judy Jacobs
Irving and Norma Shapiro

In all life one should comfort the afflicted, but verily, also, one should afflict the comfortable, and especially when they are comfortably, contentedly, even happily wrong.
—*John Kenneth Galbraith*

With [Reagan], polls were not used to change policy to follow the prevailing winds. Instead, they were tools to determine how to persuade people about an idea.
—*Michael Deaver, senior aide to President Reagan*

[Legislators and the Clinton White House] don't use a poll to reshape a program, but to reshape your argumentation for the program so that the public supports it.
—*Dick Morris, pollster for President Clinton*

My first two years here, I was totally absorbed in getting legislation passed. I totally neglected how to get the public informed. It was my fault and I have to get more involved in crafting my message—in getting across my core concerns.
—*Bill Clinton*

The Administration's silence has created a news vacuum. The vacuum has been filled by opponents and by haphazard leaks. . . . Opinion makers who are or should be allies have not been made part of a crafted information flow. They have not been armed to validate the administration's definition of concepts. . . . The Press has not been part of a crafted information flow. It has been antagonized without purpose and is being forced to negatively review and translate the reform plan.
—*Democratic Senator Jay Rockefeller, in a confidential memo to Hillary Rodham Clinton dated 26 May 1993*

[T]hose political leaders who shirk the task of popular education are misfits who do not understand the responsibilities of their jobs. And those leaders who act as if they thought the people to be fools responsive only to the meanest appeals deserve only scorn.
—*V. O. Key Jr.*

Contents

Preface and Acknowledgments

The way Congress handled the impeachment of President Bill Clinton revealed a lot about American politics. Commentators and the American public were visibly struck by the unyielding drive of congressional Republicans to remove Clinton from office in the face of clear public opposition. The Republicans' disregard for the preferences of the great majority of Americans contradicted perhaps the most widely accepted presumption about politics—that politicians slavishly follow public opinion.

There was little ambiguity about where Americans stood on Clinton's personal behavior and impeachment. The avalanche of opinion polls during 1998 and early 1999 showed that super-majorities of nearly two-thirds of Americans condemned the president's personal misdeeds, but about the same number approved his job performance, opposed his impeachment and removal from office, and favored a legislative censure as an appropriate alternative punishment.

Despite Americans' strong and unchanging opinions, congressional Republicans defied the public at almost every turn. Beginning in the fall of 1998, the Republican-led House of Representatives initiated impeachment proceedings; its Judiciary Committee reported impeachment articles; and it passed two articles of impeachment on the House floor. Neither the House nor the Senate allowed a vote on the option supported by the public—censure. For all the civility in the Senate trial of the president on the House-passed articles of impeachment, the Republicans' pursuit of Clinton was checked not by a sudden attentiveness to public opinion but rather by the constitutional requirement of a two-thirds vote and the bipartisan support that this demanded.

The impeachment spectacle reveals one of the most important developments in contemporary American politics—the widening gulf between politicians' policy decisions and the preferences of the American people toward specific issues. The impeachment of Clinton can be added to the long list of policies that failed to mirror public opinion: campaign finance reform, tobacco legislation, Clinton's proposals in his first budget for an energy levy and a high tax on Social Security benefits (despite his campaign promises to cut middle-class taxes), the North American Free Trade Agreement (at its outset), U.S. intervention in Bosnia, as well as House Republican proposals after the 1994 elections for a "revolution" in policies toward the environment, education, Medicare, and other issues.

Recent research, which we review in chapter 1, provides evidence that this list is not a quirk of recent political developments but part of a trend of declining responsiveness to the public's policy preferences. The conventional wisdom that politicians habitually respond to public opinion when making major policy decisions is wrong.

While the impeachment crisis illustrated unresponsiveness to public opinion, it was also atypical in important respects. One of its most unusual features was the attention that journalists and political observers devoted to the decision of elected officials to ignore public opinion. Politicians' disregard for public opinion on other policy decisions was never an issue.

On impeachment, however, the press devoted generous coverage to Republicans' open discussion of their unresponsiveness and their insistence that they would "not listen to polls at all" (Bill McCollum quoted in Rosenbaum [1998]). Senator Rick Santorum spoke for many Republican legislators when he defiantly announced at the end of the Senate trial that "I don't accept that . . . we should simply do what the polls say" (quoted in Bruni [1999]). Standing for "principle," "constitutional duty," and the "rule of law" against the onrush of ill-guided public opinion was the defense that Republicans offered.[1]

The Republicans' unwavering decision to sail against public opinion and then to openly defend their undemocratic actions was just one aspect of the impeachment process that was atypical. Perhaps most surprising was that Republicans rebuffed public opinion on an extraordinarily salient issue that put at risk their ambitions to expand congressional majorities and capture the White House in the year 2000. Even after the disappointing results of the 1998 elections, when Republicans unexpectedly lost seats in the House and failed to widen their margin in the Senate, they persisted in pressing onward. What happened to politicians who were easily cowered by the threat of electoral retribution?

The Republicans' handling of impeachment fits into a larger pattern in contemporary American politics. This book examines the connections of politicians to public opinion and the impact of this relationship on the mass media and the public itself.

We use the cases of Clinton's health care reform campaign and Newt Gingrich's first Congress as House Speaker to make three points that are echoed in the impeachment episode. First, Republicans disregarded public opinion on impeachment because their political goals of attracting a majority of voters was offset by their policy goals of enacting legislation that politicians and their supporters favored. The ideological polarization of congressional Republicans and Democrats since the mid-1970s, the greater institutional independence of individual lawmakers, and other factors have raised the political benefits of pursuing policy goals that they and their party's activists desire. Responding to public opinion at the expense of policy goals entailed compromising their own philosophical convictions and risked alienating ideologically extreme party activists and other supporters who volunteer and contribute money to their primary and general election campaigns. Only the heat of an imminent presidential election and the elevated attention that average voters devote to it motivate contemporary politicians to respond to public opinion and absorb the costs of compromising their policy goals.

Indeed, the Republicans' relentless pursuit of impeachment was largely driven by the priority that the domineering conservative wing of the party attached to their policy goal (removing Clinton) over their political goals (appealing to a majority of Americans). Moderate Republicans could not ignore the risk of opposing impeachment—it could lead to a challenge in the next primary election and diminished campaign contributions.

Our second point is that politicians pursue a strategy of *crafted talk* to change public opinion in order to offset the potential political costs of not following the preferences of average voters. Politicians track public opinion not to make policy but rather to determine how to craft their public presentations and win public support for the policies they and their supporters favor. Politicians want the best of both worlds: to enact their preferred policies and to be reelected.

While politicians devote their resources to changing public opinion, their actual influence is a more complex story. Politicians themselves attempt to change public opinion not by directly persuading the public on the merits of their policy choices but by "priming" public opinion: they "stay on message" to highlight standards or considerations for the public to use in evaluating policy proposals. Republicans, for example, emphasized "big government" to prompt the public to think about its uneasiness about government. Politicians' efforts to sway the public are most likely to influence the perceptions, understandings, and evaluations of specific policy proposals such as Republican proposals in 1995 to significantly reduce spending on Medicare to fund a tax cut. But even here, politicians' messages promoting their policy proposals often provoke new or competing messages from their political opponents and the press that complicate or stymie their efforts to move public opinion. In addition, efforts to influence the public's evaluations of specific proposals are unlikely to affect people's values and fundamental preferences (such as those underlying support for Medicare, Social Security, and other well-established programs). We distinguish, then, between political leaders' attempts to alter the public's perceptions, evaluations, and choices concerning very specific proposals (which are susceptible but not certain to change) and Americans' values and long-term preferences (which tend to be stable and particularly resistant to short-term manipulation). In short, politicians' confidence in their ability to move public opinion by crafting their statements and actions boosts their willingness to discount majority opinion; but the reality is that efforts to change public opinion are difficult and are often most successful when deployed against major new policy proposals by the opposition, which has the more modest task of increasing the public's uncertainty and anxiety to avoid risk.

Politicians respond to public opinion, then, but in two quite different ways. In one, politicians assemble information on public opinion to design government policy. This is usually equated with "pandering," and this is most evident during the relatively short period when presidential elections are imminent. The use of public opinion research here, however, raises a troubling question: why has the derogatory term "pander" been pinned on politicians who respond to public opinion? The answer is revealing: the term is deliberately deployed by politicians, pundits, and other elites to belittle government responsiveness to public opinion and reflects a long-standing fear, uneasiness, and hostility among elites toward popular consent and influence over the affairs of government.[2] It is surely odd in a democracy to consider responsiveness to public opinion as disreputable. We challenge the stigmatizing use of the term "pandering" and adopt the neutral concept of "political responsiveness." We suggest that the public's preferences offer both broad directions to policymakers (e.g., establish universal health insurance) and some specific instructions (e.g., rely on an employer mandate for financing reform). In general, policymakers should follow these preferences.

Politicians respond to public opinion in a second manner—they use research on public opinion to pinpoint the most alluring words, symbols, and arguments in an attempt to move public opinion to support their desired policies. Public opinion research is used by politicians to manipulate public opinion, that is, to move Americans to "hold opinions that they would not hold if aware of the best available information and analysis" (Zaller 1992, 313). Their objective is to *simulate responsiveness.* Their words and presentations are crafted to change public opinion and create the *appearance* of responsiveness as they pursue their desired policy goals. Intent on lowering the potential electoral costs of subordinating voters' preferences to their policy goals, politicians use polls and focus groups not to move their positions closer to the public's but just the opposite: to find the most effective means *to move public opinion closer to their own desired policies.*

Political consultants as diverse as Republican pollster Frank Luntz and Clinton pollster Dick Morris readily confess that legislators and the White House "don't use a poll to reshape a program, but to reshape your argumentation for the program so that the public supports it" (quoted in Cannon 1998; Morris 1999). Indeed, Republicans' dogged pursuit of impeachment was premised on the assumption that poll-honed presentations would ultimately win public support for their actions. We suggest that this kind of overconfidence in the power of crafted talk to move public opinion explains the political overreaching and failure that was vividly displayed by Clinton's health reform effort during the 1993–94 period and the Republicans' campaign for their policy objectives beginning with their "Contract with America" during 1995–96. Crafted talk has been more effective in opposing rather than promoting policy initiatives partly because the news media represent and magnify disagreement but also because politicians' overconfidence in crafted talk has prompted them to promote policy goals that do not enjoy the support of most Americans or moderate legislators.

Our argument flips the widespread image of politicians as "pandering" to public opinion on its head. Public opinion is not propelling policy decisions as it did in the past. Instead, politicians' own policy goals are increasingly driving major policy decisions and public opinion research, which is used to identify the language, symbols, and arguments to "win" public support for their policy objectives. Responsiveness to public opinion and manipulation of public opinion are not mutually exclusive: politicians manipulate public opinion by tracking public thinking to select the actions and words that resonate with the public.

Our third point is that politicians' muted responsiveness to public opinion and crafting of their words and actions has a profound impact on the mass media and on public opinion itself. In contrast to others who emphasize the nearly unlimited independence and power of the mass media, we argue that press coverage of national politics has been driven by the polarization of politicians and their reliance on crafting their words and deeds. The press focuses on political conflict and strategy because these are visible and genuine features of contemporary American politics. The combination of politicians' staged displays and the media's scrutiny of the motives behind them produced public distrust and fear of major government reform efforts. We do not treat policymaking, media coverage, and public opinion as parts that can be studied one at a time; rather, we study their dynamic configurations and processes of interdependence. Democratic governance and the process of public communications are inseparably linked.

We do *not* claim that polls, focus groups, and other indicators of public opinion play no important role in the policymaking process. Information about public opinion does play a role in the making of symbolic decisions (such as the location of presidential vacations), minor policy decisions (Clinton's proposal before the 1996 election for school uniforms), and some important policy decisions (raising the minimum wage in the summer of 1996). Our main point is that the influence of public opinion on government policy is *less* than it has been in the past and certainly less than commonly assumed by political pundits and some scholars. In addition, public opinion research in American politics does play a critical role in how politicians and other elites craft their actions and statements to elicit public support. Finally, politicians are not shy about brandishing polls that support their positions in order to justify and promote them further.

This book is motivated by the central premise of representative democracy: popular sovereignty and the notion of government responsiveness in which the public's policy preferences point government officials in specific directions. The Declaration of Independence was animated by a demand for "consent of the governed," and the promise of popular control has inspired a long and, at times, violent struggle for the right to vote by all Americans, the full and equal right to freedom of speech and assembly, and other essential rights.

This book revisits the fundamental premise of representative democracy (popular sovereignty and government responsiveness) and asks, Does the American government respond to the broad public or to the interests and values of narrowly constituted groups committed to advancing their private policy agendas? On one side lies democratic accountability; on the other a closed and insular government that is ill-suited to address the wishes or wants of most citizens. When politicians persistently disregard the public's policy preferences, popular sovereignty and representative democracy are threatened.

Can we rely on competitive elections to fend off muted responsiveness to public opinion? After all, congressional Democrats suffered stunning setbacks in the 1994 elections following Clinton's campaign for an unpopular health care reform plan, and the Republicans' congressional majorities were reduced in the 1996 and 1998 elections after they pursued policies that defied strong public preferences. We argue that electoral punishment may not be enough to improve the public's influence on government: the responsiveness of national policymakers to what most Americans prefer has declined and remained low for almost two decades despite electoral setbacks to Democrats and Republicans. Politicians have worked hard to obscure their true positions and to distort the positions of their opponents, which makes it hard for the electorate to identify the policy positions of elected officials and to punish politicians for pursuing unpopular policies. In addition, most members of Congress today attach greater electoral importance to following the policy goals of party activists than responding to majority opinion. The bottom line is that most politicians are keenly motivated and amply skilled at evading electoral accountability for long periods. Their success has impaired our system of accountability and sullied the *quality* of citizenship by eroding public trust and fuelling the news media's increasing focus on political conflict and strategy rather than on the substantive issues raised by government policy.

Our analysis should not be confused, however, with naive populism. We recognize that the sheer complexity and scope of government decisions require elite initiative, at times without public guidance. And, on occasion, elites may need to defy ill-informed and unreasoned public opinion in defense of larger considerations and, instead, rely upon the public's post hoc evaluations of their actions and their arguments justifying their actions. Franklin Roosevelt's arming of merchant marines prior to the United States' entry into the Second World War and Richard Nixon's opening to China represent such cases.

What we see today in contemporary American politics, however, far exceeds responsible leadership in a representative democracy. What concerns us are indications of declining responsiveness to public opinion and the growing list of policies on which politicians of both major political parties ignore public opinion and supply no explicit justification for it. The practice of American government is drifting from the norms of democratic responsiveness.

This book is intended for a wide audience. Chapters 1 and 2 situate our claims about the responsiveness of politicians to public opinion in the context of debates among academic scholars. Two long-standing explanations for the motivations of politicians predict contradictory behavior. One account expects competition for the median voter to motivate parties and politicians to respond to public opinion; the other predicts that politicians will engage in "strategic shirking" to pursue policy goals favored by themselves and their partisan and interest group supporters. We argue that changes in political and institutional conditions since the 1970s have elevated the importance attached to policy goals above that of majority opinion; only the threat of imminent elections produces a temporary rise in responsiveness to public opinion. The shift of politicians toward pursuing their policy goals and crafting their public stances to lower its potential political damage has contributed to changes in press coverage of politics and public opinion.

Chapters 3 through 8 examine in-depth policy debates during the 1990s. Readers uninterested in the contending claims of scholars in the first two chapters may wish to skip ahead to these sections.

Chapters 3 and 4 examine the debates that occurred within the Clinton administration and Congress over health care reform in 1993 and 1994. Here we argue that policymakers were driven by ideology, personal preferences, and political calculations about the demands of their allies. Contrary to popular belief, public opinion did not drive their policy decisions. Rather, the White House and party leaders in Congress tracked public opinion in order to carefully craft their preferred policy options in order to win (rather than follow) public opinion.

Chapters 5 and 6 examine press coverage of health care issues since the mid-1970s. Over the course of nearly two decades, the volume and content of press coverage reflected policy debates and the growing polarization among authoritative government officials in Washington. Although the media represented these genuine changes in health policy debates, they also magnified the political conflict.

Chapter 7 examines the public's reaction to the health care reform debate and, specifically, the roughly 20 percentage point decline in public support for the Clinton plan between September 1993 and the following summer. The decline resulted from polarized policy debates and the press's coverage of them, which produced a shift in public opinion from collective considerations to uncertainty and fears about personal self-interest.

Public opinion is equated by many contemporary policymakers, journalists, and scholars with the adding up of the preferences of disparate individuals and with its measurement by public opinion surveys. (For the historic evolution of the concept, see Gunn 1995.) This concept of public opinion also obscures the communal process that shapes it; its measurement by surveys also obscures some of the complexity and thoughtfulness of public thinking (Blumer 1948; Herbst 1993). For example, pollsters' probes of whether respondents "favor or oppose" Clinton's health plan corresponded with the terrain of the political battlefield (they rarely asked about support for the unpassable single-payer plan), but these survey questions reduced Americans' complex cluster of attitudes to a thumbs-up or thumbs-down choice. Despite these limitations, survey results provide a means to investigate the mass public's reasoning, complex motivations (from collective considerations to more narrow self-interest), and multiple and competing tendencies.

Chapter 8 shows that the dynamics of Clinton's health reform crusade also defined Gingrich's drive to spark a revolution in American social policy. What we found for 1993–94 continued in the quite different political context of 1995–96.

Chapter 9 turns to the larger normative issues of whether elected officials should respond to public opinion or pursue their own preferences and judgments. We suggest that the decline in responsiveness and the rise of fierce partisan conflict and opinion manipulation have reduced the effectiveness of the governing process and the public's confidence in it. Rather than accepting the false choice between responsiveness and independent leadership, we propose that each has an important place in a process in which politicians generally respond to strong, sustained public preferences. We conclude in chapter 10 by proposing several changes aimed at raising the costs of discounting public opinion and making sustained responsiveness more politically attractive.

This book was the product of a great many conversations in many different contexts—from policy debates in Washington to scholarly discussions in academic forums. We gratefully acknowledge those who have offered valuable written comments on drafts of our book or parts of it: Larry Buell, Charles Cameron, Brandice Canes-Wrone, Mary Dietz, Doug Dion, Bob Erikson, Judy Feder, Morris Fiorina, Virginia Gray, former Congressman Bill Green, Hugh Heclo, Ira Katznelson, Alan Kay, Mark Lindeman, Tom Mann, Mark Peterson, Richard Pious, Paul Quirk, Julie Schumacher, Theda Skocpol, Steven Smith, and Margaret Weir.

For valuable conversations and advice we are indebted to Steven Ansolabehere, Doug Arnold, Charles Backstrom, John Barry, Larry Bartels, Eric Black, Robert Blendon, Karlyn Bowman, Larry Brown, Joe Cappella, Jim Caraley, Karen Donelan, Bud Duvall, Margarita Estevez-Abe, David Fan, Steve Farkas, John Ferejohn, William Flanigan, Tom Ferguson, Kathy Frankovic, Grace R. Freedman, Ester Fuchs, Andrew Gelman, John Geer, Mark Goldberg, Greg Haley, Tom Hamburger, Jennifer Hochschild, Bob Holt, Kathleen Hall Jamieson, Michael Kagay, Daniel Kelliher, Jeffery Koch, Andy Kohut, Joel Krieger, Sam Krislov, Paul Light, Taeku Lee, Cathie Jo Martin, David Mayhew, Nolan McCarty, John Michel, Marilyn Milliken, Jim Morone, Paul Peterson, Richard Price, Wendy Rahn, Len Robbins, Britt Robson, Howard Rosenthal, Mark Schlesinger, Phil Shively, Kathryn Sikkink, Gordon Silverstein, Tom Smith (Director NORC-General Social Survey), Paul Sniderman, Frank Sorauf, Laura Stoker, John Sullivan, Humphrey Taylor, Lois Timms-Ferrara, Kent Weaver, Harrison White (Director of the Paul F. Lazarsfeld Center), David Wilber, John Young, Frank Zinni, Sara Zuckerbraun, and participants in the Robert Wood Johnson Investigator Award program and Russell Sage Social Policy project. The Roper Center for Public Opinion Research provided critical aid in collecting public opinion surveys. The National Academy of Social Insurance, its Director Pam Larson, and its skilled staff provided (for Jacobs) a stimulating environment for discussing the connections of social policy, American politics, and applied research.

Eric Ostermeier and Greg Shaw provided, in particular, indispensable research assistance and counsel that was far above and beyond the call of duty.

We acknowledge the assistance and collaboration of Jennifer Bag-

gette, Debi Gilchrest, Kristen Hammerback, Lynn Harvey, Ron Hinckley, Angela Hernandez, Marianne Ide, John Lapinski, Eric Lawrence,
Aida Llabaly, Shmuel Lock, Harpreet Mahajan, Brigitte Nacos, Ryan
Nagle, Claudia O'Grady, Charlie Riemann, Eli Schulman, Matt Ste-
vens, Mark Watts, Wynne Pomeroy Waller, Renee Wilson, Alan Yang,
and Michael Zis.

Lisa Disch, Susan Herbst, Ted Marmor, and Ben Page generously
commented on several versions of the book and engaged us in a running debate on its central arguments and its relevance to contemporary
policy debates.

We are especially indebted to the government officials and informal
advisers associated with the Clinton administration and Congress who
took time from their frenetic days to talk with us, often off the record.
This is our tribute to their candor and generosity with their time.

The Robert Wood Johnson Foundation is a paragon of a supportive
foundation; it devotes itself to carefully deciding on grants and then
offers full autonomy and generous intellectual support to its grantees.
Its Investigator Award to us sparked this project. The Association for
Health Services Research, which administers the Investigator Award,
offered a steady diet of nourishing conferences and encouraging words.
We particularly thank Barbara Krimgold and Alvin Tarlov.

The Russell Sage Foundation supported the research that is incorporated in Chapter 8 and funded a stimulating series of conferences
on social policy during the first Clinton administration. A McKnight-
Land Grant Professorship (to Jacobs) started our early thinking about
the interactions of public opinion, media coverage, and government
policy. A Goldsmith Research Award (to Shapiro) from the Joan Shor-
enstein Barone Center on the Press, Politics and Public Policy at the
John F. Kennedy School at Harvard University spurred our research
on the media's coverage of presidents. Later support from the Pew
Charitable Trusts has enabled us to think further about the implications of our study for public deliberation, democracy, and public
policy. Our work was conducted at the University of Minnesota and
at Columbia University's Paul F. Lazarsfeld Center for the Social
Sciences (now part of the Institute for Social and Economic Theory
and Research). We alone, however, are responsible for the contents
and arguments of this book.

We are grateful to the University of Chicago Press. Ben Page and
Susan Herbst continued their penetrating comments, sage advice, and
unwavering encouragement. John Tryneski and Randy Petilos guided
it firmly but smoothly through the publication process.

We are most indebted to our spouses, Mary De Florio and Julie Schumacher, and to Larry Jacobs' daughters, Emma Lillian Jacobs and Isabella Nan Jacobs. They have endured the drain on our time and our attention in the most personal terms and we thank them most of all.

We dedicate this book to our parents, Henry and Judy Jacobs and Irving and Norma Shapiro. Their concern about improving the world they brought us into remains a guiding inspiration.

Lawrence R. Jacobs   Robert Y. Shapiro
St. Paul, Minnesota   New York, New York

January 2000

Part One

Political Motivations, the Public, and the Media

Chapter One

The Myth of Pandering and Theories of Political Motivation

P|ublic opinion polls are everywhere. The media report them without stop and political activists of all kinds—from candidates in election contests to political parties and interest groups—pump millions into focus groups and polls. The flood of polls has fueled the nearly unquestioned assumption among observers of American politics that elected officials "pander" to public opinion. Politicians, it is charged, tailor their significant policy decisions to polls and other indicators of public opinion. Elected officials are faced with the terrifying choice of pandering or perishing in the next election and—as a 1997 article in the *Atlantic Monthly* exclaimed—are "running scared" and are settling for "poll readership" (A. King 1997; Penny 1994; Lewis 1993; Safire 1996). The *New Yorker* nostalgically wished for the golden years of "the silent majority" as it bemoaned the current era in which "what 'the American people' think trumps." Political commentators and policymakers lament that the politicians who do exercise independence from public opinion are not reelected or drop out, and the officeholders who remain have stopped "deciding, and saying, what they themselves think" in their zeal to anticipate the reaction of future voters (Hertzberg 1998). The enormous cost of "mass participatory democracy" is the abdication of responsible leadership that promotes the national interest, and the abandonment—as *New York Times* columnist Anthony Lewis put it—of "the Framers' constitutional design for a more reflective, more considered form of government" (Lewis 1993).

Bill Clinton is often singled out as exemplifying the kind of politician who "rel[ies] too heavily on polling information," "follows them

slavishly," and allows "decisions [to be] simply driven by polls."[1] Journalists (including *New York Times* columnist Maureen Dowd) seized on
Clinton's high profile relationship with his pollster, Dick Morris, as
"demonstrat[ing] that polling has turned leaders into followers" (Dowd
1997).

The idea that politicians succumb to public opinion has been accepted not only by the press and political elites but also by some scholars (Quirk and Hinchliffe 1998; Geer 1996). While research (including
our own) over the years has found evidence of government responsiveness, perhaps the strongest recent claim that politicians incessantly
follow public opinion comes from the work of James Stimson, Michael
MacKuen, and Robert Erikson,[2] who tracked the decisions of American government on domestic affairs (e.g., legislation enacted by Congress) since the 1950s and constructed global measures of liberalism
and conservatism for each year. The researchers then asked: Did
changes in government policy in a liberal or conservative direction
correspond to changes in public support for more or less government? They found that government policy followed public opinion as
it moved in a liberal direction in the 1960s, in a conservative direction
around 1980, and then back toward a liberal course in the late 1980s.
They concluded that politicians behave "[l]ike antelopes in an open
field": "When politicians perceive public opinion change, they adapt
their behavior to please their constituency" (Stimson, MacKuen, and
Erikson 1995, 545, 559).

Despite the strong claims of this account, there is much more to the
story. A growing body of evidence suggests that since the 1970s the
policy decisions of presidents and members of Congress have become
less responsive to the substantive policy preferences of the average
American.[3] Alan Monroe's (1998) research shows that government
policies in the 1980–93 period were less consistent with the preferences
of a *majority* of Americans than during 1960–79. He found that the
consistency of government policies with majority public preferences
on over five hundred issues declined from 63 percent in the period
1960–79 to 55 percent in 1980–93.[4]

Monroe's study is partly confirmed by our own preliminary study.
We compared changes in public preferences toward social policies and
congruent changes in government policy and found a noticeable decline in correspondence in opinion and policy changes during the
1980s and especially the 1990s than found during earlier periods (Jacobs and Shapiro 1997a; Page and Shapiro 1983).[5]

Another important study by Ansolabehere, Snyder, and Stewart

(1998a) examined the responsiveness of members of the House of Rep-resentatives between 1874 and 1996. They used the Republican share of the presidential two-party vote within each congressional district as an indicator of constituency opinions, and compared it to the ideologi-cal position of each party's candidates for the House of Representa-tives. They found that the candidates' ideological responsiveness to opinion within their district was weak prior to the 1930s, steadily rose between 1934 and its peak in the early 1970s, then declined into the 1990s (precipitously among Republican candidates).

A growing body of research suggests, then, that policymakers' re-sponsiveness to public opinion is complex and defies classification into the polar extremes of either persistent responsiveness (Downs 1957) or incessant unresponsiveness to public opinion (Ginsberg 1986). The challenge is to explain *variation over time* in the responsiveness of policymakers to public preferences. Evidence that contemporary pol-iticians follow public opinion less than their predecessors fits into a longer historical pattern of variation in responsiveness. One study found that responsiveness has waxed and waned over the course of 120 years (Ansolabehere, Snyder, and Stewart 1998a). Still another study reported that the correspondence between changes of public prefer-ences and subsequent changes in government policy varied noticeably between the 1930s and 1980. The incidence of changes in policy paral-leling changes in public opinion declined from 67 percent during the 1935–45 period (heavily dominated by wartime issues) to 54 percent during the 1960s, and then increased to 75 percent during the 1970s (Shapiro 1982; Page and Shapiro 1983).

The general decline in responsiveness of politicians since the 1970s is connected, we will argue, to two of the most widely debated and worrisome trends in American politics: the mass media's preoccupa-tion with political conflict and strategy, and the record proportion of Americans who distrust politicians—convinced that they no longer lis-ten to them.

The relationship between the policy decisions that politicians make and the policy preferences of ordinary citizens raises three fundamen-tal questions about American politics. First, why does responsiveness vary over time? Investigating long-term variations of responsiveness is complicated by shorter-term fluctuations. For instance, as the presi-dential election approached in the summer of 1996, congressional Re-publicans and Clinton briefly replaced partisan gridlock with a brief period of working together to pass legislation that had strong public support, such as the minimum wage law, the Kennedy-Kassebaum reform of private health insurance operations, and, arguably, welfare reform. What, then, would explain the pattern since the 1970s of a long-term decline in responsiveness interrupted by short-term rises in responsiveness that appeared tied to the electoral cycle?

Second, is there a causal connection between politicians' responsiveness to public opinion and other trends in American politics? In particular, to what extent has politicians' detachment from public opinion affected the media and public opinion itself?

Third, does representative democracy require a high level of responsiveness? Or does it require that politicians discount current public opinion in order to act in the best interests of citizens?

This chapter and the next develop a general explanation for the variation in politicians' responsiveness and how their behavior and strategies have affected the media and public opinion. In subsequent chapters, we present a large body of supportive evidence. The concluding chapters turn to the normative question of whether responsiveness is an essential feature of representative democracy.

Explaining how and why responsiveness to public opinion varies requires understanding the motivations of presidents and legislators. This chapter examines two long-standing but competing explanations for the motivations of politicians. The first account consists of "median voter" theory and the retrospective voting model and emphasizes the personal benefits politicians expect from pursuing policies favored by most voters—what we will refer to as "centrist" opinion. (We use the term "centrist opinion" to refer to the median voter or citizen in the distribution of public opinion and not to an ideologically fixed "left" or "right.") These accounts explain why many political observers assume that politicians are highly responsive. This "strong responsiveness" perspective directly connects competitive elections to the policymaking process, but it is hard-pressed to explain any general increase or decrease in responsiveness. Further, it underestimates strategic behavior by elites to attempt to change (and not simply accept) centrist opinion.

The second explanation predicts that politicians will pursue their own policy goals and those of their partisan supporters, interest groups, or other policymakers in government. This policy-oriented account challenges the widespread presumption among political observers that public opinion persistently drives policy decisions; instead, it suggests that these decisions are driven whenever politically possible by the policy objectives of politicians and their supporters. Presidents and legislators attempt to minimize the electoral risk of pursuing their policy goals by developing strategies to shield their decisions from the scrutiny of voters. This account alone, however, cannot explain politicians' comparatively high responsiveness to public opinion in the past and during election periods.

The strong responsiveness model and the policy-oriented accounts share two limitations. First, neither account explains the *variation* in politicians' responsiveness—its decline over the past two decades and its short-term rise and fall during election cycles. We need a theory of political motivations to explain the changing weight that politicians assign to following centrist opinion. Second, both accounts treat politicians' motivations as largely divorced from media coverage and the dynamics of public opinion, neglecting the interrelationships among the three.[6] The decisions of politicians to follow centrist opinion or to pursue their policy goals affect both the media's coverage of politics and public opinion and, in turn, the decisions of politicians are affected by the behavior of the media and public opinion.

We offer in chapter 2 an alternative account of politicians' motivations that both synthesizes the strong responsiveness and policy-oriented accounts and incorporates media coverage and public opinion. We argue that the motivations of politicians are dynamic and conditional on political and institutional developments. A number of factors including the increase since the early 1970s of the institutional independence of government officials and, most importantly, ideological polarization within Washington and among congressional districts have elevated the perceived benefits to politicians of pursuing the policy goals that they and their narrow group of supporters favor. Compromising policy goals in favor of centrist national opinion has become more costly to politicians since the 1970s. The approach of elections, however, still raises (over the short-term) the costs to politicians of discounting centrist opinion, thereby temporarily creating incentives to heed public opinion.

Politicians' perceptions of the costs and benefits of their behavior affect their strategy. The priority they attach to policy goals has prompted politicians to attempt to lower the potential electoral costs of discounting centrist opinion by *crafting* their arguments and rhetoric. Presidents and legislators carefully track public opinion in order to identify the words, arguments, and symbols that are most likely to be effective in attracting favorable press coverage and ultimately "winning" public support for their desired policies. Politicians' attempts to change public sentiment toward their favored position convinces them that they can pursue their policy objectives while minimizing the risks of electoral punishment. The irony of contemporary politics is that politicians both slavishly track public opinion and, contrary to the myth of "pandering," studiously avoid simply conforming policy to what the public wants.

We argue that politicians' pursuits of policy goals have created a reinforcing spiral or cycle that encompasses media coverage and public opinion. It is characterized by three features. First, the polarization of Washington political elites and their strategies to manipulate the media and gain public support have prompted the press to increasingly emphasize or frame its coverage in terms of political conflict and strategy at the expense of the substance of policy issues and problems. Although news reports largely represent the genuine contours of American politics, the media's organizational, financial, and professional incentives prompt them to exaggerate the degree of conflict in order to produce simple, captivating stories for their audiences.

Second, the increased political polarization and politicians' strategy of crafting what they say and do (as conveyed through press coverage) raise the probability of both changes in public understandings and evaluations of specific policy proposals, and public perceptions that proposals for policy change make uncertain or threaten the personal well-being of individual Americans. The presence of a vocal political opposition, combined with the media's attentiveness to the ensuing conflict and the public's skittishness about change, often prevents reformers from changing public opinion as they intended.

Third, the cycle closes as the media's coverage and the public's reaction that was initially sparked by politicians' actions feed back into the political arena. How politicians appraise the media's coverage of their initial actions affects their future strategy and behavior. Politicians latch on to any evidence of changes in public opinion that are favorable to their positions in order to justify their policies and to increase the electoral risk of their rivals for opposing them.

Our explanation for the variations in responsiveness to public opinion draws on existing research as well as an in-depth analysis of two dramatic episodes in national policymaking: Clinton's health care reform campaign during 1993 and 1994 and the Republican "Revolution" led by House Speaker Newt Gingrich in 1995–96. Clinton and then the Gingrich Congress proposed sweeping legislation based on the policy goals that they and their relatively narrow group of core supporters favored. Most Americans, however, opposed or were, at best, ambivalent toward their specific initiatives. As the 1996 presidential elections approached, however, congressional Republicans and Clinton shifted gears for a very brief period to work together to pass legislation that the public strongly supported.

Our investigation of these cases (and especially the Clinton episode) is based on a variety of in-depth evidence (including interviews with congressional and administration officials, content analysis of Clinton's statements, and detailed legislative histories) that offers an "insider" perspective on the intentions, perceptions, and decisions of elected officeholders and their staffs;[7] extensive content analysis of media coverage over a nearly two-decade period; and quantitative analysis of data from national public opinion surveys.

We are especially interested in the *collective responsiveness* of an institution like Congress or the national government as a whole to *national* public opinion.[8] (We discuss research on political representation in appendix 1.) These cases are moderately difficult tests of national policymakers' responsiveness to centrist opinion. The characteristics of the Gingrich and, especially, the Clinton health reform cases—high salience, social welfare issues, and high levels of public support for policy positions—make them likely candidates for responsiveness by policymakers.[9]

We use the Clinton and Gingrich cases of major policy innovation to generate research questions, theoretical arguments, and empirically grounded explanations for the interconnections of politicians, journalists, and public opinion. We are especially interested in investigating the mechanisms that produced the decline in responsiveness, and in breaking into the "black box" of policymaking, democratic linkages between government officials and citizens, and the process of public communications about politics. We ground the study of policymaking in the study of the press and public opinion: the institutions and practices of public communications reflect and shape the links between politicians and the mass public. Future research can examine further these issues for a wider set of cases in domestic and foreign affairs, using different methodologies.

In the next section, we examine further the contrasting interpretations of political motivations offered by the strong responsiveness theory and the policy-oriented account. In chapter 2, we distinguish our conditional model of political motivation from the prevailing accounts and discuss the interconnections of politicians' behavior, the media, and public opinion.

What Motivates Politicians

Theoretical and empirical analysis of the motivations of politicians has led to the conclusion that legislators and presidents value two goals most: enacting their desired policies and securing their reelection or that of their party by responding to centrist public opinion when making policy (Smith and Deering 1990; Bianco 1994, 36–37, 71, and chap. 4; Cohen 1997, chap. 1).[10] Richard Fenno's (1973) landmark study established, for instance, that two of the basic goals that motivate House members are making "good public policy" and reelection. While Fenno argued that exercising influence within the House of Representatives was a third goal, most subsequent analysis posits policy and electoral goals as predominant (Smith and Deering 1990).

Most career politicians prefer issues that allow them to improve their opportunities for reelection while also pursuing their policy goals. Indeed, many find that their reelection and policy goals overlap on some issues; their preferred policies are also favored by those who elect them. In addition, political leaders attempt to avoid public decisions that force themselves or their partisans into uncomfortable tradeoffs by attempting to control the agenda of decision making.

Most politicians, however, are not able to restrict their choices to issues that require little sacrifice of either policy or political goals. Actions by presidents, legislators, and other political activists force government decisions—often on salient issues that divide the political parties—that confront politicians with a choice between their electoral and policy goals. Modern presidents, for instance, often find themselves in a "no win" situation of attempting to satisfy the expectations of both mass public opinion and a narrower group of supporters in their political parties and Washington (Cronin 1980; Rockman 1984; Edwards 1983; Lowi 1985). Legislators are similarly confronted with balancing their own policy preferences against the preferences of those who elected them (Bianco 1994, 36–37, 71, and chap. 4). The result is that politicians often make tradeoffs among their goals, sacrificing one goal in order to achieve another more highly valued one.

Most presidents and members of Congress are not singularly committed either to their policy or electoral goals. The normal tactical problem facing politicians, then, is to adopt positions that fall between their own policy preferences and the preferences of centrist opinion (Stimson, MacKuen, and Erikson 1994, 31).

The tactical adjustments that politicians make between advancing their electoral ambitions and their desired policies reflect in large part their perceptions of the costs and benefits associated with each goal. Their policy positions and actual decisions or votes on specific legislation reflect the tradeoff of the personal benefits of pursuing policy goals versus the anticipated electoral costs of discounting centrist opinion. But compromising policy goals can also be costly; these costs may be sufficiently high to persuade even vulnerable politicians to support policies opposed by centrist opinion. For instance, vulnerable House Republicans voted to defy the preferences of large majorities of Americans and impeach Clinton because they anticipated that failure to support the party's policy goal would be punished by their core supporters and allies—they would suffer a drop in campaign contributions, increased support among party activists for a primary challenger, and the antipathy of their colleagues and party leaders. The political price of bucking their party's goals was high and close to certain; the ultimate electoral costs of defying centrist opinion were less clear given the nearly two years until the next election and the likelihood that most voters would move on to other matters and would be less concerned about impeachment when they cast their ballot in the next election.

The efforts of politicians to weigh the costs and benefits of policy and electoral goals are most significantly influenced by their constituents, but constituents do not provide a clear and uniform signal to politicians about which goal to favor. Presidents and legislators are most strongly concerned with two sets of constituents: the narrow group of loyal partisans who are necessary to win primary contests, and the broader group of "swing" voters who move between the parties and are often necessary to win the general election (Fenno 1978; Fiorina 1974; Mayhew 1974a, 45; Wayne 1997; Cohen 1997, 20–22). Politicians often find it difficult to reconcile the intense preferences of the narrow group of loyal party activists and the more centrist views of the general electorate on salient issues.

Despite the political importance of constituents, politicians are uncertain about the costs and benefits of policy decisions regarding their various constituents and how their constituents will react to legislation after it is implemented. The modern presidency and its administrative divisions, such as the Office of Management and Budget, developed in order to increase the executive branch's information and analytic capacity and to enable presidents to pursue effectively their various political objectives (Moe 1985; Greenstein 1988; Ragsdale and Theis 1997; Burke 1949). In reaction to the development of the presidency and to address their own institutional needs, Congress designed rules and procedures that provided incentives for members to acquire policy expertise and to widely distribute detailed, accurate information to otherwise ill-informed colleagues (Krehbiel 1991). Improved policy expertise enhanced the capacity of legislators and presidents to anticipate the consequences of their policy decisions but did not determine whether this capacity was used to pursue electoral or policy goals: policy expertise may be used to identify the most effective avenue to achieve policy goals or to lower uncertainty about what legislation would appeal to the most voters.

Obviously, there are significant differences in the choices facing House members, senators, and presidents. The composition of many congressional districts, for instance, provides individual House members with enough partisan supporters to win the general election without having to broaden their appeal to voters outside their party. Although we highlight these differences below, presidents, most senators, many House members, and legislative leaders generally engage in broadly similar calculations regarding their multiple constituents as they weigh their policy and electoral goals.

Two long-standing accounts of elections offer divergent predictions about politicians' motivations as they balance their policy and electoral goals in the face of multiple and often competing constituencies. The first account emphasizes the motivations of politicians to discount their policy goals in order to pursue their electoral objectives and respond to centrist opinion. By contrast, the second account posits policy goals as predominant. We draw on these standard models of voting in order to generate theoretical expectations about the motivations of politicians when making policy. Our purpose is not to endorse one approach over another; rather, we seek to synthesize the two in order to explain variations over time in politicians' motivations.

Strong Responsiveness to Centrist Opinion

The median voter theory and the retrospective voting model share a common prediction—that the personal benefits of electoral goals dominate the calculations of candidates and officeholders in an inclusive and competitive system of elections. Elections create strong incentives for politicians to follow the policy preferences of centrist opinion when reaching government decisions between elections. David Mayhew argues, for instance, that the Congress is "entirely motivated by reelection" and that the behavior of its members can be explained as "single-minded reelection seeking" (Mayhew 1974a, 16–17). (We use the term "electoral goal" to signify the political calculations to respond to centrist opinion.)

In both models of motivation, politicians treat their policy positions primarily as a means or instrument for holding their party supporters and appealing to the centrist opinion in their constituency. Compromising policy goals to respond to centrist opinion can be costly; it can alienate party activists and other supporters and compel politicians to sublimate their own personal beliefs about "good public policy." But, according to the strong responsiveness account, politicians perceive the personal benefits of electoral goals as outweighing the costs of compromising policy goals.

The median voter theory associated most closely with Anthony Downs suggests that the competition of officeholders and candidates to win elections creates a tendency to use their actions and statements to appeal to centrist opinion (Downs 1957; Black 1958). Although Downs does recognize situations where centrist opinion is discounted by politicians, his primary prediction is that competing candidates will minimize the distance between their announced policy positions and voters' policy preferences and will converge at the midpoint of public opinion.[11] Two predictions are especially relevant for our purposes. First, centrist opinion is posited as a critical constituent: the competition for voters among opposing candidates and officeholders drives them to pursue the centrist constituent even at the risk of alienating more extreme supporters (Downs 1957; Black 1958; Enelow and Hinich 1984). Second, the means for pursuing the electoral center are the policy positions of the politician and the median voter: candidates (including incumbents) and officeholders use their policy positions to appeal to centrist voters based on their shared positions.

The median voter model concludes that candidates will offer clear policy positions that approximate the preferences of voters. When voters fail to perceive the positions of one candidate as closer to their own, Downs and then others (Fiorina 1981) predict retrospective voting as a fallback model for producing strong political responsiveness.

The alternative model—retrospective voting—suggests that voters look back over national and international conditions during the term in office of the incumbent candidate and party with an eye to the future. In particular, voters are expected to evaluate individual candidates and their parties in terms of both their policy positions and the overall performance of the nation's economy and foreign policy. Officeholders anticipate the public's retrospective judgment at the next election and adopt policies or otherwise create conditions while in office that will appeal to most voters. Politicians, then, have incentives to be responsive to centrist opinion because they expect to be held accountable at the next election for their salient policy positions and national and international conditions during their term in office: incumbents and the party in power will be punished for unpopular policy positions and disappointing economic and foreign policy performance. Like the median voter theory, the retrospective model presumes that public opinion is critical to politicians and that policy positions (in conjunction with favorable national conditions) are an important means for winning.

The retrospective model raises a complex but important issue for studying responsiveness: politicians adopt positions to help them in the election by responding to *anticipated* future public opinion toward national economic and international conditions and discounting existing public preferences. For instance, John Zaller (1998) and Jeffrey Cohen (1997) suggest that presidents respond to anticipated future public opinion toward national and international conditions (support for economic growth and peace abroad) by adopting policy positions (e.g., cutting domestic spending) that may not be preferred at that moment by centrist voters or toward which public preferences are not well formed. (Arnold [1990] also emphasizes the responsiveness of legislators to anticipated public opinion.) Zaller and Cohen suggest that both President Reagan and President Clinton discounted existing centrist opinion (opposition to cutting specific government programs and, in Clinton's case, ambivalence to increasing taxes) in order to pursue policies that would produce strong economic performance, which voters would retrospectively judge favorably—as was apparently borne out by Reagan's reelection in 1984 and Clinton's reelection in 1996.

Two important differences distinguish the median voter and retrospective models. First, they adopt different evaluative perspectives: while the median voter theory expects voters to make prospective evaluations of whether their preferred policies will be enacted in the future, the retrospective model assumes that the evaluations of voters are based on looking back in time at the policy and national conditions that prevailed under individual officeholders and the party in control—voters use the past as a signal of future policy outcomes (Fiorina 1981; Fearon 1999). Second, each account, in reality, requires different levels of information, skills, and resources (compare part 1 and part 2 of Downs [1957]). The median voter model requires that voters possess the skills and invest the extensive time and energy necessary to assemble and analyze information on government policy, but the retrospective model imposes a much less stringent set of requirements to reach judgments—voters evaluate the everyday conditions of life and the actions of politicians based on media coverage or their own experiences and those of other people (Page 1978; Popkin 1991; Downs 1957, part 2).

In both the median voter and retrospective models, the motivations of second-term presidents are a bit unique because they cannot be elected to a third term. Even if it is an incumbent's final term, he is

expected to remain keenly attuned to centrist opinion in order to preserve his party's control of the White House, expand its ranks in Congress, and ensure the continued implementation of his agenda. In addition, a "lame duck" president is motivated to continue attracting
public approval of his performance in order to improve his bargaining
position and ability to persuade legislators and other policymakers
(Neustadt 1980; Cohen 1997).

Contributions and Limitations

Although components of the retrospective and, especially, the median
voter models have been challenged,[12] research does support their core
propositions that centrist opinion stands out as a critical constituency
and that politicians' positions and policy decisions are responsive to
it. As we noted earlier, a large body of research shows that government
policies have been strongly related to public opinion. In addition, research on the voting records of U.S. senators suggests that in states
where no party dominates, the incumbent balances appeals to party
activists with appeals to independent voters who fall in between these
extremes (Shapiro, Brady, Brody, and Ferejohn 1990; Wright 1989).
Responsiveness to independents serves to moderate the pressure from
the more ideologically extreme and pulls the incumbent toward centrist opinion.

Research also suggests that voters remove politicians who offer only
muted responsiveness. Patricia Hurley (1991) finds that the failure
of Republicans to respond to independents and disaffected Democrats (and some Republican partisans) on a number of major issues
prompted these more centrist voters to withdraw their support in favor
of the Democratic Party in the 1982, 1984, and 1986 elections. The
result was that Republicans were unable to sustain the realignment
process sparked by the 1980 election.

Although the median voter and retrospective models usefully connect competitive elections with the motivations of politicians between
elections, they suffer from two limitations. First, neither model is well
positioned to account for the decline in responsiveness since the 1970s.
The invariant motivations posited by each model—that politicians
single-mindedly respond to centrist opinion—is ill-suited to explain
change in political behavior. Second, they falsely assume that politicians accept public opinion as a given and operate under conditions
of *certainty* regarding the future contours of public preferences
(Downs 1957, part 1). Conservative or liberal legislators, for instance,
are expected to wait until centrist opinion changes before pushing their

preferred programs (Kuklinski and Segura 1995). *Uncertainty,* however, is a critical influence on politicians' perception and treatment of public opinion. If presidents and legislators perceive public opinion as unreliable and susceptible to change, they have strong incentives to engage in strategic behavior to move the public's policy preferences in the direction they prefer.

Policy Goals and Deviations from Public Preferences

The policy-oriented approach offers an alternative to models that expect politicians to be driven by public opinion. It argues that politicians perceive strong personal benefits from pursuing policy goals that they believe constitute "good public policy" and are preferred by party activists, interests groups, and other policymakers (especially political leaders). Politicians, it is suggested, perceive the benefits of pursuing policy goals as greater than the costs of compromising their electoral goals and discounting the policy preferences of centrist opinion. Second-term presidents are expected to remain committed to their policy goals because of their personal preferences and their desire to secure a venerable legacy or mark on history.

The median voter and retrospective voting accounts predict that politicians will adjust their policy positions to align with centrist opinion. By contrast, the policy orientation account expects politicians to pursue steadfastly a stable set of policies. Indeed, politicians rarely change their voting patterns in Congress (Poole and Romer 1993; Lott and Bronars 1993). Routinely altering their policy positions risks not only alienating long-time supporters but also arming their next electoral opponents with the opportunity to seize upon inconsistencies as evidence of untrustworthiness while still highlighting any earlier unpopular positions (Kau and Rubin 1993; Lott and Davids 1992; Wright 1993). In short, it is politically infeasible for politicians to regularly change their positions in response to centrist opinion.

There are two variants of the policy-oriented approach: the *party vote* model and the *strategic shirking* account.

The Party Vote Model

The *party vote model* argues that candidates and officeholders follow the policy preferences of partisans, who include committed activists and leaders within the political parties as well as voters whose sense of attachment with one party prompts them to routinely choose its candidates (Aldrich 1995; Rohde 1991; Kiewiet and McCubbins 1991;

Cox and McCubbins 1993; Ansolabehere, Snyder, and Stewart 1998a). The most important constituency, according to this model, are party activists who tend to harbor policy preferences ideologically to the extreme of centrist opinion. The influence of partisans on political motivation should not be confused, though, with the contribution of parties to governing capacity: compared to the British and other parliamentary systems of governance, American political parties are ineffective in fusing the legislative and executive branches, though the degree to which party control of both lawmaking branches facilitates American policymaking is a matter of dispute.[13]

The preferences of party loyalists are highly valued by presidents and legislators for three reasons. First, candidates are carefully screened by party elites and activists, who serve as gatekeepers and recruiters in identifying like-minded individuals to run for office (Wright 1989). Politicians are not simply a random sample of voters.

Second, candidates and officeholders are especially attentive to the preferences of committed party activists because they provide the bulk of the campaign's core votes, volunteers, and contributions to fund media advertising, consultants, and travel. The candidate's need for monetary contributions, which political parties and their activists help to generate, influences the selection of candidates and creates incentives for politicians to provide access to activists and privileged private interests; neither of which encourages the pursuit of centrist opinion.

Party activists, then, are critical to most candidates. In addition to providing a critical base of support in the general election, they control the nomination process in primary elections; the low turnout in these contests means that each party's most active and committed members exercise a disproportionate influence (Fiorina 1974; Aranson and Ordeshook 1972; Page 1978; Wright 1989).

Third, partisans are easier to represent than other voters. Compared to centrist voters, partisans are more politically active and communicate more often with candidates and officeholders, convey more detailed and plentiful information about their policy preferences, and are more homogeneous and therefore less likely to send conflicting signals. The result is an improvement in the accuracy and efficiency of politicians' efforts to identify their constituents' concerns and to respond to the preferences of partisans (Wright 1989; Fiorina 1974; Stone 1982).

The party voting model suggests, then, that politicians have strong incentives to enunciate and vote for policy positions that reflect the national parties' platforms. Compromising the party's policy goals to follow centrist opinion is quite costly. Politicians appreciate that the risk of political retribution is higher when originating from organized, narrow factions with intense preferences and politically significant resources than from generalized public opinion: alienating party activists and elites may prompt them to support a more faithful party candidate or to withhold their financial contributions and willingness to volunteer.

Substantial research supports the party vote model. Fenno's (1978) observation of House members suggested that they were more interested in, placed more importance upon, and were more responsive to their "supportive constituency" of partisans than their other constituents. More sweeping quantitative research confirmed Fenno's finding. Parties and candidates displayed consistent and significant differences on policy issues that depart from (rather than converge toward) the preferences of centrist opinion (Ginsberg 1976; Page 1978; Wittman 1983; Poole and Rosenthal 1997).

Party constituencies generate (along with other factors) the differences among the legislative parties: party voting by the electorate as well as the actions of party activists and state party leaders induces legislators to follow the agenda of their party (Kingdon 1989; Ansolabehere 1998a; Fiorina 1974; Shapiro, Brady, Brody, and Ferejohn 1990; Aldrich 1995; Rohde 1991). One set of studies has established that senators from the same state but different parties compile different voting records corresponding to their different partisan constituencies (Wright 1989; Kingdon 1989; Rohde 1991). (Senators from the same state and the same party exhibit much less difference in voting behavior than senators as a whole.) The role of party voting by the electorate in generating legislative party differences is further confirmed by district-level analysis of House elections over a hundred-year period (Ansolabehere, Snyder, and Stewart 1998a). When challengers defeat incumbents, the ideological rating of the district's representation moves strongly toward the positions of the winner's national party. According to this analysis, voters choose between candidates who represent distinct national visions regarding the role of government. For instance, in all but two cases, Democratic House candidates represented a position to the "left" of the Republican candidates.

The Strategic Shirking Account

The second variant of the policy-oriented approach is the *strategic shirking account*. It suggests that presidents and legislators prefer to maximize their policy goals but only when there is an opportunity to shirk from the median voters' policy preferences *and* avoid electoral punishment (Kau and Rubin 1979; Kalt and Zupan 1984; Nelson and Silberberg 1987; for a review see Rasmussen 1989). They are strategic shirkers, pursuing policy goals but alert to the effects of policy positions on their chance of winning reelection; they seek to maximize the enactment of their desired policies and their likelihood of returning to office. In contrast to the median voter theory, this model suggests that the goals of politicians are not simply winning elections but also enacting policies more consistent with their objectives than those of median voters (Wittman 1990).

Politicians prefer to dodge centrist opinion in favor of their strong policy goals for four reasons:

1. The policy goals of partisans are important, though unlike the party voting model they constitute only one of several influences on politicians. Partisans not only devote their time and support in the process of candidate selection, but they also are an important source of campaign contributions.
2. Nearly all politicians harbor their own conceptions, attitudes, or ideological views about what is "good public policy." Presidents, for instance, pursue policy goals to ensure their "place in history" and to build long-term public support for themselves and their party (Cohen 1997). Personal policy beliefs and the desire to enact good policy are also significant influences on legislators, according to statistical analyses of congressional roll call voting and other evidence (Kingdon 1989; Levitt 1996; for a review see Bianco 1994, 36–37 and chap. 4).
3. Presidents and members of Congress are sensitive to the demands of interest groups that can mobilize particularistic groups within a legislator's constituency and use national political action committees to provide campaign contributions to politicians (Cigler and Loomis 1983). For example, Fenno's study found that House members worked to satisfy constituent groups who could turn out narrow blocs of loyal voters like letter carriers and their families (Fenno 1978; Stein and Bickers 1995).
4. Presidents and legislators weigh the positions of other officeholders due to party loyalty, perceptions of the national interest, and calculations of political expediency aimed at avoiding positions that are unpopular with partisans back home or contribute to perceptions of stalemate (Kingdon 1989; Bond and Fleisher 1990). For instance, Ronald Reagan's crusade to reduce taxes and spending won the sup-

port of a critical bloc of House Democrats during his first term because of shared policy goals. Bill Clinton benefited from party loyalty and the support of party activists in his efforts to unify congressional Democrats against the Republican drive to impeach him.

Formal models of electoral competition as well as empirical research suggest that politicians attempt to develop political strategies to achieve their electoral and policy goals. On the one hand, politicians (especially those who are intent on attracting centrist voters) recognize that reelection is necessary for continuing in office and that discounting centrist opinion puts reelection at risk. On the other hand, politicians are "not single minded seekers of election" (Arnold 1990, 5; Wittman 1983, 1990). "When electoral calculations yield no specific recommendation, legislators are free to pursue other goals" (Arnold 1990, 6).

Two distinct political strategies are critical, then, in enabling politicians to pursue policy goals independent of centrist opinion without unduly sacrificing their chances for reelection. First, presidents and legislators capitalize on or heighten the difficulty voters have both in monitoring the policy positions of their representatives and in disciplining them for not following their preferences. Donald Wittman (1983; 1990) suggests that politicians seize on the "bias" of voters toward evaluating candidates according to considerations other than policy positions, and electoral safety is one important source of bias that benefit politicians. Legislators at any level of government can capitalize on comfortable margins of election victory (greater than 55 percent) to depart from the policy preferences of centrist opinion in favor of their policy goals (Fiorina 1973; Ansolabehere 1998a; Kuklinski 1977; Kuklinski and Elling 1977; Hansen 1975; Sullivan and Uslaner 1978). Safe seats result both from the nature of constituencies (namely, the presence of proportionally large numbers of fellow partisans) as well as from the deliberate efforts of incumbents to secure voters' support and their trust by performing constituency service (e.g., providing government spending and programs to their districts) for which they can claim credit (Mayhew 1974a,b; Fiorina 1977; Cain, Ferejohn, and Fiorina 1987). According to one analysis, "trust gives a representative voting leeway, allowing her to act as she thinks best in light of her private information, without fear that her vote will damage her chances of reelection" (Bianco 1994, 23). Legislators are most likely to win trust when they persuade their constituents that they are acting in the common interest. Politicians in safe seats, then, can capitalize on their advantageous strategic position to move closer to their preferred policy position and further from centrist opinion. Although only a relatively small subset of legislators serve marginal districts or states, it deserves emphasizing that an electorally safe seat offers only an opportunity, not unconstrained autonomy; incumbents are not "free" to do as they wish and are not immune from successful challenges (Kingdon 1989).

Even if voters evaluated representatives based on their policy positions, politicians appreciate that it is likely that voters will find it difficult to monitor and punish their representatives for any single vote. The sheer number and diversity of politicians' positions make it very difficult for voters to identify their representatives' positions on specific issues, clarify their own views, and decide if punishment is warranted (Page 1978). The result is to widen politicians' discretion in reaching decisions and shirking from centrist opinion.

In addition to capitalizing on favorable political conditions such as comfortable margins of reelection, politicians adopt deliberate strategies to diminish their chances of electoral punishment as they pursue their policy objectives. Leaders of coalitions committed to policy goals rely upon legislative rules and procedures both to obscure policy attributes that are likely to alienate median voters and to reassure their followers in Congress that their vote will not put their election at risk (Arnold 1990). In particular, coalition leaders package legislation in order to delay benefit reductions and tax hikes and to make it difficult for voters to trace the outcome of a policy decision back to a governmental action and then, in turn, to an individual legislator's vote. According to Arnold, the most effective and common strategy for deflecting the electoral threat of policy decisions focuses on legislative packaging and on national government officials and the relatively small group of Americans who are attentive to government decisions.

The second strategy politicians pursue to lower the electoral risk of shirking is to change public opinion. A critical assumption in the median voter model is that public preferences are fixed and candidates move toward centrist opinion. Officeholders facing reelection have only one strategic option: change their personal policy choices and abide by what centrist opinion favors. Neglected is the possibility that elites may attempt to change public opinion.

Benjamin Ginsberg (1986) suggests that governments and social scientists have over a long historical period redirected political participation from behavioral expressions (such as riots or strikes) to attitudinal manifestations and more passive behavioral expressions. (See also Herbst 1993.) Over the course of a century, Ginsberg argues, the systems of education and mass communications have reduced the diversity of ideas and homogenized public attitudes into a "docile," "plebiscitary" phenomenon (83). Although useful in highlighting the impact of elites on voters, Ginsberg's portrayal collapses the complex interplay of responsiveness and opinion manipulation to a single process (elite indoctrination) and neglects the strategic interaction of politicians and the mass public.

More helpful for our purposes is the analysis of legislators and presidents who attempt to move public opinion. Research indicates that politicians are uncertain about the future direction of public opinion and seize on this uncertainty as an opportunity to change public opinion rather than risk the political costs of discounting existing centrist opinion. Political leaders (presidents and legislators elected or appointed to influential leadership positions) are especially involved in attempting to change public opinion because of their superior resources and their particular incentives to achieve collective benefits such as promoting their party's reputation and establishing or maintaining their party's majority status in government office (Jacobs, Lawrence, Shapiro, and Smith 1998).

Fenno argues that House members rely on a "less policy-centered" style of representation and avoid the "substantive matter" of aligning "the policy preferences of the represented and the policy decisions of the representative." Instead, legislators use "the description, the interpretation and the justification of their behavior" to influence the evaluations and opinions of their constituents back home. Members rely on their "explanations" to "develo[p] the leeway for activity undertaken in Washington" and to build the "political support" to pursue their own policy goals (Fenno 1978, 136, 240–41, 244; Kingdon 1989).

Research on the presidency similarly emphasizes efforts to change public opinion, though on a national (rather than local) scale. Presidents face a growing number of constraints that frustrate their efforts to satisfy the demands placed on them and to fulfill their campaign promises (Neustadt 1980; Skowronek 1993; Shaw 1998; Pomper and Lederman 1976; Krukones 1984; Fishel 1985). Presidents rely on their popularity to offset the constraints on them and their office; greater presidential popularity expands their leverage in achieving their policy initiatives (especially in Congress).

Samuel Kernell (1986) argues that modern presidents have reacted to their debilitating environment of "individualized pluralism" by "going public" to augment their already scarce political resources. Their speeches and other public announcements provide a unique means to boost public support for their proposals and, especially, their approval ratings, which in turn increase the electoral pressure on legislators and other Washingtonians to compromise with the president. In other words, presidents try to mobilize centrist opinion behind them and their proposals in order to construct a supportive coalition from an otherwise splintered set of political actors within Washington. (See also Lowi 1985; Peterson 1990.) In a similar vein, Jeffrey Tulis (1987) stresses that the norms of governance shifted from "inside-the-Beltway" deliberation among Washington's elites during the nineteenth century to the "rhetorical president" of the twentieth century who made appeals over the heads of legislators in order to build public support for them and pressure to enact their policies. Although research has focused on presidents' efforts to bolster their public approval and general political influence (Neustadt 1980; Brace and Hinckley 1992; Kernell 1986), we concentrate on presidential campaigns to alter public preferences and evaluations of specific policies.

Contributions and Limitations

The theory of policy-oriented motivations offers a corrective to the presumption in the strong responsiveness account that politicians passively register public demands. Instead, party voting and strategic shirking offer cogent explanations for how and why politicians discount centrist opinion in favor of policy goals. These accounts provide the starting point for investigating the political motivation underlying the declining responsiveness since the early 1970s. They also suggest a variety of elite strategies to minimize the electoral risk of pursuing policy objectives.

There are, however, two broad limitations with the policy-oriented account. It does not explain the comparatively elevated levels of responsiveness, as we have noted, in the decades before 1980. The policy-oriented perspective is ill-equipped to explain the *change* in the motivations of politicians toward responding to public opinion. In addition, it is hard-pressed to explain the *intermittent rises in responsiveness* as elections approach during periods in which responsiveness sags.

Second, the emphasis on politicians' strategies both to capitalize on the limits of voters' efforts to monitor them and to change public opinion is informative but incomplete in important ways. While there is a broad appreciation that changing public opinion can create "leeway" to pursue policy goals, this analysis does not directly connect variations in responsiveness with the changing motivation to alter public

opinion. How can the decline in responsiveness since the 1970s be incorporated in Kernell's analysis of "going public" or Fenno's investigation of "homestyle" representation? We will argue in the next chapter
that the decline in responsiveness went hand-in-hand with systemic
pressures on a variety of political actors to pursue a strategy of changing public opinion.

The political purpose of polling, focus groups, and other sources of
information on public opinion is another incomplete aspect of the
policy-oriented model. Casual observers of American politics infer
that the enormous amount of research on public opinion is used by
politicians for governing. But if policy-oriented politicians are shirking
public opinion, why are they so interested in tracking it? Does the fact
that politicians track public opinion undermine the claim that politicians are motivated by policy goals? Or, alternatively, do politicians
respond to public opinion but not for the purposes of making government policy?

In addition, analysis of politicians' efforts to change public opinion
(such as Fenno's and Kernell's) tend to treat the actions of legislators
and presidents as discrete, isolated phenomena. Neglected is the fact
that legislators (especially congressional leaders) and presidents are
linked—they react to each other (Jacobs and Shapiro 1998; Harris
1998). The efforts of presidents to mobilize public support provoked
legislative leaders to counterattack with their own national campaigns
to "win" public opinion rather than to plod along with the decentral-
ized, district-by-district efforts that Fenno describes.

Moreover, the policy-oriented perspective overlooks the focus of
politicians on specific policies. Fenno concentrates on the "less policy-
centered" efforts of legislators to change their constituents' perceptions and attitudes; Kernell and other students of the public presidency
emphasize presidents' preoccupation with boosting their overall approval ratings. Neither of these accounts are wrong, but they are
incomplete. The next chapter suggests that both the public opinion
research that politicians conduct and their efforts to change public
opinion concentrate on specific policies.

Furthermore, the effort of contemporary presidents and legislators
to direct public opinion on salient policy issues is not simply an occa-
sional option; it has become routine. Arnold, for instance, suggests
that the manipulation of policy attributes in a legislative package to
diminish potential voter retribution is more likely and effective than
efforts to change public opinion. Politicians, though, do not perceive
these two approaches—legislative packaging and the influencing of

opinion—as mutually exclusive. In an era of competitions among elites to change public opinion (Zaller 1992), legislators who seek to lower the electoral risks of pursuing policy goals are unlikely to rely simply on carefully designing the visible attributes of legislation and trusting that this will be self-evident to Americans. Rather, legislative leaders and others have strong incentives to actively manage public perceptions of salient proposals for new legislation in anticipation that rivals will counterattack and highlight costs (even if they are delayed) and diligently work to trace specific votes to unfavorable outcomes.

Conclusion

Overall, the strong responsiveness and policy-oriented models offer competing theoretical expectations regarding the relationship between public opinion and politicians. The former predicts that politicians perceive high personal benefits from adhering to centrist opinion and minimal costs from compromising their policy goals. By contrast, the latter expects politicians to perceive high personal benefits from pursuing their preferred policies while sizing up the electoral risks as manageable. The two perspectives differ, then, on whether the policy decisions of politicians are a means to reelection or an end in themselves (with elections merely the means to achieving policy goals).

The contribution of the strong responsiveness and policy-oriented models is to lay the foundation for building a theory to explain the changing motivations of politicians to respond to or discount public opinion. Two primary challenges remain. First, neither account explains the *variations* over time in politicians' responsiveness—its decline over the past two decades and its intermittent rises and falls during this period. Each account posits a set of fixed expectations regarding the motivations of politicians: politicians either defer to public preferences or they exercise their discretion to pursue policy goals. What is needed is a theory of political motivations that explains the changing priority that politicians assign to following centrist opinion. The challenge is to develop an explanation for variations over time in responsiveness that synthesizes both accounts.

Second, both accounts treat politicians' motivations as largely divorced from the mass media's coverage of politics and from the dynamics of public opinion. The calculations that politicians make to follow centrist opinion or to pursue their own policy goals need to be connected with the dynamics of media coverage and public opinion (and their feedback effect on politicians' behavior and strategy). We must ask: What impact do the strategies of politicians have on media coverage and public opinion? How does public opinion and news reporting figure in the calculations of politicians?

The next chapter takes up the challenge of incorporating the contributions of the strong responsiveness and policy-oriented models into an account that explains the variations in responsiveness and the dynamics of political news coverage and public opinion.

Chapter Two

Crafted Talk and the Loss of Democratic Responsiveness

Political motivations regarding electoral and policy goals are dynamic and vary in reaction to specific changes in political and institutional conditions. Since the 1970s, the growth of ideological polarization in Congress, of institutional independence of government officials, and of the advantages of incumbency have increased the benefits that politicians associate with seeking policy goals and discounting centrist opinion. The motivation to pursue policy objectives has encouraged politicians to adopt a strategy aimed at lowering the potential electoral costs of discounting centrist opinion: politicians craft how they present their policy stances in order to attract favorable press coverage and "win" public support for what they desire. We refer to this strategy as one of *crafted talk*. If public opinion does not change in the desired direction, politicians change their behavior with the imminent approach of presidential elections by temporarily increasing their responsiveness to centrist opinion even if it requires compromising their policy objectives.

Politicians' pursuit of policy goals and the strategy of crafted talk affect not only policymaking but also how the mass media cover politics and what Americans think about politics and government. We suggest that competition by politicians to fulfill their policy objectives and to attempt to change public opinion generates media coverage that focuses on political conflict and strategy. How the public perceives this polarized policy struggle (as conveyed by the press) increases its uncertainty about policy change and the sense of individuals that their personal well-being is threatened. As a result, the public concludes that the proposed government action is undesirable and rejects the crafted presentations offered by the promoters of reform.

In this chapter we develop an explanation of the varying responsiveness of presidents and legislators and the wider impacts of this responsiveness on the strategies of politicians, the media's coverage of politics, and public opinion. We study each of these in subsequent chapters by using evidence that includes interviews, archival research in White House records, content analysis of press coverage, and statistical analysis.

Here we discuss our theoretical explanations and their grounding in recent and historical developments in American politics. Our discussion is organized into three parts. First, we examine the behavior and strategy of politicians. In particular, we discuss the changing institutional and political dynamics over the past two decades that have elevated the perceived benefit of pursuing policy goals and the expected utility of changing public opinion through carefully crafted presentations. Second, we discuss the impact of politicians' behavior and strategies on media coverage and public opinion. Third, we describe the design of our research.

Declining Responsiveness and Rising Opinion Manipulation

The perceived costs and benefits of pursuing policy versus electoral goals are not constant. Rather, politicians change their evaluation of these costs and benefits, which in turn produce adjustments in their policy actions. "[P]olitical actors have not a single likely policy position," Stimson, MacKuen, and Erikson (1994) observe. Rather, politicians' tactical adjustments between policy and electoral goals produce a "sequence of choices over time, made anew (but with a strain toward consistency) on each policy act" (Stimson, MacKuen, and Erikson 1994).[1]

Changing Politics and Institutions

Changes in political and institutional conditions since the 1970s altered the incentives for politicians to respond to centrist opinion. _Five systemic conditions, which are emphasized by the policy-oriented account, changed or interacted in ways that elevated the expected benefits of pursuing policy goals in the historical period after the 1990s._ The five conditions are partisan polarization, institutional individualization, incumbency bias, interest group proliferation, and divisive interbranch relations. One situational factor—the close proximity of national elections—remained in place to increase intermittently the influence of centrist opinion.

Political Parties and Partisan Polarization

The party vote and strategic shirking models emphasize, as we have noted, the influence of voters who routinely support each political party as well as party activists and leaders (Aldrich 1995; Rohde 1991; Ansolabehere, Snyder, and Stewart 1998a). The influence of these strong partisans on politicians has grown since the 1970s, pressuring candidates and officeholders to pursue policy positions that were increasingly distant from the positions of the other major party and the median American voter. The relentless partisan warfare between Democrats and Republicans from the time of Clinton's hopeful inauguration in January 1993 to the fitful end of the Gingrich Congress in 1996 illustrates the fundamental division of politicians to the left and right over the role of government (especially in matters relating to the redistribution of income). (These fierce contests foreshadowed the bitter partisan fight over impeachment not long afterward.)

Two trends explain the polarization of nation's two parties within Washington since the 1970s. First, there was greater unity *within* each political party as the proportion of moderates in both parties (but especially the Republican Party) declined dramatically from the 1970s to 1990s. Legislators who harbored policy views outside their party's mainstream and regularly voted with the opposing party—like liberal New York Republican Jacob Javits and conservative Arkansas Democrat Wilbur Mills—were replaced in each party by more ideologically extreme politicians (McCarty, Poole, and Rosenthal 1997; Bond and Fleisher 1990; Fleisher and Bond 1996). In particular, there was a severe slippage in the ranks of moderate or progressive Republicans from New England, the Middle Atlantic states, and the upper Midwest, who had regularly voted with Democrats on civil rights, the environment, and other issues. Democratic losses in the South removed a number of conservatives from the party. It is telling that the Republican surge in 1994 hurt moderate Democrats more than liberals.

The fading number of moderates and the decline of intra-party differences was evident in numerous ways. Most roll call votes on the floor of the House and Senate no longer divided each party as they did from 1945 to 1976. There was also a significant decline since the mid-1970s in the proportion of close floor votes in Congress where more than 10 percent of each party disagreed with a majority of their party. Finally, the ideological position of each party's members grew closer together. Figures 2.1 and 2.2 present McCarty, Poole, and Rosenthal's measures of the distance between the votes of members of the same

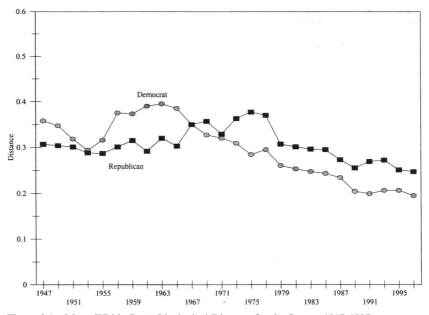

Figure 2.1   Mean Within-Party Ideological Distance for the Senate, 1947–1997
Source: McCarty, Poole, and Rosenthal 1997.

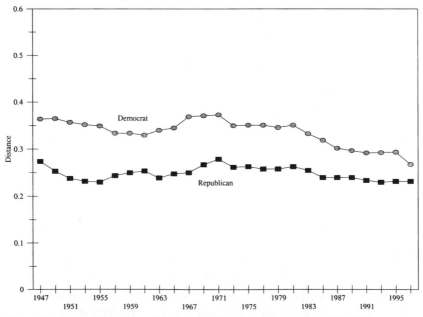

Figure 2.2   Mean Within-Party Ideological Distance for the House, 1947–1997
Source: McCarty, Poole, and Rosenthal 1997.

party in the House and Senate. They reveal less division within each party in 1996 than at any time since 1947.

The second trend producing partisan polarization was the growing ideological distance between each party. Figure 2.3, also based on McCarty, Poole, and Rosenthal's measures, indicates that the distance separating the average House and Senate Democrat from the average Republican increased over time. Roll call votes in Congress were more frequently divided between liberals and conservatives in the 1990s than at any time since 1947, when President Harry Truman faced an contentious Republican-dominated Congress. Democrats and Republican became more ideologically homogeneous and polarized; the polarization of American government policy in the 1990s was neither a sudden aberration nor simply a product of individual personalities.

The origins of polarization can be traced to the civil rights legislation of the 1960s and the exodus of white voters in the South from the Democratic to the Republican Party. After the 1960s, the Democrats became more likely than Republicans to support government action to aid minorities, and racial policy became a key distinguishing feature separating the two parties (Carmines and Stimson 1989; Poole and Rosenthal 1997). Civil rights legislation sparked defections among

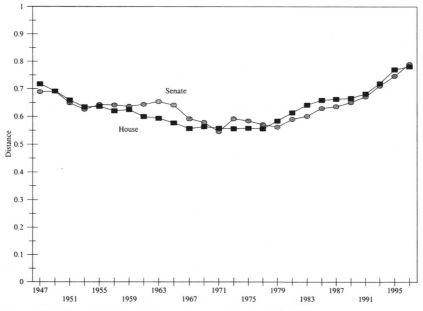

Figure 2.3   Mean Ideological Distance between Parties, 1947–1997
Source: McCarty, Poole, and Rosenthal 1997.

white southern Democrats, which appreciably reduced the percentage of voters who identified themselves as belonging to the Democratic Party. The impact of the steadily rising identification of white Southerners with the Republican Party was particularly evident in Congress: the number of conservative southern Democrats in Congress declined and the ranks of Republicans grew at a time when the rising population of the South boosted the region's representation in the House. The gradual transformation of southern politics coincided with the historic trend in Congress toward more conservative Republicans, proportionately more liberal Democrats, and fewer moderates.

The "vital center" that had bridged the congressional parties and encouraged bipartisan coalitions had eroded by the 1980s (Schlesinger 1949; Cameron 2000a). The implications are significant: the combination of fewer legislators outside their party's ideological mainstream and growing policy differences between the parties on social and economic issues increased the costs of compromising the policy goals of partisans. Responsiveness to centrist opinion becomes less likely if it means suffering great policy costs.

EXPLANATIONS FOR PARTISAN POLARIZATION   The changing partisan clustering in Congress raises a critical question: what caused the flight by each party away from moderation and toward the extremes? The changes in the South explain the shift toward the Republican Party, but it does not explain the overall rise of ideological extremism and the disappearance of moderation.

The ideological polarization among Washington elites was not simply a product of a comparable change in aggregate public opinion overall. American public opinion was not characterized at the time by a growing ideological divide between supporters of government activism (liberalism) and supporters of individual rights and minimal government (conservatism). As elites became more extreme, the distribution of Americans' preferences regarding policies and ideological orientation remained relatively stable (D. King 1997; Dimaggio, Evans, and Bryson 1996; Weisberg, Haynes, and Krosnick 1995; Page and Shapiro 1992, chap. 7). Indeed, ideology remained a relatively minor political consideration for Americans, with only about a fifth of voters in presidential elections using it to choose a candidate since the early 1970s (Hagner and Pierce 1982).

Studies comparing individual members of Congress and their congressional districts have also reported evidence of a gap between elites and the general public. One set of studies found that the income and other characteristics of a legislator's constituents fail to account for their liberal or conservative pattern of voting (Poole and Rosenthal 1997; Poole and Romer 1993). For instance, black representatives from the South take more liberal positions than justified by the characteristics of their district. Another set of studies of individual members of Congress and their constituencies have for many years revealed that the impact of public preferences on legislators' roll call votes is modest (Miller and Stokes 1963; Clausen 1973; Erikson 1978; Sinclair 1982; Page et al. 1984). Still other research concluded that House members were more attentive to the ideology of the national party than to the ideology of their constituents during the 1980s and 1990s than during the previous two decades (Ansolabehere, Snyder, and Stewart 1998a). The decline in the efforts of each party's candidates to tailor their positions to their congressional districts coincided with the rise of congressional polarization.

Although aggregate public opinion has not overall become polarized ideologically on national issues and legislators defer to their national party rather than local constituents, the ideological polarization within parties has received some encouragement from the changing distribution of voters *within* congressional districts (partly due to redistricting). A growing number of legislators have been elected from ideologically homogeneous constituencies. The growing ideological polarization of congressional Democrats and Republicans coincided with congressional districts becoming more liberal and conservative, respectively (Kingdon 1989; Rohde 1991; Fleisher 1993).

The political behavior and attitudes of the mass public, however, did not alone produce the rise of ideological extremism within the political parties and the disappearance of moderation among politicians; the evolution of political parties toward greater independence and power for individual candidates and party activists after the 1960s was a decisive factor. In particular, the widening partisan polarization within Washington was fueled by changes within political parties that expanded the independence and influence of both individual candidates and rank-and-file party activists; reforms of the political parties diminished the influence of party leaders over the selection of candidates and the behavior of elected legislators.

Until the 1960s, party organizations and a small cadre of party leaders exercised significant influence over the selection of congressional and presidential candidates, the platforms of presidential campaigns, and the financing of elections. Candidates won their party's nomination by battling for support among the small cadre of party leaders. In 1960, only two presidential primary contests (West Virginia and Wisconsin) drew attention, and in 1968 Hubert Humphrey won the Democratic nomination after spurning the primary process. The main motivation of party leaders was to win the general election, which prompted them to encourage moderation in order to attract swing voters.

By the 1970s, however, most candidates were nominated through party caucuses and direct primaries, which profoundly altered the incentives of candidates and officeholders. Campaigns for the presidency and congressional seats depended on the individual candidates' ability to organize and operate their own campaigns. Campaigns became personalized and candidates became "freebooting political privateers" out to advance their individual prospects. The influence of party leaders over the selection of candidates and election campaigns was severely curtailed and political parties developed into full service centers to facilitate the efforts of individual candidates, offering public opinion polling, media advisers, direct mail specialists, and other professional assistance.

Success in this personalized system of campaigning depends on the ability of candidates to secure the support of key groups. Political action committees (PACs) and interest groups are critical for stimulating volunteers and, especially, contributions, which we discuss more fully below (Page 1978; Stein and Bickers 1995). Party activists, however, are the "worker bees" in election campaigns: they provide the bulk of the contributions, volunteers, and votes necessary to win first the party's nomination and then the general election (Verba, Schlozman, and Brady 1995; Aldrich 1995, chap. 6; Davidson and Oleszek 1998, 67–68).[2]

Party activists became more influential during a period when their policy positions became more ideologically extreme than the general public or even their fellow (but less active) partisans. Surveys of national party conventions show that, since 1976, delegates at the Democratic conventions and caucuses became a bit more liberal while delegates to the Republican conventions and caucuses became decidedly more conservative (McCann 1996; Abramowitz 1989; Polsby and Wildavsky 1996; Wayne 1997).[3]

A study by David King tracked the ideological direction of strong partisans, who made up about a third of the electorate and were most inclined to participate in politics and party activities. Figure 2.4 indi-

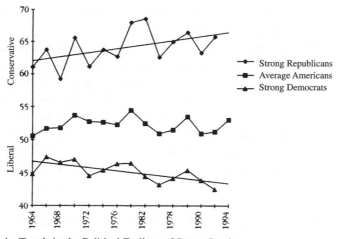

Figure 2.4   Trends in the Political Feelings of Strong Partisans

Source: King 1997, 172. The original data source was the American National Election Studies, 1952–92 Cumulative File, Variable No. 801 (question not asked in 1978).

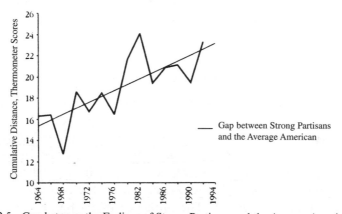

Figure 2.5   Gap between the Feelings of Strong Partisans and the Average American

Source: King 1997, 173. The original data source was the American National Election Studies, 1952–92 Cumulative File, Variable No. 801 (question not asked in 1978).

cates that while the general public's feelings remained stable with a slight increase in warmth toward conservatives, strong Republicans felt noticeably better about conservatives and, to a lesser extent, strong Democrats felt better about liberals. Figure 2.5 condenses the trends in figure 2.4 and shows the widening gap between the liberal or conservative feelings of average Americans and those harbored by strong partisans. In 1964, the distance between the ideological feelings of the average American and those of the strong Republicans and strong

Democrats was about 16 points; by the mid-1990s, the distance had grown 40 percent to about 23 points.[4]

The battle since the 1970s to win each party's nomination and cement the support of party activists and others pressured candidates and officeholders to take ideologically extreme positions that diverge both from those of the opposing party and from centrist opinion (Huntington 1950; Fiorina 1974; Aldrich 1995; Polsby 1980; Jacobson 1987, 20; Wright 1994). John Aldrich has argued that the strategic value of party activists to ambitious politicians "generat[e] incentives to act in office as they advocated on the campaign trail" (Aldrich 1995, 191–92). Indeed, the polarization of legislators corresponded with the growing ideological extremism of party activists: the growing gap between congressional Democrats and Republicans in figure 2.3 closely paralleled the rising extremism of partisans shown in figure 2.5.

The influence of partisans on politicians' policy goals, which the policy-oriented account emphasizes, increased over the last three decades. The result was to elevate the perceived benefit to politicians of pursuing policy goals shared by partisans and to discount the preferences of centrist opinion.

The Rise of Individual Independence in Congress

The empowerment of individual members of Congress increased their discretion to pursue their own preferred policy goals as well as those of party activists and others. In the past, parties exercised substantial political influence over debate and legislation; the vehicle for party influence was the House and Senate leadership during the nineteenth century and the system of committees during the first two-thirds or so of the twentieth century. The influence of parties was based on their control over the selection of candidates, election campaigns, and, during the nineteenth and early twentieth centuries, the disposition of jobs, contracts, and other forms of patronage. The political significance of this for legislative operations was that the parties possessed visible means to discipline wayward members.

By the 1970s, however, reforms in party rules and congressional institutions empowered individual legislators to take policy initiatives on their own and to resist leaders. (We refer to this development as institutional *individualization.*) The new independence was especially apparent in the House; the norms and procedures of the Senate had already afforded wide latitude to its members. The new power of rank-and-file House members was starkly illustrated by their decisions to vote out once-powerful committee chairs and to vote in new chairs who lacked seniority. In addition, the House expanded the personal staff for members and created staff agencies like the Congressional Budget Office, which equipped individual members with the analysis and capacity to pursue their own legislative interests. Although the House reforms expanded the prerogatives of the Speaker of the House, actual leadership required consultation with a wider circle of members who saw themselves as independent and possessed the capacity to pursue their own goals (Kingdon 1989).

The influence of individual senators was expanded after the 1970s by the growing use of filibusters. It became increasingly common for senators to require opponents to assemble not just a majority but a supermajority of sixty votes to overcome the filibuster.

Although the number of moderates who were uncomfortable with their party's mainstream declined, they remained critical in building majorities in both chambers and in drawing the sixty votes necessary to overcome filibusters in the Senate. Clinton's drive for health care reform, for instance, met its final end when Bob Dole threatened a filibuster in the summer of 1994 after he was convinced that he had won the battle with the White House for the votes of Republican moderates like Senators John Chafee and Bob Packwood.

After the 1970s, individual legislators were positioned to pursue their policy goals and to resist their party and leadership in ways that are not possible in parliamentary systems. American political parties fail not only to control activities within Congress but also to fuse the executive and legislative branches on the basis of shared institutional and political interests (as is the case in Britain and other countries with parliamentary systems). Both President Clinton and House Speaker Gingrich witnessed—with futility—the inclination of rank-and-file legislators to resist their party leaders.

INSTITUTIONAL INDIVIDUALIZATION AND PARTY COHERENCE   One of the most intriguing puzzles in American politics since the 1970s is that the extraordinary unity within legislative political parties (see figs. 2.1 and 2.2) coincided with the extraordinary independence of individual legislators from the control of congressional leaders.

The primary explanation for party unity in an era of political individualism is that the Democratic and Republican parties within Congress evolved into organizations that specialized in coordinating action on shared policy goals: congressional parties identified the common ground among autonomous partisans and forged coalitions on the basis of these shared preferences. Of particular importance were the party caucuses in the House and the Senate, which tracked the policy preferences of legislators within each party and generated instructions to the committee chairs and other party leaders. Reforms over the last two or three decades gave party leaders (like the Speaker of the House) powers over committees and floor debate that enabled them to coordinate the party and secure the policies favored by the caucus.[5]

The unity of parties within Congress was achieved, then, not by controlling legislators and dictating their behavior but by using the caucus system and the powers of leaders to coordinate party members and to structure the agenda of legislative action to prevent votes on policies not favored by a majority within the party. The reinforcing pressures of local and state party activists and fellow partisans within Congress pushed independent legislators in common ideological directions (Aldrich 1995; Cox and McCubbins 1993; Rhode 1991). It was in the interests of individual legislators to follow the ideological direction of the party caucus.

The party caucuses and leaders like the Speaker not only identified and promoted the policy preferences of each party's legislators but also reinforced partisan divisions within the electorate and among legislators. Candidates who won elections defined their respective party's positions through public statements and through gathering simple majorities within the caucuses for policies that appeal to partisans who would help them win next time. The policy preferences of incumbents had a somewhat contradictory impact: it contributed to more coherence within each legislative party but it also impaired the success of candidates in marginal or ideologically mixed congressional districts, depressing their probability of winning (Ansolabehere, Snyder, and Stewart 1998a; Ansolabehere and Snyder 1997).

In short, the growing independence of individuals within Congress expanded the discretion and incentives for members to pursue their policy goals. Party leaders, who were motivated by collective concerns to protect the party's reputation with the general public, lacked the power to direct their party toward policy positions that responded to centrist opinion.

The Bias of Incumbency

The effect of incumbency was the third condition that intensified over time and increased the incentives for politicians and, especially, members of the House of Representatives, to pursue policy goals at the expense of centrist opinion. Contemporary House members enjoy a larger advantage in their election contests against challengers than did their predecessors in the immediate post-World War II period. The incumbents' overall advantage grew from a 1 to 3 percentage point edge in the share of the vote in the 1940s and early 1950s to a 7 to 10 point benefit in the 1980s and 1990s (Mayhew 1974a; Alford and Brady 1989; Gelman and King 1990; Krashinsky and Milne 1993; Cox and Katz 1996; and Levitt and Wolfram 1997; Ansolabehere, Snyder, and Stewart 1998b).

This incumbency advantage, as it interacted with other new conditions, expanded the "bias" of voters against critically evaluating their representative's policy actions and increased the leeway of politicians to pursue their policy goals (Wittman 1983 and 1990). Incumbents in the large number of safe districts could reasonably calculate that the electorate is not terribly sensitive to their policy positions and is unlikely to be affected by a change in them (Koetzle 1998).

The Proliferation of Interest Groups

The fourth condition was the rapid growth in the number and diversity of national interest groups that could mobilize particularistic groups within a legislator's constituency and use national political action committees to provide campaign contributions to supporters (Cigler and Loomis 1983; Salisbury 1990; Walker 1991; Heclo 1978; Peterson 1993; Stein and Bickers 1995). Until the 1960s, interest groups were relatively few in number and those from similar sectors of society came together under relatively strong peak associations such as the American Medical Association (AMA), which dominated health policy. The dominance of a few peak organizations aggregated the demands of interest groups and provided a tangible bargaining partner for politicians as they balanced their electoral pressure to follow centrist opinion with the demands of peak organizations.

After the 1960s, however, a number of indicators—from the number of registered lobbyists to the number of corporations operating offices in Washington—revealed a dramatic growth in the number and variety of organizations engaged in pursuing their interests in Washington. New groups and new coalitions on social, economic, and political issues formed continually. Moreover, once-dominant peak organizations were replaced by associations that specialized in small policy niches or that formed complicated coalitions that cut across formal associations (Cigler and Loomis 1983; Salisbury 1990; Walker 1991; Heclo 1978;

Peterson 1993). The groups increasingly used campaign contributions, grass roots organizing, and, as we discuss below, media campaigns to pressure politicians to advance their particularistic policy concerns.

Organized labor—a decisive influence into the 1960s—saw its membership slip from over 30 percent to 14 percent of the workforce in just three decades, recording one of the lowest rates of union membership among industrialized countries. The AFL-CIO, which had been the lead spokesperson for organized labor, no longer served as a dominating peak association.

The take-off in the sheer number and diversity of interest groups was somewhat offset—at the behest of politicians—by the formation of interest group coalitions. Politicians welcomed the coalitions as a means for reducing disagreements among groups in similar areas and making their interactions with interest groups more manageable. The alliances, though, presented new challenges for politicians. Interest groups join coalitions precisely to enhance their leverage in advancing policy goals and to confront politicians with a well-organized and well-funded alliance committed to a shared policy goal. When groups conclude that a coalition may neglect their particularistic interests, they are still willing to "go it alone" in besieging politicians (Hojnacki 1997; Hula 1995).

The result was that a relatively small number of powerful interest groups no longer dominated government decision making in particular policy areas like health care. The proliferation of narrowly based interest groups increased the pressure on politicians to pursue specific policy goals; politicians could no longer negotiate with a peak organization to gain flexibility on some issues in exchange for supporting an organization's priorities.

The incentives to pursue policy goals were also increased by the growing importance of money in politics in the form of campaign contributions by PACs and well-funded lobbying campaigns during policy debates (as epitomized by the $100 million spent by opponents of the Clinton health plan in 1993–94 [West, Heith, and Goodwin 1996, 42–43]). Although researchers disagree on the nature and extent of the influence extracted by contributors to campaigns and policy initiatives,[6] there is some agreement that the pressure on politicians to fund media advertising and political consultants has produced three advantages for privileged private interests committed to advancing government policy favorable to them (McChesney 1997; Sorauf 1988; West and Loomis 1999; Ferguson 1995).

First, contributors to election campaigns and policy campaigns increase their access to politicians and the mass public. Officeholders are more likely to grant them access, introduce favorite bills, and to be at least modestly swayed by their concerns when voting in Congress (Sorauf 1988). In addition, major contributors are able to widely distribute their messages by purchasing advertisements. The result is to increase their opportunities to influence public opinion and, in the case of policy debates, to influence policymakers who treat these advertisements as indicators of potential public opinion (West, Heith, and Goodwin 1996; West and Loomis 1999). (Our analysis of media coverage of health care shows that Democrats and Clinton received significantly more attention than other government officials, which somewhat offset the purchasing of advertisements by reform opponents.) Second, the decision to fund a candidate enables contributors to advance the chances of friendly candidates and, especially, incumbents who offer the security of a well-known voting record. Third, money prevents threatened actions by lawmakers (McChesney 1997).

Divisive Interbranch Relations

Changes in the relations between the executive and legislative branches have, under certain conditions, elevated the anticipated benefits to presidents and legislators of pursuing divergent policy goals. Presidents and legislators carefully weigh the positions of the other lawmaking branch because of party loyalty, perceptions of the national interest, and calculations regarding the reactions of partisans and centrist voters (Kingdon 1989; Bond and Fleisher 1990). Discord between the lawmaking branches, although it is an old story, intensified since the 1970s.

The framers of the U.S. Constitution discouraged officials in the executive and legislative branches from developing common political interests and shared institutional responsibilities. The constitutional system dispersed constitutional authority and bifurcated the political interests of presidents, who are elected to represent national interests, and members of Congress, who are selected in subnational elections to represent more local interests.

The age-old divisions and rivalries promoted by the Constitution were aggravated by two interrelated developments since the Second World War. First, the president's party rarely enjoyed a majority in both chambers in Congress during the postwar period. Although important legislation was enacted even during periods of divided government (Mayhew 1991), the parceling out of the national government to different parties tended to discourage sweeping legislation and to give an institutional foothold to presidents and legislators to pursue increasingly divergent policy goals.

Second, the growing influence of ideologically extreme partisans (combined with split party control over the lawmaking branches) intensified the importance of policy goals in the relations of presidents and legislators since the mid-1980s. Fleisher and Bond (1996) demonstrate that Bill Clinton was more successful during his first two years in office than previous post-war presidents whose party also enjoyed legislative majorities but during periods of less partisan polarization (736–37). Even when the same party controls both branches of government, however, policy goals may add yet another obstacle to interbranch cooperation when members of Congress disagree with the president's position. Clinton's overall legislative record during 1993–94 benefited from the shared policy goals of congressional Democratic majorities, but his drive for health care reform was blocked in part by fellow Democrats who followed their strongly held policy preferences.[7] Indeed, the support for Clinton by Democratic loyalists in the House during 1993–94 was far below the levels for Kennedy and Johnson (though higher than for Carter). Presidents and legislators are both attuned to party activists but the chief executive is also attentive to his broader and more moderate national constituency.

The debilitating effect of partisan polarization was most apparent when neither party controlled both lawmaking branches. Presidents whose party was in the minority won considerably less often following the onset of partisan polarization in the mid-1980s than their predecessors during the previous three decades (Fleisher and Bond 1996). Clinton discovered in 1995–96—like presidents Reagan (during his second term) and Bush—that partisan polarization greatly complicates the already difficult job of a minority president: Clinton found few moderate Republicans who were outside their party's mainstream and open to defecting after the Republicans seized control of Congress.

Split party control, ideological polarization, and individualistic behavior in institutions widened conflict between the legislative and executive branches after the 1970s (Peterson 1990). The wishes of centrist public opinion were often sacrificed as legislators and presidents clashed over divergent policy goals.

The Proximity of Elections

After the 1970s, many of the conditions that the policy orientation approach identified became more prominent and influential in American politics. Indeed, these conditions interacted in ways that intensified the pressure on politicians to pursue policy goals.[8]

One situational factor—the close proximity of elections—temporarily elevates the perceived benefit of responding to centrist opinion and prompts politicians to absorb the costs of compromising their policy goals. When elections are no longer imminent, politicians return to their preferred positions and move away from the positions preferred by centrist opinion.

The nearness of elections boosts the perceived benefit of responding to centrist opinion for two reasons. First, politicians pursue policy goals under conditions of uncertainty regarding the future preferences of the mass public, anticipating that they can steer it in the direction they desire. As we noted in chapter 1, Fenno (1978), Kernell (1986), and others argue that legislators and presidents communicate with their constituents in order to change their opinions. The approach of elections, however, diminishes politicians' uncertainty as the time and opportunity to change voters' opinions before they cast their ballots dwindles. Faced with imminent elections, it is less risky and faster to respond to public opinion than to attempt to change it. Politicians have incentives to claim credit, then, for responding to the public's preferences.

Second, politicians appreciate that the electorate is most attentive to their most recent actions and attach a disproportionate attention to them (Wittman 1983 and 1990). Politicians (especially leaders) are particularly concerned about the "swing vote" of weak partisans and independents, who tend to be less well informed and more easily influenced by recent actions than partisans. The proportion of independents—voters who identify with neither major party—has risen since the 1960s to a third of the electorate (Stanley and Niemi 1995; Weisberg, Haynes, and Krosnick 1995).[9] In addition, parties have witnessed the defection of voters who weakly identify with them and vote for candidates of the other party.[10]

The behavior of the Clinton administration and the Gingrich Congress fits this pattern: their sustained pursuit of policy goals was temporarily suspended as the 1996 election approached and each shifted toward a strategy of working together to pass legislation strongly supported by public opinion such as the minimum wage law, the Kennedy-Kassebaum reform of private health insurance operations, and welfare reform. This pattern of responsiveness as the 1996 election approached is supported by other research. The clearest evidence comes from studies of senators, who were found to moderate their earlier positions and to increase dramatically their responsiveness to their state's median voters as election day neared (Levitt 1996; Kuklinski 1978; Amacher and Boyes 1978; Elling 1982; Wright 1989; Wood and Andersson 1998). One study found a similar pattern for presidents; a comparison of the publicly enunciated positions of Lyndon Johnson with his private polling revealed a pattern of rising responsiveness as the 1964 presidential election approached (Jacobs and Shapiro 1993).

Presidential election years may exert greater influence than midterm contests on the calculations of presidents and legislators toward responding to centrist opinion. Compared to congressional election years when the White House is not up for grabs, presidential election years affect a wider swath of politicians, with the White House and over 460 House and Senate seats up for grabs. In addition, politicians fully appreciate that the average voter devotes unusual attention to presidential election years as evident by their higher turnout. The characteristics of voters for each set of elections is quite different: while midterm congressional elections are more dominated by voters with strong partisan orientations, presidential elections attract a wider spectrum of voters including those who are more moderate and skip the less salient congressional elections.

In short, in a period when partisan activists, incumbency, and other factors have tilted politicians toward pursuing policy goals, the approach of presidential elections may temporarily increase the incentives to respond to centrist opinion and absorb the costs of compromising policy. After election day, the pressure to respond to centrist public opinion fades and the incentives to pursue policy goals return with full force. The decline in responsiveness since the 1970s may have made the upswing in responsiveness during election campaigns more noticeable. During periods when responsiveness was higher, the effect of the election cycle may have been relatively muted because politicians were already intent on following centrist opinion.

The Political Strategy of Orchestrated Public Appeals

Politicians' pursuit of policy goals since the 1970s has elevated the perceived importance of orchestrated national appeals—"crafted talk"—as a strategy to win the support of centrist opinion for their desired policy positions. Changing public opinion in the nation as a whole makes the preferred positions of politicians electorally expedient. Politicians attempt to *simulate responsiveness* by changing centrist opinion to support their positions; if their efforts are successful, enacted policies are (in the end) in accord with public opinion. Policy-oriented politicians aim to achieve both their policy and electoral goals: they pursue what they consider "good public policy" and what their partisans and interest group allies want even as they appear responsive to centrist opinion. This apparent responsiveness provides electoral protection for themselves and their core allies and political capital among politicians who want to appeal to swing voters.

On salient issues that tap into partisan divisions, the campaigns of politicians to win public backing for their policy objectives have become a routine part of American politics. Competition among legislators, presidents, and other political activists to promote their favored policy positions generates a barrage of (perhaps unequally funded) campaigns and counter-campaigns. Even legislators who prefer to rely on legislative packaging or on evading the monitoring of voters launch orchestrated campaigns in anticipation that rivals will highlight the costs to the general public (even if they are delayed) and attempt to trace specific votes to unfavorable outcomes.

The Strategic Attractions of Changing Public Opinion

A constellation of six factors has prompted legislators and presidents to attempt to change public opinion in order to mitigate the electoral costs of pursuing their policy goals.[11]

1. Politicians are uncertain about what the public will prefer by the time of the next election, but they view the unsettled nature of public opinion as an opportunity when election day is more remote. They believe that public opinion is susceptible to change and that it is possible to obtain public support for their positions.[12]

2. Changing public opinion does not require politicians to modify their policy goals and absorb the costs of compromise. It allows politicians to try to satisfy their electoral *and* policy objectives.

3. In the calculations of policy-oriented politicians, moving public opinion not only mitigates the electoral hazard to themselves but it can also generate valuable political resources for pressuring other politicians and securing the votes of the small but critical cluster of congressional moderates who tend to be most sensitive to centrist opinion.

4. The introduction of new technologies, from radio and television to sophisticated telecommunications, expand the ability of politicians to circulate political messages widely and visibly. The cheap and attractive distribution of information surmounts the age-old limitations inherent in face-to-face exchanges in a large and heterogeneous population. Ninety percent of American households owned televisions by 1959 and the average number of viewing hours has risen dramatically.

In addition, the visual medium of television makes it possible to induce individuals—and the public overall—to subconsciously make inferences and draw associations. The combination of television's unique visual mode with verbal and print presentations produces gripping drama and deep emotional and visceral reactions that can short-circuit the audience's search for evidence (Jamieson 1988, 1992; Calhoun 1992; Robbins 1993; Poster 1989). The speed, scope, and intensity of communications make it possible for politicians to reach audiences on an unprecedented scale and sway them through their message.

5. National campaigns by presidents and legislative leaders to move public opinion are more effective and efficient than the retail approach of reassuring voters constituency-by-constituency and lobbying policymakers one at a time. As Fenno (1978) explains, the legislator's task of finding and communicating with constituents is time-consuming, difficult, and prone to error. By contrast, a wider campaign generates efficiencies of scale; efforts by presidents and legislative to change national opinion are cheaper and faster than selling proposed policy actions person to person.

For instance, Bill Clinton's national speech on health care reform in September 1993 was a classic—even electrifying—illustration of a president capitalizing on the unique visibility of his office. Only nine months into his term, Clinton found his initiatives under attack; the White House expected a national speech to "win" national support, which would simultaneously boost his own sagging standing, help political activists who shared his goal, and make negotiations with ambivalent legislators and interest groups easier and less costly in terms of policy compromises.

6. The norms and practice of public appeals have spread from presidents to other political actors. Presidents have long enjoyed the fabled power of the "bully pulpit." Presidents alone—according to textbook accounts of presidential influence—have the distinctive power to "go public" to "monopolize" national debate and pressure Washington elites to cooperate (Kernell 1986; Tulis 1987; Miroff 1982). Public appeals, however, are no longer the tool of presidents alone. The combination of polarization, the emphasis on policy goals, the rise of political consultants, and the emergence of a new breed of media-savvy political leaders have dramatically widened the use of opinion manipulation strategies from presidents to members of Congress and interest groups.[13] They launch orchestrated appeals to gain public support and counteract real or anticipated campaigns by political rivals pursuing divergent policy goals.

Not unlike presidents, congressional leaders publicly promote their positions in order to satisfy their "policy-oriented members while simultaneously providing electoral cover for colleagues" (Harris 1998, 206). Interest groups have also changed tactics. E. E. Schattschneider described the "distinguishing mark" of the old style of pressure tactics as "not attempt[ing] to persuade a majority" (emphasis in the original) (Schattschneider 1960a, 189). The point, according to political consultant Carter Eskew, was to talk to people inside the Beltway because "the right connection [will] fix things" (Barnes 1995). By contrast, the new style (in Eskew's words) is "all about getting the people involved" and "tak[ing] our case to the broader public" in order to win support (Barnes 1995). A particularly memorable illustration of interest groups' use of crafted presentations to pressure politicians was the "Harry and Louise" health care advertisement, which portrayed a fictional couple worrying over the impact of the Clinton health plan. The Health Insurance Association of America (HIAA) sponsored the spots because, one of its vice presidents explained, it "allowed a little old trade association to have an impact way beyond its size" (Barnes 1995).[14] The actual influence of interest groups on public opinion may depend on the way in which they are representative of public opinion (Kollman 1998). Interest groups, legislators, and others use political advertisements, mass media coverage, and computer-based direct mail campaigns to stir up public attention and support for their policy goals (Cigler and Loomis 1983).

The result of the competition to "win" public opinion is that orchestrated presentations by presidents and legislators provoke reactions and counteractions. Clinton's masterful speech in September 1993 generated immediate replies by his political opponents; the networks carried the official Republican response, and journalists interviewed legislators and interest groups for their reactions. In the days and weeks following the president's speech, journalists, members of Congress, interest groups, and others countered Clinton's message with what became a familiar incantation of the faults with Clinton's health reform effort—too much big government, an unwieldy and secretive task force, and overly ambitious policy objectives. Crafted presentations breed a cycle of reaction and counteraction.

Crafting Presentations to Change Public Opinion

Legislators and presidents rely on three techniques in their efforts to change public opinion on specific policy issues: tracking public opinion through polls, focus groups, and other related methods; managing press coverage; and using the tactic of "priming" to influence the public.

RESEARCHING THE MESSAGE   Presidents, legislative leaders, and other political activists commonly conduct extensive research on public opinion. Beginning in earnest with John Kennedy, presidents have developed a "public opinion apparatus" to routinely track Americans' attitudes and reactions to ongoing or potential policy actions (Jacobs 1992a; Jacobs 1993, chap. 2). The polling and focus group research conducted by the Clinton White House continued activities that began decades earlier and were expanded most dramatically under Richard Nixon and Ronald Reagan, his Republican predecessors (Jacobs and Shapiro 1995, 1996a; Heith 2000). Congress and its leaders have also developed the capacity to regularly track public opinion (Harris 1998; Jacobs and Shapiro 1998).

Another puzzle of contemporary American politics is that elected officials devoted significant organizational and financial resources to tracking the public's policy preferences during a period that showed declining responsiveness. Why do presidents and legislators monitor the public's policy preferences only to discount them in making policy decisions?

Politicians respond to public opinion in two qualitatively different ways. In one, politicians track the content of the mass public's substantive policy preferences in order to guide their policy decisions. The median voter theory predicts this kind of *substantive responsiveness* and it appeared to decline since the 1970s. In the second, politicians track public opinion to identify the words, arguments, and symbols about specific policies that the centrist public finds most appealing and that they believe to be most effective in changing public opinion to support their policy goals. In this case, "responsiveness" to public opinion is an instrument for changing it in order to *simulate* responsiveness. *Instrumental responsiveness* is a pervasive aspect of contemporary politics and it has been underestimated in the study of politics.

Gauging public thinking in order to more effectively sway voters is certainly not new. In the past, politicians used face-to-face canvassing or other informal methods to hone their presentations and improve their effectiveness. What is different today is that scientific techniques supply more detailed and reliable information about public thinking and emotions; modern research can pinpoint words or phrases that evoke particular feelings and thoughts and measure the intensity of those reactions. Politicians can use this sophisticated research to target the full brunt of mass communications on public opinion. Just as military strategy has shifted from carpet bombing to targeted bombing, political communications has moved from sweeping addresses to crafted presentations honed to spark specific public reactions. The words of presidents, legislators, and other political activists are guided by public opinion research like a laser-guided "smart" bomb.

Interest groups have joined presidents and legislative leaders in using polls, focus groups, and other methods to calibrate their public presentations into "messages the public would find believable." For instance, HIAA hired public opinion analysts to maximize the impact of their "Harry and Louise" ads on Americans and to pinpoint the most appealing presentation, investigating whether the couple should sit in a community center, a living room, or a kitchen (research pointed to the latter option).

POLITICAL USE OF THE MEDIA   Efforts by presidents and legislative leaders to change centrist opinion elevated the political importance of managing the press—it was the critical conduit for affecting Americans (for historical treatment see Jacobs 1993, chap. 2; Cook 1998, chaps. 2, 3, and 6). For instance, during the first part of 1993 Senator Jay Rockefeller and White House aides issued a telling warning to Mrs. Clinton, who directed the president's health reform initiative: passing health legislation required the "ability to define the health care reform debate on our own terms" and to incorporate journalists in a "crafted information flow."[15] The distinctiveness of the White House's efforts to craft positive news coverage in order to capture public support is highlighted by the style of government management of news in Germany and Britain, which focus on solidifying the support of political elites (Pfetsch 1998).

American politicians rely on two tactics to influence the press. First, they attempt to saturate the press with their "message"; blanketing the country with their message would integrate the press in their "crafted information flow," inundate Americans with it, and, by extension, crowd out the opposing message from their rivals. Second, they package their presentations in terms of simple, attractive themes that would both satisfy the media's economic pressures to draw audiences and override the press's preoccupation with the maneuvering of politicians. The Clinton White House, for example, settled on the simple theme, "Security for All," to boost the interest of Americans and to direct the story about health reform toward the needs of patients rather than the strategy and bickering of politicians.

PRIMING THE PUBLIC   Politicians place considerable political stock in changing public opinion, but they rarely count on directly persuading the public of the merits of their position by grabbing the public's attention and by walking it through detailed and complex reasoning. Their skepticism stems in part from their low regard for the public's capacity for reasoned and critical thought. Our interviews with Clinton White House officials and senior congressional staff revealed, as we discuss in subsequent chapters, that the public is generally perceived as inattentive to the details of policy debates and misled by false information and unthinking ideological or partisan predispositions. In addition, politicians assume that the kind of reasoned discussion that is necessary for persuading Americans would be short-circuited by the media and their political opponents. The Clinton White House, for instance, rejected the idea that a presidential speech devoted to a substantive discussion of its health plan could, in practice, persuade Americans to convert to their perspective; the anticipated outcome of such a speech was that the administration's opponents would distort it and that the media would ignore or repackage the substantive discussion to focus on strategy and the attacks by their opponents.

Politicians adopt as a more realistic and effective approach to changing public opinion what social psychologists refer to as "priming" (Jacobs and Shapiro 1994a; Krosnick and Kinder 1990; Zaller 1992; Iyengar and Kinder 1987; Iyengar 1991; Neumann, Just, and Crigler 1992; Cappella and Jamieson 1997; Aldrich, Sullivan, and Borgida 1989; Lavine, Sullivan, Borgida, and Thomsen 1992). A priming approach concentrates on raising the priority and the weight that individuals assign to particular attitudes already stored in their memories. Politicians use public statements and the press coverage they can generate to influence which attitudes and information individuals retrieve from memory and incorporate into their judgments. For instance, opponents of health reform consistently voiced the warning that the Clinton plan would create "big government," intending to prompt many Americans to put whatever conservative attitudes they harbored toward government to the forefront of their minds and to use them as the yardstick by which to evaluate health reform. The political fight, then, was over the salience of different yardsticks that the public would use in its evaluation.

"Priming" is, of course, not a term that legislators and presidents use, but its effectiveness in changing the public's preferred policy choices is widely recognized by politicians (though in different terms). They perceive three advantages to a priming strategy. First, priming is seen as simpler and more likely to be effective than a strategy aimed at persuading the public to change its values and fundamental preferences. The aim is to boost the sheer quantity of statements about simple themes—identified through public opinion research as favoring their position—and news coverage of them in order to highlight specific criteria for the public to use in evaluating specific policy proposals. In the language of politicians, they and their allies must "stay on message." Opponents of health reform aimed simply to immerse Americans with their "big government" message.

Second, a priming strategy is less susceptible to distortion by journalists and opponents than a strategy to directly persuade Americans on the merits of a policy proposal (though opponents may counter it with their own efforts at priming). Opponents of the Clinton health plan successfully deployed this strategy to counter the White House's commitment of enormous resources and the unique visibility of the president to override its message. Ironically, counterattacks can inadvertently help to highlight oppositional themes; Clinton's counterattack against the charge of "big government" in the "Harry and Louise" ads raised the salience of governmental dread as a yardstick for evaluating health reform.[16]

Third, efforts at priming impose less stringent requirements on the public. Americans (and journalists) do not have to acquire and process the kind of extensive information about policy details that a direct persuasion strategy can demand; they need not pay attention to and follow detailed and complex reasoning. Nor are Americans expected to change their existing values and fundamental preferences; Clinton's "Security for All" message attempted to activate the public's preferences toward universal insurance, which were overwhelmingly positive and stable (Jacobs, Shapiro, and Schulman 1993).

Both the advocates and opponents of proposed policies utilize fairly predictable tactics to prime the public. Advocates of policy reforms generally prime benefits and avoid a discussion of costs. Clinton's "Security for All" message publicly highlighted the benefits of health reform as a substitute for a detailed discussion of how to pay for the plan and implement it. Public promotion of benefits is often emphasized in terms of the national good; Clinton stressed that health reform would stimulate the economy by reducing waste and provide *all* Americans with health care "when you need it." The "common good" arguments can be quite encompassing; Clinton's message appealed to the leaders of large corporations, the middle class anxious about not affording care, and the politically vulnerable uninsured.

By contrast, opponents of reform prime its costs and encourage the public to perceive reform as threatening their personal well-being.

From "Harry and Louise" ads to Senator Bob Dole's warning about
Clinton's convoluted "Rube Goldberg" scheme, opponents of the president's health reform proposal consistently stuck to the simple message
that "big government" would reduce quality. Their aim was to prompt
Americans to evaluate the Clinton plan by focusing on whether it expanded government and on the consequences of the plan for the quality of health care.

The Politics of Technological Change

Public presentations by politicians have always been used to sway lis-
teners. They have never represented a transparent and neutral means
for political communication. A long-standing tactic in eighteenth-
century election campaigns in America was to hire orators (much like
today's political operatives) to praise a candidate, castigate the opponent, and tirelessly "contrast" the two rivals. Nineteenth-century elections were fought by armies of party workers and volunteers who can-
vassed face-to-face in wards and precincts in order to sell their party's
candidates and policy positions.

By the 1990s, however, political efforts to change public opinion had
been transformed into a qualitatively different exercise than had existed before. New technologies in mass communications and public
opinion research increased the speed, reach, and effectiveness of political efforts to target public feelings and thoughts. Indeed, it is tempting
to conclude that changes in technology alone caused politicians to
craft their presentations to change public opinion. But a simple technological explanation neglects politics.

It was change in American politics that created the environment in
which new technological capacities were perceived as strategically valuable and then adopted. A simple technological explanation has two
limitations. First, improved public opinion research did not provide a
clear advantage to either responding to public opinion or attempting
to move it; rather, advances in opinion research improved the effectiveness of both responding to the public and directing it. Second, the
technology existed *before* the decline in responsiveness and the rise of
routine efforts to change public opinion. Presidential administrations
and congressional leaders were aware of the technological capacity to
track and influence public opinion earlier in the early twentieth century but did not capitalize on it as politicians did in the 1990s.[17] Kennedy was the first president to track public opinion in earnest and to
use television regularly to reach Americans, but the new technological

advances did not prompt him to adopt orchestrated campaigns aimed at changing public opinion as a routine strategy. The technology existed but was not used because Kennedy and other politicians did not perceive it as offering a clear strategic advantage (Jacobs 1993, chap. 2; 1992a).[18]

The political incentives in the decade or so before the 1970s—when technological changes were afoot, partisan polarization relatively subdued, and the ranks of moderates comparatively large—prompted presidents and legislators to rely on bargaining and negotiation. Negotiations occurred with identifiable partners who could deliver votes (if they were leaders in Congress and political parties) or organizational support (if they headed an industry or provider group). The political calculations in making policy were based on identifying constituents and their material stakes. "Farm, business, labor, and veterans organizations represented the material interests of farmers, firms, unionists and veterans" (Wilson 1995). If quiet discussions hit an impasse, political leaders would mobilize their constituents into action—whether it was to lobby a member of Congress or attend a rally. Indeed, several studies indicate that this kind of political participation by the mass public was more common before the 1970s than after, precisely because of elite mobilization strategies (Rosenstone and Hansen 1993; Verba, Schlozman, and Brady 1995).

President Kennedy's highly charged drive to establish Medicare illustrates the change in political strategies. Kennedy began his health care campaign in 1961 by sending a written message to Congress. His first and primary focus was on solidifying support from constituencies like labor and on opening quiet negotiations with members of Congress, the American Medical Association (AMA), and others with a stake in the existing health system. More than a year after introducing legislation, Medicare was stalled in Congress and Kennedy chose a nationally televised address at Madison Square Garden in New York City to restart the legislation (Jacobs 1993).

In contrast to Clinton's speech in September 1993, Kennedy's national address was poorly planned and controversial.[19] It was only in the limousine on the way to Madison Square Garden that Kennedy carefully read his speech and concluded that it was unacceptable; he then quickly scribbled some notes for his speech. The speech itself was pronounced a "disaster" by the president's supporters not only because of his poor preparation but also because of the controversy sparked by the novelty of using a national appeal to go over the heads of Washington elites. The *New York Times* complained that "Presi-

dents have tried to marshal public opinion before this for a favored
and politically potent bill, but probably never on such a scale." Opponents of reform such as the AMA capitalized on the controversy to
ominously warn in their own national address that "doctors fear that
the American public is in danger of being blitzed, brainwashed, and
bandwagoned." Kennedy's national appeal was equated with "skillful
manipulation" rather than with the legitimate public leadership that
greeted Clinton's address (Harris 1966; Jacobs 1993).

Another telling difference with Clinton's public presentations was
that Kennedy aimed his address at encouraging an ongoing set of political actions, including secret negotiations with legislators. By contrast,
Clinton's speech in September 1993 preceded (rather followed) the introduction of legislation. Interviews and internal records indicate that
Clinton's initial and primary concern was not to bargain quietly with
Congress (as Kennedy had done); that was not considered a realistic
option in the 1990s. One White House official complained that "we
were begging to negotiate [with interest groups and Republican members of Congress. But] we could never pin them down on anything."

What distinguishes the efforts to pass health reform by Kennedy and
Clinton are their distinctive political environments, not the technology
of mass communications and public opinion research that were available to both of them. Kennedy's speech was carelessly planned and
widely denounced as inappropriate because elite bargaining and negotiation were the primary means for influencing policy. Clinton's address
was expected, carefully crafted, and favorably received because it reflected the political incentives of his time; his action was entirely consistent with an era in which politicians routinely used orchestrated presentations to minimize the electoral risk of pursuing their desired
policy goals. The political incentive structure of the 1990s made crafted
presentations—targeted by public opinion research to swing the public
behind the desired policies—a common feature of debates over salient
policy issues that divide the parties.

Technological and political explanations are not mutually exclusive.
Technological innovations take form through political decisions about
whether to seize upon or ignore opportunities for using advances in
communications and public opinion research.

Making Policy Goals Electorally Attractive

The behavior and strategies of contemporary American politicians appear contradictory: politicians discount centrist opinion to pursue
their policy goals, while at the same time they struggle to change public

opinion in order to appear responsive. Politicians are both avoiding responsiveness and claiming to be responsive.

The reality is that politicians try to have it both ways—to pursue their policy goals and make their positions electorally attractive. When elections are not imminent, legislators and presidents struggle to change centrist opinion precisely because they have discounted the public's preferences and appreciate that their reelection chances improve if their positions approximate those of most Americans by election day. In addition to protecting their own electoral situation, moving centrist opinion also influences presidents, electorally vulnerable legislators, and legislative leaders concerned about securing a majority in their chamber.

The Spiral of Crafted Talk

The full interconnectedness of elite politics, media coverage, and public opinion has been neglected by pundits and scholars alike. Their analysis of American politics has, in practice, tended to treat each as a discrete phenomenon or to consider each in simple ways. Even when analysis has shifted to the media's impact on public opinion, it has often neglected the political roots and context in which press coverage and public opinion form; scholars in particular too often treat news reporting on politics as a sterile "independent variable" with an under-appreciation of its context or origins in a larger system of political and institutional developments.

We argue, however, that each component of the political process adapts to the routines of the others. The change in the behavior of American politicians since the 1970s toward pursuing policy goals and orchestrated presentations largely (but not exclusively) drove the news media's preoccupation with political conflict and the public's perception that government action threatened their personal well-being. Genuine change in politics provoked journalists to alter their reporting to focus on political conflict and strategy, and the public tended to recoil from proposed policy reforms. Changes in the behavior and strategy of politicians affected not only policymaking but also the mass media and the public.

The Political Cycle of Media Coverage

The Media-Centered Explanation for Political Coverage

In an age in which political power is equated with controlling public debate, few observers of American politics doubt the power of the press. The press can blunt or help policy advocates mobilize public support through its decision over what to cover and how to report it. While pundits, journalists, and scholars have focused on the political influence of press coverage, their media-centered accounts tend to underplay the driving influence on news reporting: the actual behavior and strategy of government officials and their allies.

THE EFFECTS OF MEDIA COVERAGE   Research into the effects of the media on policymakers and public opinion stretches back to the early twentieth century (see Graber 1993b). Since the early 1970s, the most sophisticated studies of media effects have focused on the impact of the press on the political matters that policymakers and the general public select as important and worthy of their attention.[20] These agenda-setting studies generally compare the volume of media coverage of specific issues with policymaking activity and public opinion on those issues. The common finding is that media reporting on an issue (often instigated by committed political activists) precedes both the initiation of legislative activity and a rise in the issue's salience to the public.

For example, Baumgartner and Jones (1993) report that media coverage of pesticides after World War II and, especially, in the 1960s slowly brought the issue of its dangers onto policymakers' radar screens; this led to major laws, regulations, and court decisions in the late 1960s and early 1970s. In the case of nuclear power, when previously favorable media coverage turned unfavorable in the 1960s and 1970s, congressional committees, state governments, and elected officials moved into action (Baumgartner and Jones 1993). Studies of agenda setting have suggested, then, that media coverage usually changes first and therefore largely causes subsequent government decisions; the press affects what subject or issue government officials and Americans consider important.

THE CONTENT OF PRESS COVERAGE   Because of the influence of media coverage on policymakers and Americans, the style and content of news stories about politics have drawn intensive scrutiny from scholars, politicians, and even journalists themselves. These and other observers of American politics are in remarkable agreement in criticizing the press for its obsession with political conflict and strategy (Jamieson 1992; Cappella and Jamieson 1997; Patterson 1994; Fallows 1996). Press coverage of the debate over government policy now resembles its coverage of elections: journalists assume the guise of a political campaign consultant (or theater critic) who dissects policy debates to reveal the big-stakes and the strategic ins and outs of the political game. The news media, it is charged, have artificially imposed their fascination with political tactics and conflict on otherwise substantive policy debates; the high cost is proportionately less coverage of the substance of problems and issues and of politicians' own statements.

The news media's coverage of the health reform debate, for example, was criticized by Kathleen Hall Jamieson and others for avoiding both the complexity of the substantive issues and the actual words of policymakers. Instead, journalists and editors repackaged the debate to concentrate on the political scheming by Clinton and his opponents (Jamieson and Cappella 1995; Cappella and Jamieson 1997; Times Mirror Center for the People and the Press 1995).

Blame for the media's preoccupation with political conflict and strategy has typically been assigned to factors internal to the press—the concerns of journalists, editors, and investors for economic gain and professional respect and advancement. The mass media are businesses. Money in the media business follows audiences because that is what attracts advertisers. Newspapers and television intensely compete for a fragile and shrinking audience. The circulation for daily newspapers stagnated since the 1960s: excluding *USA Today,* readership continued to decline after the early 1980s. Entertainment shows challenged television news for audiences. The mergers of news and entertainment organizations have further intensified commercial pressure (Bagdikian 1992; Underwood 1998).

Because the media's bottom line is to attract and keep audiences, news journalists and editors cannot ignore the eroding marketplace for their product and the imperative of courting viewers and readers, especially general audiences that are neither well versed in political issues nor especially interested in them. Journalists and editors respond to economic pressures when covering politics by avoiding complexity in favor of simplicity, easy-to-sell stereotypes, and audience-grabbing plots. The marketing calculation (within news organizations) is that political conflict and the "horse race" or war between competing political factions will captivate and draw audiences addicted to titillating entertainment. (The extent to which audiences are in fact drawn by "horse race" coverage is open to dispute [Jamieson and Cappella 1998; Cappella and Jamieson 1997].)

Media observers also attribute the press's fascination with the political "horse race" and conflict to the professional norm of "objectivity" and covering "both sides" of political controversies. Reporting the charges and countercharges of politicians is considered "factual." The press is also expected to serve as watchdogs that question rather than simply accept official pronouncements, which encourages journalists to scrutinize politicians' presentations in order to unveil their "true" intent and to report the "behind-the-scenes" strategy. Journalists are trained with a sense of professional obligation to inform citizens and cover what matters most in the activities of government officials. The press is pressured, then, to deliver information but in an entertaining and "sellable" form.

BRINGING POLITICS INTO MEDIA WATCHING   Previous analysis of the effects of media coverage and its emphasis on political conflict and strategy has tended to center on the media—their independent impact on politics and the internal incentives generating their horse-race orientation. The media-centered analysis, however, is incomplete. In particular, it does not give full weight to the original political impetus for media coverage—the actual political and policy developments that drive press reporting.[21]

Recognizing the impact of actual politics on press coverage addresses a widespread limitation with the existing study of media effects and its horse-race content. Research on media effects and, particularly, on the role of the press in agenda-setting has overemphasized the influence of the press in incubating issues, and it has neglected the larger effects of real-world political developments—such as ideological polarization and the rise of policy-oriented politicians—on what issues the press covers and how it presents them. The media's focus on political strategy and conflict may well reflect a genuinely high level of partisan conflict and reliance by politicians on orchestrated presentations targeted at the press. Analysis needs to consider the impact of politics on the press, and not just the reverse.

Both intense economic pressures on news organizations to maintain or expand their audiences and professional norms to carry "both sides" have influenced news reporting, but they are at most only part of the story—and not the most important part. Bringing politics back into the study of the press is essential to making sense of the content and character of media coverage and how this feeds back on political activity.

The Political Impetus for Media Coverage

W. Lance Bennett (Bennett 1990; Alexseev and Bennett 1995) persuasively argues that the contemporary press routinely represents the broad contours of major government policy discussions (for discussion of historical evolution see Bennett 1996). Journalists (not unlike politicians) react to their incentive structure—the rewards and sanctions associated with their actions. A set of common incentives, as was already mentioned, have pressured competing news organizations to converge on similar stories about the political world: the economic need to cover the audience-grabbing "big" political story and the adherence to journalistic norms to inform citizens about government deliberations. A third factor is the "beat" system for gathering news, which distributes reporters based on perceptions about where government power routinely resides (e.g., more journalists generally cover the White House than the Supreme Court).

Bennett usefully identifies three dimensions of news reporting that follow political and policy developments. First, the content of press coverage generally represents the broad contours of government actions. The coverage of most national policy debates is "indexed" to the public statements of authoritative government officials who exercise significant influence over decisions. For instance, a strong position by a prominent politician like the president will receive wide coverage in the mainstream press. Second, strong opposition and conflict among authoritative government officials expand the range of viewpoints and the volume of coverage devoted to the policy debate. Scattered criticism by junior legislators of a presidential initiative is not likely to receive coverage or to boost the media's attention to the policy area, while opposition from congressional leaders who can block White House proposals is likely to be reported and to expand coverage of the policy debate. Third, the actions and statements of authoritative officials are more often used as news sources or subjects than those of other political actors (Blumler and Gurevitch 1981; Brown, Bybee, Weardon, and Straughan 1982; for a review see Bennett 1996). In short, Bennett offers a set of clear expectations regarding the ways that press coverage reflects the general contour of political debate.

We use Bennett's propositions to develop three theoretical expectations regarding the impact on press coverage of policy-oriented politicians and their emphasis on orchestrated presentations since the 1970s.[22] First, we expect variations in the volume and content of press reports about policy debates to represent the ebb and flow of actual discussions by government officials. Changes in the volume and content of press coverage of health policy issues over time should reflect the evolution of policy discussions.

Second, we expect the media's presentation of policy disagreements to be sensitive to political changes over time. "Negative" press coverage can take one of two forms: the *directionality* of news coverage (what we call "*issue* negativity") may disproportionately be negative ("con") rather than positive ("pro") concerning a specific issue; or the press can excessively cover the political motivations, intentions, and strategic behavior of officeholders and candidates (what we call "*political* negativity") instead of substantive policy issues. Increases in genuine policy disagreements expand press coverage of political negativity—political conflict and strategy. On the other hand, the directionality of press reports may be less affected by policy disagreements; describing the policy proposals by authoritative government officials requires, as a practical matter, a substantial amount of print and broadcast time. The press would require disproportionate space to explain, for instance, the contents of the Clinton health care plan in order to provide the context for reporting the questions and criticisms of the plan offered by its opponents.

Third, policy actions by authoritative government officials expand the media's selection and use of them as sources. We expect the citation of presidents and congressional leaders, in particular, to rise when the White House or the House and Senate take action or issue significant statements on government policy.

In short, we offer a political account of the content and cycle of media reporting. The overall pattern of the media's reporting mirrors the intensity, content, and relative degree of dissensus in ongoing policy debates among authoritative government officials. Media coverage of politics, then, is largely driven by forces external to the media—by statements, behavior, and events in the political world.

The Media's Feedback Effect

News reports offer an interpretation of reality—one that represents some aspects while magnifying or downplaying others. The impetus for press coverage lies in the realm of actual politics, but the combination of needing to sell a business product, to inform citizens, and to capitalize on ever-expanding technological capacity creates incentives for journalists and editors to magnify policy disagreement and its threat to their audiences. In conveying politicians' presentations, journalists and editors also insert their own interpretations that emphasize the strategy of political activists and the personal stake of the audience; the media exercise their own standards of quality and interests (Cook 1998). This kind of journalistic intervention is consistent with Thomas Patterson's findings that American reporters, when compared to their counterparts in other industrialized countries, are distinctively active in shaping political news even as they claim political neutrality (Patterson 1998).

The ironic result of the media's feedback effect is that the already crafted presentations of politicians are amplified further by journalists. Press efforts to unmask the very real strategic calculations of politicians magnify the conflict imbedded in the statements of their news sources and lead the press to neglect political developments that are considered unlikely to produce government action. (The scant coverage of the single-payer plan during the 1993–94 health care reform debate illustrates the inclination of the press not to report on a policy that seemed unlikely to become law.)

The feedback effect of the media into the political process suggests, then, that the press clearly retains a significant influence on policymaking. Serious and acrimonious policy debates draw media coverage, but press coverage also influences the behavior and strategies of politicians as they weigh their future strategy.

The speech that Bill Clinton delivered in September 1993 was a product of how he expected reporters and political opponents to behave; it reflected not so much his own personal character as his realistic adaptation to the current structure of American politics. The White House's "launch" of its health plan was shaped by its perception that the near defeat of the administration's first budget proposal in early 1993 stemmed from the media's focus on the criticisms of opponents and on the "horse race" and political battle rather than on substance. Clinton's speech was designed to exploit the media's well-known routines and to preempt his opponents by sticking to a simple message that relied on emotionally charged stereotypes of American life and on unsubstantiated promises to save free choice and avoid big government.

In short, the behavior and strategies of politicians affect not only policy debates but also the media coverage of them. Genuine policy disagreements instigate the press's focus on conflict, which then intensifies the determination of politicians to orchestrate their statements and actions. Journalists and editors reflect and contribute to this political cycle of media reporting.

The Political Cycle of Public Opinion

Many politicians and scholars operate on the assumption that politics and media coverage have a significant impact on public opinion. A generation of scholars has followed V. O. Key's advice to "plac[e] the newer knowledge about public opinion in a political context" (1961, vii) and now accepts that public opinion is endogenous to the process of politics and media coverage (Page and Shapiro 1992; Zaller 1992; Carmines and Stimson 1989; Hill and Hurley 1999). For their part, politicians treat the public—as discussed above—as largely a passive object, which absorbs the messages that are most effectively crafted and that receive the most favorable media coverage.

The focus on the influences on public opinion is an important feature of academic study and political strategy, but it too has limitations. The first limitation is a tendency to exaggerate the propensity of public opinion to change in the wake of political developments and media coverage. Despite a history of research that (until recently) emphasized the limited effects of the media, there has been a consistent tendency to overstate the influences on public opinion and downplay the stability and resilience of the public's own attitudes (cf. Kuklinski and Segura 1995, 9; Klapper 1960; Bartels 1996). Politicians and political observers have adopted a more extreme perspective—that the public's attitudes and beliefs are manufactured and prone to sudden change in reaction to a well-crafted and widely circulated message. The reality, though, is that Americans' fundamental policy preferences—like its support for Medicare or government spending on health care—change little over time, which makes them resistant to simply following politicians' persuasive messages (Page and Shapiro 1992). In addition, Americans cannot simply "obey" politicians because the information they receive is rarely uniform or dictated by one individual or group. Intense partisan disagreement and the media's portrayal of it tend to generate conflicting messages on specific policies (Lazarsfeld and Merton 1948). Moreover, ordinary citizens interpret political information, rather than uncritically consume it. The public is equipped with the skills to select, reject, or ignore information offered by the media and instead to draw on their interactions with peers and their personal experiences (Gamson 1992; Neuman, Just, and Krigler 1992).[23] People are influenced by politicians and the media, but it is through more subtle processes than direct and willful manufacturing.

There is a tension between the strategy of crafted talk and the actual dynamics of public opinion. Although politicians' confidence in their capacity to move public opinion reinforces their inclination to discount the public's policy preferences, the nature of public opinion (and news coverage) poses barriers to efforts to win public backing for a specific policy reform. In fact, both Clinton's efforts to win public support for his health care reform plan and Gingrich's similar campaign to gain public backing for the Contract with America failed. Their political opponents were more successful in moving public opinion because they faced the more manageable task of stimulating uncertainty.

A second limitation applies most directly to scholars and stems from the gaps in their investigation of political and institutional developments. Research concerning the influences on public opinion recognizes the significance of politics but has not yet examined adequately the nature of politicians' motivations and strategies for handling media coverage and public opinion. For instance, Zaller (1992) emphasizes how the character of policy debate (namely, the degree of elite consensus or dissensus) affects public opinion by tracking political information carried by the media. It remains unclear, however, where the political content of the media originates—from journalists, politicians themselves, or, as we argue, some combination of both. Accounting for politicians' motivations and strategies is essential to connecting political and institutional dynamics to changes in public opinion. What needs to be incorporated is the intentional strategy of politicians to change public opinion and to pinpoint particular public considerations. The specific content of the information reaching the public today is at least partly the result of a calculus by policy-oriented politicians to use public opinion research to change public opinion. Studying "how variations in . . . elite discourse affect both the direction and organization of mass opinion" (Zaller 1992, 14) is important but remains one important step removed from political and institutional dynamics; we need to understand the political source and content of this influence.

Although Americans' preferences cannot be willfully manufactured by political actors, the public's heavy (though not exclusive) reliance on the media for information makes them vulnerable to subtle processes of influence. The concept of priming is useful not only as a heuristic for discussing political strategy (as shown above) but also as an analytic tool for studying public opinion change.

The character of political behavior and strategies elicits identifiable patterns of media coverage and public reaction. The pursuit by politicians of policy goals and orchestrated presentations and the resulting media coverage of strategy and conflict raise the likelihood that the public will focus on the uncertainty and risks of altering the status quo (Kahneman and Tversky 1984). The public's perception of uncertainty and its inclination toward risk-aversion increases the prospects that favorable evaluations of specific proposed policies will decline and that the public's motivations will shift away from broader concerns about the nation as a whole to more narrowly self-interested considerations.

The interaction of politics, media coverage, and public opinion is illustrated, as we discuss in later chapters, by the 20 percentage point decline in public support for the Clinton health reform plan between September 1993 and the following summer. The highly partisan policy debate and its coverage by the press primed the public to focus on its ambivalence about "big" government and on its uncertainty about the future of their personal medical care. The result was that many Americans reversed their once favorable evaluation of the Clinton plan.

Connecting Politics, Media Coverage, and Public Opinion

Politics, media coverage, and public opinion are interconnected. Figure 2.6 summarizes the most important causal connections we have described. We focus our discussion here on the four most important sets of nested relationships.[24]

The first set of relationships involve the effects of political and institutional conditions on the behavior and strategy of politicians. We have argued that the policy choices of politicians and their strategy of orchestrated presentations have resulted from a set of historically variable political and institutional conditions. Since the 1970s, ideological polarization, interest group proliferation, institutional individualization, incumbency, and acrimonious interbranch relations have elevated the benefits politicians associate with pursuing policy goals that they and their supporters favor (as opposed to responding to na-

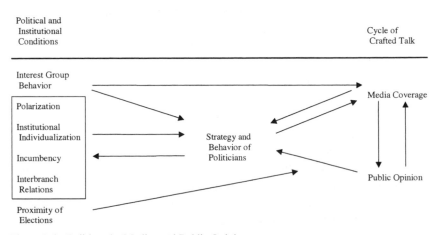

Figure 2.6   Politics, the Media, and Public Opinion

tional public opinion). They attempt to lower the electoral risks of discounting centrist opinion to pursue their policy objectives by attempting to manipulate public opinion. The approach of imminent elections, however, temporarily raises the expected benefit of responding to centrist opinion and briefly interrupts the drive of politicians to reach their policy objectives.

National interest groups have not only raised the benefits that politicians perceive from pursuing policy goals at the expense of centrist opinion, they have also used huge sums of money to intervene directly in political communications with the public. In particular, organized groups have used paid ads to impose their views on the public. For instance, HIAA used its well-funded "Harry and Louise" spots to contribute directly to (and manipulate) the information that the public received about Clinton's health care reform plan.

The second relationship involves the impact of political behavior and strategy on the media's reporting of political news. Conflicts among authoritative government officials over government policy draws the media's spotlight. The press reports on the content of the proposals and counterproposals of authoritative officials by expanding the scope and volume of its coverage to capture the conflict among government officials and other political influentials. The result is that the press conveys some of the themes crafted by politicians and focuses heavily on political conflict and strategy. The media's coverage has indirectly reflected, then, the genuine changes in political and institutional conditions since the 1970s that have elevated the pursuit of policy goals by politicians and heightened conflict; the press reported on political conflict in the past but it did so far more after the 1970s.

The third relationship is represented by the path from politicians' policy choices and political strategy to public opinion *through* the media's coverage of these developments. Although the public's fundamental preferences and values are generally not altered, the media's coverage of politicians' presentations and policy debates primes the public to reconsider its evaluation of whether specific policy proposals represent desirable changes in the status quo. In the health care debate, political actions and media coverage of policy disagreements prompted Americans to reactivate their existing attitudes about "big" government and to conclude that health reform threatened their personal well-being and was therefore undesirable.

The interrelationship between the media and public attitudes is complicated. The press influences public opinion in ways that extend beyond its priming effect; it also influences the public's collective perceptions and understandings of "public opinion" itself. While this may be a general "media effect" (Mutz 1998), it can also occur due to the press's use (and reporting) of polls. The media influence the agenda of opinion polling and the selection of topics on which the public is surveyed (Dearing 1989). The result is that some issues are neglected; polling on Canada's single-payer system was limited during the Clinton reform initiative because of the media's focus on authoritative government officials. More fundamentally, though, the media's reliance on standard survey questions that restrict a respondent's reaction to a policy proposal to "favor or oppose" obscures the complexity and thoughtfulness of the public's thinking (Herbst 1993). The process of polling and the media's reliance on it unwittingly shapes the way public opinion is understood by Americans and by policymakers.

In addition to the influence of the media on public opinion, the public may affect the media. A common argument is that the public essentially gets what it wants from the press (e.g., Zaller 1998b). The problem, however, is that the public's choices or even "tastes" in news reports are at least partly induced by the press itself; the media's amplification of political conflict and strategy helps create the interest in and demand for more accounts "inside" the political campaign to win an election or enact a policy proposal.

The fourth set of nested relationships involve the feedback effects of politicians' behavior and strategy. The first and most important feedback for our purposes involves the paths or processes emanating from political actions and interest group promotions to media coverage, through public opinion, and back to politicians. This loop captures what we describe as *simulated responsiveness* in which successfully crafted public opinion influences politicians' ultimate policy decisions.

Having pursued their policy goals and discounted centrist opinion, policy-oriented politicians can claim to be responsive to public preferences. They trumpet their responsiveness in order to pressure other politicians who are sensitive to centrist opinion and to bolster their own electoral prospects as well as those of their allies. For instance, Republicans gloated in September 1994 that the majority of Americans got what they wanted when Congress defeated Clinton's health care reform proposal by refusing to even vote on it. For their part, the Democrats (who controlled the White House as well as majorities in the House and Senate) decided on the brink of the 1994 elections to accept quietly the defeat of the *unpopular* Clinton health plan. In short, Democrats and Republicans adjusted their policy choices to the public's reaction, which itself had been the successful result of the well-orchestrated campaign by the opponents of health care reform (as conveyed by the press).

A second feedback shown in figure 2.6 involves the influence of politicians' actions and interest group's ad on media coverage, which rebounds back to influence politicians. The reaction by politicians can take two forms. In one, politicians alter their political strategy. For instance, the Clinton White House became more attentive to orchestrating its activities and presentations in the late spring of 1993 by introducing the "war room" to counter what they perceived as the media's unfavorable coverage of the budget debate. A second reaction by politicians is to adjust their policy goals. For example, our interviews indicated that the "Harry and Louise" ads confirmed for some moderate legislators their own trepidation about government activism and contributed to their tepidness toward the Clinton plan. These politicians may have perceived the "free media" reports on "Harry and Louise" as an indication of public opinion. (A 1998 Pew survey of members of Congress and executive branch officials indicated that their perceptions of public opinion were formed more by media reports than polls themselves [Pew 1998]).

The reciprocal interaction of press coverage and the actions of politicians may powerfully influence how the press and politicians perceive each other. On the one hand, politicians' actions confirm and further encourage the perceptions of journalists and editors that their portrayal of politicians as wheeler-dealers is accurate. For instance, our content analysis of media coverage and Clinton's statements regarding health care shows that the media's zeal for uncovering political machinations prompted it to underreport the president's actual comments about containing health costs. On the other hand, the media's amplification of the disagreements and strategizing by politicians reinforces politicians' worst impressions of the press and encourages them to plan their actions and public statements in anticipation that the press will reconstruct them along predictable lines. Ironically, the media's reporting of genuine policy disputes reinforces the inclination of presidents and legislators to orchestrate their actions and rhetoric.

In short, the changes in the behavior of politicians and the media that were prompted by systemic changes in political motivations have turned into a reinforcing cycle of crafted talk and action—a process that satisfies the distinctive career interests and professional considerations of political actors and the press while also addressing (though not necessarily well) the public's demand for information.

Our Research

Theory Building

Our purpose for studying two cases of major policy innovation—the Clinton health care reform campaign and the Republican "Revolution" to enact the Contract with America—is to generate research questions and explanations to account for the variation in politicians' responsiveness to centrist opinion and the impact of this variation on media coverage and public opinion. These generalizable questions and explanations can be examined and tested further by others.

Most studies of public opinion and policymaking adopt an "outsider" perspective: they focus on aggregate relationships and do not directly study the strategic calculations and usages of public opinion by policymakers. Although it has made valuable contributions, this research has not adequately disentangled the causal connections between public opinion and policymaking (see appendix 1). In addition to wrestling with whether opinion influences policy or the reverse, researchers have struggled to incorporate the impact of media coverage and other factors on policymakers and public opinion (Page and Shapiro 1983, 185; Page 1994).

In contrast, we offer an "insider" account that intensively studies the calculations of legislators and presidents toward policy issues and public opinion. Our aim is to penetrate the black box of policymaking and investigate how politicians understand, evaluate, and use public opinion (Jacobs 1993, 1992a, 1992b). Our analysis more generally is geared to addressing a gap in the existing analysis of aggregate data; we identify the concrete mechanisms that link political behavior and strategy, media coverage, and public opinion.

Our methods and evidence, then, are designed to investigate the intentions and perceptions that drive the actions of politicians. We rely on White House memoranda and other records, congressional votes, content analysis of the statements and decisions of President Clinton and legislators, and semi-structured interviews with senior advisers in Congress and the Clinton administration, which allowed them to discuss decisions in their own words and in the terms familiar to them. The contribution of this intensive case study approach is that it supplements aggregate-level analysis; it adds another analytic perspective to efforts to disentangle the relationship between public opinion and the policymaking process.

Our analysis of media coverage is also in-depth. We conducted an intensive study of health care issues in order to track trends in media coverage and public opinion over time, as well as to examine interrelationships among media coverage, public opinion, and policy debates. In particular, our systematic content analysis of media coverage of health issues over a nearly two-decade period tracks trends in the volume, content, and sources of press reports. In addition, we use aggregate- and individual-level analysis of public opinion data on health care issues to examine trends in public preferences and to study changes in the influences on these preferences as the health care debate and media coverage of the debate progress.

Studying Existing and Anticipated Public Opinion

Politicians evaluate both existing and anticipated future public opinion: they examine the public's current attitudes and estimate its likely future opinions. Indeed, many politicians take the next step and downplay or ignore existing opinion in favor of anticipated public preferences. A critical question looms, however: what is the purpose of discounting existing opinion and anticipating future opinion? Are politicians attempting to respond to the public's own well-considered opinions or to design strategies to change existing opinion in order to support (in the future) their desired policy goals? Are politicians motivated by electoral or policy goals when they anticipate opinion?

Politicians motivated to appeal to the median voter may have strong incentives to tailor policies they propose to their estimates of the public's preferences in the future. Presidents and legislators may ignore existing centrist opinion to enact policies (e.g., cuts in government spending) that are currently unpopular but will produce in the future the kind of favorable national conditions (e.g., economic growth) that voters traditionally reward (Zaller 1998). In other words, politicians anticipate retrospective voting and therefore attempt to create favorable national conditions even if it means disregarding the public's immediate policy preferences. Politicians may also calculate that voters will make policy-specific evaluations and punish officeholders who burden them with legislation that imposes high costs and minimal benefits. Arnold (1990), for instance, implies that legislators constantly adjust their decisions in Washington to satisfy the anticipated reaction of constituents back home to whether legislation immediately imposes large and concentrated costs while delaying benefits. Politicians may have particular incentives to anticipate public opinion when they perceive the public as relatively uninformed.

There are two difficulties in assuming that politicians anticipate opinion in order to respond to the public's autonomous preferences. First, the changing political and institutional conditions that produce variations in responsiveness to existing public opinion also apply to anticipated opinion. The incentives of politicians to respond to the anticipated future direction of the public opinion is offset by institutional and political developments that encourage politicians to reach decisions based on the policy goals that they or their partisan or interest group supporters favor. Under these conditions, which have developed since the 1970s, politicians are motivated to change (and not simply follow) future opinion to support their desired policy goals and avoid the costs of policy compromises. Indeed, Fenno (1978), Kernell (1986), and our own research suggest that politicians count on communications with constituents to change their evaluations and create, as Fenno put it, more "leeway" to pursue policy goals. Research that fails to incorporate fully a conditional model of political motivations risks stripping policy debate and public opinion of its dynamism, its political context, and its wider informational context.

Second, it is more risky for politicians (and scholars) to anticipate future opinion than to evaluate existing opinion; even genuine attempts at anticipating substantive preferences are prone to miscalculation. Arnold (1990), for instance, presumes that the public's reaction to policy debates can be reduced to "predictable" calculations about the costs and benefits of policy attributes. Previous research (in addition to ours) does not support the proposition that politicians can confidently estimate future public opinion based on predetermined laws of policy attributes; politicians' crafted actions and statements are designed precisely to manipulate public perceptions of policy attributes. For instance, the Clinton administration chose to propose an "employer mandate," which would require employers to provide health benefits for their employees, rather than a direct payroll tax to fund its health plan partly because it anticipated that the former would obscure the plan's costs. The administration's opponents, however, orchestrated their own messages to offset the administration's calculation and paint Clinton's plan as introducing immediate and massive new costs—a huge tax increase and an abandonment of high quality health care. The risk of error in responding to existing opinion is lower than that for anticipated opinion because it relies on observable and more certain comparisons of policy choices and public attitudes.

Conclusion

We argue that changing institutional and political dynamics since the 1970s raised the personal benefit to politicians of both pursuing policy goals, which decreased their responsiveness to centrist public opinion, and crafting their messages and actions to win over public opinion. The current level of responsiveness, however, is not fixed; it varied in the past and may well vary in the future in reaction to changes in political and institutional conditions. Changes in political and institutional dynamics could shift the incentives from policy-oriented behavior toward greater responsiveness to centrist opinion (as was the case in previous historical periods).

The next chapter turns to evidence on policy debates. It examines the behavior and strategies of officials in the Clinton administration as they formulated the president's health reform proposal and attempted to build a supportive coalition for it. We ask: What drove the administration's health policy decisions? Did it respond to public opinion and, if so, how?

Part Two

Health Care Reform

Chapter Three

The New Democrats and the Crafting of Public Opinion

The Roosevelt Room in the White House normally holds twenty people and is often used for cabinet meetings. The cabinet members sit around the large table that dominates the room and their most senior aide sits behind them along the walls. May 20, 1993, was different, as President Bill Clinton, the First Lady, Vice President Al Gore, Mrs. Gore, and at least fifty of the top officials in the Clinton administration packed the room. The cabinet and top officials squeezed around the table; others scrambled for seats along the walls but many were forced to sit on the floor. The heart and soul of health care reform seemed to be on the line in the Roosevelt Room, and for the first time the health policy wizards, the White House's political operatives, and senior administration officials all gathered for what they saw as a momentous opportunity to hash out the direction of health care reform.

What transpired was unusual in the annals of presidential decision making; the Roosevelt meeting was transformed into a kind of Oxford on the Potomac. Ira Magaziner, who coordinated the White House's health care reform efforts, appointed two debating teams; their assignment was to marshal detailed and factual arguments on whether the health benefit package scheduled to take effect at the beginning ought to be comprehensive or scaled back and then gradually expanded. Many participants in the Roosevelt debate who had worked in Washington for years were struck by the focus on substance. While some found it ill-advised, favoring instead a political focus, one official from an academic background found the experience reassuringly familiar: it was "great to watch the level of discussion taking place at that level."

This nearly full-blown Oxford-style debate over detailed and substantive health reform issues contradicts the persistent criticism of
Clinton as "hyper-responsive" to public opinion and elevating his pollster to a "prominent and unprecedented role" in policymaking (Perry
1994; Drew 1994; Berke 1993; Center for Public Integrity 1994, 64; A.
King 1997). Did Clinton and his advisers design their health care reform proposal (as commonly assumed) by following what most Americans wanted or, alternatively, did they discount public opinion in order
to pursue the policy goals of the president and his supporters?

White House documents and interviews confirm the argument in
chapter 2: far from the next presidential or congressional election,
Clinton and his advisers discounted centrist opinion, fully understanding that their favored approach (managed competition) had little public support. Instead, they pursued the policy goals of party activists,
interest groups, critical groups of legislators, and Clinton's personal
preferences regarding "good policy." The substance-heavy debate in
the Roosevelt Room genuinely reflected the priority that the president
and his aides placed on policy objectives.

But how can we square the way the Clinton White House pursued
policy goals and discounted centrist opinion when formulating legislation with its routine practice of closely monitoring public opinion?
White House records, interviews, and other evidence indicate that the
president and his aides used polls and focus groups to craft their presentations in order to most effectively "win" public backing. They attempted to move public opinion to close the gap with what most
Americans preferred (or, in our shorthand, "centrist opinion"); the
strategic attraction was lowering their electoral risk and, at the same
time, increasing the pressure on politicians sensitive to public opinion
to support Clinton's reform plan. Public opinion research, then, did
not guide policymaking; rather, policy decisions guided the research
on public opinion in order to identify the language, arguments, and
symbols most likely to persuade Americans.

The battle for public opinion among political elites and organized
interests in Washington focused on the mass media. While journalists
were recognized as the conduits for reaching the public, they were seen
as prone to distortion. Indeed, the White House's expectation of media
distortion was confirmed the morning after the Roosevelt Room debate when the *Washington Post* and the *New York Times* ran misleading and explosive stories about the First Lady battling against the
president's economic team.[1] Faced with the prospect of distorted news
coverage, White House aides as well as those opposed to the Clinton

plan for health care reform turned to the same strategy—crafted talk—to evoke favorable media coverage and public support for their cause. The actions of the press and the White House were mutually reinforcing: the press reflected the genuine political conflict over policy and the crafted presentations of the combatants, but its amplification of these patterns drove the White House's dependence on manipulation of public opinion. White House officials came to accept it as inevitable that an effective communications strategy would require incomplete or even misleading presentations of their decisions.

This chapter and the next one examine the formulation and attempted passage of the Clinton health care reform plan. We first look at the formulation of the plan during the first nine months of 1993 and the development of a political strategy for passing it, which the president "launched" in his nationally televised address in September 1993. Chapter 4 then analyzes the political conflict over health care reform from the onset of the legislative debate in the fall of 1993 and its quickening pace in the spring of 1994 to its demise in September 1994. In these chapters, we show that the actions of politicians and political activists sparked a cycle of actions and counteractions, which fueled media coverage and public debate and stimulated more determined efforts by policy advocates to craft their presentations more effectively.

We draw on a diverse body of evidence: White House records, interviews, presidential speeches and other public comments, polls and focus groups conducted for the White House and for the media, as well as secondary sources. The interviews used in this chapter were conducted with high-ranking officials within the White House and the executive branch departments as well as with influential Clinton advisers outside of government. Most of the interviews were conducted in person during or just after the tumultuous final months of the president's campaign for health reform in 1994. The prominence of our sources, the delicate timing of our discussions, and the importance of candor made it necessary to offer anonymity. We have omitted citations to the interviews to shield the identity of our sources unless the sources agreed to be quoted; this follows the practice of other scholars (e.g., Kingdon 1989; Fenno 1973, 1978).

The Formulation of Clinton's Health Care Reform Proposal

Existing analyses of the Clinton administration and health care reform have focused on its elephantine 630-person task force and its formulation of a highly detailed and complex plan.[2] Political observers and

White House officials emphasize two factors in explaining the task force process and the complexity of Clinton's plan. First, White House officials and Johnson and Broder (1996) pin Clinton's approach on pressure from Democratic congressional leaders, who uniformly advised Clinton to propose detailed legislation.[3] Second, they point to the president's cognitive style and demand (as one senior aide put it) for an "all-encompassing look at the health care system" that thought through even the most intricate policy options. This side of Clinton was on display in the Roosevelt Room. Clinton's insistence on substantive deliberations encouraged his aides (as they recalled) to "sit with many of the best experts and practitioners, consult with the best of the best, [and] analyze the best numbers available." Clinton himself committed hundreds of hours to "get[ting] up to speed" on the detailed issues, participating in meetings, and wading through long reports from Magaziner. The White House's approach, it was claimed, reflected the president's approach to making decisions.

Both congressional pressure and Clinton's personal style contributed to the task force process and the complexity of the White House plan, but focusing on them alone ignores the White House's larger set of political calculations. The task force and the complex plan resulted from the White House's determination both to impose the policy goals favored by Clinton and his allies and to rally public opinion behind its approach in order to create a winning coalition in Congress.

The New Democratic Creed

Chroniclers of Clinton's rise to the presidency assume that electoral pressures both to respond to centrist opinion that favored health reform (as captured in Harris Wofford's 1991 Pennsylvania Senate race following the death of John Heinz) and to appeal to swing voters in the 1992 campaign produced the broad structure of the plan that Clinton publicly unveiled in a September 1992 speech at Merck Pharmaceuticals and forwarded to Congress a year later (Johnson and Broder 1996, 82–92). It is certainly true that Clinton's campaign team was intimately familiar with Wofford's successful campaign (two of Wofford's consultants later worked for Clinton), and that the Clinton team designed its health reform positions to reduce the risk that anticipated Republican attacks on Clinton as a "tax and spend" Democrat would alienate centrist voters.

But simply attributing Clinton's health care reform proposal to his responsiveness to centrist opinion during the 1992 presidential campaign is an overstatement. Policy issues other than universal health insurance reform were politically safer, which explains why no Demo-cratic presidential nominee had aggressively campaigned for it since the early 1950s. In addition, the Clinton campaign could have deflected Bush's "tax and spend" charges by choosing reform packages other than the novel approach it proposed (a liberal variant of managed competition that combined market competition with government mandates to create universal coverage and a budget cap). Clinton's se-lection of the risky issue of universal health insurance reform and a novel approach to achieving it resulted from an amalgam of electoral and policy goals, with particular emphasis on the latter. Electoral pres-sure reinforced the policy preferences of Clinton and his supporters but did not drive them.

Clinton's primary goal from the outset of his 1992 presidential cam-paign was economic growth and deficit reduction. He was committed to using government policy to achieve both of these, but his use of government was guided, according to aides who worked with him dur-ing the campaign and in the administration, by his "philosophical at-tachment to the concept of a New Democrat." Clinton's philosophy stemmed from his long-standing beliefs and policymaking experience as governor in Arkansas and from his political struggle to distance himself from the label of "tax and spend" Democrat (Hacker 1997).

Clinton's New Democratic philosophy favored incorporating the pri-vate sector and economic competition in government policy and avoiding new taxes or a heavy reliance on regulation. It was an article of faith among Clinton aides that "not taxing really mattered to him." The overall political environment in Congress and in the country only reinforced Clinton's personal aversion to taxes: "We were working in a world," one aide explained, "where there was not going to be any broad-based tax increase, other than maybe a sin tax or two" (see also Bruck 1994). Another of Clinton's "basic values" was to promote a visible role for private markets that would complement and offset gov-ernment activity, or what he called "micro-regulation." Summarizing the views of the president and his aides, one adviser suggested that "a fundamental philosophy was that regulation doesn't work, never has, never will. And that it was time to let the market try to work."

Health reform rose to the top of Clinton's agenda because he and his advisers identified it as the means for achieving his overriding goals of economic rejuvenation and deficit reduction.[4] Responsiveness to public opinion did not put it on his agenda, though public attitudes reinforced Clinton's interest in health care. One senior aide who worked on economic and health issues in the campaign and in the

administration explained that Clinton promoted health care reform
from the start of the 1992 presidential race because "he viewed health
care primarily as an economic issue first, and as a social issue second."
In particular, Clinton and aides like Magaziner were alarmed that rising national health care costs were swelling the government's budget
deficit and gobbling up national economic growth and real personal
income.

It was primarily Clinton's commitment to economic growth and
deficit reduction that led, according to a wide spectrum of Clinton's
aides, to his support of universal health insurance; humanitarian concerns and political pressures from Democratic activists and officeholders reinforced this decision but did not drive it. Clinton accepted
the view vigorously promoted by Magaziner and his economic advisers
during the campaign that universal coverage would control government and business costs (1) by putting an end to the rampant practice
of shifting the expenses for treating the uninsured to the insured, and
(2) by focusing Americans on remaining healthy and efficiently using
the health system. One adviser to the campaign and later to the administration explained that Clinton's "goal was not a social goal of coverage expansion per se." He "went in as a way to save and reduce the
deficit" and, perhaps, to "finance high priority new initiatives in such
areas as education or the environment."

The novel approach to health care reform that Clinton embraced
was the offspring of his New Democratic philosophy; it seemed to
promise an approach to health care reform that would expand insurance coverage while avoiding a visible government role and a massive
tax increase. Clinton backed a liberal variant of managed competition
that proposed to establish universal access to health insurance by requiring employers to contribute to their employee's insurance and by
creating new regional bodies that negotiated with private health plans
and monitored competition between them. Clinton first signaled his
interest in this approach in *Putting People First,* which Magaziner
helped to write in June 1992, and more fully outlined his position in a
September 1992 campaign speech at the Merck Pharmaceutical company in Rahway, New Jersey. In this speech, Clinton publicly spelled
out the general structure of the plan that he would forward to Congress
as president a year later. He became president, his advisers emphasize,
locked into the broad structure of managed competition.

One aide recalled, "The president philosophically wanted to say 'I
have a competitive bill, not a regulatory bill.'" Managed competition
was seen as reducing the government's role to a situation where "you

steer, don't row"; government rules would be restricted to "leveling the playing field" and promoting private market competition. "We've got to quit having the federal government micro-manage health care," Clinton announced in his September 1992 campaign speech, "and instead set up incentives for the private sector to manage the cost."

Clinton was also attracted to managed competition because it promised to finance health care reform by squeezing waste out of the system rather than imposing enormous direct tax hikes. According to several officials active in the 1992 campaign and the administration, "the president viewed the system as incredibly costly, inefficient, unwieldy, and overpriced." White House officials and especially Magaziner, who coordinated health care reform, repeatedly assured the president and Mrs. Clinton that by eliminating "waste in the current system, . . . system savings will exceed system costs significantly" and would "cover universal access and possibly contribute to deficit reduction."[5] Managed competition seemed to promise "something for nothing." (Analysis by the Congressional Budget Office [1994] would later report that Clinton's managed competition approach did not produce greater savings than costs.)

The twin sins of the New Democratic creed—direct taxes and government regulation—ruled out approaches that were popular among some groups of Democratic Party legislators and activists. Health policy experts who proposed such direct government regulation as price controls for all payers were labeled "Old Democrats" and were derided as "Washington people" out of touch with the "competition ideas" being tested nationally.[6] Not surprisingly, the Canadian-inspired single-payer plan, which enjoyed significant support among the public and upwards of a third of congressional Democrats was—as campaign and administration advisers recalled—"never anything that was ever entertained, anywhere" because it relied on "direct . . . tax increases of a large magnitude and also relied on regulatory approaches that the president was not fond of."

Clinton, Magaziner, and other aides preferred the liberal variant of managed competition over alternative approaches because of their strong views of what constituted "good public policy." They also calculated, however, that it offered two political advantages. First, Clinton and his advisers were convinced that their judgments about "good public policy" and their mastery of health policy would translate into political capital. "[O]ur strongest asset may be the merits of our case," one set of health policy advisers reported to the president and Mrs. Clinton.[7] The emphasis on merit was fueled by their supreme confidence in their policy wizardry or "arrogance," as even White House aides put it. Officials compared the Clintons' policy discussions with those of "eighteenth-century salon intellectuals"; they believed that "anything the specialists have to say is something they can fit into their framework, interpret back in their own way and move beyond it."

The second political calculation made by Clinton and his advisers was that managed competition would provide a means to appeal simultaneously to the policy goals of Democratic and moderate Republican legislators—"bridg[ing]" together liberals with moderates in both parties and "win[ning] widespread support."[8] During the 1992 campaign and especially after the election, it was clear to the Clinton camp that they faced a daunting political environment. The Democrats were split into warring factions, each supporting a different approach to health care reform. Clinton aides as well as House Majority Leader Richard Gephardt and Senate Majority Leader George Mitchell agreed that no proposal (from the single-payer approach to more incremental alternatives that reformed the insurance market and partially expanded coverage) had a "majority behind it."[9]

Clinton's predicament was further complicated by the need—as White House aides insisted from the outset of the president's term—to "win some real, not just token, support from Republicans." The White House anticipated that Republican support would be necessary both to overcome a certain filibuster in the Senate (sixty votes were required and Democrats held but fifty-seven seats) and to offset inevitable defections by Democrats in a closely divided Congress. But bipartisan cooperation was obstructed by polarization in the political parties toward their ideological extremes. Even as Clinton depended on moderate Republicans (and Democrats), their numbers were evaporating. To make matters worse, the polarization of the parties had sown distrust within the mainstream of each party (Brady and Buckley 1995). The mutual antagonism was especially apparent in the House. Democratic House leaders, who had become accustomed to passing major bills by relying on their own ranks, demanded a "Democrats-only strategy" on health care reform and warned the White House that working with Republicans (or even conservative Democrats) would spark a revolt by its liberal Democratic base.[10]

The Clinton camp calculated that the "only way" to pass health care reform in Congress was for the president to propose "a relatively detailed and unambiguous" plan for managed competition that offered "conservative means to liberal ends."[11] They expected to appeal to the policy goals of Democrats by promising universal access and comprehensive benefits and to woo moderates in both parties by "focus[ing] on our reliance on competitive forces and a private sector solution" that avoided taxes and massive government regulation.[12] Indeed, Magaziner and other aides stubbornly backed this political calculation by optimistically reporting throughout 1993 that Clinton's managed competition plan represented "both good policy and the best initial political position."[13] White House officials counted on holding the support of almost all liberal and moderate Democrats, winning a majority of conservative Democrats, and attracting 8–10 moderate Republicans in the Senate and 15–20 in the House.[14]

In short, Clinton's adoption of a complex and comprehensive proposal to establish managed competition resulted from his own policy goals and his political judgment that this proposal would unite a coalition of disparate elements within the Democratic and Republican parties. Jacob Hacker's (1997) insightful study of the origin of Clinton's health care reform proposal in the 1992 campaign similarly concludes that Clinton embraced managed care because of his policy preferences, personal values, and political judgments about the policy goals of potential supporters.[15] The underlying assumption within the White House, as we discuss below, was that the president could sell the public on his plan and this would solidify congressional support.

The New Democratic Redux

Clinton's New Democratic philosophy drove his fundamental decisions, but in directions that were unintended and that eventually contradicted the core of his philosophy—avoiding taxes and government regulation. Seasoned health policy experts were quite vocal in the 1992 presidential campaign and afterward in refuting the amount of Clinton's projected savings from comprehensive system reform. As one administration adviser recalled, the argument by Clinton and Magaziner that the cost of covering nearly forty million new people could be covered by savings and perhaps a small sin tax made policy experts "flinch every time" because it could not be achieved. Judy Feder, who worked on the campaign and later in the Department of Health and Human Services, repeatedly warned Clinton that it was a "mistake to talk about no new taxes" because reform could not be financed by system savings.[16] But their New Democratic philosophy blinded Clinton and Magaziner to the warnings by Feder and others, who were dismissed as captives of the Washington establishment.[17] "If the president had a better understanding of these issues," one administration official predicted, "he might not have touched health care reform with a ten foot pole."

But the president did buy the "something for nothing" argument, which later forced him to retreat further from his New Democratic creed. By September 1993, Clinton had been pushed to propose a relatively severe budget cap on health care premiums and substantial government regulation. Faced with incontrovertible evidence that his plan would produce (as Feder and others had predicted) higher-than-anticipated taxes and deficits, Clinton was forced to impose cost containment measures that were, in the words of one adviser, "much more aggressive than anything we contemplated."[18] The president also found himself cornered into accepting far more regulation than he initially intended. Part of the problem, several administration advisers explained, was that Clinton and Magaziner did not understand that the philosophical commitment to encouraging market competition would require extensive regulation of the private sector's behavior.

Clinton's embrace of the "something for nothing" argument also locked him into a plan for comprehensive reform and into accepting a quite narrow range of policy options. One senior health policy aide explained that "the scope of health reform depends on the problems you're setting out to solve." Once Clinton, Magaziner, and other senior advisers defined the problem as controlling costs and using the savings to finance reform, then incremental reform lost its attraction and there was an overriding need to implement the whole package as soon as possible. "If we took it on piece by piece," Clinton insisted, "we might solve some problems but we might make others worse" and, aides added, ensure that a "significant portion of anticipated savings cannot be realized."[19] Indeed, when prospects for reform grew bleak in 1994 and Democrats struggled to salvage a scaled-back reform package, Magaziner argued—with the support of the president and Mrs. Clinton—against a tactical retreat because it would not reduce the budget deficit and would therefore cause more harm than good. Clinton later conceded that his resistance to pulling back from comprehensive reform to a staged reform over several years was a "blunder" and "entirely my mistake" (Johnson and Broder 1996, 127). The source of the "mistake," though, lay in the original "something for nothing" approach that Magaziner pushed and Clinton adopted. The irony is that the goal of achieving health reform without relying on government regulation or new taxes ended up creating the kind of policies and political problems Clinton and his advisers sought to avoid in the first place.

The Political Purpose of the Task Force

Politicians, journalists, and others have devoted enormous attention to the task force and assigned it great importance in the formulation of the Clinton health plan. Most accounts identify two factors to explain the decision to staff the task force with health policy experts and to command them to find the "right" approach. One was Clinton's personal preference for substantive discussions in reaching decisions; the other was Magaziner's background as a business consultant and his inclination to create complex scenarios (Johnson and Broder 1996). There is no question that the president felt comfortable with the intricate process Magaziner recommended and that he was personally committed to designing the details based on the principles he had enunciated during the campaign.

It is wrong to assume, however, that the White House established the task force to formulate its policy on health care reform. Correcting the misperceptions about the task force clarifies the White House's approach both to formulating its health policy and to designing a political strategy to enact it.

The primary purpose of the task force was not to generate new information and expert analyses. Its participants insisted that the task force was "not in any way a decision process and was never intended to be"; they almost uniformly concluded that the administration did not "gain that much knowledge" from the process. Administration officials in the executive branch departments also complained that the White House set up a process for "endless debate over minutia that should never have been on the radar screen of cabinet members . . . and that chewed up a lot of time of the principals, including the president." Many of the administration officials we interviewed pointed to alternatives to the task force's "academic bull sessions"; all involved an avoidance of intricate "unanswerable questions" and a return to the practice of all presidents since Franklin Roosevelt of relying on a small group of officials to formulate health policy.

A puzzling question naturally arises: why did the White House establish a task force with unprecedented manpower, intricacy, and commitment by senior officials if it never intended to use it to design its health plan? The principal purpose of the task force was political. Clinton approved of the task force and its publicly promised search for expert answers not to formulate his health plan but rather to serve as a political strategy to advance his own policy goals. In particular, Clinton and his senior advisers used the task force to pursue two aspects of their

political strategy: to build consensus within a fractious policy community and to establish the credibility of the administration's plan among
the general public and political observers. The task force illustrated
how the White House's internal policymaking process had been compromised to serve its political strategy and to bolster its effectiveness
in selling administration proposals to experts and to the general public.

Building Consensus among Policy Experts

When John Kennedy decided to campaign on health care reform in
the 1960 presidential election, the Democratic health policy community within Congress and outside government had already coalesced
around a policy framework and a political strategy that produced
Medicare (Jacobs 1993). Bill Clinton had no such luck; the Democratic
health policy community and other experts committed to reform were
populated, Magaziner warned, by competing "theologians who are
prepared to wage holy war on behalf of their own ideologies" under
the banners of "single payer," "pure managed competition," and "pay
or play."[20] If the splits among reform-oriented experts were not addressed, they would resurface (it was anticipated) in the form of opposition within Congress and the executive departments and in the stories
by journalists who would turn to these experts as sources. While Clinton and his advisers accepted that "very strongly held views on opposite sides" of the Democratic health policy community would block
full consensus, they adopted the task force process as part of their
effort begun during the campaign to "pull people together" behind
their managed competition approach.[21]

The tactic of using the task force process to build consensus was,
a trusted administration adviser recalled, one reason that the White
House "decided to literally start at the very beginning, with fact finding and sorting through all of the options, mostly having to do with a
managed competition approach." Laboriously sifting through the evidence was expected to steer experts to the conclusions that Clinton
and his advisers had reached; the power of evidence and arguments
would win them over.

Cooptation required inclusiveness. For the task force process to
generate meaningful agreement and to serve as an effective part of
its "outreach initiatives," the White House invited policy experts from
outside government as well as from within both the cabinet departments and Congress (with staff drawn from legislators who held quite
different philosophies).[22]

The White House put a high priority on building cooperation and

loyalty within the cabinet departments because administration officials, members of Congress, and journalists often turned to career civil
servants in the executive branch for analysis and advice. These civil
servants possessed valuable expertise in health policy as a result of
their work for the Bush and Reagan administrations (Glied 1997, 195).
The task force began, according to several senior health policy advisers, as a tactic to "revolutionize the way government thought by pulling career civil servants out of their government agencies, bringing
them up to speed on the proposal, and then telling them to 'keep the
force' when they went back to their agencies." The aim was to "get
rid of the institutional constraints" and to make these career officials
"responsible to the task force" rather than to the "old ways of thinking
in their agency."

Building Credibility with Americans and Political Observers

The White House was acutely aware of Americans' strong distrust of
Washington and the constraints it put on new government activity.
Reversing the public's distrust was a persistent concern in the White
House, and it led to prominent initiatives like Vice President Al Gore's
drive to "reinvent government." Indeed, the White House's pollster,
Stanley Greenberg, advised Clinton and his senior aides that it was
"hard to overestimate how important reinventing government is to the
entire Clinton program," and specifically health care reform; the "reinventing government" initiative was counted on to "reinforce Clinton's
commitment to non-bureaucratic solutions" and to "accountable and
responsible government."[23]

The White House's second reason for establishing the task force process was to build the credibility and legitimacy of its proposal with
the general public and, especially, political observers whom Americans
would trust to "validate" Clinton's plan. The White House expected
the task force to clearly distance policy development from the world
of politics that the public reviled. Separating policy from politics was
driven partly by Clinton's concern to leave political judgments for himself, but also by the calculation that Americans would be more inclined
to support the administration's proposal for managed competition if it
could be plausibly presented as apolitical—a product whose structure
and details were well thought out by experts and defensible on substantive (and not simply political) grounds. Apolitical policy development would depart from "business as usual" and, paradoxically, yield
political benefits.

Indeed, from every account of the task force's operations, Magaziner defined his role as "policy development" and instructed the policy specialists—to their dismay—to design policy apart from political judgments.[24] With an apolitical policy process, the White House expected (as officials put it) to win "credibility [for being] able to say that we really had consulted widely" with the best and the brightest and for having its efforts "viewed as the most comprehensive, thorough, and all-encompassing attempt to put together a health-reform proposal." Operating a policy process on the "higher plane" of substance would lay the basis for the president and First Lady to "argue against special interests in favor of the human interests."

Controlling the Decision-Making Process

The persistent fear of Clinton and his senior advisers was that their process for reaching decisions and, specifically, its task force operation would allow their managed competition approach to be "taken over by the Washington insiders [who would] turn it into the same old [regulatory] proposal we've seen before." They were haunted by a generalized "distrust of anyone who had a lot of Washington experience," namely, longtime Democratic health activists and the "regulators" in the Health Care Financing Administration (HCFA) and its home department (the Department of Health and Human Services).[25] "A competitive model," they assumed, could not be "developed by people who basically believed in regulation."

Although the White House attempted to seduce the "Washington insiders" through participation in the task force, it planned from the outset to establish "tight control" to guarantee that the president's policy goals would "driv[e] the substance of policy formation."[26] The White House's solution was twofold: politicize the appointment of senior health policy advisers and centralize final decisions in the Oval Office.

Clinton attempted to control policy formulation by selecting individuals to lead his health care reform effort who had demonstrated personal loyalty and shared his political values; demonstrated competence in health policy or Washington politics was not required. The president's appointment of Hillary Rodham Clinton to direct the effort showed his commitment to health care reform, but he also put in place (along with his selection of Magaziner to coordinate the task force's everyday operations) proven loyalists who would have the president's "interests at heart" and share his New Democratic commitments. Clinton bypassed scores of seasoned Washington hands who were experts in health policy and the legislative process but who lacked a track record of supporting him and his values.

The second part of Clinton's strategy to assert control was to establish a centralized chain of command through Magaziner that maximized the president's opportunities to make decisions. Magaziner was widely criticized in Washington (as administrations officials complained) for "keeping opposing views away from the president and the First Lady and filtering evidence to give them only an incomplete view." But this criticism is better directed at his assigned institutional role than his personal drive to suppress arguments that challenged his own positions. Clinton put Magaziner near the apex of the chain of command in order to coordinate the presentation of information and options and to leave the decisions to the president. Criticisms of Magaziner for preventing arguments from reaching the president or Mrs. Clinton fail to appreciate that most of these arguments were "heard, but were not successful."[27] (Magaziner's personal style may well have exacerbated, rather than dampened, the resentment toward his institutional role and the White House for establishing a centralized process.)

Under Magaziner's direction, health care reform was concentrated in the White House and distanced from the Departments and Cabinet Secretaries, marginalizing even the Department of Health and Human Services (DHHS), which had nominal responsibility for federal health policy. Information is power and Magaziner took the unprecedented step (from the perspective of rivals within Washington) of preparing policy options and quantitative analyses in the White House. The departments and cabinet secretaries were "cut out" from the "innermost circle" and were not even trusted (as was the normal practice) with conducting their own sets of technical analyses because Magaziner (at the behest of the president and his most senior aides) insisted on being "in charge of what the cabinet knew." Even cabinet members and senior officials who were experienced in the ways of Washington and health care reform, such as Treasury Secretary Bentsen and White House Budget Director Leon Panetta, were excluded "because they weren't in the campaign and weren't long-standing allies whom the president could trust."

The White House's strategy for maintaining control over the task force produced a hierarchical process that, according to interviews and White House records, pushed mountains of thick briefing books, memoranda, and other materials up to Clinton, preserving for him a staggering number of decisions.[28]

Clinton's decision to appoint politically sympathetic and loyal advisers and to centralize final decisions in the Oval Office was not unique. It was a common presidential strategy since Richard Nixon's terms in office to resist encroachments by the bureaucracy and policy professionals (Moe 1985). What distinguished Clinton from previous presidents was that he invited widespread participation as part of an attempt to coopt them.

Misguided Faith in the Task Force Process

Although the task force initially received a few favorable stories in the media, the White House's strategy of using the task force to win support for its proposal unleashed a destructive epidemic of new political problems—internecine warfare within the health policy community and even within the administration.[29] Because inclusiveness was seen as critical to building support, Magaziner's initial plan envisioned the "daunting" size of ninety-eight people.[30] The promise of inclusiveness, however, created irresistible pressure for unintended expansion. The plaintive query, "Why didn't you include me?", armed Cabinet Departments and members of Congress with a persuasive argument for gaining access (and intelligence) regarding the White House's thinking. Once the First Lady and Magaziner advertised the task force as an inclusive process, "everybody thought that they had a right to be part of it," and the White House felt compelled to allow in hundreds of those who complained about not being included. The result was that membership on the task force ballooned to 630. What was intended as a political strategy to induce cooperation sparked an insatiable demand for inclusion and an unwieldy process for any kind of satisfying deliberation. The kicker was that the task force *still* alienated specialists who felt slighted because they were not included.[31]

In addition, the White House's solicitation of input raised expectations that were crushed by the president's demand for a hierarchical process that left him in control. The irony was that Clinton's strategy to win support produced just the opposite outcome: the task force created a damaging dynamic in which task force members—with great frustration—discovered that the invitation to participate was restricted to "endless discussions" and precluded actual influence on policy decisions. Contrary to Clinton's stated intention to break the mold, the closer the decision got to the top, the smaller the number of participants and narrower the range of views considered. Those who were excluded felt the bite of being "cut off" and were "portrayed as traitors, document leakers, undercutters." The task force process spewed forth disaffected and vocal complainers, instead of a cadre of specialists who "bought in" to the Clinton plan and who would "validate" it publicly as originally intended. When the White House "looked for expert endorsements at the end," one administration official explained, they found few.

The White House's promise of inclusiveness through the task force process also alienated members of Congress and their senior staffs. The White House's presumption that participation in the task force represented negotiations offended legislators and their staff. It undercut the traditional pecking order in Congress by abandoning the practice, as one senior congressional aide fumed, of "negotiating among people who represent different power centers in our government." The task force process treated "all staff as co-equal when Dan Rostenkowski's representative is not equal to Joe Blow congressman's junior assistant who happens to handle health." The task force process (and hundreds of meetings with members of Congress) also jettisoned the typical give-and-take exchange between the White House and legislators. Frustration and outrage mounted as input was collected through the task force and through individual meetings but was not used in truly shaping the output.[32] Finally, giving members inside access to White House deliberations spawned destructive reports of "disarray . . . and significant delay."[33]

One of the most damaging consequences of the task force was to set off a fierce internal struggle that inspired senior administration appointees to undermine Clinton's plan. The president established a hierarchical process that designated Magaziner as the coordinator of the task force and health policy development. But administration officials perceived the task force process as a "shield that Magaziner put up" to facilitate his personal drive to control information and decisions. Officials protested against the constant "battle with Magaziner over getting pieces of paper that we needed." Magaziner defended his tight control over information as a precaution against damaging leaks, which had been ordered by the president and his top advisers. In the eyes of administration officials, however, Magaziner's control over information helped to ensure that "he was the only one who knew all the pieces" and allowed him to keep senior officials ill-informed.

Officials also blamed Magaziner and the task force process for blocking major changes in the structure of Clinton's plan. Some of the most prominent administration officials—from Department of Health and Human Services Secretary Donna Shalala to senior economic advisers National Economic Council Chairman Robert Rubin, Deputy

Treasury Secretary Roger Altman, Treasury Secretary Lloyd Bentsen, Council of Economic Advisers head Laura Tyson, Office of Management and Budget Director Leon Panetta, and Deputy OMB director Alice Rivlin—criticized the establishment of health alliances, the cuts in Medicare spending, and the tight restraints on health care prices. Senior officials were, one White House aide recalled, "truly worried about how little access they had to the president" and, in particular, how little influence they exercised. Bentsen was moved to write a detailed thirty-eight-page memorandum to the First Lady. Clinton's advisers agreed that "it was not just liberal views that were being lost, it was also conservative views." The president and Magaziner expected the task force process to build support within the administration; instead, its outcome was that "nobody in the administration believed in virtually any of it."[34]

The animosity generated by the task force process and by the president's rejection of senior officials' advice isolated his plan within the executive branch; instead of administration officials using their powerful connections to boost Clinton's plan, they schemed to undermine it. Leaking information to journalists was a favorite tactic by the "warring factions" within the administration; each side jostled for advantage in "playing up the struggle and glorifying their own role in the struggle." Even to an inside critic, the leaks created an "unbelievable state of affairs" in which "complicated, sensitive meetings would appear the next day in the newspaper" in a distorted form. With Congress closely divided over the president's budget proposal, "the enormous fear in the White House during the spring of 1993 was that any kind of static on health care was going to upset the apple cart in the Congress." For instance, leaks that the Treasury Department was analyzing a tax on liquor and wine prompted a letter from every member of the California congressional delegation threatening not to support the president's budget, which was already teetering on defeat.[35] The effect of the leaks by critics within the administration was to "sabotage everything"; Clinton was politically compelled to instruct Magaziner to stop making decisions, circulating written materials, or even holding general discussions of health care reform.[36] The opposition within the administration shut down the White House's deliberations from May until August 1993 when the budget finally passed.

The use of leaks by disgruntled administration officials intensified the distrust and opposition within the administration and Congress. Officials who had used leaks to resist White House decisions now bitterly complained that Magaziner used the leaks to withhold information and enhance his control over the process by seizing on it as a pretext to cloister the president off alone. The suspicion that Magaziner was secretly "mesmerizing" Clinton grew so widespread that the president was reduced at one cabinet meeting to pleading for his own relevance by itemizing his credentials on health care reform and insisting that he was calling the shots. But distrust was corrosive. Although Magaziner cheerfully reported to Mrs. Clinton early in the administration that "our cost estimates . . . will provide consensus,"[37] administration dissidents complained (sometimes to reporters) that he was "hyping the numbers." These suspicions prompted the president to request from Magaziner a formal report on his process for generating cost estimates, and they led Bentsen and other officials to refuse to "go out and really back the numbers until their own people had read it in the vetting process themselves."[38]

Leaks were a tactic for high-level opposition; delay was a more subtle form of resistance. The political isolation of health care reform created a coalition of officials in the White House and the departments who, at critical junctures when reform could have been moved faster, came together and promoted (rather than discouraged) delay.[39] Magaziner and the First Lady fought a running battle against officials who seized on the budget fight, NAFTA's upcoming deadline, and other issues as pretexts for pushing health care reform off until 1994.[40] During one battle, Magaziner candidly acknowledged to the president and Mrs. Clinton that pressure for delaying health care reform stemmed from the uncertainty of "most of your senior economic and political advisers" regarding a health plan that "they neither have seen nor have confidence that they or the American people would support."[41]

White House officials "trace 99 percent of our problems" to Senator Robert Byrd's decision to oppose the incorporation of health care reform into the expedited budget reconciliation process because it did not directly contribute to deficit reduction.[42] Although Byrd relished his role as guardian of parliamentarian rules, his decision was facilitated by suspicion of the president's plan within the administration and Democratic congressional ranks. Several administration advisers explained to us that "If the White House had allies in the administration, health care reform wouldn't have been so separate from the budget process." One official recounted a meeting Clinton conducted with Senators Daniel Patrick Moynihan and James Sasser, the chairmen of the Senate's budget committees, at which Bentsen fully supported their argument that the committees could not handle health care reform at the same time as the budget. Bentsen stressed the impossibility of

simultaneously handling the budget and health care reform, because
in the view of this official he "shared Moynihan's and Sasser's and
Panetta's concern to first get the deficit reduction and then worry
about health care when maybe we'll have more time to impact on it."

Bill Clinton and his senior advisers created—on their own—a major
political problem. The task force process alienated senior officials to
the point that they decided not to invest their political capital in pushing Clinton's plan and instead were "distancing themselves from it."
Distrust, opposition, and muted support from *within* the administration created and fanned the doubts of legislators and journalists over
an ambitious reform project. White House officials reported that the
warfare within the administration was fueling the unmistakable "perception of internal squabbling" within Congress and was reinforcing
legislators' own questions about the reliability of the White House's
plan.[43] Nearly a year after the task force had been formed, senior
White House aides fumed that the attacks by reform opponents were
"backed up by some in our administration whose cocktail party con-
versation has given [the charges] credence" and prevented a "uniform
message to the Hill and the media."[44]

Most presidents find that their internal process for reaching decisions
rarely receives widespread attention. Clinton's task force was different.
His personal miscalculations in creating it (or at least in supporting its
creation) sparked intense criticism from policy specialists, members of
Congress and their staff, and administration officials who should have
been the White House's natural allies. Instead, their chorus of suspicions
and complaints about the task force process fed journalists an ample
supply of leaks, and reform's opponents were handed a set of irrefutable
criticisms. This chorus, we argue in chapters 5 and 6, cycled back to the
public as a steady barrage of negative news stories.

Although Clinton's mistakes in designing policy and his political
strategies created serious problems, he entered a political environment
in which any health care reform proposal—including those designed
by conservative Democrats and moderate Republicans—would face
intense public scrutiny and unsteady support. Clinton's strategy complicated an already daunting political situation.

What Drove Health Policy Decisions in the White House

Another puzzling question remains: if the preferences and calculations
of elites dominated how the White House formulated its health care
reform proposal, what affect did public opinion exert on policy deci-

sions? After all, the White House's attention to Clinton's New Democratic philosophy and to strategically circumventing political and professional divisions coincided with a steady flow of public opinion analysis.

By all accounts, Clinton avidly consumed the findings produced by the White House's public opinion apparatus, which presidents since John Kennedy had developed (Jacobs 1992a, 1993; Jacobs and Shapiro 1995; Heith 1998). Clinton immersed himself in polls (one official explained) as a "substitute for being able to walk down the street and talk to people" as he did as governor in Arkansas. During the first year of the health care debate, he reportedly spent $2 million on polling and met at least once a week with his pollster, Stanley Greenberg, who conducted monthly focus groups and surveys of policy issues, presidential job performance, perceptions of Clinton, and other matters.[45] Greenberg's analyses combined excerpts from focus groups with sophisticated statistical results from regression analyses, multivariate time series, and factor analysis. Greenberg also worked closely with a number of administration officials engaged with health care reform, keeping them abreast of public attitudes.[46]

Public opinion had a varied and complicated influence on health care reform decisions, especially during the campaign in 1992 and the critical months in early 1993 when Clinton's plan was formulated. The agenda of issues that Clinton addressed coincided with what the public felt required action. But the relationship between public preferences and the actual policies that the administration formulated was more mixed. We took two approaches to unravel the influences of public opinion. We interviewed White House aides in order to identify their intentions and calculations in reaching decisions.[47] To balance and corroborate the information provided by the interviews, we also relied on independent evidence—secondary sources and comparisons of White House decisions with polls conducted by the press and other organizations.

Clinton's attention to health care reform coincided with the public's high ranking of the issue as one of its leading national concerns. By the early 1990s, health care had risen to near the top of the public's policy concerns; only pressing economic problems ranked higher. Senator Harris Wofford's Senate campaign in the 1991 special election and Clinton's 1992 campaign highlighted the need for health care reform. President Clinton moved quickly after his inauguration to make the issue one of his top priorities. It would be a mistake, though, simply to conclude that Clinton responded to the public's wishes. Clinton's interest in health care reform primarily stemmed from his policy goals of achieving economic growth and reducing the federal government budget. The attention that Clinton, along with other politicians and journalists, devoted to health care reform raised the issue's visibility in the media and helps to explain its high ranking on the public's agenda (Iyengar and Kinder 1987). It is telling that once the Republicans assumed control of Congress in 1994 and focused on other issues, health care reform dropped from its high ranking. During Clinton's two terms in office, policies such as crime and the budget deficit similarly moved up the public's priorities as political leaders and the media shifted their attention.

The relationship between public opinion and the health policies that the White House formulated is more mixed. The Clinton plan followed the broad contours of public preferences on the important issues of universal coverage, employer mandate, sin taxes, and benefits. Figure 3.1 shows that through September 1993 clear majorities (close to two-thirds in some cases) favored prominent policies that Clinton embraced—namely, the principle of universal insurance coverage and a government requirement that employers provide health benefits for their employees (the so-called "employer mandate"). In addition, Americans as a whole backed sin taxes—levies on liquor and cigarette sales—to finance health care reform, an option that Clinton also selected. Finally, interviews with administration officials indicated that the White House's own research identified support for comprehensive benefits and provided grounds for anticipating public opposition to limiting benefits. Greenberg and others feared that limiting benefits to catastrophic care would force the average American "to pay more . . . to cover less and less"; given "the ability of the opposition to attack," they anticipated that future public opinion would oppose any plan lacking comprehensive benefits.

While the public apparently supported critical components of Clinton's plan, *public opinion did not drive the decisions that were made on these and other issues.* Indeed, administration officials repeatedly insisted that their "plan [was] constructed by the policy people" and that "polling didn't drive the policy decision." They fully accepted that "*the most compelling features of our package in policy terms may not yield the highest public support.*"[48] Greenberg confirmed—with disappointment—that the White House formulated policy "some distance from political advice and polling" and kept him "out of the process . . . of designing the content of health care reform."

The influence of public opinion was limited for three reasons. First,

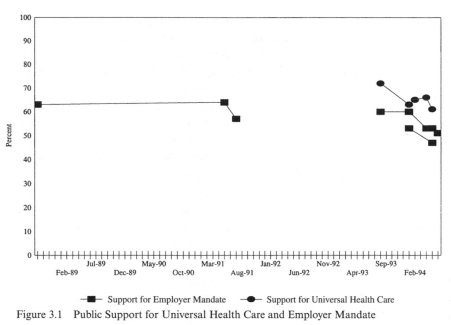

━■━ Support for Employer Mandate   ━●━ Support for Universal Health Care

Figure 3.1   Public Support for Universal Health Care and Employer Mandate

Source: See appendix 2 for question wording and polling organizations.

centrist opinion was less influential on White House decisions than the policy goals that arose from Clinton's own philosophy and policy preferences, interest group pressure, and White House judgments on "what would sell in Congress" to its various ideological factions. Advisers who were both defensive and critical of the administration agreed that the president's New Democratic philosophy and positions regarding universal coverage and other issues were "uppermost in Clinton's mind." Greenberg complained that the preferences of most Americans had been sacrificed to Clinton's policy goals; "our problem is not being political enough and focusing on doing the right thing in public policy."[49]

Even in those cases where Americans supported a White House decision, public opinion was not the cause of the decision. This is important because it is tempting to infer from polls showing support for aspects of the reform proposal that public opinion drove its decisions. For instance, a *Wall Street Journal* survey in March 1994 found that large majorities favored components of Clinton's plan when the president's name was omitted; this finding may appear to corroborate the influence of public opinion on White House policy decisions (Stout 1994). This analysis, however, confuses the correlation of public opinion and policy with causation, and imputes motives to policymakers without exploring their own perceptions and decision calculus. Officials who were both critical and supportive of the Clinton plan agreed that public opinion was not the source of the president's decisions. At best, "polls were only one form of political analysis" that "described a landscape and the general lay of the land."

For instance, the enthusiasm of most Americans for universal coverage "bolstered" Clinton's commitment to it on other grounds—it was expected by Clinton aides to reduce government and business expenditures and spur economic growth. More politically meaningful to the White House than national opinion were the supermajorities of loyal Democratic partisans among the public who favored universal coverage as well as employer mandates and the use of taxes to finance national health insurance.[50] Indicative of the importance of partisans in White House decisions, Greenberg's reports to the president and his senior advisers emphasized that passing the Clinton plan was "the single most important accomplishment for . . . the Democratic base."[51]

The issue of taxes offers another critical illustration of the pitfall of assuming that public opinion drove policy decisions. The White House adopted the popular employer mandate for reasons not directly related to public opinion and only after rejecting a more popular approach. Americans were willing to support a direct and explicit tax. Figure 3.2 presents a series of *New York Times*/CBS News polls that indicate that by January 1993 about two-thirds of the public had steadily supported tax-financed national health insurance; this support was 10 to 20 points higher than it was a decade earlier and had reached record levels.[52] Greenberg conducted focus groups and surveys that explained the different approaches to financing health care reform and found greater support for a broad-based payroll tax than the employer mandate.

Magaziner and several of his policy analysts favored the popular payroll tax because it was simpler than the employer mandate, which required a more complex organization and system of subsidies to businesses. They also focused on future public opinion and anticipated (correctly) that the employer mandate would not prevent Republicans from calling it a tax and delivering a political "hit."

Clinton, however, rejected the findings of public opinion research and brushed past his advisers' warnings, and adopted the employer mandate instead of a payroll tax. His primary objections to the payroll tax stemmed from policy considerations (it would diminish the role of managed competition) and philosophical qualms (his own "strong preference" against raising direct taxes). Clinton and his advisers also anticipated future public opposition to a payroll tax because it in-

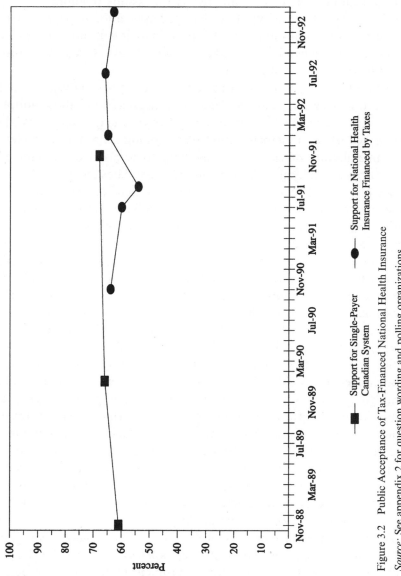

Figure 3.2   Public Acceptance of Tax-Financed National Health Insurance

Source: See appendix 2 for question wording and polling organizations.

Support for Single-Payer
Canadian System

Support for National Health
Insurance Financed by Taxes

creased the payments of the middle class and upper middle class and would (no one doubted) provoke a hostile "ten million dollar campaign" that highlighted these costs. White House officials discounted polls indicating that "taxes would fly" (with existing opinion) as "very unsolid, to say the least." While anticipated opposition to payroll taxes was one reason for avoiding this form of financing, it did not provide a rationale for an employer mandate, which was also (accurately) projected to spark public opposition.

The bottom line, according to a senior health policy adviser, is that polls and focus groups did not "enter into the decision" about adopting an employer mandate and rejecting a payroll tax. Even the White House's efforts to anticipate future public opinion produced no clear recommendation; officials were unwilling to respond to anticipated public opposition by abandoning employer mandates and payroll taxes altogether. Indeed, one senior health policy official suggested that the uncertainty about the future strengthened the White House's focus on "policy integrity" and its inclination to discount both existing and anticipated public opinion.

On other issues that enjoyed strong support in polls, Magaziner's memos to the president and Mrs. Clinton (as well as additional evidence) confirm that appeasing interest groups and Democratic Party constituents also drove White House decisions. Long-term care and drug benefits were added to "make the Medicare and Medicaid savings possible for the American Association of Retired Persons [and other senior and disability groups] to support"; the early retiree discounts were created to "solidify large business, labor, senior and state and local government support"; and numerous other policies were designed to curry favor with small businesses, urban areas, provider groups, and single-payer advocates.[53] Even on the issue of comprehensive benefits for which Greenberg's research reported strong national support, several administration officials suggested that aggregate public opinion was not as influential as "a lot of pressure from a lot of seniors." "We knew," one political adviser recalled, "that if we didn't have long-term care we wouldn't get the AARP."

The preferences of members of Congress also weighed heavily in White House decisions. For instance, polls in early 1993 revealed highly lopsided public support for government limits on the amounts charged by private health insurers, drug companies, doctors, and hospitals; the public also backed government controls to restrict increases in health spending—even if it meant that some health services would be harder to obtain.[54] Administration officials were fully aware of the public's support for regulations but embraced a less popular and alternative approach based on managed competition. Clinton's own preference for managed competition was reinforced, as one longtime adviser noted, by the fact that using "competition in the market to control the costs was popular in Congress, [while price controls] were the least popular with members."

Finally, Clinton rejected the Canadian single-payer system even though some polls indicated that it was supported by as much as two-thirds of Americans (fig. 3.2).[55] As we indicated earlier, Clinton rejected the single-payer approach because of his philosophy and his evaluation of congressional sentiment.

The second factor that limited public opinion's influence was that many policy decisions were neither examined in polls nor matters on which Americans had opinions. White House documents described hundreds of detailed issues that the public could not offer clear opinions on because it had hardly thought or known about them. Many policy options—from the functions of the national health board, which monitored the new health system's operations and expenditures, to important measures for generating revenues (such as lifting the tax exemption on employers' health insurance premiums or imposing a tax on providers or insurers)—were areas that had not appeared "on the radar screens" of Americans nor pollsters because there was little information or discussion of them.[57] On still other issues, such as the treatment of abortion, the public was divided and could not offer clear direction to policymakers. On most policy questions, it was simply not possible to say, as one official pointed out, "Here are the four policy choices, we should go with that one because the polling data says it's more popular." Instead, administration officials exercised substantial discretion in formulating policy.

Third, the White House decided to ignore or contradict public preferences on important policy issues (such as government regulation and payroll taxation) because of its judgments about the quality of public opinion and the role polls should play in policymaking. Some administration advisers bypassed public preferences because they believed that public opinion was fickle and easily manipulated by the opponents of reform. As noted above, advocates of the payroll tax within the White House acknowledged that "even if the polls show that people will support a tax, my guess would be that support would be very unsolid" after a well-funded campaign by its opponents. Others argued that "you can't be a slave to what polls say" because the public is not sufficiently knowledgeable on a wide set of issues—from the composition of the uninsured population (the vast majority are employed) to public health. The problem with public opinion surveys is that "people [do not] understand what it is that they're being asked to vote for or against in a poll." Finally, administration officials found it inappropriate and "wrong" to allow polling and public opinion to "drive the process" and "dictate every tiny step you take." The president was elected, one White House official explained, "not to follow public opinion, necessarily, but to lead by making decisions about the best way to get to an ultimate end point." This was hardly, as we noted earlier, the common lore about Bill Clinton at the time (or since).

The persistent criticism of the public's competence that emerged in our interviews with Clinton administration officials (and congressional staff in the next chapter) during 1993 and 1994 is echoed by a 1998 Pew Center survey of members of Congress, presidential appointees, and senior civil servants. This survey found that less than a third believed that "the public knows enough about the issues you face to form wise opinions about what should be done" (Pew 1998). (A similarly dim evaluation of the public as insufficiently informed and emotionally distanced to provide sound guidance on policymaking emerged from interviews with officials responsible for foreign policy [Kull 1999; Kull and Destler 1999].)

In short, White House officials persistently discounted existing and anticipated public opinion when formulating health policy. They primarily pursued the policy goals favored by the president and his allies within Congress, the Democratic Party, and the interest group community within Washington. When confronted with a choice between Clinton's policy goals and centrist opinion, the White House ignored or contradicted the preferences of most Americans. On many other policy decisions, public opinion was not perceived as sufficiently formed nor detailed enough to warrant serious consideration.

Public Opinion and White House Presentations

The evidence that polls and focus groups did not drive health policy decisions raises an intriguing question: why did the White House systematically track public opinion? The answer is that the administration used information about public opinion to craft the presentation of Clinton's plan—a plan that had been formulated to reflect the president's philosophy, policy preferences, and political judgments. Senior White House officials studied polls and focus groups to find the language, arguments, and symbols that would win public support and unify Washington elites behind the president's managed competition proposal.

The White House, like other Washington elites, treated public opinion as a political resource to pressure policymakers. Their motivation for monitoring public opinion was neither to follow it in making decisions nor to accept it as it existed. Rather, they tracked public opinion after deciding on what they wanted to do; their purpose was to exert the "leadership skills to shape public opinion" and "educate people." Using public opinion research to change (and not follow) public opinion was considered "absolutely normal." Of the eleven administration officials who explicitly discussed with us the White House's interest in public opinion, seven indicated that public opinion should be led and not followed. Polls and focus groups were an aid to leadership, identifying (as White House memos explained) "how best to sell a health care reform plan that is constructed by the policy people."[57] It is telling that, according to administration advisers, the White House restricted Greenberg's first direct involvement to *after* the proposal was set.

Political leaders today, much like Clinton and his aides, attempt to manipulate public opinion by continually monitoring it.

The Politicization of Public Opinion

Bill Clinton's 1992 campaign was infamous for its "war room" and its rapid reaction to damaging media reports. When he came to Washington to be inaugurated, however, he left the war room and its campaign style of public relations behind in Arkansas. Clinton's approach to governing in January 1993 did not start out, according to Stanley Greenberg, as simply an extension of his campaign strategy in 1992.[58]

Bill Clinton's assumptions and approach to governing dramatically changed, though, after a series of early controversies, including the "Gays in the Military" episode and the congressional votes over his budget during his first six months in office, which he nearly lost even after he agreed to unpleasant compromises of his policy goals. These early political debacles heightened the White House's appreciation of the political risks of damaging media coverage and the constraints on the president's influence over policymaking as he struggled to overcome his weak electoral mandate, small Democratic majorities in Congress, relatively few legislative moderates, and each political party's shift toward their ideological extremes. Watching Democrats desert him and Republicans withhold support, he concluded (according to advisers) that bipartisanship was unlikely and that many members of his own party were "independent operators" who were driven by their personal policy goals and electoral interests.

The cumulative impact on the White House of the early budget battles and controversies was to underscore the critical importance of using supportive public opinion as an "ally" and "tool" to counteract political rivals and to draw Congress and interest groups toward the president's policy goals. Perceived public support, administration officials concluded, "affect[ed] the perceived strength of a policy initiative [and] the way that people rate you." *After* Clinton's early political setbacks, he changed his approach to governing and earnestly imported his campaign techniques into the White House. "The first time a war room was created," Greenberg recalls, "was to pass the budget ... and [to address] trouble on many fronts."[59] The White House turned to campaign tactics because it perceived public opinion as uncertain and vulnerable to change if the administration and its allies did not aggressively counteract the promotional efforts by advocates of opposing policy goals.

Moving majority opinion was critical, in the White House's view, to achieving a specific political objective—making its policy goals electorally expedient for themselves and others. Public backing, according to White House calculations, translated within Congress into "clout" and "leverage" to engage effectively in "arm twisting" and "persuasion" with other politicians and, especially, the small but critical cluster of legislative moderates who tend to be most sensitive to centrist opinion. Several White House officials observed that "polls that demonstrate large public support for something that is running up against a wall in Congress" created "pressure that is reflected back to Congress." On health care reform, the White House banked on "creating legislative push because of public support." Overwhelming evidence that majorities of Americans wanted health care reform was expected to provide in Congress the "necessary comfort level and support to pass a plan."[60] The administration believed that the Clinton plan's "bipartisan appeal" among Americans strengthened its general "strategy [to] rise above partisanship" and to woo moderate Republicans in Congress or at least reassure them.[61]

Administration officials also counted on public support for Clinton and his policies to enhance their "leverage" with interest groups because they "respond to their constituencies who are part of the general public."[62] White House officials found that "when the president's ratings have been up, interest groups tended to come in and say 'we want to cut a deal' because they were more afraid of us." During the period of strong public support for health care reform in March 1993, Magaziner reported to the president and Mrs. Clinton that "interest groups, afraid of being left behind . . . are coming to the table with incredible offers to support positions they have historically opposed."[63] On the other hand, officials found that "when the president and his policy have been low [in public support], interest groups come in here a lot more cocky and a lot less willing to deal."

Because of the political importance of public opinion, Greenberg and White House officials actively worked to manage elite perceptions of public opinion, downplaying signs of public doubt and promoting any indications of public support. Compared with previous administrations who were leery of openly discussing public opinion or polls, Clinton and his aides consciously took a "much more aggressive role" in "arguing with the media's interpretation of polls" and not "letting [congressional] opponents and interest groups announce their polls" without rebuttal.

Manufacturing Public Support

Administration officials did not assume that the public would support its plan. On the contrary, they worried from the outset that "public opinion was divided" on health care reform and not supportive of managed competition, and they were uncertain about its future direction, fearing that criticism from opponents of reform (as conveyed by the press) would further splinter Americans. Carefully crafted public presentations or (in White House jargon) "communications" and "message" development were latched onto as the means to "educat[e] the public" and secure politically vital support. In effect, the White House aimed, as Clinton's political consultant Mandy Grunwald put it, for a "*bank shot*" off the public and into Washington: their strategies to "portray," "fashion," and "spin" Clinton's plan were expected to mobilize public support and in turn enhance the White House's leverage with Congress and interest groups.[64] Greenberg, who had been locked out of policy formulation, spearheaded the presentation of Clinton's plan along with Bob Boorstin (a key 1992 campaign aide and White House communications specialist).

The unquestioned assumption among Clinton and his advisers was that—with the right strategy—they could "go out and sell a program to the public" and "lead public opinion." For Clinton, relying on crafted presentations was a natural step; it was a strategy with which he was familiar, comfortable, and successful from his experiences in Arkansas and national politics. His own aides acknowledged that the president exhibited "unbelievable arrogance" regarding his ability to change public opinion; he boasted after his first year in office that presidents "can create new political capital all the time, because you have access to the people through the communications network."[65]

Clinton's hubris was echoed by his aides who believed, as one explained, that the White House could "get away with anything provided you believe in something, you say it over and over again, and you never change." Even well after the White House had been pounded by advertisements like the "Harry and Louise" spot, aides continued to count on "us[ing] the power of the White House to control the message against this barrage of spending."[66] Their faith in the White House's ability to "market the plan" and "achieve a large scale public response" rested on combining the White House's institutional resources to deploy a "campaign organization" with the skills of the president and First Lady.[67]

The White House's confidence in its ability to change public opinion rested on deploying a specific strategy—*priming*.[68] Their fundamental objective was not to persuade Americans based on the merits of reasoned and detailed arguments to convert from doubters of managed competition into supporters; administration officials, as mentioned earlier, believed the public lacked the necessary skill and interest to acquire and process the required information. Rather, their strategy was simpler: prompt individuals to think about attitudes, considerations, and information they already had stored in their memories, which favored the Clinton plan, and to use them as their standard or yardstick in evaluating competing health care reform proposals. Greenberg, Boorstin, and other political advisers implemented their priming strategy by pursuing two closely linked tactics: crafting a simple message that resonated with Americans, and saturating Washington and the country with their message.

Honing the Message

At the outset of Clinton's presidency, several White House aides pressed for a communications strategy that conveyed the "concrete benefits of reform and the mechanisms for delivering them" and warned that "elites, pressure groups and even the general public will not be satisfied if we don't."[69] Indeed, the autopsies of Clinton's health care reform by Theda Skocpol (1996) and Haynes Johnson and David

Broder (1996) lampoon the president precisely for not discussing the detailed workings of his plan and persuading Americans based on its merits.

The president and his advisers considered presenting their plan's concrete design but rejected it. They accepted that Americans could not understand the plan's design and that concentrating on its design would, according to a senior health policy official, "*focus the debate* on the details of the policy in which case we lose" (emphasis added). Clinton and his political advisers anticipated that journalists "weren't going to get into the details of health care reform" and restrict their coverage to substantive comments on the merits of reform. Instead, they expected journalists to allow opponents to seize on the White House's discussions of details to portray its health care reform plan in oversimplified and misleading terms as a complex and "huge government-run system" that would impose burdensome taxes. Presenting a detailed defense of the Clinton plan, on its merits, would enable its opponents to control what Americans (and the media) "*focused*" upon—what information and considerations were in the forefront of their minds.

Clinton's advisers were already fearful by the summer of 1993 that the administration was endangered because the president's "identity as president is intimately caught up with health care" and, yet, the battle over the administration's first budget had forced Clinton to break his campaign pledge to propose health care reform legislation within the first hundred days of his term.[70] According to confidential memos, the delay meant that the administration had "los[t] the ability to define the health care reform debate on our own terms."[71] Senator Jay Rockefeller privately warned Mrs. Clinton that the White House had failed to incorporate journalists and others in a "crafted information flow."[72] Instead, Rockefeller and White House aides soberly concluded that reform opponents had "succeeded in defining health care reform" by creating a damaging cycle of crafted information: opponents were casting reform as "more taxes and government control," reporters who were "ripe for manipulation" "serv[ed] as the vehicle for attacks," and the public was falling prey to having their "fears—[that they would] pay more [and] get less—fueled."[73] White House advisers agreed that the battle for public opinion would be determined by which side controlled the issues Americans focused upon, and that opponents were already more successful only nine months into the Clinton administration.

The solution, the White House decided, was to calibrate its "communications war" to craft specific messages that would present the complexity of the Clinton plan in simple terms that Americans found familiar and appealing. Greenberg, Boorstin, and other political advisers decided that White House presentations that "focus[ed] on principles and not on the details of the policy" were more likely to produce public support for Clinton's plan. Their objective was to design specific messages that captured these principles and "control[led] the definition and debate of policy options."[74]

The White House used polls and focus groups to "craft the communication strategy and the message" to most effectively appeal to the public. White House aides candidly acknowledged that the purpose of public opinion research was to move Americans toward supporting what "you care about . . . and believe." "We didn't poll the policy," one well-placed aide explained, to discover what "people really wanted policy-wise," but rather "we polled the *presentation* of the policy." The purpose was to figure out what presentations would "reassure [Americans] against the serious doubts that lie just below the surface."[75] Of the twenty-two administration officials who explicitly discussed polls and focus groups, thirteen of them (about 60 percent) specifically mentioned using it to frame already-decided policy.[76]

Polls and focus groups were employed by White House officials to evaluate existing public opinion and to detect "what people don't know" and whether the administration's message was "getting across to people." This research answered the question, as one official put it: "Where are people in relationship to where you want them to be, based on your strong beliefs?"

The White House most consistently used polls and focus groups, officials insisted, to identify the language, symbols, and "arguments that will resonate with people." One administration official described the White House's efforts to move public opinion toward supporting its plan in the following terms: "If people are thinking X and you know Y, how do you start trying to shape public opinion so more people will understand Y?" Pinpointing the "words that people use" in everyday life told the White House how to "talk, describe, and sell" its reform package in a manner that effectively appealed to public opinion. The White House used its public opinion research, then, to identify existing public attitudes and information that were supportive of aspects of the Clinton plan (e.g., universal coverage) as well as unfavorable (e.g., concerns about costs and government bureaucracy); then, the White House crafted its presentations to prompt Americans to bring attitudes and information favorable toward the Clinton plan to the top of their minds.

In particular, public opinion research directed the White House's decisions on three aspects of its "message" development: its choice of "security for all" as an overriding theme, its emphasis on the personal benefits of reform, and its selection of specific words to describe its plan.

Clinton's most important speech on health care reform—his September 1993 address that "launched" his campaign—powerfully illustrates the White House's calculations regarding the importance of public support and its use of "Security for All" as a theme in securing this support. President Clinton strode into the crowded and sweaty House Gallery on the assumption, as his advisers and other political observers warned, that the viability of his presidency was in question and its success or failure rode on his speech. Public support would decide the outcome of health care reform, and his address was the ultimate weapon for "pursuing the issue with a vengeance" and for mobilizing public support and thereby solidifying the backing of the Washington community.[77] Greenberg promised that "the speech can change the mood of the country" and "bring a substantial lift for the president— giving us the space to make our case to the American people and Congress."[78]

Public opinion research influenced "how to sell the plan" in Clinton's momentous September 1993 speech. Guided by polls and focus groups, White House aides and then the two Clintons carefully crafted the president's address to preempt the charges of reform opponents that the administration's plan would introduce higher taxes, fewer jobs, more government bureaucracies, and lower health care quality.[79] Instead, they aimed to "reassure" Americans about the Clinton plan by emphasizing "non-threatening, non-aggressive, middle-class themes" and by promising to "preserve and protect what is valued" in the current health care system.[80] Greenberg's suggestion was that the president focus on the broad goal of health care security—as symbolized by a new card—and avoid discussing details. The "simple, core idea" of health care security "captures the whole complicated exercise" in ways that "resonate with the public" and equip it to "pick through a lot of criticism and scare tactics." Greenberg assured the White House that the "Security for All" theme would tap Americans' support for universal coverage and be perceived as credible with a public that was "not sure we can deliver on cost control," evoking an "emotion[al] [reaction] that empowers our rationale for bold change." To cinch his case, he reported his research findings that the new health insurance card "outdistanced everything else in the plan by about 4 to 1."[81] Clinton's decision to highlight the health security card in his speech aimed at using this symbol to demonstrably identify his plan with the popular Social Security program and to encourage Americans to believe that the government had the means to implement reform.

What remains unclear, though, is whether the strategies recommended by White House aides actually corresponded with Clinton's public comments. We independently evaluated Clinton's public campaign through a systematic analysis of his public statements on health care in 1993 and 1994. (A discussion of our methodology is available in the appendix 3.)[82] Our analysis of Clinton's recorded statements confirms in part his strategic approach to presenting his proposal in September 1993 and other periods. The White House's determination to control the specific focus of its public message produced a striking consistency: the president devoted 60 percent of his time to just three issues—promoting the Clinton plan, extolling its control of costs, and dramatizing its expansion of access. Although White House aides insisted that their communications with the public were intended to "educate people," the education that the administration offered was not open and balanced. Rather, it was dominated by a programmatic and political agenda devoted to plugging the administration's plan and directing public opinion. Clinton's statements were largely self-promotional and self-serving. Out of all of the president's declarations, Clinton gave more attention to promoting his plan than to any other issue such as cost or access.[83]

Clinton embraced health care reform in order to control costs, yet his political advisers warned against focusing Americans on cost control. Figure 3.3 suggests that Clinton listened to his advisers' recommendations; over time he devoted less and less of his public discussion of health care reform to costs. After March 1993, when he devoted just over half of his public statements to cost, the proportion of such statements plummeted; by the spring and summer of 1994, cost generally received less than a fifth of his monthly attention—and often quite a bit less. Indeed, seasoned observers of the media and health policy criticized Clinton for ignoring this issue (Hamburger, Marmor, Meacham 1994, 37). By contrast, the president increasingly singled out universal coverage (access) as time went on, devoting as much or more attention to it than cost control in some months. He particularly stressed universalism whenever he addressed the general public; he gave less attention to it in statements to interest groups and other audiences. Overall, the only issues to receive more attention than universalism were his own plan and cost control.[84] Drowned out in the administration's presentation was the issue of quality; other than the brief attention it received in April 1993, it was essentially ignored.

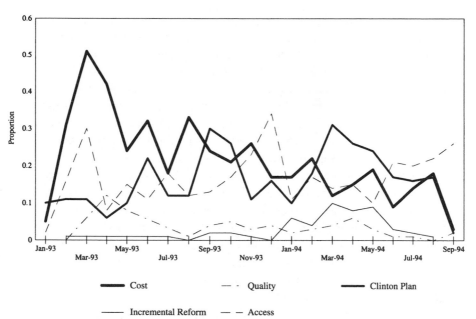

Figure 3.3 Proportion of Clinton Statements Dedicated to Top Health Care Issues
Source: Compiled by authors; see appendix 3 and text.

Although cost—the paramount issue in Clinton's mind—received less attention over time, it is nonetheless striking that the president continued to raise the issue against the strategic advice of Greenberg and others. The reality is that while strategic calculations influenced the president, they did not fully determine his public presentations. Clinton continued to weave substantive concerns (as illustrated by cost control) into his crafted presentations.

Public opinion research influenced a second aspect of the White House's presentations—its emphasis on the personal benefit of Clinton's plan for "you and your family." Greenberg's findings that "health care reform is very personal to people" contributed to the administration's decision to focus Americans on their self-interest concerning reform. White House officials encouraged Americans to draw "personal comparisons" of "how it affects you personally."[85] The bottom line for the White House was to "convince the happy insured that our program was good for them." Part of the White House's motivation was to preempt the media's portrayal of the personal consequences of Clinton's plan and to neutralize journalists' expected focus on how the plan would affect everyday Americans.

White House officials were convinced, according to our interviews, that focusing on the plight of a poor person or disadvantaged groups such as Latino immigrants would antagonize middle America. As a result, the White House's efforts to sell its plan as promoting Americans' personal interests did not, on average, focus on the experience of a single individual or group. Rather, the president tended to pitch his plan in terms of national or general consequences—its impact on stimulating the economy by reducing waste and especially its provision of health insurance to all Americans. Based on an analysis of a sample of Clinton's statements, nearly 90 percent of Clinton's statements mentioned health care reform in a general or abstract context rather than narrowly in terms of a particular individual case or episode. In addition, 65 percent of the president's messages emphasized national patterns or consequences rather than a specific group that was at risk.[86] Clinton's statements were directed at the "common good" and a national payoff of reform—they were encompassing messages that appealed to a wide and diverse audience.

The White House used its public opinion research for a third purpose: to pinpoint, as one adviser put it, the very words to "describe what it is that's being done." For instance, there was a long debate over what to call the new entities that were to purchase health insurance for consumers. Policy analysts labeled them "health insurance purchasing cooperatives" or HIPCs. Mrs. Clinton preferred "co-ops" because this seemed to have an appealing agrarian sound. But these names were trumped by focus group and poll findings that HIPCs was "not a word people understood" and that "'alliances' went over better" and would be the "most palatable to people when they listen to it."[87]

Saturating the Country

After designing simple messages that resonated with the public, the White House devoted itself—as political consultants say—to "staying on message" and saturating the public (through the media) with it. The aim was to boost the sheer volume of its messages that reached Americans. The mechanism, White House officials repeatedly explained, was a highly choreographed and "massive public communications campaign" that "deliberately and relentlessly communicate[d] our health care message."[88] Blasting the country with White House messages was expected to raise the salience of its messages and to drown out critical commentary by reform's opponents and journalists.

Analysis of Clinton's statements and actions indicates, though, that the White House's plans for saturating the country were never fully implemented. The public was not, in fact, the subject of an uninterrupted barrage. While Clinton did target the general public in 1993, the battle to woo Washington elites in 1994 supplanted the president's outreach to Americans. In 1993, 62 percent of Clinton's public discussions of health care reform issues were directed to general public audiences during national speeches, town hall meetings, or statements to journalists; only 38 percent were directed to elite audiences such as interest groups and party or government officials. (His favorite forums for championing his plan were public gatherings like town meetings, where he devoted nearly 20 percent of his public comments.)[89] Clinton's emphasis changed in 1994: 63 percent of his public discussions were aimed at elites and only 37 percent at the general public. The focus on winning congressional votes in an inhospitable Washington shifted Clinton's attention in 1994 from rallying the public—as the White House had originally hoped—to lobbying elites.

Figure 3.4 also shows that the White House did not in fact "relentlessly" saturate Americans with Clinton's message; his outreach on health care reform was intermittent and declined over time. The amount of attention that Clinton devoted to health care reform (measured by the number of lines of text in his statements) was largely limited to one major event—his September 1993 speech to Congress,

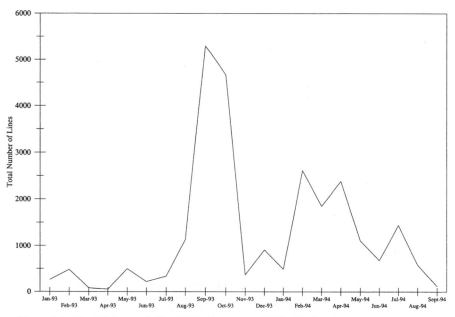

Figure 3.4   Total Volume of Clinton Statements on All Health Care Issues

Source: Compiled by authors; see appendix 3 and text.

which was followed by Mrs. Clinton dramatic appearances before five congressional committees. The president's first address to a joint session of Congress in February 1993 produced a slight rise in his public effort but then fell in March and April. Although Clinton's State of the Union speech in January 1994 was designed to "relaunch" health care reform, his overall attention to the issue in January was relatively low. He engaged in short bursts of activity in the spring of 1994, but this public campaign declined further during the summer, as our interviewees complained. None of the activity in 1994 even approached its 1993 peak.

Administration officials repeatedly found their elaborate plans to plaster the country with their message sabotaged by national and international events—foreign policy crises in Somalia and Haiti, legislative battles over NAFTA and the Brady bill, and the Whitewater political scandal. They watched helplessly as they "lost the president" on health reform and found their message "go off screen." That the president would be distracted and forced to delay or abandon well-laid plans was predictable but underestimated by the White House. Before Clinton's inauguration, the powerful Chairman of the House Ways and Means Committee, Dan Rostenkowski, was reported by his senior health policy adviser to have warned the president and Mrs. Clinton that they should plan for the event that "something's going to blow up and it's going to take all of your attention."

In short, the White House pursued a strategy of priming public opinion by anticipating the reactions of journalists and their political opponents. It struggled to adhere to a specific message that primed or highlighted the national or collective benefits of its health care reform plan, while deflecting attention from its costs and from a detailed discussion of how to pay for the plan and implement it.

The Fantasy of Winning Public Opinion

The rap on Clinton's health care reform campaign was that the president, Magaziner, and other senior health policy aides were consumed with policy and ignored the political obstacles facing them (Heclo 1995; Hacker 1997). It is certainly true that the debate in the Roosevelt Room in May 1993 captured a genuine immersion in the minutiae of health policy. But the absorption with the substance of policy did not prevent the Clinton coterie from accurately forecasting the political and institutional obstacles facing reform and underscoring the long

odds against success. Magaziner and other senior policy aides appreciated the political risks (Johnson and Broder 1996, 150).

The fundamental political mistake committed by Bill Clinton and
his aides was in grossly overestimating the capacity of a president to
"win" public opinion and to use public support as leverage to overcome known political obstacles—from an ideologically divided Congress to hostile interest groups. Clinton and his political advisers,
White House officials observed, interpreted each uptick in public support for the president and his health care reform plan as confirmation
of their ability to direct public opinion, "ensur[ing] a heightened and
particularly naive amount of confidence" that public support would
compel Congress to support the president's plan.[90] The initial poll results after Clinton's September 1993 speech seemed to fulfill the White
House's hopes, with more than half of the country favoring the Clinton
plan.[91] Greenberg gushed that his focus group research indicated that
the president's plan was "enthusiastically received by voters who
viewed the speech [and that it enjoyed] almost unanimous support."[92]
Within six months, however, public support had plummeted by more
than 20 percentage points.

The White House's unquestioned faith that the president could rally
Americans produced a rigid insistence on comprehensive reform in the
face of souring political fortunes. Neither the delay caused by the budget fight in early 1993 nor the growing opposition in 1994 prompted
Clinton and his aides to reconsider seriously their plan or even, according to one aide, to "imagine a scenario where we go to Plan B,
which rolls our plan out in detachable pieces that goes into the next
Congress." Downturns in support prompted new White House
schemes for public "education" rather than a fundamental reconsideration of the premise of its strategy—that the president possessed the
capacity to lead public opinion on a contentious social policy issue.

The White House's inflated confidence in its ability to win over and
hold public support also lulled it, as one official put it, into "underestimating how easily our plan could be used to tap the public's cynicism
and distrust of the government." Interviews and White House records
show a clearheaded appreciation of Americans' uneasiness with government and the political danger this uneasiness posed. The White
House anticipated that the health alliances, the National Health Board
that oversaw benefits and expenditures, and other components its plan
could readily be "painted by opponents as big government requiring
many new bureaucracies."[93] But Magaziner and other officials down-

played the danger posed by government bashing, because they over-estimated their ability to drown out their opponents. They mistakenly reassured Mrs. Clinton in preparing for the president's September speech that "our opponents, while powerful, will not have a cohesive message."[94]

It was not until 1994 that the constraints on the president's ability to lead public opinion began to dawn on the White House. Indeed, our analysis of Clinton's statements and White House records reveal a sobering shift away from moving opinion and public appeals toward an emphasis on elites. In the wreckage of his crusade, Clinton con-ceded that he had "overestimated the extent to which [he] could achieve a sweeping overhaul of the health care system."[95]

The fundamental reason for the defeat of the Clinton plan was the White House's inflated expectations about its ability to direct public opinion and use public support to overcome the well-known political and institutional obstacles facing health care reform. These expecta-tions prodded the White House to design a plan whose scope and de-sign defied public ambivalence and was unlikely to win congressional approval.

Managing the Media

The White House's efforts to "win" public support elevated the politi-cal importance of managing the press; it was perceived as the critical conduit for affecting Americans. White House officials harbored a top-down model for moving opinion in which decisions by the media di-rectly affected the public's evaluation of issues. They credited the media with "setting the agenda [by] the stories it picks" and with largely de-termining the public's policy evaluations. The president's advisers ap-preciated that the expected influence of the press on public opinion magnified its political power; one influential Clinton health adviser ex-plained that the press "shapes members of Congress" because they anticipate its impact on their constituents.

It was precisely because of the media's perceived influence that the White House "worr[ied] about the media affecting public opinion" and attempted to manage it. "What scares me," one White House official confided, "is how easily manipulated public opinion has become through the mass media," especially because the rules of press coverage make it vulnerable to "serv[ing] as the vehicle for attacks." A number of administration officials pointed to the pressures on journalists and editors to "grab" audiences who have limited knowledge of health care issues and to adhere to the professional norm of "presenting the other side, which means that at best you get 50-50 in most stories." The most consistent complaint by White House aides was that their perspective was underrepresented or distorted and that the political "horse race" had become "the prism for all the coverage." From the White House's perspective, journalists turned to administration critics and their own interpretation in order to uncover Clinton's overriding "concern about getting elected." The result, officials repeatedly complained, was that media reports bore "little or no resemblance" to administration meetings or activities; "much of what [the president and vice president] think is most important is never covered because it's not personality driven, it's not confrontational, it's not conflict."

White House officials struggled to counter the biases of journalists by adjusting their strategies to the media's routines and styles of reporting. At the outset of Clinton's term, Magaziner and other advisers argued unsuccessfully for regularly briefing journalists on health care reform and even inviting them to task force meetings. Welcoming the media, they reasoned, was the most effective means for "controlling the news flow" and "focusing [reporters] on explaining the White House's activity and options," because they would "understand what we had gone through" and their demand for material would have been satiated.[96] Only a few weeks after Clinton's inauguration, aides prophetically warned that failure to incorporate journalists would invite a situation where decisions "will randomly leak and dribble out to be interpreted by others to advance their own agendas."[97]

But George Stephanopoulos and other officials who oversaw the White House's relations with journalists persuaded Hillary Clinton that the threat of media distortions was best avoided by walling off administration officials from the media. They feared that journalists would exploit their access and file explosive stories that would unnecessarily unsettle allies and divert attention from tenuous budget negotiations. The result, officials later conceded, was an "insulated process" that "didn't communicate with the press" and that prohibited Magaziner and other health policy specialists from even taking phone calls from journalists.[98]

The political battles and controversies during the administration's first months in office, however, convinced the White House, as aides later acknowledged, that its initial strategy was "totally defective" and that journalists must be "fed" stories as part of a "national media campaign." The White House, according to a variety of administration officials, used three tactics to offset the inclination of the press toward framing policy debates in terms of conflict and "who's winning or losing." First, it established "a buddy system": senior administration officials and task force members were "assigned" prominent journalists to contact and "educate." The buddy system was complicated by the fact that editors were constantly rotating their staff, passing the story from reporters who specialized in health care issues to those who covered the Congress or White House. Second, administration officials tried to push journalists away from "horse race" stories by spending "countless hours explaining the plan and answering substantive questions"; they were ultimately disappointed that the "coverage was just never reflective" of the briefings because journalists "don't really talk about the substance."

Third, the White House ultimately abdicated to the journalists' fixation with conflict and recreated (on Magaziner's suggestion) the "war room" from Clinton's 1992 campaign. The war room's capability to monitor news coverage and blitz journalists with the White House's immediate reaction gave officials the ability to rapidly "counter what the other side was doing" and the critical stories that were filed by journalists.[99]

Clinton's public statements remained substantive, however, even during the White House's campaign to offset the media's addiction to insider politics. Our analysis of presidential statements shows that three-quarters of his comments focused on substantive policy issues and less than one-fifth on politics.[100] Moreover, as we suggested earlier, his attention to cost control (against the strategic advice of his aides) also demonstrated the way Clinton weaved in substantive considerations: his public statements combined policy concerns with strategic ones.

Journalists appreciated that Clinton was using substantive presentations for strategic purposes and concluded that all of his statements and actions were simply orchestrated. The White House's adaptation to media routines encouraged, officials acknowledged, the presumption among journalists that "anything the administration says is biased and wrong." As we discuss in chapter 5, however, journalists' were driven by genuine political developments to unpack the calculations behind the crafted statements by Clinton and other political activists, leading the press to neglect the substantive policy issues at hand. In effect, journalists treated the substantive issues as mere window dressing to adorn a pervasive strategy of manipulation. But their preoccupation with the means of White House political strategy (namely, the use of crafted talk) came at a high cost: the press neglected the ends of politics and, specifically, the genuine substantive issues raised by Clinton's philosophical beliefs and policy positions.

Conclusion

Bill Clinton's policy preferences, philosophy toward government, and political judgments about the policy goals of his potential supporters drove the formulation of his health care reform plan. Only after he and his advisers reached their decisions did they focus on public opinion as part of a strategy to win over the public to their policy positions and thereby induce cooperation from policymakers and interest groups. Their decision to manipulate journalists and craft White House presentations to avoid the mechanics of health care reform reflected neither the personal or moral failings of Clinton nor a coup by political consultants. Rather, the White House's strategy stemmed from a realistic assessment of how journalists and the opponents of reform would behave in the political system of the time.

Clinton and his allies turned to crafted presentations after their tortuous first six months in office as a desperate attempt to insert themselves in a policy debate that they perceived to be dominated by the media's rules and by opportunistic opponents. The content and style of their public presentations were shaped by how they expected reporters, political opponents, and the public to react. Clinton and his advisers calibrated their public comments and activities to play by the media's rules of engagement; they expected the press to reconstruct Clinton's statements along predictable lines, spotlighting the personal stakes of policy debates and the political strategy at work. White House advisers calculated that the failure to follow the media's work patterns would enable opponents to capitalize on the media's routines to their own advantage. From this assessment of the likely reactions by journalists and political opponents, the White House publicly presented simplified or misleading versions of its arguments, which were charged with potent symbols and warnings about the personal stakes of Americans in health care reform.

Even the White House's presentation of its political strategy was crafted to obscure its actual intentions. In public, the president repeatedly welcomed recommendations for changes and presented his plan as a starting point. The White House's speechwriters were instructed to lace their prose with promises to pursue "consensus building rather than [being] negative and divisive" and to project an appealing image of a president who is searching for the "right kind of changes" and

who humbly recognizes that "we don't have all the answers and that
we would seek to incorporate good ideas."[101] Back in the White House
bunker, however, Magaziner and other aides promoted the invitation
to dialogue as a political gambit; this "*strategy gives us the opportunity
. . . to appear to be listening*" (emphasis added). The political payoff
was seen as significant: "If people feel they had a chance to participate
in a national discussion, they may be more supportive of the outcome."
In addition to coopting supporters, the expected payoff for projecting
an image of openness was to enhance the administration's flexibility
and to remove it from the "defensive posture [of] defending every detail.[102] But Magaziner made it clear that despite the promise of open
discussion, he did not expect the administration's plan to "fundamentally change."[103]

This captures the internal dynamics of the White House that produced its health care reform plan and its political strategy. Administration officials did not view the public as a genuine partner in policymaking. On the contrary, it was an object to be manipulated for political
purposes. The next chapter examines the external circumstances in
Congress and in the interest group community and how they reacted
to Clinton's plan and the White House's strategy of crafted talk.

Chapter Four

Storming the Bully Pulpit

P residents have long been fabled to have the power of the "bully pulpit." The power of public persuasion, however, is no longer the tool of presidents alone but is shared by members of Congress and interest groups. The combination of political incentives to pursue policy goals rather than centrist opinion, the rise of political consultants, and the emergence of a new breed of media-savvy political leaders has dramatically widened the use of opinion manipulation in debates over government decisions that divide the parties. Legislators and interest groups calculate, not unlike presidents, that crafted appeals can offset the electoral risks of pursuing policy objectives and increase the likelihood of attracting support from the small but critical number of moderate members of Congress who remain sensitive to centrist opinion (Jacobs and Shapiro 1998; Jacobs, Lawrence, Shapiro, and Smith 1998; Harris 1998).

The debate over health reform in 1993 and 1994 ignited a cycle of dueling presentations. Clinton and his advisers hatched their strategy for moving public opinion to counter the expected campaign by reform opponents to swing opinion against health reform and to rally the divided and relatively small Democratic majorities in the House and Senate.[1] The Clinton team's preparations fueled efforts to influence public opinion by interest groups and members of Congress opposed to health reform. Much like the White House, they appreciated that winning public support would lower the risk of retribution at the next election for pursuing their policy goal (defeat of health reform), and it would pressure legislative moderates in both parties to join coalitions to block the president's plan. Like the White House, interest groups and Republicans also used polls and focus groups not to make policy but rather to orchestrate appeals to win Americans over to their side.

Interest Groups Go Public

Clinton's health reform legislation was cursed by intense resistance from a diverse set of interest groups. The groups of stakeholders who were threatened by health reform—representatives of small- and medium-sized health insurers (Health Insurance Association of America) and small business (National Federation of Independent Businesses [NFIB])—harbored intense concerns about defending their livelihoods. Clinton's plan was also opposed by large umbrella organizations such as the Business Roundtable and the Chamber of Commerce. The umbrella organizations represented employers who stood to benefit from reforms that controlled the escalation of health care costs and the incidence of uncompensated care. But they ultimately opposed Clinton's plan because of the combination of deep-seated ideological hostility toward government and weak organization, which enabled the intense opposition of a few members, namely, health insurers, to set their policy (Martin 2000; Brown 1993). The influence of reform opponents was further boosted by the formation of a loose coalition of thirty small and large organizations that coordinated their lobbying and public attacks on Clinton's plan (Johnson and Broder 1996).

On the other side of the divide, organized interests that favored health reform were, to the surprise of the White House, far less intense than reform's opponents. Before Clinton announced his plan in September 1993, the White House expected pro-reform groups like the American Association of Retired Persons (AARP) and representatives of labor, consumers, and public interest organizations to "dedicate their resources and membership base to the health care cause"; aides comfortably predicted in July 1993 that "we will have a strong coalition that will be able to lobby the package through Congress."[2] Within a year, though, the White House declared these groups a "great disappointment" because they held back their full support in an ongoing drive to secure still more concessions. "When they got 90 percent of what they wanted," one White House official protested, "they withheld their support, energy, and resources to get the 10 percent."[3]

Both advocates and opponents of reform focused on securing the same political resource—public support—in order to provide cover for allies who shared their policy goals and to pressure moderate legislators to join their coalition. The political importance placed on winning public opinion changed the nature of interest group influence on health reform and created opportunities for relatively small stakeholders to boost their influence.

The age-old approach to wielding influence had been to lobby members of Congress in backrooms and to organize support among a legislator's constituents back home on a district-by-district basis (Fenno 1973, 1978; Schattschneider 1960a). By the 1990s, however, public opinion research had honed mass mailings and paid advertisements into new weapons for interest groups. They provided a fresh means for "educating" the public and supporters of interest group positions and for mobilizing them all across the country to attend local meetings with members of Congress and to write or call them. For instance, the NFIB launched the largest grassroots effort in health reform to communicate its message and mobilize supporters; it used Rush Limbaugh, mass mailings, and faxes to alert tens of thousands of small business owners. Although HIAA lacked NFIB's community ties, it instigated nearly half a million phone calls, visits, and letters from constituents to members of Congress (Johnson and Broder 1996, 213).

Most of the techniques of mass communications deployed in the health reform debate had been available for decades but were not fully exploited during previous policy debates. (They were of course staples of electoral politics.) What changed in the 1990s were the political incentives: interest groups recognized the increased political importance of winning public opinion to secure or strengthen the backroom deals. Relatively small groups like HIAA viewed their political ads and their other mass communication tools as weapons to amplify their positions beyond what their limited resources could previously deliver and to catapult these groups from relative obscurity to positions of prominence and influence. Part of HIAA's success stemmed from parlaying its paid "Harry and Louise" ads into much greater "free" media coverage of the ads themselves, which in turn increased the attention to its arguments and boosted its fund raising, as it demonstrated its ability to draw attention to its claims.

"[W]e realized," explained John Motley, the chief lobbyist for NFIB, "that the battle is not going to be a typical inside-the-Beltway battle. . . . This battle is going to be waged across the country with the American people" (Johnson and Broder 1996, 219). The danger, according to HIAA officials, was that an unstoppable "bandwagon" would form for Clinton's plan if "the President has the field to himself and the poll ratings show a great acceptance" (205). The interest groups opposed to Clinton's plan sank $100 million into influencing the debate. The money that poured into defeating Clinton's plan (about $60 million) purchased a nearly unparalleled advertising blitz, allowing antireformers to distribute their messages in a way denied others. If the press is a gate through which information is passed, antireformers purchased the equivalent of a season's pass (West and Loomis 1999; West, Heith, and Goodwin 1996).

Clinton and his advisers list interest group spending as the principal reason for the defeat of their plan. In their account, they got their "clock cleaned because opponents put up more resources in their public opinion messages" and were able to "change public opinion" and the "perception of the people."[4]

The financial and organizational resources that antireform opponents poured into fighting Clinton's plan gave them an opportunity to widely distribute their claims that was shared neither by unorganized groups such as the uninsured nor by less well-funded organizations such as single-payer advocates. The Clinton administration, however, was not the overwhelmed victim it claims. Our analysis in chapter 6 shows that the "free" media devoted far more attention to the president and Democrats than opponents. Although the ability to communicate with the mass public was not equally shared, there was competition among authoritative government officials and privileged private interests.

In short, the changed political incentives heightened the perceived benefits of mobilizing public support. New methods of mass communications and a tidal wave of special interest funding equipped antireform groups of even modest size with the capacity to challenge the president's bully pulpit and to redefine the issue of health reform.

Congress and Public Opinion

It is not surprising that interest groups would hatch plots to shape (and not follow) public opinion toward health reform. But political observers would find it surprising that during the health reform debate many members of Congress also refrained from following public opinion in favor of trying to shape it. After all, legislators are widely presumed to follow public opinion in reaching significant policy decisions in order to curry favor with constituents and boost their prospects for reelection (Mayhew 1974a). Indeed, in-depth interviews with thirty-nine senior staff members from House and Senate offices during the summer of 1994 indicated that they fully expected the 1994 congressional elections to be influenced by voters' preferences about health care reform.[5] In fact, 75 percent of the staff associated with legislators running for reelection believed that health reform would be a central issue in the next campaign and agreed that a member's position would need to coincide with his or her constituents' policy preferences to win reelection.

Public Opinion's Muted Influence

Since the 1980s, congressional leaders (especially in the House of Representatives) gradually developed the capacity to track public opinion by commissioning polls and focus groups. But the persistent (though not uniform) theme from our interviews was that public opinion and polls were not decisive influences on congressional decision making. Only five of thirty-six staff (13 percent) indicated that the purpose of information about public opinion was to drive policy.[6] (This contrasts with 40 percent of legislators in the early 1940s who reported "consult[ing] a reputable public opinion survey for aid in determining your attitude toward a measure concerning which you were doubtful.")[7] They attributed their refusal to "utilize polls as a finger in the wind" in reaching decisions to four factors, which parallel those listed by administration officials. First, the nearly endless stream of opinion polls from the media, party organizations, and lobbyists were generally not considered credible; congressional officials presumed that the findings were manufactured through the use of slanted question wordings and biased sampling. Wordings and sampling allow a poll's sponsor to produce the results they want and, as one staff member put it, "move a survey from an 80–20 split to a 20–80 split."

Instead of relying on polls, nearly three out of four staffers indicated that they used long-standing practices for tracking constituency opinion—face-to-face meetings, letters, or phone calls. Although they of course belittled "manufactured" or "artificial grass roots" campaigns run by interest groups, they valued a "heartfelt" or "thoughtful" letter, phone call, or personal contact because it indicated strongly held and well thought out beliefs. Many offices compiled daily or weekly reports on the number and subject of phone calls and letters received.

The second reason staffers discounted public opinion surveys in making policy was that polls were considered too crude to pinpoint public sentiment about the package of policies contained in a complex proposal. Eliciting public reaction to just one component of a proposal invited "confusion" and false choices. For instance, several staff for

Republican members complained that polls reporting majorities in favor of universal health insurance coverage neglected the public's offsetting apprehension or even skepticism regarding the means for achieving it—namely, higher taxes and greater government regulation.

A third factor was that staffers acknowledged genuine uncertainty about the public's preferences. Many staffers emphasized the complexity and fuzziness of public attitudes, with as many as a third of the respondents indicating, for example, that their constituents had no opinion on several major policy issues. We asked staff members to characterize public opinion toward six aspects of the health reform debate—universal health insurance coverage, competition among health plans, cost control mechanisms, financing arrangements, health care benefits, and the role of the states. Aside from universalism where 86 percent of our respondents believed that their constituents' supported it, there were large differences across congressional offices in how they appraised their constituents' beliefs. The greatest divisions occurred on the issues of cost control and financing; nearly equal groups of staffers expressed diametrically opposed appraisals of their constituents.[8]

Congressional confusion and disagreement on constituents' policy preferences had important implications: it prevented congressional majorities—even if they wanted to—from following national public opinion on health reform. The divergence in congressional perceptions of public opinion may have, in part, resulted from the reliance on subjective judgments of scattered sources. Skepticism regarding polls and faith in their informal contacts with constituents meant that members did not rely on a common source of information that presented a unified appraisal of public opinion.

Finally, individual legislators considered public opinion an inappropriate consideration in responsible governing. Letting polls drive their decisions was considered "goofy," irresponsible, and dangerous due to the volatile nature of surveys and public opinion.

The consistent message from our interviews was that the policy positions of members were guided by their policy goals and their personal views regarding health policy and the role of government. When asked to account for the placement of issues on the policy agenda and legislative decisions, most congressional staff pointed to a member's personal beliefs or judgments on "what is best" for their constituents. While most Democrats favored some kind of health care reform, the policy and philosophical preference of most Republicans was for no more than modest reform, with a relatively large and vocal bloc of conservatives favoring no legislation at all.[9] Although most members discounted what Americans preferred, public opinion may nonetheless have influenced a small number of legislators, whose decisions were critical in a closely divided Congress.

While the interviews with congressional staff are telling, they have a potential pitfall: the staff may simply have offered the expected "appropriate" or politically acceptable answers to our questions. Legislators and their staff might have anticipated that acknowledging the influence of public opinion (rather than personal philosophy and beliefs) on their policy decisions would reflect badly on them (especially among their peers and other elites). Indeed, we would not trust the interviews if they were the only evidence we had to offer. But they are not.

Previous studies of the relationship between individual members of Congress and their constituencies corroborate the pattern in our interviews. They indicate that public opinion has a modest and highly contingent impact on members' voting decisions and electoral prospects and that this impact has been declining since the 1970s (see chapter 1). Although reelection is a haunting worry, legislators pursue other goals including policy objectives and exploit the difficulty that voters have in monitoring the positions and behavior of their representatives (see chapter 2).

Public opinion surveys conducted by the media and academics provide another independent basis for evaluating the impact of opinion on policy decisions. In a variety of ways, the behavior of the five congressional committees that were primarily responsible for health reform did not coincide with public preferences as measured in media and academic polls.[10] Congressional committees adopted policies that lacked clear public support; many policies were neither the subject of poll questions nor matters on which Americans had opinions. The result was that the committees exercised discretion in designing a host of policies including the formula for reimbursing health care providers, the authority of the new National Health Board, and the taxing schemes that states could use to pay for health benefits that exceeded those offered in the basic reform plan.

In addition, committees ignored public preferences that already existed. The single-payer approach enjoyed public support, certainly enough to justify inclusion in the debate within Congress (and the media). But aside from its approval by the House Education and Labor Committee it was altogether ignored by four committees. Government regulations that limited the amounts charged by private insurers and drug companies were also popular with Americans, but none of the congressional committees voted on them. On financing health reform, there were no recorded committee votes on adopting a direct and explicit payroll tax, which also enjoyed public support; there was only one vote—in a House subcommittee—to raise tobacco taxes, which Americans strongly supported. Instead, legislators chose to follow the policy goals that they and their supporters favored.

Polling and Crafted Talk

If public opinion did not drive the policy positions of interest groups and most legislators, why did they monitor public opinion? According to interviews and other evidence, Republican congressional leaders and interest groups adopted the same strategy as the Clinton White House: they used information about public opinion to identify the language, arguments, and symbols for countering the Clinton administration. Legislators' use since the 1970s of public appeals to gain the support of centrist opinion for their policy goals coincided with the development of the capacity by congressional leaders (especially in the House of Representatives) to launch campaigns to influence public opinion by managing press reporting (Harris 1998).

Congressional efforts to lead public opinion solve the puzzle of legislators simultaneously discounting public opinion on health reform while acknowledging that their reelection would be affected by their constituents' preferences toward it. Legislators defused the threat to reelection by working to move the public toward supporting their positions and simulating responsiveness.

Managing the Media

Journalists were treated by politicians and interest groups as kingpins because of their presumed impact on the public. The White House eventually focused on the press because it was the principal source of political information and the conduit to reach ordinary citizens and voters. Interest groups and members of Congress who opposed reform reached the same conclusion and used the press as their primary means to shape public opinion. Echoing the sentiment of many congressional officials, John Motley, who directed NFIB's campaign against health reform, boasted that "we have never structured a campaign in the past which was as press-focused or press-conscious as this one" (Johnson and Broder 1996). Interviews with congressional staff revealed that nearly half of those who discussed their media strategies (42 percent, 11 of 26) said that they monitored advertisements and news stories and publicly countered what they considered inaccurate or harmful messages. Our interviews and research by others indicate that the attention to the media was even more acute among congressional leaders (Sinclair 1995; Harris 1998; Hess 1986).

Although reform opponents utilized paid advertisements like HIAA's "Harry and Louise" spots, critics in Congress and elsewhere also appreciated that the "free" news media boosted this ad's direct influence on the public. Indeed, HIAA was forced by its limited budget to restrict its broadcasts to Washington and a few other locations; but its message was spread far and wide because of the "media multiplier effect"—journalists devoted extensive coverage to "Harry and Louise" and to the reaction of political activists to the spot. Reform opponents also schemed to channel the "free" media against the Clinton plan by planting critical questions in administration briefings and reaching out to sympathetic media outlets like the *Wall Street Journal,* Rush Limbaugh, and the conservative talk radio network (Johnson and Broder 1996, 196–98).

The Public Opinion Guidance System

Interest groups and members of Congress used information about public opinion (much like administration officials did) to target the messages that they transmitted through the media. The opponents of reform (especially Republican leaders) relied on the polls and focus groups of Bill McInturff, Frank Luntz, and, to a somewhat lesser extent, Bill Hamilton.

They used public opinion research to influence Americans in three ways, which closely parallel the White House's practices. First, legislative staff reported that polls "enable members to find out what the public is thinking" in order to build on areas of support and challenge pockets of opposition. A plurality of congressional staff (36 percent) reported using their public opinion information to lead and educate Americans to change their preferences. Polls showing that a majority approved the Clinton plan were interpreted by Republican legislators as signaling that "we needed to educate the public regarding what we didn't like about the plan" and its "negative unintended consequences."

Second, polls provided symbolic or rhetorical ammunition to "prove your own point." About two thirds of the legislative staff sample indicated that public opinion information was helpful in justifying their position.[11] For instance, when reform was teetering on defeat in May 1994, Gingrich used McInturff's analysis to reassure moderate Republicans that outright opposition to reform was acceptable to Americans (Johnson and Broder 1996, 428). Polls showing public opposition to the Clinton plan, which Republicans worked hard to create, were used to portray the GOP's policy goals (defeating health reform) as electorally expedient.

Third, congressional officials used polls to identify existing public attitudes that were ambivalent or opposed to aspects of the Clinton plan (e.g., expanded government bureaucracy) and then crafted their presentations to prime these considerations as Americans evaluated health reform. As one congressional official explained, "polls help to *focus and define messages*" (emphasis added). Research by reform opponents identified an ambivalence in Americans' attitudes towards health reform: public support for the goals of reform coexisted with uneasiness about the means for achieving it and, especially, with distrust of the government and bureaucrats. The implication was that support for Clinton's plan could be eroded by accentuating and arousing Americans' dread of government and the personal costs of health reform. HIAA, for instance, designed its "Harry and Louise" ad to prime the public's uneasiness; following its public opinion research, the ad warned that "the government may force us to pick from a few health care plans designed by government bureaucrats" and pleaded, "there's got to be a better way" (Johnson and Broder 1996). Two thirds of those we interviewed in Congress reported using information on public opinion to frame policy decisions in their statements or speeches.[12]

Marshalling Republicans and Public Opinion

Republican leaders in Congress and in the party coordinated the Republicans' campaign to turn Americans against Clinton's plan and against all but modest health care reform.[13] Congressional leaders were more inclined than the rank and file to direct public opinion because they were especially concerned about securing collective benefits for the Republican Party—improving the party's overall standing or reputation with centrist, swing voters and thereby winning majorities in the House and Senate in 1994 and the White House in 1996. Congressional leaders were also especially active in directing opinion because of the expectations of rank-and-file legislators, who looked to them—according to our research and that of others—to assume primary responsibility for using the media to influence public opinion and create "electoral cover."[14]

Republican leaders struggled throughout the health reform debate to balance their electoral and policy goals: their commitment to protecting the party's reputation among centrist voters and the party's prospects in upcoming elections clashed with the objective of conservatives to block all health reform. Senate Minority Leader Bob Dole and other Republican leaders agreed that explicitly setting out to "blow up the bridges and watch the trains wreck" would paint the party as obstructionist with centrist Americans and cost it dearly in the 1994 and 1996 elections. Echoing the concerns of Republican leaders, Fred Grandy (R-IA) warned against "just stand[ing] on the sideline and systematically shoot[ing] at everything that moves into your crosshairs" because the party will become perceived by many Americans as heartless and uncaring about an issue that touches voters very personally (Dewar and Priest 1994). To respond to the public's general concern about health care, Dole and other leaders emphasized their commitment to "responsible" health reform and to working with Democrats to control costs and expand access.

Even as leaders responded to the public's support for health reform, they cautiously used a range of tactics to prod the public toward preferring what most Republicans favored—minimal, if any, reform. Republicans leaders collaborated with other reform opponents in blitzing the country with the simple message that "big government" would threaten the quality of health care in order to highlight, or "prime," the costs (rather than the benefits) of reform in the public's mind. The aim, as mentioned above, was to prompt Americans to evaluate the Clinton plan by focusing on the expansion of government and on the consequences of this for threatening their personal well-being. Republican leaders turned to well-known tricks of the trade to amplify their message: they leaked "trial balloons" to the press, promoted alternative plans, introduced cross-cutting issues such as abortion, and advanced alarming scenarios about the Clinton plan. Republican leaders coordinated their messages with the rank and file and interest group allies and used a "rapid response" system to fax out the immediate responses of leaders to Democratic health care announcements (Merida 1994; Johnson and Broder 1996).

In short, Republican leaders pursued a dual strategy of both responding to and shaping public opinion. On the one hand, they responded to public opinion by adjusting the timing of their actions, the wording of their statements, and the alternatives they proposed while voicing general support for the popular idea of reform. On the other, they attempted to gradually build the public's opposition while maintaining the guise of responding to its concerns.

Leading public opinion required Republican leaders to pursue not only an outward looking strategy but also an inward strategy of shepherding their rank-and-file Republican members to specific proposals. If the Republican ranks splintered, the party's leaders would be unable to appeal to the public with a coherent message, build the party's reputation, and seize majority status. Bob Dole, Newt Gingrich, and other Republican leaders feared that Democrats would capitalize on divisions within the GOP to "pick off enough Republicans to get the [health reform] bill to pass (Balz 1994). "Our most important problem," Gingrich confided, "was not letting [Republicans] defect and pass a health care plan" (Johnson and Broder 1996).

The potential for Republicans to break ranks was real. The White House, according to its confidential records, was indeed "actively (but quietly) working to sign up" moderate Republicans who were "sending encouraging signals about at least the possibility of supporting the [President's] proposal."[15] Based on reports that John Chafee, a Senate Republican and influential moderate, was working with twenty-three other Republican senators to draft a plan, White House aides concluded that half of the forty-four Senate Republicans supported compromising with Clinton and passing significant reform.[16]

The struggle of Republican leaders to prevent the defection of moderates to Clinton through private negotiation and compromise was facilitated by the shrinking number of Republican moderates and the growing ranks of hard-edged conservatives who opted for open warfare with Democrats rather than compromise.[17] Former Dan Quayle chief of staff William Kristol became the most prominent spokesman for the conservatives' position: just months after Clinton's electrifying September 1993 speech launching his reform plan, Kristol openly argued for "defeat[ing] the President's plan outright" by adopting an "aggressive and uncompromising counter-strategy."[18]

Republican leaders faced a major challenge. Appealing to Americans by proposing moderate reform conflicted with the positions of conservative Republicans who opposed any reform. On the other hand, simply following the conservative wing of the party risked alienating moderate Republicans and appearing obstructionist to centrist opinion. The contest for the Republican Party's presidential nomination further complicated divisions among congressional Republicans; Bob Dole's ambitions for the White House heightened his sensitivity to conservative legislators and party activists and his determination to keep them on his side even as he courted centrist opinion.

Republican leaders, then, faced the daunting challenge of bridging the divide in their ranks and channeling members toward points of convergence that would protect the party's reputation. The conflicting electoral and policy pressures on leaders prompted them to alter regularly the proposals that they formulated or endorsed and those that they attacked as unsatisfactory. The most dramatic illustrations were the shifts in Dole's policy positions as he responded to perceived changes in centrist opinion and Republican sentiment in Congress: he endorsed Chafee's comprehensive plan during the zenith of the Clinton plan's popularity; he remained open to compromise legislation when the public was split on it; and he dropped both Chafee's and his own bare-bones package during its nadir as conservative opposition to any reform intensified.

Reformers and Opponents Square Off

Competing efforts by the advocates of reform and their opponents to "win over" public opinion proceeded roughly in four different stages. In each stage, Clinton and his Democratic allies, Republican leaders, and interest groups adapted to their rivals' strategies and to changes in public opinion. The policy debate over health care reform was caught in a spiral of crafted talk. To complement our analysis of Clinton's strategy, we tracked the behavior of Republican leaders through our interviews as well as by chronicling legislators' votes and positions.[19]

September 1993: Clinton Engages a Cautious Opposition

The White House Makes Its Case

The debate over health care reform began in earnest with Clinton's national speech and flurry of activities to unveil his plan in September 1993. Before the speech, White House's pollster Stanley Greenberg counted on the speech to "change the mood of the country" and "bring a substantial lift for the President—giving us the space to make our case to the American people and Congress."[20] Clinton and his advisers interpreted the findings from polls and focus groups as fully confirming their high expectations, with Greenberg reporting to the White House that "President Clinton's health care plan was enthusiastically received by voters who viewed the speech."[21] Independent polls reported that nearly 60 percent favored Clinton's plan when given the narrow choice of either approving or disapproving of it. Gallup surveys showed that Americans who considered themselves Democrats supported it overwhelmingly (83 percent to 13 percent) and a majority of independents also backed it (55 percent to 34 percent); Republicans opposed it, 35 to 56 percent. The White House had won the enthusiastic support of its Democratic base and wooed independents.

Clinton and White House aides were also pleased that the congressional reaction "went as expected." The reassuring soundings (both in public and private) from Republican Senate Minority Leader Bob Dole, Senate Republican and influential moderate John Chafee, moderate House Democrat Jim Cooper, and others confirmed for White House officials their strategy of bridging liberals and moderates. Although they presumed that Dole was a "highly doubtful supporter," they were convinced that strong public and congressional support for the president's plan equipped them to "g[o] around Dole and buil[d] a . . . viable bipartisan deal."[22] Magaziner reported to the president and Mrs. Clinton that "I am increasingly confident that we are positioned correctly for the political discussions ahead." He recommended preparing for negotiations by "think[ing] backwards from the 'end game'" and outlined a range of compromises that would, he predicted, produce legislation.[23]

Buoyed by Americans' initial "enthusiastic" reaction, the White House was confident that support from the public and Congress could be maintained and expanded by capitalizing on the abilities of the president and the "war room" to shape the debate. Following their strategy to saturate the country with their message, aides repeatedly developed new "short- and long-term calendars" for Clinton to "undertake a massive media affairs campaign" to "promote" his plan.[24] Aides plotted an elaborate "'national discussion' strategy . . . to keep the debate centered around the President's plan"; a series of forums with health professional and business leaders was expected to encourage the "public [to] associate them with the Clinton plan [and] neutraliz[e] those who may otherwise speak out against the plan."[25]

Storming the country with the White House's messages was repeatedly identified as "critical to the ultimate success of health care reform."[26] In addition to hammering the "Security for All" message, Greenberg and other aides emphasized that "our primary communication focus" should be pitched to a "personal level" in convincing people that reform will help "their own well-being." Greenberg bolstered his recommendation by presenting the results of multivariate regression analysis that identified specific components of Clinton's plan that "reassure[d] voters on how their families will fare."[27]

One of the most striking features of the White House's reactions to

Clinton's speech was its presumption that favorable public opinion and congressional positions in September 1993 represented fixed commitments rather than initial positions that would change. Missing at the top of the White House's chain of command was a serious appreciation of the possibility that the president's effective unveiling of his proposal, the media's glowing reports, and vague congressional reassurances were the high-water mark and might not be sustained as reform opponents launched their own crafted presentations.

Opponents React Cautiously

The opponents of health care reform reacted to Clinton's campaign and its initial public support with a strategy that was carefully calibrated to gradually build opposition over time. They acknowledged the problems in health care and voiced general optimism about the need for reform while "planting seeds of doubt," as HIAA's president Bill Gradison put it (Johnson and Broder 1996, 206).

While HIAA launched its "Harry and Louise" ad in early September to begin stirring up public uneasiness with government, Republican leaders in Congress started out by confirming the problems in health care and endorsing alternatives to the Clinton plan. Dole and his chief aide, Sheila Burke, optimistically observed (in their public comments) that health reform enjoyed the support of a "solid core of Republicans" and would win passage by the spring of 1994 (Priest 1993; Marcus and Devroy 1993). Dole told Clinton that he expected that they eventually would "work something out," and he gave the impression of believing that a compromise plan would eventually be adopted (Johnson and Broder 1996, 35).

Dole deferred the job of designing a Republican health plan to Senator John Chafee, who proposed achieving universal health insurance by using an "individual mandate," which would require individuals to pay for insurance. More than half of the Senate's forty-four Republicans backed the so-called "Chafee-Dole plan" and signed a "statement of principles" that promised universal coverage. Dole supported Chafee's negotiations with conservative House Democrats and publicly signaled that he was ready to line up Republican support for key elements of the emerging Clinton proposal (Broder and Rich 1993). Even the more conservative House leadership publicly held out the possibility of incremental health care reform and pleaded in public for bipartisanship, with Newt Gingrich promoting a reform proposal.[28] The initial

public reaction of Republican leaders to the Clinton plan reflected
their view that it was popular and that the party needed to protect
itself from Democratic attacks.

Fall 1993: Opponents Begin to Engage a Distracted Clinton

In the several months following Clinton's speech, the White House became distracted by domestic and foreign policy crises, Congress was
unable to begin serious action on health reform, and criticism of reform became more direct.

No Longer Focused Like a Laser Beam

The White House remained optimistic of public and congressional
support and was unyielding in its strategy. In mid-October, Greenberg
declared that the White House's public campaign had achieved a
"powerful impact on public thinking about health care" and had succeeded in "establish[ing] a principle" of universalism and in preparing
the public to "conside[r] the attacks with some skepticism."[29] He continued to insist in a subsequent report to Mrs. Clinton that the White
House had "successfully launched health care" and was sufficiently
confident that he recommended "develop[ing] a devastating line of attack" against the alternative proposed by moderate Democrats like Jim
Cooper rather than seek compromise.[30]

White House advisers continued to count on the transformative
power of presidential promotions, with Greenberg challenging the
White House to "expand rather than protect our present level of support."[31] Clinton's advisers outlined yet another round of activities that
would capitalize on the White House's capacity as "educator" to saturate the country with its message and steer public opinion.[32] Although
Greenberg's analysis in October acknowledged some public concern
that reform could produce unemployment and bureaucracy, he confidently predicted that the public's uncertainty could be offset by a "second launch" that "ke[pt] our principal goal [of universal coverage] before the public" and hammered the "facts that provide the necessary
reassurance."[33] Greenberg and other political consultants reempha-
sized the "Security for All" message and the effectiveness of pitching
the White House's case to the public's self-interest by reassuring
"people [who] want to know how this will help or hurt their families."[34]

The White House was equally upbeat in evaluating congressional
prospects and interest group positions. Senior aides reported that the
"winning coalition is essentially in place," and Magaziner continued to

insist on "end game scenarios" that ranged from a slightly altered version of Clinton's plan to a "minimum bill" that nonetheless maintained the framework of the president's plan; no other alternative bill or dramatically scaled-back version was apparently considered even in private.[35]

Opponents Take the Initiative

As the afterglow of Clinton's September speech faded, Republican leaders began more regularly to intersperse public criticism of the administration's plan and its procedures with their soothing promises to find "common ground" with Democrats (Broder 1993b). In October, Dole publicly pledged not to be "Dr. Gridlock" and largely limited his criticism to congressional Democrats' "unprecedented" step of rushing to begin hearings before the administration had prepared a bill for submission to Congress (Broder 1993a). After Clinton formally presented his plan to Congress in late October, Dole emphasized the possibility of passing legislation, but stressed the policy differences between the two parties. He refrained from making major new statements on health reform in November but attempted to seize control over the definition of health care as a national problem by arguing in December—at the behest of conservative Republican advocates William Kristol and former House member and Secretary of Defense Richard Cheney—that health care "is not a crisis, it's a problem."[36]

Even while holding out the promise of bipartisan cooperation, Newt Gingrich and House Minority Leader Robert Michel offered harsher public assessments than Dole and began the Republican counterattack. On TV's "Meet the Press," Gingrich called the Clinton plan a "monstrosity," a "disaster," and "the most destructively big government approach ever proposed." Michel charged that the plan required "upwards of 50,000 additional bureaucrats to meddle with our health care" and pointed to "substantive and profound policy differences" with the administration (Broder 1993a; Rubin and Connolly 1993). By December, Gingrich equated the Clinton bill to "socialism" (Broder 1993c).

As reform opponents countered Clinton's messages by warning about government interference, they also competed with the White House, as Kristol urged, to "appeal to the enlightened self-interest of middle-class Americans." Support for Clinton's plan would shrivel, Kristol counseled, if Republicans "shifted [the] debate toward . . . the effect of Clinton's proposed reforms on individual American citizens and their families, the vast majority of whom . . . are content with the medical services they already enjoy."[37]

The escalation in Republican criticism coincided with an ebbing in public support for Clinton's plan during the fall, as presented by Gallup and other independent polls. Public support for Clinton's plan was no longer climbing as it had in September but had actually slipped between 7 and 14 points by November. Kristol seized on these findings as evidence that "[public] support has now sharply eroded" and as a justification for a frontal assault on Clinton's plan.[38]

Interest groups added to the growing chorus of Republican complaints. Although the "Harry and Louise" spots ran before Clinton's September speech, it was afterwards that journalists and Washingtonians took serious notice and relayed its criticisms to the public. White House officials watched in horror as the advertisements became a "touchstone" in the minds of journalists and legislators for the claim that the Clinton plan was "too much too fast."[39]

By December, the muted public campaign for reform by advocates and the fierce criticisms by opponents had produced a creeping unease in the White House. Howard Paster, who oversaw relations with Congress, sounded a loud alarm. Aiming in an only slightly veiled way at Magaziner, Paster warned chief of staff Mack McLarty of his "fear" of White House officials who are "anxious" and "quick to see the endgame." Reminding McLarty that "overconfidence and arrogance, like indecisiveness, are dead certain losers in the legislative process," he pointedly warned that the White House suffered from the "tendency to underestimate or belittle the opposition." The reality, he argued, was that "[r]ight now the safest political route is to vote for change on the margins, not the kind of bold change the President so rightly seeks."[40]

From the perspective of White House aides in December, the problems were the stubborn limitations on the president's attempts to guide public opinion to pressure Washington. The president simply did not have the time to maintain the public campaign envisioned by aides. The analysis presented in the previous chapter (fig. 3.4) confirms that the amount of attention Clinton addressed to health care issues fell to a low level in November and remained quite low in December despite a slight rise.

White House advisers also came to realize that the mass media could not be consistently managed in the ways they had calculated. Officials found that journalists felt compelled to present the other side, which at best gave the administration half of most stories, while paid advertisements allowed opponents to beam their unadulterated message.[41] Advisers (including those responsible for reaching out to interest groups) complained that "the groups are not doing enough, but when they are doing positive things they aren't getting covered"; the announcements of support from the groups were brushed off by journalists as "old news."[42] The activities of reform's opponents combined with the media's inclination to report attacks put the White House "behind the curve in educating the public" and "allowed the elite debate to get away from us." The damaging result, White House advisers observed, was that "[o]ur enemies" are "stir[ring] up a great deal of fear" and effectively defining the Clinton plan in "[c]onventional Washington punditry [as] 'old Democrat,' liberal big government."[43] The White House still clung to the hope that sustained presidential promotions would "seize the initiative" back.[44]

White House officials also began to file candid evaluations of the problems in Congress. In a report on a critical House committee, they concluded that "our list of possible problems is considerably longer" than the number of Democratic votes. Aides also humbly warned Clinton's top advisers that it would be a "mistake" even to consider the cosponsors of the president's bill as "solid yes votes"; a group of important moderates in both parties were "moving away from, rather than closer to, the Administration."[45]

It began to dawn on White House officials that the initial favorable reactions by members of Congress were hardly fixed positions. Members who praised Clinton's plan in September were by January backing out of their initial positions by refusing to negotiate and work with the White House; this would later escalate into full-scale retreat from earlier positions. Senior White House officials complained that they were "begging to negotiate," but "there was no one to talk to on the other side" and that congressional officials on the Republican side began to report "tremendous pressure" from their leaders not to work with the administration. It became apparent to one official that "something had already happened" by November when "I called all these Republicans who had told us to our face that they would be able to support something and not one of them would even go on the bill as a cosponsor."

January–Spring 1994: All-Out War

The advocates and opponents of reform adjusted their strategies during 1994 to changing public opinion and political conditions in Washington. The noticeable drop in public support for Clinton's plan during the fall of 1993 and the open attack by opponents fed back into the ensuing debate in 1994.

The Clinton Mirage

White House officials were frustrated by losing the president to the unexpected crises of NAFTA, Whitewater, and other events during the fall, and by "not having something out of some committee to rally around." Officials were disappointed that even with Democratic control over both the House and the Senate, divisions within their own party prevented the committees from moving faster. House committee chairs were caught in a nasty crossfire between Republicans opposed to reform altogether and Democrats, such as moderate Representative Jim Cooper, who were intent on thwarting what they considered Clinton's overly ambitious and regulatory proposal. In the Senate, reform was slowed by Democratic divisions over Clinton's proposals regarding benefits and regulations, as well as by a battle over turf between Ted Kennedy's Labor and Human Resources Committee and Daniel Patrick Moynihan's Finance Committee.

The absence of a legislative rallying point and a sustained presidential campaign undermined the White House's strategy to win public support by blitzing the country with well-crafted messages. It was simply beyond the capacity of the Clinton White House (and perhaps any White House) to "coordinate reform supporters around a message," as aides had planned. The difficulty of unifying the disparate collection of reformers behind a disciplined strategy to hammer home a few coherent messages was illustrated, several White House officials lamented, by an AARP advertisement that was "supposed to be positive but hurt us." The ad urged support for long-term care and prescription drugs without mentioning the Clinton plan that included these benefits; but participants in focus group discussions of the advertisement reacted against the Clinton plan because they mistakenly assumed that it neglected these benefits.

The inability of the White House and reformers to launch a sustained public campaign, White House officials realized, opened the door for opponents to control what issues received sustained attention in the media and in policy debates. Again and again, reformers watched as opponents successfully seized on opportunities to "demonize the president's bill." Clinton's encouragement of competition was supposed to have a "tremendous appeal to conservatives" but, as one official lamented, "we lost that image and allowed others the opening to say 'this isn't competition, this isn't market oriented, this is regulation.'" Another aide complained that during the deliberations in Congress "all the publicity and attention focused on relatively marginal" issues, which obscured the efforts of committees to "rework" heavily criticized areas of Clinton's plan involving the growth of bureaucracy and the threat to small businesses. The result, White House officials steamed, was that the committees' solutions to the "political problems generated" by Clinton's plan were just not "reported on or focused on"; they were in effect suffocated by the crafted messages of opponents.

The attacks by Clinton's opponents and the drop in public support for his plan coincided with the arrival of new political advisers in the White House (most notably, Harold Ickes) and a renewed sense of urgency in promoting health reform. A new strategy emerged that focused on using the State of the Union address in late January to restate the president's commitment to comprehensive reform by threatening a veto of any legislation that excluded universal coverage. Some White House aides, however, fought the idea of a veto threat because it would restrict the "flexibility" of reformers to compromise later; Clinton himself would concede after the session that it was a mistake.[46] But in January 1994, Clinton and his senior advisers resorted to the veto threat because they were grasping for some way to energize supporters and renew attention to the common goal of most reformers.[47]

It was soon clear to the White House, however, that the veto gambit and the reliance on "something big to stir passions and transform the debate" were not winning the hearts of Americans. Soon after the State of the Union address, pollsters reported a major drop in public support for the Clinton plan; it had fallen from its high of near 60 percent after Clinton's September 1993 speech to below 45 percent where it essentially stayed. Aides were now openly conceding that "generating passion on this issue has not been as easy as we had hoped." The communications juggernaut envisioned just a year before was left sputtering to "gear up a serious communication" effort and to find some way for "educating, energizing, and mobilizing" even liberal Democrats who were initially expected to form the rock-solid base for reform but whose support and intensity had also waned.[48]

As the White House hit a brick wall in galvanizing the public, it reconsidered the heart of its strategy—that public support could be won and used to pressure elites. Our analysis of Clinton's statements confirms that he shifted from rallying Americans to score a "bank shot" into Washington (as was originally hoped) to lobbying elites.

After the State of the Union address, there was an uptick in Clinton's statements on health reform; but the distractions of Whitewater, Bosnia, anticrime legislation, and telecommunications regulation combined with the White House's frustration in winning Americans' support for health reform to discourage the president from resuming the intensity of his earlier public campaigns.

It is especially striking that most of Clinton's public comments in 1994 were directed at elite audiences and not at forums geared to reaching the general public. The peak of Clinton's public campaign in 1994 was February; rather than pitching his comments to the general public, over 90 percent of the president's remarks were directed to party and government officials such as in meetings with the Democratic National Committee or executive branch personnel. The pattern continued in March and April when a majority of the president's presentations were also pitched to elites. By May, the president's public campaign plummeted, never to rise again. What comments Clinton did make remained targeted to elites, commanding over 60 percent of his attention in May and June. In June, Senate Majority Leader George Mitchell privately reiterated the conclusion that the White House had been inching toward: that public opinion could not be turned around to pressure members of Congress (Johnson and Broder 1996, 438).

Spring Mayhem

Opponents of health reform encouraged and reflected the growing public opposition to the Clinton plan by launching more overt and unequivocal attacks on health reform. Dole used his response to Clinton's State of the Union address to portray graphically the president's proposal as a "Rube Goldberg" scheme of staggering complexity and stifling bureaucracy. Paralleling the plan's sinking public support, Dole now openly declared that "there are more things [about Clinton's plan] that bother us now than bothered us six or eight months ago" (Balz 1994). As spring approached, Dole reversed his earlier public receptiveness to compromising with conservative Democrats and attacked Representative Cooper's alternative, which had begun to attract support from major business groups and some Republicans (Devroy 1994). Other Republican leaders reiterated Dole's criticisms by seizing on the Congressional Budget Office's report that Clinton had (slightly) underestimated the cost of his plan and that his proposed Health Alliances were new government bureaucracies.

Even as Republican leaders worked vigorously to signal openly their displeasure with Democratic reform proposals and to feed public doubts about them, they were mindful to shield their party's reputation from charges of obstructionism and to project an image of coopera- tion to middle America. Representative Dennis Hastert, the head of the GOP task force on health, acknowledged to the *Washington Post* on 15 April 1994 that outright opposition to health reform had to be avoided to protect the Republican Party's reputation with centrist opinion: "some people on our side want to kill health reform, [but] that is not the image we want to portray." Following the public script, Gingrich disingenuously claimed to the *Post* on 5 March 1994 that "We think there is a real opportunity to write a bipartisan bill."

Dole took the lead in preventing "the public [from] think[ing] all we're doing back here is playing politics." He abandoned his "no crisis" comment, listed areas of agreement with Democrats, called for biparti- sanship, and gingerly offered that compromising with Clinton was still "worth exploring" (Dewar 1994; Broder and Claiborne 1994; Devroy 1994; Dewar and Priest 1994; Novak 1994). Dole also took charge from Chafee in designing a Republican alternative that would provide a legislative focal point for channeling the GOP rank and file. He ap- peared to believe that public support for reform was still sufficiently strong that Republican senators should find a plan that they all could support (Johnson and Broder 1996, 363). In March, he convened a retreat of mostly Senate Republicans to weave together competing GOP proposals into an incremental package. What became clear, though, was that any form of health reform was fiercely opposed by conservatives—especially Dole's rival for the Republican presidential nomination, Phil Gramm. The contradictory pressures of reassuring centrist opinion and abiding by the policy goals of conservatives were echoed in Dole's behavior: he publicly offered comforting comments and searched for a Republican alternative, while he also openly aban- doned his initial position favoring the "Dole/Chafee" plan (Priest and Balz 1994).

The professed interest in bipartisanship by Republican leaders was geared not only toward mollifying the general public but also toward reassuring moderates in their own party and discouraging them from supporting any reform. Senator David Durenberger, a moderate Re- publican, wrote two "Dear Colleague" letters in early 1994 opposing the confrontational strategy advocated by Kristol and warning that "Republicans must assure Americans that they understand the prob- lem and are committed to genuine and meaningful reform" (Barnes 1994).

After the spring's antireform mayhem and sinking public support for reform, Republicans and Democrats in Congress were now abandoning their positions supporting universal coverage, which they had embraced only months earlier. This experience showed the White House not only the barriers to leading public opinion but also the fact that congressional positions were not fixed and were subject to sharp change. It was a revelation, one senior official confessed, to discover that the "center was not a static phenomena" and that legislators were "moving far away from where the president started." The White House's shift to the right by dropping its insistence on full universal coverage was aimed at garnering more votes, but it actually had the opposite effect. Members who were already right of center moved further to the right, and those on the left were unwilling to move to the center. Officials felt trapped in a surreal world in which "everything was sand"; "we could never pin members of Congress down on anything" or "ever get to the point of bargaining."

Summer 1994: Finishing the "Perfect Crime"

The White House Orders a Casket

By summer, four of the five congressional committees reported major health reform bills to their respective chambers, but White House officials stumbled in their attempts to construct even a "fragile coalition that would maintain your base, but build outward." Although officials recognized the obstacles to galvanizing Americans, they concluded with reform advocates that they had no choice but to launch a last ditch effort to win back the public. In late July, the White House and reformers started a bus caravan of "real" Americans who had been hurt by the current health system—doctors, nurses, and the sick and their families. The objective was to spur an outpouring of public sympathy and support that would turn the heat back on Congress to act. Yet again, the White House's public campaign failed to elicit the expected support. By July, pollsters reported that support for the president's plan had sunk to below 40 percent and that polls were picking up a general conservative shift against health reform. Support from politically pivotal groups of Americans plummeted from September 1993: Gallup surveys showed that those who declared themselves independent flipped from supporting the Clinton plan (55 percent–34 percent) to opposing it by a nearly equal margin (56 percent–39 percent), and even support among Democrats dropped by 14 percentage points from 83 percent to 69 percent.

Clinton conceded the inevitable and essentially abandoned his public campaign in August and September. Even his last gasp campaign in July was largely pitched to elites and not the general public.[49]

The White House efforts to build a supportive coalition in Congress also fizzled. The influential Energy and Commerce Committee in the House, which was chaired by the committed John Dingell, was forced to concede in June that it was deadlocked and unable to report any bill. The critical Finance Committee in the Senate could not muster the votes for a employer mandate, which was the financial engine of Clinton's plan. White House debates during the summer raged between helping Senator Mitchell design a scaled-back bill that would salvage something and deciding when and how to accept defeat.

Opponents Bury Reform

During the summer, the opponents of reform moved in for the kill by intensifying their public and private campaigns against any legislation. One of Clinton's major obstacles in leading public opinion was that antireformers—under the watchful eye of journalists—forced themselves on to the bully pulpit and prevented the president from monopolizing it. The bus caravan flopped partly because interest groups conspired to turn it into health reform's Waterloo. A coordinating committee of interest groups opposed to reform staged fierce protests at each of the caravan's stops—turning out larger, louder, and more intense crowds than did reform's advocates. The result was the opposite of what reformers intended: the media beamed pictures of protesters, conveying the unmistakable impression that small town America was fervently opposed to health reform (Johnson and Broder 1996, 464–66).

The all-out attack by congressional Republicans was slightly tempered by increasingly vague and empty promises by its leaders that they remained open to the kind of minimal package that Clinton had demonstrably ruled out. Dole maintained the public face of compromise by insisting that he supported both universal coverage as a "goal" (rather than a principle to be enshrined in legislation) and bipartisan compromise—albeit a far more bare-bones package than he had originally endorsed.

The plunge in public support, though, lowered the anxiety of congressional Republicans over retribution by centrist voters; they were now ready to move in for the kill under the pretense, as Gingrich put it, of responding to the fact that "support for [Clinton's] health bill is collapsing" (Broder 1994b). Neither Gingrich nor other Republicans mentioned that the shift in public sentiment that they now claimed to be following was one they had worked to create. Republicans were practicing the art of simulated responsiveness.

Republican leaders openly retreated from earlier positions and worked to disconnect Democratic reform proposals from their life support systems. Dole reversed his earlier support for Chafee's proposal to use an individual mandate and now criticized both a compromise plan being fashioned by a bipartisan group of senators and the bill passed by the Senate Finance Committee in early July. By the end of the summer, he backed away from even his bare-bones proposal that focused on mild insurance reforms and explicitly threatened to filibuster any legislation that used an employer mandate. Gingrich gave "marching orders" to Republicans in the House not even to participate in committee work on health reform (Johnson and Broder 1996, 426–29). Republicans avoided alarming centrist opinion by dressing up their opposition to reform in the guise of constructive delay; unlike Democrats, they wanted to "get it done right" rather than simply "rushing" to "get it done fast" (Devroy 1994b).

Republican leaders reached out to moderate Republicans, who remained willing to support the policy goal of health reform, by appealing to their electoral ambitions. They unified the conservative and moderate wings of the party behind a shared belief that their constituents were not clamoring for reform and that denying Clinton any legislation would catapult the party into control of Congress and perhaps the White House. The efforts of the bipartisan group of senators working on a "mainstream" compromise fizzled out in the face of opposition from both liberals and conservatives. As a senior White House official put it, support for reform "evaporated" with nobody on the right or left backing the compromise being negotiated.

Health reform was put to a final (and quiet) rest when Gingrich and Dole announced that Democratic insistence on a definitive vote on health care would ensure that the General Agreement on Tariffs and Trade (GATT) would be "killed." Mitchell threw in the towel in late September and Republicans rejoiced at committing the "perfect crime." Senator Bob Packwood celebrated the Republicans' success in achieving their policy goal without alienating centrist opinion: "We've killed health care reform. Now we've got to make sure our fingerprints are not on it" (Cohen 1994, 2357).

The White House's initial plan to mobilize public support to pressure moderate Republicans and Democrats lay in tatters. The public had turned against the president's plan (and reform more generally). By the end, no Republicans supported reform even though twenty-three of the forty-four Senate Republicans had endorsed Chafee's comprehensive plan just a year earlier. Although the House and Senate were controlled by Democrats, neither came close to passing legislation, which had been a top priority for the Democratic president.

Conclusion

The False Promise of Public Appeals

One account of Washington politics claims that congressional elections set the basic parameters of what presidents can achieve by determining the ideological and partisan composition of the House and Senate (Bond and Fleisher 1990; Edwards 1989). The implication of the electoral determinacy account for Clinton's drive for health reform is that it was always doomed because comprehensive health reform lacked the votes in Congress. While Democrats held majorities in both chambers, they lacked the sixty votes in the Senate to prevent a filibuster and their proposal contradicted the basic ideological principles and policy preferences of most legislators. Enough Democrats were willing to defect to form majorities that preferred the status quo over the central planks of the Clinton plan (Brady and Buckley 1995).

Our tracking of the positions of legislators and the policy options they weighed reveals that the political possibilities were more open than suggested by the electoral determinacy account. There was enormous change. The White House and, especially, members of Congress in both parties continually floated alternative proposals and policy designs in an effort to capture the shifting ideological, policy, and partisan considerations of their colleagues. Dole and half of his colleagues in the Senate swung from endorsing comprehensive reform that would establish universal coverage to embracing a more incremental package and finally a bare-bones proposal. The shifting positions of Republicans were related to shifts in public opinion and in other political factors.

The initial position of some Republican reformers may have simply reflected political posturing and not been sincere. But this simply begs the question: Why would so many Republicans feel compelled to align themselves with centrist opinion by supporting the Dole/Chafee comprehensive reform? The answer lies in their political calculations: openly supporting popular reform promised political benefits to legislators sensitive to centrist opinion, while openly opposing it from the outset risked alienating swing voters and was unnecessary if most of the public could be swayed to favor their desired policy goals.

Centrist opinion was probably of marginal or passing importance to Republican legislators (including half of Senate Republicans) who leaned in an ideologically conservative direction. They were primarily motivated by policy goals favored by themselves, party activists, and other supporters. Most Republican senators who endorsed the Dole/Chafee proposal may well have harbored contrary policy goals and were simply posturing perhaps as part of a strategy to move public opinion. But centrist opinion was, as the White House calculated, quite important to bolster the policy positions of a small but decisive group of moderate Republicans. Indeed, White House advisers pinned their failure to hold moderate Republicans on losing public opinion. Administration officials reported that congressional moderates who pulled back reported to the White House that "there's no public opinion to support the president's plan, therefore we don't have to do anything." The souring of public support by 1994 not only spooked moderates but also emboldened the consistent opponents of Clinton's plan who concluded, according to administration officials, that "you can go after health reform without any political peril.

The evidence suggests, then, that the positions of at least a critical core of legislators were not predetermined by their ideological and partisan affiliations. Instead, these members were acutely sensitive of their political environment and shifted their positions in response to changes in centrist opinion and partisan coalitions.

Clinton's strategy to win public opinion failed. Part of the reason was that the president faced tough odds; any president who pursued health reform in 1993 would have confronted a daunting political environment (Heclo 1995). The reality, as one White House official concluded, was that "we couldn't control a lot of what happened."

The Clinton White House's preoccupation with the political significance of public opinion and its overconfidence in "winning" it obscured the enduring constraints presented by ideological cohesion, politically influential party activists, and the perennial institutional obstacles in the American political system. Even though Republican moderates endorsed comprehensive reform, their positions remained susceptible to partisan pressure on them and on centrist opinion. Their initial support for reform coincided not only with favorable public opinion but also with the approval of other Republicans including the party's leadership (especially in the Senate). But as 1994 progressed, the inclination of moderates to support reform was offset not only by sagging public support (which antireformers instigated) but also by the lure of partisan electoral goals—Republican victories in the 1994 congressional elections and the 1996 presidential race.

White House officials eventually conceded that they overestimated their control over public opinion and their ability to overcome the enduring draw of partisan politics. That moderate Republican would desert their initial positions and ultimately not support any reform was, Mrs. Clinton conceded, "not in our political calculations" (Johnson and Broder 1996, 521; Starr 1995).

The System of Crafted Talk

Soon after Clinton's inauguration, the White House actively recruited the Democratic National Party (DNC), the AARP, and unions to "unleash [on behalf of health reform] the biggest grass roots campaign in which any of us have ever been involved."[50] The White House planned to supplement its national blitz for health reform with a grass roots campaign in the states and congressional districts.

The White House discovered, though, that local organizations failed to materialize and mobilize local support in congressional districts for health reform (Skocpol 1996 and 1992). Although they "tried to . . . target our efforts on congressional districts," Clinton's advisers became frustrated: they could "not [be] there on the ground," and the "DNC effort . . . began to break file" and the local AARP chapters and labor unions were "not as vociferous" as opponents who felt personally threatened by health reform. With the White House lacking "heeled boots," administration officials and members of Congress reported that legislators attended town meetings dominated by reform's opponents (especially small business organizations) who had been mobilized by national phone trees and direct mail operations, and "said to themselves, 'Hell, I've got to worry about this thing.'"

What stands out about the failed grass roots campaign is that it never prompted the White House to question or alter its strategy of solely relying on a national campaign run from Washington. It was only after the defeat of health reform that Clinton's advisers conceded the "devastating" impact of lacking a network of local organization to challenge the federated efforts of reform opponents.

The White House's dependence on a national campaign to change public opinion and surmount enduring political obstacles reflected an overestimation of its control over public opinion and a failure to appreciate the constraints of operating within a system of political communications. White House officials began their health reform campaign assuming that political communications consisted of malleable and discrete components. What they missed was that the routines and incentives of politicians, journalists, and public opinion were linked. The interconnections of the political communications system prevented the White House from monopolizing public debates on health reform and created opportunities for counterattacks by political opponents who also recognized the strategic value of winning public opinion. With journalists only too eager to spotlight the conflict among elites, Americans were treated to conflicting messages that highlighted the uncertainty of health reform and the personal risks they might face.

The White House's failure to sway the public was starkly captured by a *Wall Street Journal* poll in March 1994, which found that more Americans opposed the Clinton plan than supported it even as they strongly backed its basic provisions. Highlighting the limits of presidential influence on public opinion, the *Journal* concluded (after the deployment of enormous White House resources) that "Clinton is losing the battle to define his own health-care bill" and has, its pollster added, "communicated very little to the public" (Stout 1994).

Given the intertwined motivations and routines of competing politicians, journalists, and public opinion, no president or other political activist—even if they command impressive resources such as those of the presidency—can consistently dictate media coverage and dominate public opinion. After health reform was laid to rest, White House advisers conceded that their "greatest mistake . . . was underestimating the severity of the attack and the success of the attack"; the system of political communications made it impossible to "get public opinion back untarnished" and to prevent the "distortion of public opinion and turning it against the plan."

Although the White House failed to appreciate fully the constraints created by this process of public communications, the reality is that its public appeals (as well as those of its rivals) were ultimately products of and an influence on the cycle of policy debate, media coverage, and public opinion. The White House as well as opponents of reform calibrated their campaign to play by the rules of journalistic engagement in order to influence the public's evaluation of the policy debate. They expected journalists to reconstruct their statements along predictable lines, spotlighting the bickering and political strategy at work and the personal consequences of policy debates for everyday Americans. Indeed, press coverage of the "gays in the military" controversy and the administration's first budget proposal confirmed the White House's expectation of distortion and the political necessity of relying on orchestrated presentations, which spurred it to create the war room to manage its drive for health reform. The results were speeches, public comments, and events that were charged with potent symbols, simplified messages, and dire warnings about the personal stakes of Americans in health care reform.

The crafted presentations of health reform's advocates and adversaries fed back into the policy debate, with each side eager to highlight evidence of simulated public support for their desired policy goals. After the president's September 1993 national speech, White House officials seized on the surge of public support and urged legislators to respond to the demands of Americans, which they had plotted to create after discounting centrist opinion themselves during the formulation of their health care proposal. Similarly, in September 1994 Republicans claimed to respond to the public opposition they had assiduously cultivated for their policy goal of defeating the Clinton plan. Indeed, with the 1994 congressional elections fast approaching, Democrats conceded that they failed to direct public opinion and quietly accepted the defeat of health reform in September.

Explaining the Defeat of the Clinton Health Plan

Washington insiders and journalists blamed the defeat of Clinton's health reform plan on the characteristics of the persons involved—the president's failings as a leader and the difficult personalities of key officials (from the Rasputin-like Magaziner to the tempestuous Daniel Patrick Moynihan) (Clymer and Toner 1994; Drew 1994; Woodward 1994). Students of American politics have also emphasized the immediate context or situation facing Clinton's drive to enact health reform, such as a weak electoral mandate and narrow majorities in Congress (Heclo 1995; Skocpol 1996).

The defeat of the Clinton health plan, however, was not simply the result of these personalistic or situational failings. Although these factors contributed to the demise of the Clinton plan, the primary cause was the change in the structure of American politics that created incentives for politicians to pursue relatively extreme policy goals, discount centrist opinion, and compete with political rivals and journalists to direct public perceptions in order to minimize the risk of electoral retribution.

The structure of American politics created the context for personal and situational factors to take hold. The "personal failings" of Clinton and his advisers lay in not comprehending the system of political communications that prevented any one policy advocate—including the president—from "winning" public opinion and using it to overcome the daunting political and institutional obstacles facing health reform. The scope and design of the Clinton plan could not pass; but the reason for its impolitic contents originated in the White House's trust in its capacity to move public opinion and in its determined pursuit of policy goals that were neither shared by centrist opinion nor most legislators.

The next two chapters shift the analysis from politicians and political activists to the process of public communications and its effects—to the mass media and public opinion. Politicians' pursuit of policy goals and their reliance on crafted presentations affected not only policy debates but also media coverage of them and public opinion.

Part Three

The Media, Public
Opinion, and Health Care

Chapter Five

Political Cycles of Press Coverage

Few national political events are as combustible as a prominent politician challenging a sitting president from his own party in the presidential primaries. Nineteen seventy-nine was a year of real political fireworks. Democratic President Jimmy Carter, who was more conservative than his party's mainstream, faced growing criticism from liberal stalwart Senator Edward Kennedy, who was preparing to challenge him in the Democratic primaries that began February 1980. On 21 June 1979, little more than six months before the primaries, the Associated Press's Janet Staihar filed an extensive story on three major health reform proposals before Congress: Carter's plan to control costs and insure Americans against catastrophic illness; Kennedy's call for comprehensive health reform; and a scaled-down version of Carter's plan introduced by Senator Russell Long, chairman of the powerful Senate Finance Committee.

Staihar devoted just over half of her story to the very real political divisions both within Congress and between the liberal and conservative wings of the Democratic Party. She reviewed the political hurdles facing each bill and emphasized that Kennedy's proposal was meeting "strong [opposition] among Democrats and Republicans on the Finance Committee." Staihar reserved the other half of her account for describing the financial costs of each plan and the benefits that they offered. She emphasized the implications of these costs and benefits for the country as a whole. For example, she presented Long's proposal as "mainly aimed at helping working Americans," committing money to catastrophic insurance for the employed and to the poor. Staihar largely depended on Democratic senators and the president as her story's sources.

Flash ahead fifteen years to 27 February 1994, the day that Congress began consideration of President Clinton's health reform plan. Once again, the Associated Press (AP) ran an extensive story on health reform. AP reporter Jill Lawrence opened with her thesis that "it's increasingly unlikely that President Clinton's 1,342 page [plan] will survive." The story zipped into the declaration by a Democratic subcommittee chair that "he'll be starting from scratch" and it emphasized that Clinton's plan harvested only a "few outright endorsements." Lawrence then chronicled the maneuvering for advantage among Washington insiders and the "common complaints . . . that it is bureaucratic and complicated." She portrayed the president as struggling to counter the opposition with a political strategy of "determinedly highlighting the more appealing aspects of the plan," noting that "this week the theme will be reassurance." Nine out of ten lines described the political conflict and strategy engulfing Clinton's plan. Lawrence based her story on the comments and analysis of the president and administration officials and, most strikingly, herself; the space devoted to her own interpretations was more than three times that devoted to other sources such as policy experts, interest groups, or members of Congress.

These two AP stories—fifteen years apart—could be interpreted as ammunition for a critique of political reporting that emphasized the news media's independent influence. Policymakers, academics, and journalists themselves claim that the media constitute a "fourth branch of government" that uses its power over news reporting to significantly misrepresent and damage the exchanges among political candidates and officeholders. This media-centered account offers a simple explanation for this book's central concern with the interconnections of politics, news reporting, and public opinion: the media are a critical independent influence, motivating politicians to rely upon crafted presentations and shaping public opinion (Cappella and Jamieson 1997).

The press, according to the media-centered account, exerts an independent impact on political dynamics and public opinion in three distinct ways. First, the press sets the agenda: it takes the initiative to define the subjects and issues on which politicians and the public focus their attention.[1] The AP stories in 1979 and 1994, for instance, drew attention to health care and to the financial and bureaucratic burdens of health care reform rather than on other policy areas or even other health care issues.[2] Indeed, as we noted in chapter 3, White House aides credited the press with possessing the power to independently "se[t] the agenda [by] the stories it picks."

Second, journalists willfully slant their story, media critics warn, by determining whom to quote or whether to rely upon themselves as the unattributed narrator of the story (Cappella and Jamieson 1997; Jamieson 1992; Patterson 1994; Steele and Barnhurst 1996; Hallin 1992; Just et al. 1996; Just, Crigler, and Buhr 1999). The AP's 1994 health reform story downgraded and replaced the standard sources— legislators and policy experts—who formed the backbone of the 1979 piece, with the reporter's own commentary and interpretation. Instead of representing political reality and the substance of policy, the information that is conveyed to the public, according to the media-centered account, is distorted. Politicians recognize this and, in anticipation, they focus on controlling reporters' interpretations at the expense of commenting on substantive issues and concerns.

The third and perhaps most widespread complaint about the press by political activists, practicing journalists, and scholars is that reporters and editors have imposed their preoccupation with the "horse race" and the jockeying for political advantage on otherwise substantive policy debates during both election campaigns and the periods of governing (Fallows 1996; Jamieson 1992; Patterson 1994). The focus of the AP stories in 1979 and, even more so, in 1994 on political conflict and strategy confirms the widespread criticism among scholars and policymakers that the press, as Clinton White House spokesman Mike McCurry put it, have replaced the "hard-news lead and story" with interpretation of who is up and who is down (Auletta 1996, 51, 59).

Although the media-centered account has highlighted the significance of news coverage for politics, it has tended to examine the press in isolation from political and policy developments. It has focused excessively on the impact of the media on American politics at the expense of considering the reverse effect—the affect of American politics on the media.

By contrast, we offer a political account of the content and cycle of media reporting. Press coverage is largely driven by forces external to the press—namely, the behavior and strategy of authoritative government officials and other political influentials. These external forces are more consequential than the independent influence of the press on the agenda and other aspects of the political process.[3] In particular, we argue that politicians' pursuit of policy goals and use of crafted talk since the 1970s have largely determined what issues the press has covered and how it presented them.

We do not, however, ignore the media's influence on political dynamics nor the interaction of political dynamics, media coverage, and public opinion. The impetus for news coverage lies in the actions of government officials and other influentials, but journalists and editors magnify and exaggerate political and policy developments, which in turn feed back into the political process. In addition, we show in chapter 7 that the policy debate in 1993–94 and the press coverage of it influenced public opinion, depressing support for the Clinton plan and creating the perception among many Americans that government action threatened their personal well-being.

Our political account of press coverage attributes press behavior to its incentive structure: economic and professional rewards and sanctions encourage journalists and editors to be attentive to political and policy developments. Increasing economic pressures among news organizations to maintain or expand their audiences create incentives to cover the "big" political story that features famous politicians and that promises to affect large numbers of people. Journalists and editors are also encouraged to represent authoritative government actions by the professional norm of serving as a "watchdog" that provides accurate and independent information to allow the public to hold government officials accountable. In addition, professional training and routine practice have led journalists to implement the norm of "objectivity" by presenting "both" sides of a story on the assumption that the truth lies somewhere between the competing claims. As a result of economic pressures and professional norms, the news media distribute the regular "beat reporters" to where government power routinely resides (Bagdikian 1992; Graber 1993; Underwood 1993; Donohue, Tichenor, and Olien 1995; Tuchman 1972).

We draw on the analysis of W. Lance Bennett's (Bennett 1990; Alexseev and Bennett 1995) and others to develop four theoretical expectations to account for how press coverage of policymaking has been affected by politicians' widening pursuit of policy goals and crafted rhetoric since the 1970s.

First, we expect news reports to represent or "index" the behavior, statements, and strategies of presidents, legislators, and other political actors who influence or wield authority over government policy under debate. In particular, we expect the ebb and flow of policy deliberations among authoritative government officials and other influentials to be reflected in changes in the volume and content of press reports. For instance, a president's adoption of a strong position on a policy issue will generally receive wide coverage in the mainstream press because he is the most influential individual in the government policy process, he is known to a large audience, and he is under the watchful eyes of an unparalleled number of beat reporters. Indeed, the content of the

AP stories in 1979 and 1994 followed the new proposals by presidents and senior legislators to reform significantly the health care system.

Second, we anticipate that press attention to political conflict and strategy as well as its representation of the range of viewpoints among establishment figures will expand in reaction to widening disagreement among policy influentials and their reliance upon crafted presentations (Bennett 1990; Alexseev and Bennett 1995; Donohue, Olien, and Tichenor 1995).

The AP stories in 1979 and 1994 illustrate that when intense disagreement among policymakers on significant health policy issues erupted, journalists reported the conflicting viewpoints of authoritative government officials and focused heavily on the political "game." What clearly stands out is that the AP's coverage of conflicting views and political strategy was transformed from a partial concern in 1979 to a near exclusive focus in 1994. This transformation in media coverage reflected genuine political changes during this period, not simply the independent initiative of the press: as described in previous chapters, the perceived political benefits of taking relatively extreme policy positions grew, political polarization widened, and the incentives for manipulating journalists and public opinion expanded. Journalists reacted to the increased political jousting and staged displays by intensifying their scrutiny of government leaders and their health policy proposals. It was political and policy developments, then, that prompted the AP to replace its attention in 1979 to the consequences of health reform for the nation or large groups like the working uninsured with coverage in 1994 of political conflict and strategy.

Third, we expect the press to disproportionately use authoritative government officials as sources because they possess the capacity to affect or determine future events (Blumler and Gurevitch 1981; Brown, Bybee, Weardon, and Straughan 1982; Entman and Page 1994; Zaller and Chiu 1996; for review see Bennett 1996). Both AP stories relied on government officials: even with the strong voice of the AP reporter in the 1994 piece, President Clinton and administration officials were still used as sources twice as frequently as the reporter and five times more often than interest groups.

Fourth, we expect journalists to react to serious and contentious debates among polarized authoritative government officials and establishment figures by exercising their own standards of quality and interests to cover the story and to unmask the strategic calculations of politicians (Cook 1998). The impetus for the media's expanded attention to political strategy and conflict lies in the realm of actual politics, but journalists and editors magnify policy disagreements (as exemplified by the AP's obsession with the political "game" in 1994). The result is that the press has a feedback effect into the political process, amplifying the already crafted presentations of politicians and contributing (as we argue in chapter 7) to heightening the public's perception that policy initiatives threaten its personal well-being.

In short, the behavior and strategies of politicians affect not only policy debates but also the media's coverage of them. Genuine political disagreements instigated the press's focus on conflict, which then intensified the determination of politicians to orchestrate their statements and actions. Journalists and editors reflect and contribute, then, to the political cycle of media reporting and to the larger spiral of crafted talk involving politicians, journalists, and the public.

Studying the Media

The clearest way to understand how press coverage has developed and changed is to examine it closely and systematically *over time.* We used two approaches. First, we tracked news stories on health policy by the Associated Press between 1977 and 1994. Editors and journalists widely use the AP wire service throughout the nation; while regional news outlets have a narrow geographic scope and audience, AP stories get reported nationally. The "bias" in AP coverage is toward a straightforward chronicling of the "facts"; therefore, we would expect our analysis to underrepresent inclinations toward commentary, interpretation, or speculation about political strategy or other trends found in other media. Second, we analyzed the news coverage in television or broadcast media and print reports by magazines and newspapers for the period between Clinton taking office in 1993 and the summer of 1994. This press coverage provided a basis for corroborating patterns in the AP reports during 1993–94, for analyzing short-term variations within this narrow period, and for studying variations in the reporting by different media, especially television. Previous research suggests that the coverage of broadcast and print media varies because of differences in their audiences, professional styles, journalistic cultures, and written versus visual forms of presentation (Graber 1984; Just, Crigler, and Buhr 1999). Comparing these two types of news reports allowed us to examine differences over time and across media.

We were especially interested in examining the *content* of news reports in a way that went beyond relying on anecdotes or settling for generalizations about the content of an entire story. Our approach classified stories according to 228 separate categories of health care and health policy issues. Our investigation offers a comprehensive analysis of the detailed content and historic trends of media coverage between 1977 and 1994. (See appendix 3 for a fuller discussion of our content analysis.) Health and health policy encompass a broad and diverse set of issues ranging from government regulation to redistribution of resources and spanning political outcomes—from passage and failure to repeal. Our analysis, however, excluded topics such as personal hygiene that did not raise significant questions of public policy.

The remainder of this chapter analyzes variations since the 1970s both in the volume and content of press coverage and in the media's attention to political strategy and conflict in reporting on health issues. The next chapter examines the press's disproportionate use of establishment sources and challenges the notion that the media are uniformly "negative"—critical and disparaging of policy proposals.

Surges in Media Reporting

Rises and Falls in Coverage

The news media devoted more and more attention to health care issues since 1977. We tracked the broad sweep of media coverage of health policy by totaling the separate messages concerning 228 health care issues for each year.[4] Figure 5.1 shows that journalists devoted increasing attention to health care and health policy issues over time.

The trend in media coverage is stair-step like, steadily ratcheting up during the 1970s and 1980s before taking off dramatically in the first half of the 1990s. Each step up beginning in 1977 produced new plateaus that exceeded the previous peak. Four periods stand out as peak periods in reporting: 1978–79, 1981–82, 1987–89, and 1993–94. Most strikingly, coverage during Clinton's presidency more than doubled the previous high in 1987.

The peaks in media coverage reflect important, identifiable changes in actual health care conditions and policy debates. Each peak corresponds with the general pattern of high and rising levels of uninsurance and of national health care expenditures on health services, which produced bursts of intense policy debate. After the mid-1970s, American health care expenditures steadily rose from 8 percent of gross domestic product in the mid-1970s to 14 percent in 1992, at a time when trends in Europe and Canada leveled off (Congressional Budget Office

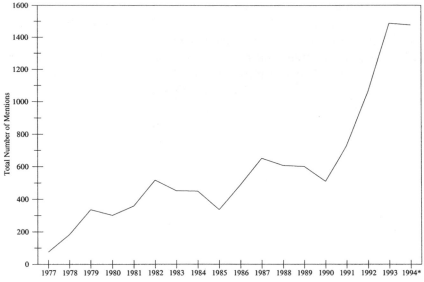

Figure 5.1   Total Number of Mentions of All Health Care Issues in AP Coverage,
1977–1994

Source: Compiled by authors; see appendix 3 and text.
* Coverage ends in September 1994.

1993). The proportion of Americans lacking health insurance also steadily grew from about 10 percent in the mid-1970s to over 15 percent in 1992.[5]

The apexes in media coverage in 1979, 1982, 1987, and 1993 occurred during periods of governing, not periods of presidential electioneering. This is somewhat surprising because media observers typically portray journalists as eager to foment discord and conflict during presidential election years, and health care issues such as abortion certainly offer tempting opportunities to hype the divisions between Republicans and Democrats. In contrast to the presumed motivations of journalists, the leaders of both political parties have no great political interest in casting these elections as referendums on abortion and other related issues. Democrats have little to gain from flaunting or deviating from their "pro-choice" position while Republican leaders run the risk of alienating either their core "pro-life" supporters or centrist swing voters who are more pragmatic in accepting contraception, fetal tissue research, and some forms of abortion.

In fact, journalists' relative coverage of abortion and other issues connected to reproduction fell to one of its lowest levels during the Republican-dominated presidential elections in 1980, 1984, and 1988 and peaked during nonelection years such as 1977 and 1989.[6] In addition, the coverage of abortion and other divisive health issues never came close to matching the attention that other health issues received whether during or after elections. At the very peak of media coverage of reproduction issues in 1989, fewer than 10 percent of news reports on health care were devoted to abortion and related issues. In short, journalists gravitated to important health care issues when political leaders settled down to govern; presidential elections did not drive their timing.

The Issues Covered

Apart from the volume of press coverage, the content of news reports was remarkably stable from 1977 to 1994. A handful of topics received steady attention in AP reports between 1977 and 1994, laying the foundation of its coverage: high health care costs and the need to control them; expanding access to health insurance and health care; dissatisfaction with employer health benefits and efforts of labor unions to expand them; improving public health by for instance cutting smoking; and reproductive issues like abortion. Although we tracked a broad range of issues, journalists concentrated overwhelmingly on health policy debates or real-world developments like health costs that raised obvious policy issues. Narrower reports on medical developments (such as innovations in medicine or government efforts to promote medical breakthroughs) were not a significant component of the AP's total coverage, accounting for only 5 percent of its reports.

We simplified our analysis by sorting the issues covered in the media into two categories: government efforts to change health policy or health care (what we call "*reform*" issues) and the state of affairs in health care more generally (what we call "*generic*" issues). Reform issues included specific government initiatives to expand access to health care and insurance as well as, to a much lesser extent, support for comprehensive government health reform, government controls over Medicare costs, and government promotion of public health by improving nutrition and cutting smoking. The coverage of generic issues was dominated by news reports about rising health care costs, dissatisfaction with employer health benefits and, to a lesser extent, quality of care, breakthroughs in high-tech medicine, and treatment of cancer.

The volume of news coverage on reform issues held a moderate but unstable edge over reporting on generic topics until the mid-1980s, when reform issues consistently began to constitute 60 percent to 70

percent of media reporting on health care, topping out at 80 percent
in 1994 (90 percent in August 1994). The growing dominance of reform
issues in the media stemmed from the rising concern of authoritative
government officials with escalating health care costs and other aspects of health care and from a series of high-profile and contentious
health reform initiatives after the mid-1980s.

Broadcast and print news outlets generally devoted similar amounts
of attention to health care issues. There were, however, a few notable
exceptions: television devoted about a third less coverage to the issue
of cost than did newspapers and magazines, and television (along with
newspapers) gave greater coverage to health care access than did magazines.[7] In short, news reports on health issues generally converged—
with remarkable consistency over time—on a handful of topics relating largely to debates over government reforms.

Real-World Developments and Peaks in Media Coverage

A critical test of our political account of media reporting lies in
whether the content and cycles of media coverage match or diverge
from the dynamics of policy debates. An ideal approach would be to
compare press reports with concrete, observable government actions
like congressional hearings or addresses by legislators in the House
and Senate (e.g., Althaus et al. 1996). While this approach works under
particular conditions, it is not an appropriate method for analyzing
government deliberations over health care because they often occurred
within the cloistered confines of the executive branch (the Department
of Health and Human Services or the White House) rather than in
public forums. For instance, the major reform of Medicare to establish
a prospective payment system in the early 1980s as well as the momentous Clinton health reform initiative generated relatively minimal congressional floor debate; simply measuring floor activity would be a
poor measure of the political and policy significance of these health
reform initiatives, the intensity with which they were pursued, and their
movement through the policymaking process.[8]

We pursued an alternative approach that drew on David Mayhew's
(1991) method for independently distinguishing significant from insignificant political and policy developments. In particular, we carefully
tracked (for each year between 1977 and 1994) and compared the judgments of specialists on health policy, the legislative process, and the
political process more generally. We relied on several textbooks on

health care and health policy (Weissert and Weissert 1996; Litman and Robins 1984) as well the Brookings Institution's long-standing series, *Setting National Priorities,* to identify the importance that health policy specialists placed on particular health issues in any one given year. For instance, all the sources identified President Ronald Reagan's push to cut government health care spending in 1981 as an unusually significant development.

We turned to the *Congressional Quarterly Almanac* to identify the years and issues that legislative specialists pinpointed as significant. For instance, *Congressional Quarterly* increased its coverage of health issues by 50 percent in 1981 as it picked up Reagan's proposed reductions in health care spending as well as other issues.

Finally, the end of the year wrap-up stories by the Washington experts of the *New York Times* and *Wall Street Journal* provide an informed judgment of official Washington's ranking of all critical policy debates and decisions at the end of each year (i.e., the ranking of health issues compared to other issues). Among an entire year's debates over domestic and foreign policy, only highly significant developments on health issues generally stood out. For instance, the *Times* and *Post* filed end-of-the-year stories in 1981 that devoted unusual attention (two paragraphs in a seventeen-paragraph story) to health care; Reagan's cuts in health care were ranked alongside fervent debate over an historic tax cut, unprecedented peacetime hikes in defense spending, and the controversial sale of AWACS (Airborne Warning and Control System) planes to Saudi Arabia.

These three sets of sources together produced diverse and independent judgments on real-world developments in health care and health policy. Our test of whether media coverage reflected reality is a stiff one: AP reports consist of a wider array of issues than our independent sources, which focus on high-profile developments in health policy and politics. Our analysis is biased toward finding issues in news reports that are not likely to be covered in the independent sources.

Our findings offer confirmation of our political account of media reporting. The independent evaluations, which tended to agree, persistently highlight the high costs of health care, limits to access, and abortion. Several of the independent sources discuss the less prominent issues of dissatisfaction with employer health benefits and improving public health by cutting smoking. The clearest support comes from the close match between ups and downs for the pool of issues reported by the AP and the changes in the analyses of our independent sources.

The four peaks in the volume and substantive focus of media reporting coincided with upsurges in discussions of real-world developments and fierce political debate over policy reforms.

1978–79: Rising Health Care Costs

The uptick in overall coverage of health issues that began in 1978 and crested in 1979 was driven by alarm over soaring health care costs. Health care costs, as we suggested above, reached startling new highs in the second half of the 1970s, which were unparalleled among advanced industrial countries. President Carter came into office in 1977 with Democrats controlling both chambers of Congress, and he proposed an ambitious plan to contain hospital costs by prohibiting inpatient care of acute illness from growing more than 9 percent a year. By 1978, the legislative process and political action began in earnest: the Senate floor voted on and defeated Carter's proposal for cost containment, and Kennedy introduced a modified bill for national health insurance (NHI) in 1978. In 1979, the House defeated Carter's plan and the president's public disagreement with Kennedy over health policy intensified. Experts on health policy, the legislative process, and sentiment in Washington agreed that 1978 and 1979 were an unusually important period of health policy debate, with particular attention concentrated on health care costs and the failure to enact either Carter's plan or an expansion of access through NHI legislation.

The reports by the AP echoed the real-world developments. The absolute level of its coverage related to controlling health expenditures rose to one of its highest levels in the wake of Carter's proposals to control hospital costs. AP reports on the topic of expanding access also rose after Kennedy's proposals for NHI—though it did not reach its highs of 1987 and 1993–94 nor receive nearly as much attention as costs. Journalists reacted to the heated policy debates on reforming the health care system by devoting more attention to comprehensive government reform as a proportion of their total coverage than in any other period until the 1990s; though, again, it received less coverage than costs.

The predominance of costs as a news topic is evident in an AP story appearing on 14 March 1979, which extensively outlined the escalation in hospital expenditures and "President Carter's hard sell for a lid on hospital cost." A 10 April 1979 piece zapped hospitals for their rising costs; the story moved from an acknowledgment by the National Hospital Association that its members had been unable on their own to contain their costs, to an administration official who trumpeted the president's plan as a means for controlling hospital costs. An unusually long AP story in October 1979 was devoted to the arrival of "400 elderly activists [who] swarmed over Capitol Hill . . . to complain [about] explosive health care costs."

1981–82: The Continued Push against Costs

Carter's push to control costs was revived by Reagan's drive during his first year in office to make good on his campaign platform of reducing government, as well as by Congress's effort to slow Medicare's hospital costs. Although Reagan's proposals had to clear the Democrat-controlled House of Representatives, moderate and conservative Democrats deserted their party in 1981 because they agreed with the president's policy goal of reducing government spending. (Republicans were in a majority in the Senate.) By 1982, though, Democratic opposition to Reagan's cuts in health care was more unified and intense. All of the independent sources highlighted the significance of Reagan's success in reducing federal spending on health programs by 21 percent and consolidating twenty-one health programs into four block grants in 1981, as well as the growing congressional opposition in 1982 for more budget cuts.

In 1982, Reagan won billions of dollars of cuts in Medicare by introducing new ceilings on payments to hospitals and doctors. Republicans and Democrats agreed to the changes after becoming alarmed that Medicare's rising hospital costs were rapidly draining its trust funds. Congress went a step further than Reagan intended by requiring his administration to develop a cost-control plan that relied on setting a binding payment arrangement before the beginning of each year—a prospective payment system. After discussion in 1982, the administration proposed that Medicare's reimbursement of hospitals be based on a prearranged schedule for treatment of individual diagnostic related groups (DRGs). The DRG payment plan was quickly passed in early 1983 and produced "the most significant change in Medicare policy since the program's enactment" in 1965 (Weissert and Weissert 1996, 285). Reagan's budgetary initiatives removed the issues of NHI reform and the expansion of access from serious, sustained consideration by authoritative government officials; after extensive discussion of these topics during Carter's presidency, the Congressional Quarterly Almanac failed to even mention them in 1981 and 1982.

Both the surge of media attention and the issues covered paralleled the reality of health policy and politics. AP journalists in 1982 flocked back to the cost of health care and, specifically, Medicare. Coverage of the general issue of high health costs exceeded (just barely) the level of 1979, and this was only surpassed by the tidal wave of attention that arrived in 1993. With a potential financial shortfall in Medicare's trust fund and lawmakers gearing their efforts toward reforming it, journalists lavished more attention on controlling Medicare's costs during 1982 than during any year between 1977 and 1994. This coverage of Medicare's costs dropped sharply in 1983, mirroring the pattern of intensified legislative discussion in 1982 and quick enactment in early 1983.

Reflecting the real shift in policy discussion since Carter's presidency, the AP's increased attention to cost control coincided with one of its lowest levels of coverage of comprehensive reform and expanding access. An AP story in early March 1981, for example, reported Reagan's Faustian offer to the states: they could gain control over forty health and social programs, "but the price tag for that release from the federal grip is 25 percent less money from Washington." In October 1982, the AP ran an extensive story that reviewed the Reagan administration's proposal for using DRGs to regulate the payment of hospitals under the Medicare program.

Debate over health care among authoritative officials and other influential leaders stalled between 1982 and 1985. The health policy specialists as well as the wrap-ups in the *Times* and *Post* also indicated a drop-off in activity. Likewise, figure 5.1 shows that the AP's coverage of health issues entered its steepest period of decline during this period, returning to 1979–81 levels.

1987–89: Renewed Push to Expand Health Benefits

Our independent sources highlighted 1987–89 as an important period, marked by major health policy initiatives and divisive relations between Democratic congresses and Republican Presidents Reagan and Bush. Escalating health care expenditures and difficulties controlling them remained important, and, indeed, Congress passed controls over Medicare's fees to physicians in 1989. But the issues related to expanding access received the most attention from experts on Congress, health policy, and Washington politics. Rates of uninsurance continued to creep up, and the elderly lacked protection through Medicare for handling the rising costs of long-term care.

Reagan began 1987 by proposing in his State of the Union address to help the elderly avoid financial devastation because of long-term illness. Despite disagreements within the administration over the merits of the initiative and how to pursue it, congressional Democrats enthusiastically pressed for including the new coverage in the Medicare program. The House approved an expansion of Medicare to offer catastrophic health insurance in July and the Senate followed suit in October, which virtually assured its ultimate enactment. The conservative president signed the legislation into law in 1988, enacting "the largest expansion of the Medicare program in twenty-three years" (Litman and Robins 1984, 461). But a backlash among some seniors, who were stampeded by false charges of crushing new Medicare taxes to pay for catastrophic insurance, prompted Congress in 1989—for the "first time in its history"—to repeal a major social benefit (Litman and Robins 1984, 463; Himelfarb 1995).

There were other legislative efforts in 1987 to expand access. The *Congressional Quarterly Almanac* (1987) pointed to the "widespread attention" within Congress to aid Americans who lacked health insurance coverage (21). Senator Kennedy's proposal to expand health insurance coverage by using a limited employer mandate drew the attention of legislators and other political activists, as did Representative Henry Waxman's success in enacting "a number of significant changes in the Medicaid program" that expanded benefits for pregnant women and children (Litman and Robins, 460). Waxman's incremental expansion of Medicaid hit paydirt in 1989.

A simmering congressional dispute with the Reagan administration over abortion gradually escalated during this period. The battle began over stripping administration restrictions on the abortion activities by participants in the federal family planning program. The dispute dramatically intensified in 1989, when the Supreme Court's decision in *Webster* approved some state government restrictions on abortion and provoked a surge of pro-abortion legislation in Congress. It took repeated vetoes by Bush to fend off the legislation.

Lawmakers devoted serious attention to AIDS during 1987, though they had begun to increase spending on research and education earlier in the decade. The *Congressional Quarterly Almanac* spotlighted AIDS legislation for the first time in 1987 and noted that it received "intense scrutiny and occasionally heated floor debate," with legislators approving a "tremendous boost" in funding for research and information activities. In 1988, Reagan's Commission on AIDS stirred further debate in Washington, and the Department of Health and Human Services launched the country's largest mailing devoted to health in order to inform Americans about the dangers of AIDS and the methods of prevention.

Media coverage closely followed the issues that were flagged by legislative, political, and health policy experts. The general topic of expanding access to health insurance and health services received its second highest level of total coverage in 1987 (its highest was reached during Clinton's reform crusade). As a proportion of total health care reporting, access received its highest level of attention, constituting a third of the AP's coverage; no other health issue came close to drawing comparable levels of attention. News coverage of catastrophic insurance easily reached its highest points in 1987 and 1989 after receiving few (if any) reports over the previous decade. For instance, the AP ran a series of stories on the alternative approaches that Reagan could pursue to fulfill his 1987 State of the Union commitment and capped it off with a 2 February 1987 story that explained the president's choice for adding catastrophic insurance to the Social Security system. The AP's coverage of abortion also reflected the sharpened debate in Washington, with the issue receiving its greatest proportional attention during the heated debate in 1989.

AIDS also broke through in the AP, receiving its greatest coverage in 1987, though it failed to dominate overall health care reporting (the issue of access received over twice as much attention). The media's reporting on AIDS has been harshly criticized for ignoring the disease until it reached epidemic proportions and consumed thousands of lives. Randy Shilts (1987) bitterly complained that only the death of Rock Hudson in 1985 caught the attention of journalists (Backstrom and Robins 1998; Colby, Cook, and Murray 1987).

Our analysis suggests, however, that the AP's coverage reacted in a predictable fashion to political developments. AIDS coverage peaked not in 1985 with Hudson's death but in 1987 when legislative debate intensified and drew the attention of authoritative government officials and other political influentials. Before 1987, the AP ignored the issue or gave it a fraction of the attention it would later receive. Although the media reflected the reality of lawmaking activity, it did not alert policymakers to new developments before they reached crisis proportions. Clearly, though, the media share responsibility with policymakers who did not sound earlier alarms on a devastating public health issue.

1992–94: The Health Care Tidal Wave

Our legislative, political, and health policy sources experts all point to the combustible ingredients that mixed together in the early 1990s.

Well before Clinton arrived on the national scene, the issue of comprehensive health benefits rocketed back on to the national radar screen with Harris Wofford's stunning 1991 upset of Pennsylvania Republican Richard Thornburgh in a special U.S. Senate election. Economic stagnation and the loss of jobs and health benefits further heightened interest in health reform among policymakers and journalists. The 1992 presidential campaign and, especially, Clinton's crusade for managed competition after his inauguration provided a specific plan that lawmakers and political activists converged on. The single-payer approach had strong support in Congress and among several powerful House leaders, but it clearly lacked, in the eyes of Washington observers, the necessary commanding majorities to pass in Congress.

The media's health coverage largely followed the policy discussions over reform that took off in the early 1990s. By the 1990s, press coverage rapidly rose as issues related to government health reform efforts received greater attention from establishment figures. "Generic" issues concerning the general state of affairs in health care received proportionately less coverage in the face of these major political and policy developments.

Even before President Clinton took office, the topics of health care costs, comprehensive benefits, and public health all experienced a surge in media interest during 1990 and 1991.[9] But Clinton's inauguration opened the floodgates: the volume of AP coverage of health issues in 1993 and 1994 more than doubled any previous level (fig. 5.1).

The media's enormous attention to managed competition and Clinton's health reform plan drove much of the surge in reporting in 1993–94. The AP as well as print and broadcast media showered the Clinton plan with just over a quarter of their total health care coverage, nearly double that of any other health issue. Various Democratic and Republican alternatives to Clinton's plan received a smattering of reports, none of which amounted to more than 1 percent of total coverage.

Clinton's crusade also boosted interest in a cluster of long-standing and related health issues such as expanding access, high costs, and Medicare expenditures. The volume of reports on health costs also rose in 1993 to absolute levels that more than doubled its level in any previous year before falling off in 1994 to below its 1979 and 1982 levels; relative to the total media coverage of health care, the attention to costs in 1993 was considerably below what it was in the 1970s. The overall volume of coverage of comprehensive government reform was five times greater than its highest previous levels;[10] the volume for expanding access to health insurance and health services also reached

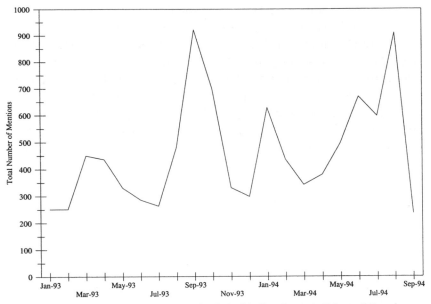

Figure 5.2   Total Number of Mentions of All Health Care Issues in Print and Broadcast Media, 1993–1994

Source: Compiled by authors; see appendix 3 and text.

new highs.[11] There was virtually no coverage, however, of the single-payer approach to reform, despite its large contingent of congressional supporters. Its poor prospects for passage and the fact that authoritative congressional and administration officials did not seriously consider a single-payer option discouraged reporters from covering it.

The media's coverage of health issues fluctuated in reaction to the political and policy developments in 1993 and 1994. Figure 5.2, which displays the total monthly volume of coverage from print and broadcast reports during this period, points to four primary periods of especially extensive reporting.

MARCH AND APRIL 1993   The first uptick in the volume of coverage occurred in March and April 1993 when the Clinton White House and congressional Democrats began to reach critical decisions about policy and politics. White House records and interviews with administration officials, which we discussed in chapter 3, reveal that the president and his cabinet officers were weighing critical early decisions concerning financing, the scope of benefits, and how to slow rising national expenditures on health care. It was also during this period that the White House was blocked by Democratic Senator Robert Byrd from incorporating health reform into the budget reconciliation process. Debates within the White House and Congress over the impact of health reform for the budget and for slowing national health expenditures were particularly strong during this time. In addition, our analysis of Clinton's public statements found that he devoted his most extensive comments during early 1993 to controlling health care costs; after this period, his public discussions of costs declined significantly, never matching their early level (fig. 3.3).

Reflecting the political debates, press coverage of costs peaked during this period and then steadily declined with subsequent rises falling short of this surge. Reports on the Clinton plan noticeably picked up, contributing to about a quarter of news reports on health care, but they did not quite match the coverage of health costs. The volume of press reports on achieving comprehensive reform also picked up, though it fell far short of costs and the Clinton plan as subjects.

From May to August, the attention of members of Congress and the administration shifted from health care to the president's budget. White House aides involved in health reform fumed during this period because they found their discussions closed down to prevent damaging leaks as Congress faced a series of highly contentious and close votes on the budget. The slide in media coverage of health care issues mirrored the lull in policy developments.

SEPTEMBER 1993   September 1993 produced the highest peak in the volume of media coverage shown in figure 5.2; it corresponded with a surge of activity by authoritative government officials. Jockeying for jurisdiction over the Clinton plan broke out in Congress and legislators leaked a still unsettled draft of Clinton's plan to the press. Republicans released their own health reform bill, which was formally endorsed by more than half of the party's members in the House and Senate.

The big bang, though, in this swirl of activity was the president's riveting national address to a joint session of Congress outlining his principles for health reform. The president's commitment to launching his plan was evident in his own public comments; we found in chapter 3 that he devoted more time to health care issues in September than during any other month, topping his comments prior to August by tenfold (see fig. 3.4). Hillary Clinton closed out the month with a series of impressive appearances before congressional committees.

The content of the media's reports echoed the political debate. The Clinton plan dominated the coverage, consuming nearly half of all health care reports and reaching its highest peak. The standard issues of health costs, expanding access, and achieving comprehensive reform also received more attention than in the past, though these three issues combined still could not match the coverage of the president's plan.[12]

Reformers' euphoria in September was quickly replaced by alarm as the fall brought another protracted lull in policymaking. Somalia, Whitewater, and other controversies distracted the White House from health reform, and members of Congress treaded water as the administration waited until late November to transmit an actual legislative proposal. The media's coverage of alternatives to the Clinton plan surged and reached its second highest peak in the fall, only surpassed by the last-ditch search for more options in August 1994 before health reform was abandoned.

JANUARY 1994   The third peak in the volume of media coverage came in January 1994, when serious differences over the urgency and direction of health reform were publicly debated in earnest. As we discussed in chapter 4, Clinton concentrated on using his State of the Union address to reemphasize the urgency of reform and to focus legislators on conducting hearings. His threat to veto any legislation short of universal coverage was a stark statement of his bottom line to legislators that dramatized his continued commitment to reform.

But Senate Minority Leader Robert Dole countered by launching his most direct and open challenge to Clinton's crusade. In January, he insisted that there "isn't a crisis" in health care, and he openly criticized the president's plan as bureaucratic and overly complicated. The month closed with the nation's governors meeting in Washington and candidly chiding the federal government for not moving faster with health reform.

Print and broadcast reports gave Clinton's plan renewed attention after a drop off during the fall—nearly a third of their health care coverage. All other health issues were overshadowed, even with the increased coverage of expanding access and comprehensive reform. The media's proportional attention to abortion also rose, though still only attracting 5 percent of health reports in January 1994.[13]

There was another break in serious policy debate from February to April as government officials and other influentials geared up for hearings by the major congressional committees. Political activists on both sides cheered on their preferred approaches to reform, and some early congressional action took place during this period. Clinton made a greater effort to rally his forces, but his public comments, according to our independent analysis, reached levels that were only a quarter of what they were in September. The health subcommittee of the House Ways and Means Committee met in March and the Congressional Budget Office released several studies, but members of Congress were still unprepared to start their formal deliberations in earnest. Press coverage in February, March, and April paralleled this dip in serious policymaking activity, dropping to one of its lowest levels during 1993 and 1994.

MAY–AUGUST 1994   The congressional lawmaking process hit its stride between May and August. All the major committees met and voted; several committees approved the major components of the Clinton proposal but the most important committees rejected the employer mandate, universal coverage, and other critical parts of the president's plan. The Senate conducted a heated debate on the floor but was unable to approve any legislation. All during this period, Senate Majority Leader George Mitchell and other leaders conducted fruitless rounds of intense meetings to stitch together a coalition. Clinton cheered Congress on; the volume of his own comments noticeably picked up in July, though they did not reach their earlier highs. By the end of August, a majority of legislators opposed all proposals for comprehensive national reform and were now weighing scaled-back changes such as revising insurance rules. If Clinton's national address in September 1993 started the public debate over health reform, then the period between May and August 1994 was the grand finale.

The increased intensity and seriousness of the legislative process and the actual debate among authoritative government officials was matched by the fourth peak in media coverage. Journalists flocked back to the Clinton plan as a favorite topic, but the amount of coverage was at nearly half the level of September 1993 and much of it focused on criticism. Coverage of expanding access also approached its zenith in August 1994. But the reports of legislative efforts to scale back or abandon reformers' initial objectives reached new highs, although positive statements on the Clinton plan and access continued to receive relatively more attention. The Mitchell plan was one of the few alternatives to the Clinton plan that received more than 1 percent of media coverage of health care.

In short, the issues addressed by journalists and the volume of press coverage between 1977 and 1994 paralleled the health care debate among authoritative government officials. The sharply greater press coverage in 1993–94 (fig. 5.1), when compared to any period since 1977, reflected the extraordinary scope, ambitiousness, and political acrimony of the Clinton health plan.

What made Clinton's episode extraordinary, however, was the change in the nature of press coverage. The media's presentation of health issues in 1993–94 dramatically accelerated existing trends, which in turn initiated qualitative changes in press coverage. In particular, we analyzed three important dimensions of media coverage: the way in which the news media portrayed or "framed" health care issues; the extent to which the press focused on agreement or disagreement regarding health issues; and the sources journalists cited in health care stories. We examine the framing of health issues in this chapter and devote the next chapter to the media's use of different sources and to the "negativity" found in news reporting.

Framing Issues

Since the 1970s, journalists have committed themselves to bringing readers behind the scenes of election campaigns to see the "inside" conflict and strategizing. Clinton's health reform initiative has been described by media observers as heralding a new era: journalists took their focus on political intrigue in election campaigns and applied it to policy debates, producing a dramatic new pattern in news coverage of policy debates (Jamieson 1992; Cappella and Jamieson 1997; Jamieson and Cappella 1995, 1998; Patterson 1994). But how new was this pattern? Was it simply a product of changes within the press during the 1990s? Additional historical evidence is necessary to understand if the Clinton coverage was new or a continuation of previous trends. Drawing conclusions without systematic evidence on changes over time runs the risk of overidealizing the past and miscasting later practices. What we need is evidence on rising and falling *trends,* not just absolute amounts of coverage.

Historical evidence indicates that press coverage of health care reform in 1993–94 was not unprecedented compared to previous episodes of health reform. The content of AP reports from 1977 to 1994 reveal that the degree of attention to political conflict and strategy did intensify significantly in the early 1990s, but this did not represent an altogether new pattern; the coverage of conflict and strategy had accompanied divisive policy debates since the 1970s. The extensive coverage of conflict and strategy that accompanied the politically acrimonious debate over Clinton's health reform efforts was preceded by rises in coverage of political maneuvering (though at comparatively low levels) during the contentious health policy debates of the 1970s and 1980s. What we find, then, is that news reports on health care in 1993–94 followed the trajectory of an established pattern—but accelerated to a higher level than before.

We tracked the way in which the media characterized or "framed" health issues since 1977. Media reports regularly use clearly identifiable frames or ways of organizing a story in order to direct and focus the way their audience thinks about and understands events and conditions.[14] An illustration of framing is the decision of journalists and editors to portray a public demonstration as a "disruption of public order" rather than frame it as an "exercise in free speech" issue (Nelson, Clawson, and Oxley 1997).

The media primarily relied on two frames to characterize debates on health policy—a strategy and conflict frame, and a national problem frame.[15] The strategy and conflict frame is evident when journalists present political events in terms of the motivations of political activists, their maneuvering for advantage, and their conflict with opponents. Observers of the media's coverage of election campaigns complain that the press relies on this one frame. Journalists have also been widely criticized by policymakers and others for casting the 1993–94 debate in terms of a battle between the Clinton Administration and its highly partisan Republican opponents; the debate was portrayed for audiences through the lens of political conflict and strategy.[16] The Associated Press's February 1994 story that opened this chapter illustrates the strategic frame (we consider political conflict as part of this single frame): it depicted the start of the congressional policymaking process in terms of opposition to Clinton's plan even from Democrats, and the White House's competition with Republicans for the most effective strategy for "selling" their position.

In contrast, the national problem frame focused the audience on the direct impact of proposed policies or health care developments on the country as a whole. An example of this is a portrayal of the country's health care expenditures as threatening the national economy. In this case, journalists would, in effect, be presenting health care as a national or collective issue, with implications that extended beyond the narrow self-interest of an individual. For instance, the AP story in June 1979 that began this chapter focused on the *wide* significance of rising health care costs; it reported that Senator Long's proposal would help the *country's* many working "individuals and families pay big medical and hospital bills that could wipe them out financially."

   Our analysis of media framing was based on counting each instance
in which a frame—a strategic versus a national frame—was used in
reporting on a specific policy issue.[17] We tallied both the frequency
with which a frame was mentioned each year as well as the number of
times a frame was mentioned as a proportion of the total number of
times all health care issues were mentioned each year. The proportional measure of media framing controls for the overall upsurges in
coverage that periodically catapulted health care into the spotlight.
This enabled us to detect changes over time that were independent of
the rising volume of reports on health care issues.

   The trend in media framing is presented in figure 5.3, which shows
the proportion of AP coverage using conflict and strategy versus national problem frames. At first glance, the most striking feature of figure 5.3 is the media's extensive emphasis on the national consequences
of health care over political strategy and conflict. This frame was the
most common portrayal of health issues for the entire period from
1977 to 1994. The dominance of national problem frames is most apparent in the period stretching from the mid-1980s until the early
1990s.

   What is critical, however, are the trends. Two patterns stand out.

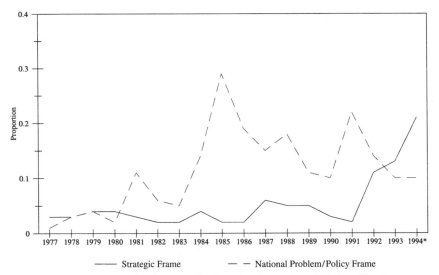

Figure 5.3   Proportion of AP Coverage Dedicated to Strategic and National Problem
Framing of All Health Care Issues, 1977–1994

Source: Compiled by authors; see appendix 3 and text.
Note: The proportions are calculated with frame mentions for each year as the numerator
and the total number of mentions per year as the denominator.
* Coverage ends in September 1994.

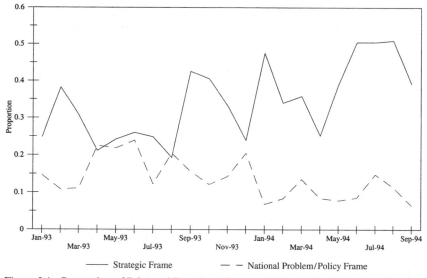

Figure 5.4   Proportion of Print and Broadcast Coverage Dedicated to Strategic and
National Problem Framing of All Health Care Issues, 1993–1994

Source: Compiled by authors; see appendix 3 and text.

Note: The proportions are calculated with frame mentions for each month as the
numerator and the total number of mentions per month as the denominator.

First, the overall trends in the national problem and strategic frames
appear to move in opposite directions.[18] When the use of national
problem frames rose through 1985, strategic frames fell or remained
low. After 1985, however, national problem framing fell and strategic
framing rose (especially after 1991). Reporting on politicking has come
at the expense of covering the national consequences of health issues
and vice versa. Our content analysis of print and broadcast media during Clinton's health reform campaign corroborates the pattern for the
AP reports. Figure 5.4, which combines the print and broadcast media,
shows that the national frames increased from January until June 1993,
and then declined. In contrast, the strategic frames fell from February
to August 1993, and then rose. (The national problem frame was more
common in print media than in broadcast messages, which is consistent with the expected inclination of television to consider pictures of
sparring politicians as audience-grabbing and the tendency of print
media to cover policy issues and their larger significance in greater
depth [Just, Crigler, and Buhr 1999].)

Second, figure 5.3 shows that strategic framing rose dramatically
during Clinton's health reform effort but this was hardly a new development. Changes in the use of strategic frames in the media had im-

portant precedents. In the past, politicized debates over health care
were also marked by at least a moderate rise in strategic framing and
a fall-off in national problem frames. Media framing, then, also follows
a political cycle.

The trends in strategic framing become clearer when we examine the
connection between media framing and policy issues. The way journalists organize their reports is influenced by whether the subject matter
is government reform, which attracts political disputes among authoritative government officials, or generic health issues that rarely engen-
der immediate political conflict.

Figures 5.5 and 5.6 track strategic and national frames for the two
categories of policy issues—reform and generic. The first important
pattern in these figures confirms that national problem frames are not
nearly as prevalent on health reform issues (fig. 5.5) as on generic issues (fig. 5.6). The domination of national problem frames over strategic frames during the 1980s, which is evident in figure 5.3 and especially figure 5.6, considerably narrowed when health reform issues are
considered alone.[19]

Figures 5.5 and 5.6 suggest a second finding regarding the trends in

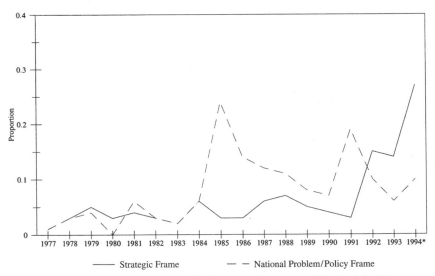

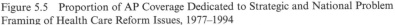

Figure 5.5   Proportion of AP Coverage Dedicated to Strategic and National Problem
Framing of Health Care Reform Issues, 1977–1994

Source: Compiled by authors; see appendix 3 and text.

Note: The proportions are calculated with frame mentions on reform issues for each year
as the numerator and the total number of reform mentions on reform issues per year as
the denominator.

* Coverage ends in September 1994.

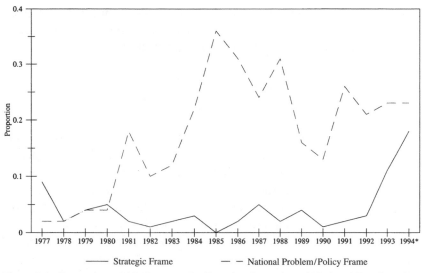

Figure 5.6   Proportion of AP Coverage Dedicated to Strategic and National Framing of Generic Health Care Issues, 1977–1994

Source: Compiled by authors; see appendix 3 and text.
Note: The proportions are calculated with frame mentions on generic issues for each year as the numerator and the total number of generic mentions per year as the denominator.
* Coverage ends in September 1994.

framing and the precedence for strategic framing. The media's proportional attention to the strategic framing of reform issues crested when political debate intensified during three of the four peaks in health reform coverage—during 1979, 1987, and especially 1992–94. Debates among political leaders on expanding the government's involvement in health care tapped into ideological divides over the role of government and politicized discussions of health care. Journalists focused substantial attention on political bickering during these periods of genuine political conflict. We examine these particular variations further in the next section.

The predominance of national problem frames is most apparent for generic health care issues (fig. 5.6). The political explosion ignited by Clinton's reform efforts failed to consume media reporting on nonreform topics. Contrary to some prevailing criticism of journalists, issues like health costs were not completely engulfed by "horse race" coverage on any topic related to health policy.

In short, when journalists reported on health reform issues in the context of intense and contentious policy discussions, they were more likely to latch on to strategy and conflict and to downplay the larger national consequences of the issues. In contrast, they gave relatively greater attention to national consequences when the subject shifted to the state of affairs in health care more generally.[20]

Health Reform Debates and Media Framing

1979

The media were slightly more likely in 1979 to cast health reform issues in strategic terms as in national problem terms (fig. 5.5). The debate over health care transpired in the context of Kennedy's challenge to President Carter when the senator's proposal to expand access to insurance pinched ideological nerves in both political parties. Journalists reported on the political infighting over the rival proposals.

The media also devoted attention to the national consequences of reform, which is not surprising given Kennedy's and Carter's common emphasis on controlling health costs. Carter's primary goal was to reduce the burden on taxpayers, while Kennedy hoped to marshal resources from the waste in the health care system in order to pay for the cost of shrinking the ranks of the uninsured. Both Democrats' emphasis on cost control was certainly welcomed by Republicans. In the June 1979 story described earlier, the AP reporter divided her piece between an account of the congressional hurdles facing reform and a run-down of the support for cost containment by Kennedy, the Carter administration, and congressional Republicans.

1981–82

The slight rise in strategic and national framing of reform issues from 1980 to 1981 corresponded with President Reagan's efforts to cut spending with the support of conservative Democrats in the House (fig. 5.5). As in 1979, the policy debate was politically charged and yet there was some bipartisan support for cost control. As figure 5.6 shows, the press's attention to the national consequences of generic issues shot up, which reflects the intense focus on the economic impact of government spending on health during the deep recession and the rising costs of health services.

The more puzzling year is 1982, when both strategic and national framing dipped. The explanation probably lies in the bipartisan and technical approach to controlling health costs (especially Medicare costs). Although Democrats resisted further budget cuts in government spending on health care, both Congress and President Reagan were concerned with high costs and controlling Medicare expenditures. In an era of tax cuts and attacks on government, no serious attention was given by Congress to significantly altering benefits or expanding access to the degree recommended by Kennedy in the 1970s. Both Democrats and Republicans in Congress requested legislation from the Reagan administration to slow Medicare's rising costs, and the Department of Health and Human Services responded with an intricate formula for tying Medicare's reimbursement of hospitals to diagnostic related groups. There was no intense disagreement among political elites over controlling Medicare's costs; civil servants were the decisive policymakers working quietly behind the scenes (with lawmakers later ratifying their decisions), and the relevant policy instruments were technical formulas.

The drop in strategic framing was consistent with the technical and bipartisan approach to controlling Medicare's costs. Absent a political shootout among authoritative government officials, there was relatively little political conflict and intrigue to report.

The drop in national framing is a bit surprising; the emphasis of policymakers on health care problems that affected all Americans presented journalists with a story that welcomed such framing. Indeed, the dip is partly an artifact of our measure of media coverage in figures 5.5 and 5.6. The actual attention devoted to national frames rose by more than 50 percent over its previous high in 1979, but the media's overall coverage of health care rose faster; the result was a proportional fall in national framing. This is one of the very few cases where the trends in proportions and the trends in the volume of coverage did not coincide during the peaks of coverage. Indeed, the October 1982 AP story cited earlier solely characterized the Reagan administration's proposal for Medicare DRGs in terms of national policy, not political strategy or conflict. The title of the story whispered, "Administration Proposes to Set Medicare Fees."

When the political debate and conflict over health reform lulled in the mid-1980s, news reports with national frames rose dramatically. The use of national framing shot up more than fourfold by 1985 for both reform and generic issues (figs. 5.5 and 5.6).

1987–89

Authoritative government officials resumed their debate over health care reform in 1987 and media framing shifted in reaction to the political change: figure 5.5 shows that strategic framing rose and national problem frames receded. A relatively small group of issues ignited heated debate between Democrats who controlled Congress and Republican Presidents Bush and Reagan: widening access to health care and health insurance, expanding Medicare to cover catastrophic illness, restrictions on abortion, and spending on AIDS testing and treatment. On 17 June 1987, for instance, the AP opened its story on expanding Medicare to cover prescription drugs by spotlighting the strategy of a Democratic leader to design legislation that would tap the "tremendous pressure from the seniors" and "win enough House support to override a presidential veto." The story continued by chronicling the struggle of Democrats against the Reagan administration and congressional Republicans who opposed expanding government.

As the Bush presidency proceeded and largely avoided health reform issues (until the 1992 election heated up), the use of the national problem frames once again rose during these off-reform years (fig. 5.5). By 1991, reform proposals had not yet returned to the political agenda, although health care problems were incubating. Because authoritative government officials were not fighting over reform issues in Washington, press coverage of health care's national consequence rose more than twofold, as the economy took a downturn and Harris Wofford's Senate campaign highlighted the nations' problems in this area.

1992–94

Chapters 3 and 4 examined the fierce political combat ignited by the Clinton crusade for health reform; our content analysis showed that the press reframed its reporting of governmental policy to reflect this political battle. As the debate heated up during the 1992 presidential campaign and Clinton's presidency, the use of strategic framing soared and national framing fell off (fig. 5.5). In 1993–94, print and broadcast media as well as AP coverage used the strategic frames two to three times more often than the national problem frames.[21] Television coverage was especially prone to using strategic frames instead of national frames—a pattern that accelerated as the debate evolved (the use of strategic frames rose by over 50 percent from 1993 to 1994). Television's particular attention to political conflict and strategy stems, in part, from its orientation toward visual images that draw audiences; prominent politicians sparring over health care certainly fit the bill.

Figures 5.3, 5.5, and 5.6 all reveal that press coverage of political conflict and strategy abruptly changed beginning in 1992. Compared to the way journalists had framed their reports since 1977, the use of strategic frames shot up in the 1990s to extraordinary levels—more than four times any previous high. Although all three figures show a similar sharp rise in strategic framing, national frames continued to dominate coverage of generic issues (fig. 5.6).

As journalists concentrated on strategy and conflict, they gave less and less proportionate attention to national health care problems. The proportion of national frames dropped by more than half from 1991 to 1994 in reports of health reform issues (fig. 5.5). Even reporting on generic issues became less dominated by national frames, though they still held a slight advantage. Common headlines in the Associated Press on reform issues capture the heightened emphasis on strategy and conflict (recall that the AP represents the melba toast of print journalism): "Clinton's Revolutionary Idea: High States, High Hurdles," "No Health Care at Expense of Welfare, Moynihan Warns," "Clinton Defends Momentum in Health Debate," "Clinton's Senate Point Man Faces Greatest Challenge," "Clinton's 1,342 Pages May Be DOA But His Goals Are Alive," and "Hillary Clinton Shouts to Pitch Health Overhaul."

A closer look at the media's framing of health care between Clinton's inauguration and the withdrawal and defeat of his efforts in September 1994 reveals short-term variations that parallel the political cycle found during earlier periods. Figure 5.4 shows that conflict and strategy dominated journalists' presentation of health care, with variations in the media's framing following the changes in the policy process.

Figure 5.4 indicates that the first major spike in overall strategic framing and the drop in national framing occurred in September 1993 when Clinton launched his health plan and the White House and opponents of reform began in earnest to maneuver for political position. A comparison of strategic framing of reform and generic issue, which is not shown, reveals a similar pattern: press reports of reform issues in September were particularly prone to strategic framing, while coverage of generic issues was more often presented in national problem terms. (In general, press framing of reform and generic issues in broadcast and print news coverage during 1993–94 followed the trend in our parallel analysis of AP reports [figs. 5.5 and 5.6].)

Consider, for instance, the coverage of Clinton's speech on 23 September 1993 by the *New York Times, Washington Post,* and *Los Angeles Times.* What is striking is that even reports by these newspapers, which are most likely to offer detailed and substantive coverage, devoted over twice as much space to the political maneuverings and calculations of politicians than to the national problems facing the country. The

Times's Clifford Krauss devoted his story to reporting the "fault lines" and the immediate efforts of lawmakers to "pick fights." Ann Devroy and Ruth Marcus kicked off their report for the *Post* by highlighting the "fundamental differences" and "grueling fight" that had already developed. Spencer Rich filled out the *Post*'s coverage by literally cataloguing the positions of competing interest groups. None of these papers ran a story that simply reported the president's plan or charted broad areas of agreement on the problems to be solved (Rich 1993; Stolberg 1993; Chen and Lauter 1993; Krauss 1993; Clymer 1993; Toner 1993; Marcus and Devroy 1993).

The second major peak in strategic framing and dip in national problem framing occurred in January 1994 (fig. 5.4). Again, this shows the media's reaction to significant changes in the policy debate: Dole demonstrably shifted his comments from receptiveness to direct opposition to Clinton's plan, and Clinton countered the Republican attack and his loss of momentum during the fall with his dramatic State of the Union address. Reflecting the political disagreement and maneuvering, the media's use of strategic framing on reform issues shot up, while its presentation of national frames declined sharply.

The third and largest overall spike in strategic framing occurred between May and August 1994. The cresting of strategic frames, shown in figure 5.4, reflected the culmination of the policy debates of authoritative government officials. Political leaders and other influentials in Washington focused during this period on the legislative process, with Democratic leaders directing frantic, but futile, efforts at building a coalition to support health care reform, while the opponents of reform maneuvered to suffocate these efforts altogether. Even as strategy and conflict dominated press coverage of reform issues, national considerations were still evident when the subject turned to generic health care issues: the use of national problem frames for these issues increased to their highest level in 1994 (data not presented). In particular, news reports on health costs or inadequate access were pitched in terms of their national significance.

Conclusion

This chapter shows that changes in media framing followed a fairly predictable political cycle over the period from 1977 to 1994. The media's use of strategic framing increased in three of the four major reform eras, while their use of a national problem frame rose during the off-reform years. Strategic and national framing moved in opposite directions during two of the four reform eras: strategic frames rose and national frames dropped in 1987 and 1993–94. When debate among authoritative government officials and other influentials heated up, the media framed their coverage in terms of conflict and gamesmanship and turned away from the national implications of health issues. When the combat over health care wound down, journalists tended to shift their emphasis from political strategy and conflict to the consequences of health care and health policy for the nation. The ebb and flow of political and policy developments have largely driven the decisions by journalists and editors over how to portray health care issues.

The media's framing was not only sensitive to political changes over time but was also tailored to the particular policy issues raised when the debate over government reform of health care attracted authoritative officials and other establishment figures. News reports reflected the relative attention of the political establishment to reform issues compared to generic issues: when reporters covered reform issues during periods of contentious policy discussions, they latched onto political strategy and conflict that unfolded and downplayed the national problem aspect of the issues; but when the subject shifted to generic health issues or when contentious policy discussions subsided, the press gave greater attention to how these problems affected the nation. In short, the overall pattern of the media's reporting mirrored the conflict, intensity, and policy content of the ongoing political debate.

The next chapter continues our analysis of the political cycle of press coverage, focusing on our investigation of the media's use of different sources and the "negativity" found in news reporting.

Chapter Six

Loud Messages, Loud Voices

P|erhaps no charge against American journalists and editors has been as widely accepted among political observers as the complaint that news coverage is "too negative." Thomas Patterson summarized the views of many observers when he chastised press coverage of presidential elections for making "negative reporting . . . the norm" (1994, 204). Bill Clinton's presidency, Patterson (1993) observed in a *New York Times* editorial, "has been dogged from the start by hyper-critical coverage" and "overly negative" news reports (also see Just, Crigler, and Buhr 1999). White House officials eagerly joined the bandwagon, complaining bitterly in our interviews that press coverage of health care reform was "all negative" and preoccupied with "trashing the president" and his proposal for reform. One study of press coverage of managed care offered a more balanced analysis but nonetheless concluded that "the tone of coverage has become more critical over time" and that the most visible media (albeit television and special series) were "the most negative" (Brodie, Brady, and Altman 1998, 10, 19).

Few terms seem as clear-cut as "negativity" and yet it can be used in at least two quite different ways to describe press coverage of health care and government policymaking. One usage refers to whether the press excessively reports critical messages about health care conditions (e.g., growing national expenditures on medical care) or a specific policy such as Clinton's health reform proposal. The focus here is on the *directionality* of news coverage ("pro" versus "con" messages); the overreporting of opposing or critical messages represents what we call "*issue* negativity." A second type of negativity applies to news reports of the political motivations, strategy, and conflict involving elected officials or election candidates. The focus here is the framing of coverage and embodies what we call "*political* negativity"; this is the emphasis on political conflict and strategy that we examined in the previous chapter.[1]

We study both "issue negativity" and "political negativity" as part of our investigation of the impact of politicians' pursuit of policy goals, crafted talk, and fierce counterattacks. This chapter explores the extent to which the press conveys issue negativity and how this has varied over time. Although increases in genuine policy disagreements expand press coverage of political conflict and strategy (political negativity), we expect the press overall to portray policy issues in positive or constructive terms more than negative ones. The journalistic norm of informing citizens encourages policy descriptions and, as a practical matter, the press requires substantial space and broadcast time to describe policy proposals—it is hard to be critical without first describing the subject, and that requires coverage.

This chapter explores a second topic related to the media's connection to policy debates: the extent to which changes in policy debates affect both the media's use of government officials and others as sources, and the range of viewpoints they cite. How do the political dynamics of governing affect whom the press cites and what viewpoints it conveys? We expect the citation of authoritative government officials (namely, presidents and congressional leaders) to increase when the White House or the House and Senate take action or issue significant statements on government policy. Widening disagreement among government leaders and other influentials is also expected to widen the range of viewpoints among establishment figures that the press represents. We begin this chapter by examining "issue negativity" and then turn to studying the media's sources.

Issue Negativity

Overall Patterns

Our analysis of issue negativity challenges the pervasive assumption that negativity is ubiquitous in the press. Press coverage of health policy *issues* has overall been more positive than negative since 1977. We consider positive coverage to include messages that express outright support for changes in government policy (such as President Clinton's health reform proposal) or that tacitly acknowledge that proposed reforms are serious and well-constructed. For instance, the Associated

Press (AP) story in October 1982 on the Reagan administration's proposal to use DRGs (diagnostic related groups) to control Medicare payments to hospitals overwhelmingly conveyed favorable messages about the purpose and design of the proposal; it devoted little attention to criticisms of DRGs.

In contrast, we considered press accounts as negative when they portrayed developments such as rising health care costs or inadequate health insurance coverage as unwanted problems. A negative message included, for instance, the quote in the AP story on DRGs from the Secretary of the Department of Health and Human Services (HHS) who warned of the "constant litany of upward hospital costs." (See appendix 3 on how we tracked and coded the positive, negative, and neutral content of media messages.)

Fully half of the AP's messages on health care were positive while 40 percent were negative (10 percent were categorized as neutral). Figure 6.1 reveals that positive messages outweighed negative ones in all but three years between 1977 and 1994. Positive coverage moved upward during the peaks of reformism—1979, 1981, 1987, and the 1990s.

The patterns found in the AP coverage was mirrored in print and

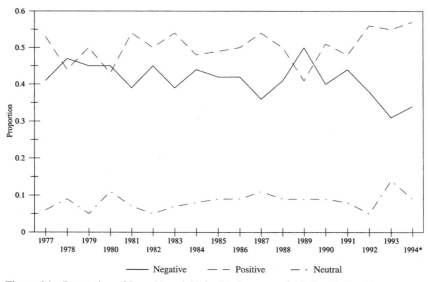

Figure 6.1   Proportion of Issue Negativity in AP Coverage of All Health Care Issues, 1977–1994

Source: Compiled by authors; see appendix 3 and text.

Note: The proportions are calculated with positive, negative, or neutral mentions for each year as the numerator and the total number of mentions per year as the denominator.

* Coverage ends in September 1994.

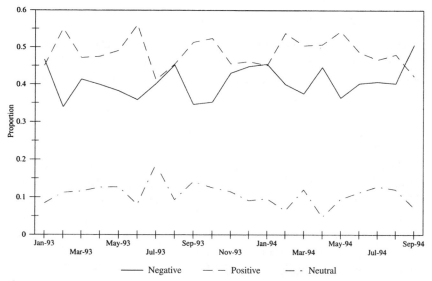

Figure 6.2   Proportion of Issue Negativity in Print and Broadcast Coverage of All Health Care Issues, 1993–1994

Source: Compiled by authors; see appendix 3 and text.
Note: The proportions are calculated with positive, negative, or neutral mentions for each month as the numerator and the total number of mentions per month as the denominator.

broadcast reports between January 1993 and September 1994. Nearly half of these reports were positive (49 percent) and 40 percent negative (11 percent were neutral). Figure 6.2 suggests two findings. First, positive messages were greater than negative ones during most of what was an extremely contentious policy debate; this is an indication of the positive orientation of the press reports on health issues. Second, the trends suggest that positive and negative coverage varied in keeping with the evolution of the policy debate. The highest levels of positive reports came during the first half of 1993 when hope still ran high and before the Clinton plan was publicly available for direct attack. The White House's "launch" of its plan in September 1993 coincided with much more positive than negative coverage. When NAFTA, Whitewater, and other controversies or crises distracted the White House in the fall of 1993 and when Senate Republican Minority Leader Robert Dole and other prominent counterpunchers took off their gloves in January 1994, the proportion of positive messages dipped while negativity rose. The proportion of negative messages steadily climbed during the final period of critical legislative activity in the summer of 1994, peaking in September as positive coverage declined.

Issue Negativity and the Content of Policy Issues

The overall positive and negative content of press reports on health care masked significant variations across issues. The issues themselves affected—in an understandable manner—whether the press conveyed positive or negative messages. Figure 6.3 reveals that the media's messages about health care reform issues were quite different from other more general or, as we defined it in the last chapter, "generic" health care issues.

Analysis of the AP's coverage of reform issues contradicts the suspicion that the media were out to give health care reform a hard time. The AP consistently conveyed positive messages over negative ones for every year between 1977 and 1994. Overall, 58 percent of the AP's reports on reform issues were positive and 33 percent negative. (Our study of print and broadcast media during Clinton's campaign in 1993–94 found a similar split of 51 percent positive and 37 percent negative.)

Figure 6.3 shows that positive messages about health care reform issues peaked during the four reform episodes, with the exception of

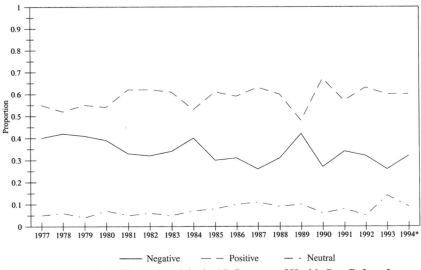

Figure 6.3   Proportion of Issue Negativity in AP Coverage of Health Care Reform Issues, 1977–1994

Source: Compiled by authors; see appendix 3 and text.

Note: The proportions are calculated with positive, negative, or neutral mentions of reform issues for each year as the numerator and the total number of reform mentions per year as the denominator.

* Coverage ends in September 1994.

1989 when Congress took the unprecedented step of repealing the Catastrophic Insurance Act. The overwhelmingly favorable comments about the Reagan administration's DRG proposal in the AP's October 1982 story (which was mentioned earlier) were indicative of press reports on reform issues. Ten years later, when Clinton propelled health care reform back onto policymakers' agenda, positive messages continued to dominate reporting of proposals to improve the quality and efficiency of American health care and to pass comprehensive government reform.

While health reform issues regularly attracted positive reporting, the Clinton plan in particular attracted varying degrees of favorable and unfavorable coverage in the AP as well as print and broadcast media. Republican leaders began in the fall of 1993 by backing particular reform proposals and expressing strong support for reform in general (see chapter 4). Reflecting the apparent support among authoritative officials for health reform, positive messages regarding the Clinton's plan peaked in September 1993 (they surpassed negative ones by at least a third). For instance, CNN's anchor Brian Christie announced on 19 September 1993 that "President Clinton pitched his plan for health care reform to some of America's black leaders." Christie then passed the story to CNN's correspondent, Jill Dougherty, who reported no explicit criticism of the president's plan; the closest she came to a negative message was to acknowledge support among members of the congressional Black Caucus for a single-payer plan.

Negative messages about the Clinton plan picked up noticeably in 1994, however, when the Republicans led by Dole ratcheted up their criticism of the Clinton plan and Democrats expressed rising concerns about the president's proposal as the legislative process moved into high gear. In January, the increasingly open battle at the apex of government between Clinton and Dole produced a conspicuous change in the tone of the media's coverage of Clinton's plan from just a few months earlier. For instance, ABC World News Tonight ran a long story on 26 January 1994 that gave extensive coverage to the phone callers who flooded Senator Arlen Specter's office because they were "angry with the Clinton health plan." Show anchor Peter Jennings and correspondent John Cochran then continued by cataloguing Republican criticisms of particular aspects of Clinton's plan. But the time they devoted to the president's side lacked the kind of detailed positive comments that would have counterbalanced the attacks. Vague references were made to the importance of health reform and to unimportant issues such as the president's laryngitis. By August, ABC correspondent Brit Hume reported that criticism of Clinton's bill meant that passing it was "uphill all the way" and that it "stood a better chance without the Clinton name on it."

Our analysis of the AP's coverage of generic issues produced a nearly opposite finding: negative messages dominated for nearly the entire period, with 54 percent of the coverage negative and 35 percent positive. A similar pattern emerged in our study of print and broadcast media in 1993–94 when 50 percent of the news reports were negative and 42 percent positive. For example, alarming reports about rising costs were evident throughout 1993 and 1994 (though they were less prominent as a proportion of all coverage than in the 1970s). CNN's story on 21 March 1993 was typical: Sharyl Attkisson reported on the trauma of one elderly American who, like others, lacked the funds to "cover the costs of the nursing home [and was forced] to give up her [retirement] check [and] her furniture."

The press considered the general state of health care as "newsworthy" and deserving of coverage when real-world problems developed or government officials accented developments as threatening. Economic pressures to attract audience attention as well as the media's watchdog responsibility meant that generic issues drew attention when they were problematic; favorable developments rarely seemed to draw comparable attention.[2]

Judging the Media

Media watchers and the Clinton administration cast journalists and editors as subversives who offered up explosive negative coverage of health care reform. News coverage on health care, however, was not relentlessly critical. Press reports described the general state of affairs in health as having problems and inadequacies, but negative reports on rising costs or on inadequate access or quality were understandable; these were hardly positive trends.

What departs more strikingly from the standard critique of the press was the media's tendency to portray the debate over government reforms as constructive and serious. This finding is surprising but it fits both with the press's professional norm of informing the public about the seriousness that authoritative officials assigned to major proposals for reform as they cranked up the legislative machinery and with its commercial interests in attracting audiences. The press described what reforms government officials were considering in sufficient detail to create a context for making some minimal sense of the health care debate and criticisms of reform proposals. In balance, this predisposed press accounts toward positive messages about health issues.

The inclination to report government reforms in positive or constructive terms does not mean that health reform debates are easy to follow for the public. Issue negativity is only one dimension of press reports. Fierce partisanship and the media's portrayal of it may obscure or at least complicate the positive portrayal of any issues themselves. Our point is that the negativity commonly attributed to media coverage is a product of the political tenor of policy debates, which leads the press to heavily use a conflict and strategy frame (as shown in the previous chapter), and not of the media's independent criticism of government proposals as flawed and unworkable.

Central Casting: The Media's Sources

The Clinton administration and its rivals utilized a political strategy of crafting talk to attempt to "win" public support. Politicians equated the success of their strategy with insuring that their "message" dominated the "information flow" through the media. "Reaching" reporters and inducing them to quote sympathetic sources who would effectively deliver or substantiate their message was a common tactic utilized by both proponents and opponents of health reform. The Clinton White House eventually developed an elaborate campaign that included: pairing administration officials with individual journalists as part of a "buddy system"; encouraging the press to quote and rely upon the president and administration sources; and incorporating into the White House task force experts who were expected to "validate" the Clinton plan when asked by reporters to evaluate it. The opponents of reform also scrambled to make sure their side got a "fair hearing" by wooing reporters and encouraging them to use sources sympathetic to their position.

Johnson and Broder's *The System* (1996) conveys a vivid picture of the battle over whom the press used as sources on Clinton's health reform initiative. The victors, according to this account, were the opponents of health reform; they out-positioned the White House and other reform advocates to become the primary sources for reporters and consistently snatched the media spotlight. Johnson and Broder attribute the reformers' failure to control whom the media chose as sources to tactical errors that reflected the complexity of the White House's message—it was just not ready for prime time. They quote one prominent reporter as complaining that the president's plan was "virtually unexplainable" and that the administration's explanations were "awful" (230). Reporters, according to Johnson and Broder, snubbed the convoluted proposals and explanations served up by Clinton and the Democrats in favor of the clear and snappy commentary of their staunchest opponents—the representatives of the health insurance industry and business.

We offer two challenges to this account. First, economic and professional pressures create incentives for the press to disproportionately use authoritative government officials and others influential in health care as sources; their institutional positions equip them with the capacity to affect substantially future events. Our systematic analysis of the media's sources, described below, challenges Johnson and Broder's conclusions that the opponents of reform such as representatives of health insurers and business overwhelmed the Clinton administration and Democrats in Congress. The sources whom journalists and editors selected in covering health issues largely reflected the institutional and political power of presidents and legislators. In addition, variations over time in the use of sources reflected actual developments in the formulation of policy proposals and the dynamics of the lawmaking process.

The selection of sources was a product of the structure of American politics and the process of press reporting rather than personal miscalculations over tactics or policy design; even a "virtually unexplainable" proposal from the president will generally stimulate the press to use executive branch officials, owing to their institutional place in American government. The preponderance of attention to authoritative officials in news reports on health care is amply confirmed by research on other subjects (Reese, Grant, and Danielian 1994; Blumler and Gurevitch 1981; Brown, Bybee, Weardon, and Straughan 1982; Entman and Page 1994; Zaller and Chiu 1996; Gans 1979; Bennett 1996).

The second challenge is that the press rarely allows one perspective to monopolize a contentious policy debate (even as it slants toward authoritative officials). The media's watchdog function and professional commitment to "objectivity" create pressures (when political conflict increases) to expand the range of reported viewpoints among government officials and others influential in the relevant policy area; this may still fall short of the full range of opinions. Even if the president and legislators in his own party dominate health reporting overall, the emergence of health care as a contentious issue is likely to prompt the press to increase its use of legislators in the opposition party and individuals influential in health care—especially providers and policy experts.

We tracked the volume of media coverage for forty-six categories of sources cited in the AP reports from 1977 to 1994 and in our sample of print and broadcast media from 1993 to 1994. "Source" refers to the originator of a policy statement and may include individuals who are quoted (e.g., the president, members of his administration and his party in Congress, legislators in the opposite party, and representatives of organized groups) or the unattributed narrators of the stories— namely, the journalists offering their own interpretation, commentary, or analysis. This detailed coding enabled us to identify a source for each quote, reference, or observation in health care stories.

Reformers versus Opponents

The most blunt analysis of the notion that reform's opponents domi- nated press accounts in 1993–94 is to compare how frequently advo- cates and opponents of reform were cited as sources in news coverage of health care. We found no evidence that the press gave more atten- tion to the opponents (Republicans and representatives of business and insurance) rather than the proponents of reform (Clinton adminis- tration officials, congressional Democrats, and seniors who depend on Medicare). For most of 1993, reformers received more coverage, peak- ing in September at a level nearly triple that given opponents. Even in 1994, reformers received more attention than opponents in the reports of the AP as well as in print and broadcast media.

The inaccuracy of the presumption that journalists were lackeys for reform's opponents becomes clearer when we compare the coverage of specific types of sources. The media's practices during 1993–94 also become clearer by looking more historically at the media's sources be- tween 1977 and 1994. Figure 6.4 displays the proportional attention given the major types of sources cited in AP reports. (We also discuss other findings that are not presented in this or in other figures.) Al- though we studied many more categories of sources (see appendix 3), we present data here on the sources that were most prominent.

Overestimated Sources: Business and Health Insurance

One of the most striking features of figure 6.4 is the set of sources that *failed* to break into the upper ranks of media coverage. In particular, representatives of business and the insurance industry were used as

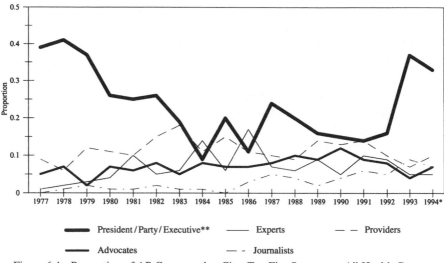

Figure 6.4   Proportion of AP Coverage that Cites Top Five Sources on All Health Care
Issues, 1977–1994

Source: Compiled by authors; see appendix 3 and text.
Note: The proportions are calculated with mentions of specific sources for each year as the
numerator and the total number of mentions per year as the denominator.
* Coverage ends in September 1994.
** This includes the president, members of his party, and officials in the executive branch.

sources much less frequently than implied by Johnson and Broder's
account. Business representatives did not break into the top five
sources; they were cited in only 4 percent of AP reports and print and
broadcast stories in 1993–94. Although print and broadcast reports
turned to business 10 percent of the time in May 1993, this proportion
dropped over time; by August 1994, business officials constituted only
2 percent of the sources cited in health care stories. Insurance officials
fared far worse in the media line-up—less than 2 percent in AP and
print and broadcast reports.

Underestimated Sources

Johnson and Broder (1996) emphasized the prevalence of business and
insurance representatives as media sources and underestimated the reliance of journalists on Clinton and other Democrats.

PRESIDENT   No individual was cited more extensively than President Clinton—he alone represented over 7 percent of all sources mentioned in print and broadcast reports in 1993–94. Reflecting the institu-

tional prerogatives of the presidency to initiate changes in government policy, Clinton constituted 15 percent of all sources cited when he promoted health care in September 1993 and 12 percent in January 1994 when he presented his State of the Union address.

But the media did not mechanically follow promotional campaigns by the president. Comparing press sources and the volume of Clinton's statements in figure 3.4 reveals that the press discounted his spurt of activity in February, March, and April 1994, while it devoted extensive coverage in January 1994 when the volume of his own comments hit a low point. The performance of official government functions clearly mattered: the press reported Clinton's comments during the period of his official State of the Union address even though the total volume of his statements was, in reality, relatively low; it devoted less attention to his relatively extensive statements that were unrelated to the direct exercise of his government authority.

The long-term evidence from AP coverage indicates that presidents were 6 percent of the sources between 1977 and 1994. But there were clear rises and falls in the AP's use of presidents and presidential candidates. In terms of press use of presidential candidates as sources, Clinton's decision to give health reform greater prominence than Bush in 1992 (and other candidates since 1977) was reflected in journalists' unparalleled use of him compared to his predecessors.[3] Among sitting presidents, Clinton's relative visibility on health issues was greater than Reagan or Bush but comparable to Carter. The proportion of Carter's citations matched Clinton's: during reform peaks the Democratic presidents were 8 percent of media sources, while the Republican presidents constituted 3 percent or less. Media attention, however, reflected political circumstances: presidents as sources jumped when they took a leading role in developing and promoting health issues (Carter and Clinton), but they dipped when the chief executive deferred to other administration officials or members of Congress (Reagan and Bush).

The news production process may account for the media's disproportionate attention to presidents and their administrations when they address health care. Reflecting the perceived distribution of governmental power, the media assign more journalists to administration "beats," such as the White House and other relevant executive branch departments (e.g., Department of Treasury, Department of Health and Human Services) than to Congress (Althaus et al. 1996). When the president or senior administrators make an important announcement, crowds of journalists are generally already on hand to file stories.

White House aides as well as pundits generally laud the power of the president's bully pulpit, but the truth is that the president's single voice can be drowned out by the chorus of other establishment figures. Although no single person was quoted as often as Clinton, important groups of authoritative government officials and others influential in health policy received far more combined attention.

The general pattern is that journalists went to sources who occupied decisive institutional positions in analyzing or formulating changes in health care and government policy. In practice, this often meant that journalists relied on sources who were sympathetic to health reform or aggressively promoted it.

DEMOCRATS AND REPUBLICANS   Democratic members of Congress were more dominant as sources than either the president or Republican legislators. Democratic legislators accounted for 7 percent of AP sources from 1977 to 1994 (12 percent in 1993–94) and 9 percent of print and broadcast sources in 1993–94; their Republican counterparts constituted 4 percent of AP sources (8 percent during 1993–94) and 5 percent in the print and broadcast reports in 1993–94.[4] Television was more likely than print media to rely on Republican and, even more so, Democratic legislators as sources.[5]

The greater prevalence of Democratic as opposed to Republican legislators since the 1970s stems from the fact that they initiated most of the major health reform legislation (from national health insurance to controlling Medicare's costs), and they seemed most attentive to changes in the state of affairs in health care. Republicans' ideological hostility to government made them generally unprepared to take the lead in proposing (let alone supporting) significant changes in health policies.

Even during major presidential initiatives, congressional Democrats held their own. Journalists cited Democratic legislators (as a group) more often than Clinton even as he crusaded for health reform. Print and broadcast reports used them as sources more frequently than Clinton during his launching of health care reform in September 1993, and they held a slight edge in January when the president presented his State of the Union address. Democrats opened their widest margin over Clinton when legislative activity heated up in the summer of 1994; by August, they constituted nearly 30 percent of press sources compared to less than 10 percent for the president. Clinton's experience was shared by his predecessors: during periods of intense health policy debate, members of the president's party received up to two or three times more attention from the AP than did the president.

What is striking, though, is that when debate over health reform heated up under Democratic Presidents Carter and Clinton, the Republicans' share of coverage consistently rose (even though Democrats still held a considerable advantage). In 1978 and 1994, the Republicans' proportion as media sources at least doubled (peaking around 10 percent for each year). In the summer of 1994 when Clinton's health reform initiative entered its final stages, the Republicans' share jumped to over 15 percent. Similarly, the media's use of Democratic sources rose when Republican administrations initiated health reform (though, again, the opposition party trailed the presidential party). These trends are significant: The surges in the Democratic and Republican share as press sources *when they were in the opposition* suggests that the media expanded the range of these partisan viewpoints during heightened conflict over health care.

The media's use of legislators as news sources reflected not only variations in the policy debate but also critical institutional changes. As we discussed in chapter 2, Congress became increasingly individualized after the mid-1970s, with legislators winning a "bill of rights." Although there is a presumption that congressional leaders dominate media coverage (Sinclair 1995; Hess 1986), the AP cited the rank and file in both political parties to a greater extent since 1977 than committee chairs and elected leaders like the Speaker of the House.

PRESIDENT AND HIS PARTY   When Clinton teamed up with congressional Democrats they were quoted in print and broadcast news at a rate that was 5 times higher than Republicans: the Democratic team accounted for 25 percent of the sources cited and were especially domineering in September 1993 when they constituted 40 percent of journalists' sources. Although the Republicans' share jumped to over 15 percent in the summer of 1994, Democrats still held an edge. The dominance of the Democrats reflected the clear reality of lawmaking: Democrats would determine the destiny of health reform because of their control over the White House and their majorities in Congress.

Even before the 1990s, though, the president and his party were the commanding voice in the media on health care (fig. 6.4), receiving three times as much attention as the opposing party. Our data reveal that the widest margins occurred during the reform-oriented Carter and Clinton presidencies, although the Republicans also received their greatest attention during the reform periods of 1981–82 and 1987–89 under GOP presidents. When a president becomes involved in health reform (even reluctantly as Reagan was), the press listens; the president's ability to initiate or formulate health policy in the sprawling executive branch clearly attracts the attention of beat reporters, who have been stationed to capture such initiatives.[6]

ISSUE NEGATIVITY AND CONGRESSIONAL SOURCES   The media's selection of government officials as sources was closely related to the tone of their reports. Clinton and congressional Democrats were consistently cited in print and in broadcasts during 1993–94 as offering more positive rather than critical statements—often by wide margins. In September 1993, positive comments attributed to them were about four times greater than critical ones. As the legislative process heated up, though, the margin narrowed to about threefold but held steady throughout 1994.

While conveying mostly positive statements from the president, journalists reported the genuine divisions between and within the Republican and Democratic parties during 1993–94. The press more frequently quoted individual legislators than congressional leaders as critical on health issues; this was true for both parties. The media's penchant for attributing criticism to the rank and file reflected the political calculations and behavior of leaders within Congress and the parties. The Democratic leadership calculated that helping Clinton would promote their interests by protecting their party's reputation and majority in Congress. Their Republican counterparts balanced their criticism with promises of cooperation in order to fend off charges of obstructionism and boost their chances of seizing control of Congress and the White House. By contrast, the rank and file exercised their considerable independence and expressed their own often critical views. Compared to leaders, journalists cited rank-and-file members of each party as more negative than positive (especially as the legislative process heated up by the summer of 1994). The Democratic rank and file were cited as critical nearly twice as often as their leaders.

The Forgotten Sources

Observers of American politics and the press have neglected not only the dominance of Clinton and congressional Democrats in news reports but also the prevalence of health care providers, advocacy groups for seniors, health policy experts, and executive branch officials.

HEALTH CARE PROVIDERS   No account of American health reform before the 1990s would have given short shrift to the representatives of hospitals and doctors. And yet, Johnson and Broder (1996) devote barely a handful of pages to them.

In reality, providers were among journalists' favorite sources, accounting for 8 percent of news sources cited by both the AP since the 1970s and print and broadcast reports in 1993–94. The variations in the media's attention to health care providers during the 1993–94 reform episode reflected different stages in the policy process. In April 1993, when journalists were sorting out how the emerging Clinton plan would actually affect health care, their use of providers constituted nearly 20 percent of their sources. During the final stages of the legislative process in the summer of 1994 when reform was in the hands of government officials, providers received their least attention, accounting for merely 2 percent of press sources on health care issues.[7]

Historically, the use of providers as news sources in the 1990s was generally comparable to previous episodes of health care reform. Figure 6.4 shows that providers were consistently the second most popular source after the president and his party. Their citations as sources rose most dramatically during the debate about controlling rising payments to doctors and hospitals in the 1970s and early 1980s—rising from 6 percent in 1978 and 11 percent in 1979 to 18 percent in 1983 before receding to the 10–14 percent level during the 1987–89 reform activities. Further confounding common presumptions, journalists did not flock to providers for critical comments. Positive statements by providers were more commonly cited than negative ones during every reform episode, except in 1989 when new controls were placed on Medicare's payments to doctors and when catastrophic insurance legislation was suddenly repealed leaving seniors without coverage for long-term care.

ADVOCACY GROUPS   Johnson and Broder (1996) credited advocates for seniors like the American Association for Retired Persons (AARP) with a greater presence in the media than health care providers, but they actually received a bit less coverage. Advocates represented about 5 to 6 percent of news sources in AP coverage since 1977 and in print and broadcast reports during 1993–94.

In addition, the media's citation of advocates declined during periods of reform, falling in 1979, 1981, 1989, and 1993. Although they were cited most frequently in the Clinton episode as the legislative debate heated up in 1994, the increase was not large and their use as a source was starting at a relatively low level, having declined sharply from its 1990 high.

Between 1977 and 1994, AP journalists most cited advocates when reporting on the national consequences of health issues and shunned them when concentrating on political strategy and conflict. Advocates were cited most often during the 1980s as debate focused on the costs of treating seniors (fig. 6.4). During the debate on Clinton's plan in 1993–94, however, television and print media behaved somewhat differently; they avoided advocates even when covering the national consequences of health issues.[8]

When the press did cite advocates, they used them more often for positive rather than negative comments during every reform period except 1981–82 when Reagan cut spending on health programs. Compared to the AP reports, print and broadcast news were more likely to cite critical comments by advocates.

In short, our findings contradict the presumption that advocates were a favorite source during policy debates when conflict intensifies and journalists follow the political maneuverings. Journalists are no fools; advocates are treated as tainted sources when their interests are at stake (Kollman 1998).

EXPERTS AND EXECUTIVE BRANCH OFFICIALS   Clinton and his senior aides anticipated that journalists would turn for information to executive officials from the White House and HHS and health policy experts from the academy and think tanks. Indeed, in chapter 2 we suggested that one reason for establishing the White House's task force was precisely to win the support of these groups. In addition, research on the press confirms the importance of experts both as news sources for reporters (Reese, Grant, Danielian 1994; Steele 1990) and as an influence on public opinion (Page, Shapiro, Dempsey 1987).

As anticipated, journalists regularly used administration officials and health policy experts as sources, but neither group dominated the news in 1993–94 nor matched their high levels of previous coverage. Overall, the AP and print and broadcast media used administration officials and experts as sources nearly as often as health providers and more often during certain months.[9]

In the spring of 1993, Clinton and his senior aides decided to lock journalists out of their contentious deliberations, but this did not stop some administration officials, frustrated at losing within the White House, from fighting back by promoting their "side" through leaks. Hungry to take advantage of information about the heated disputes within the White House over a major government initiative, the press's use of administration officials rose from 5 percent of health care sources after Clinton's inauguration to 10 percent in March 1993 and 20 percent in May 1993. As the debate shifted from the White House bunker to the more open process in Congress, the attention given to executive officials steadily fell, bottoming out at 2 percent by the summer of 1994.

Not surprisingly, the overall negative tone of print and broadcast reports citing administration officials hit its high in May 1993, with another lower peak in September before trailing off. Quotations of administration officials who criticized the president's plan followed a similar pattern, peaking in June 1993 before falling off. But the rises in the media's attribution of critical comments toward health care issues and Clinton's reform plan to administration officials were consistently dwarfed by overall positive comments throughout 1993–94; there were more than twice as many positive statements than negative ones for most of 1993. The press more than balanced the critical leaks from disgruntled officials with supportive comments.

Much as Clinton's aides anticipated, experts were used by the press as independent arbitrators. As print and broadcast news worked to identify the critical issues and make sense of leaks about White House policy debates, the media's use of experts rose from 3 percent of sources cited on health care in February 1993 to about 6 percent between May and September 1993. This peaked at 14 percent during the lull in policy discussions in December 1993 when the press tried to size up the looming debate in Congress. During 1994, the media turned to experts again as congressional debate intensified in order to make sense of different reform proposals and to assess the consequences of failing to pass any reform; experts accounted for 9 percent of sources compared with the noticeably lower attention to providers.

The media's use of administration officials and experts during the Clinton reform effort was consistent with previous reform episodes, though less frequent. Jimmy Carter's promotion of health reform elevated administration officials to an unrivalled position, accounting for 35 percent of all sources cited on health care in 1977. No other source came close. Government officials were again relatively heavily cited during the 1981 debates over cutting health costs (constituting 20 percent of all sources). But Reagan's disinterest in expanding government involvement in health care coincided with a dramatic decline after 1981 in the use of administration officials. This bottomed out at below 10 percent of news sources on health care in 1984 and 1986. The push for catastrophic insurance, which was spearheaded by HHS, propelled executive officials back into favor in 1987, when they again were 20 percent of the sources cited.

Health policy experts in the 1990s were not the media darlings that they were in the past. Figure 6.4 makes clear that expert sources were used more heavily during Clinton's reform push than Carter's but noticeably less than in the 1980s. With Reagan avoiding health reform and focusing on cutting costs and government spending, the press turned substantially to experts between 1983 and 1986, when the lull in government activity prompted the press to frame health issues in terms of their national consequences.[10] Indeed, experts briefly eclipsed executive branch officials as sources in 1984 and 1986 before falling off as government activity resumed.[11]

Sensing the declining press interest in policy experts during the 1990s, Yale health policy specialist Theodore Marmor (1995) longingly contrasted the media's heavy reliance on legal experts in covering the O. J. Simpson murder trial with their scantier use of health policy specialists to sort out the Clinton health reform episode. The result, Marmor asserts, was that Americans were left ill-informed about health reform even as they were "treated to an extraordinary public education in the most complicated corners of our law" (496).

New Developments

Media observers have loudly warned that journalists themselves (reporters, columnists, and commentators) have been increasingly inserting their own commentary and interpretations into their reporting and forgoing standard sources as well as the actual words of political actors themselves (Cappella and Jamieson 1997; Jamieson 1992; Patterson 1994; Steele and Barnhurst 1996). The intrusion by reporters has augured, it is claimed, an era of unprecedented media domination, which has profoundly distorted political reality. Summarizing its analysis of press coverage of elections, one study concludes that "the more candidates speak in campaign media, the more positive the messages, and the more journalists speak, the more cynical the tone" (Just, Crigler, Buhr 1999, 38).

Our study confirms some of the complaints of the media critics. We compared the attention devoted to the standard news sources (government officials, experts, advocates, and others) with the prominence given to the unattributed narration of reporters and the observations offered by commentators and columnists.

Figure 6.4 shows that the propensity of AP journalists to offer their own interpretation steadily increased since the mid-1980s.[12] Journalists themselves were the second most popular source in print and broadcast coverage in 1993–94; only the combination of the Clinton administration and Democratic members of Congress inched above the over-all attention to reporters' own comments. From the longer term perspective of AP reports since 1977, journalists' comments displaced the attention that had been given before 1993 to health policy experts, health care providers, advocacy groups, and business representatives.[13]

In addition, the statements of AP journalists regarding the Clinton plan were predominantly negative, with negative messages outstripping positive ones two-fold for most months. One of the highest levels of negativity occurred in September and October 1993 when opponents of reform had yet to launch their assault. Journalists who emphasized political strategy and conflict were especially inclined to insert their interpretation and commentary.[14] Our analysis confirms (at least partly) that journalistic commentary is increasing and that it tends to be critical.

We would offer, however, three qualifications to the charge of journalistic dominance. First, reporters' own comments did not monopolize coverage of health issues even in 1993–94. In both the AP reports for 1993–94, as well as in print and broadcast news where journalists were most prominent as sources, coverage was still dominated by political actors—Republican and Democratic members of Congress, Clinton, and administration officials. Figure 6.4 starkly illuminates the Democrats' more than three-fold edge over journalists. Additional analysis, which is not presented, indicates that the volume of coverage devoted to comments by AP journalists in the 1990s had risen since the 1970s, but that each citation of politicians and political activists still received more space.[15]

Second, the prominence of journalists on health care issues during 1993–94 was not unprecedented. Journalistic commentary in AP reports peaked during each of the reform episodes, with a slightly larger proportional increase in 1987 than 1993: journalistic sources rose from 2 percent in 1982 to 5 percent in 1987; but the increase to 9 percent in 1993 represented less than a twofold jump from the previous peak in 1987. The level of media commentary in the 1990s is an extension of a long-standing trend rather than a completely new development.

Third, journalists tended to be guided by real political dynamics. During 1993–94, print and broadcast reporters relied on their own commentary when authoritative government officials and other newsmakers were less active, and they withheld their commentary when political and policy activity on health care intensified. The appearance of journalists as sources peaked at 30 percent in June 1993 when the Clinton White House put its reform efforts on hold in order to focus

on its imperiled budget legislation. With no new and tangible developments, journalists offered their assessments and interpretations. In contrast, they refrained from offering their own commentary when political
events flared up—when Clinton launched his plan, when he gave his
1994 State of the Union address, and when legislative activity heated
up in 1994. (Journalists as sources reached their low in August 1994.)

POLLS AND PUBLIC OPINION   Observers of the media have increasingly claimed that public opinion polls have become a large and growing presence in election campaigns and policy debates. Journalists, it
is charged, have turned to polls as sources in order to offer their own
interpretations and forego the job of tracking down standard sources
(Jamieson 1992; Patterson 1994, 81; Frankovic 1998). One study found
that news organizations were more inclined to report polls on controversial social issues than on less salient issues of particular concern to
elites like U.S. foreign policy (Bennett and Klochner 1994).

    Public opinion, however, was not especially prominent in media cov-
erage of health care. References to polls and public opinion made up
less than 3 percent of all health care sources in AP reports and print
and broadcast news coverage. We also found no evidence that journalists used polls more frequently when they reported on political strategy
and conflict. The relatively infrequent references to public opinion and
polls clustered far more in 1993 than during 1994 when the legislative
fireworks erupted.

    Instead of constituting a regular source (as presumed), polls were
infrequently cited in health care reporting. Polls provided the means
for charting major changes or fluctuations in Americans' thinking,
which then fed back into the political struggle to "win" public support.
Indeed, we argue in our conclusion that public opinion should be
treated as real news, and it should receive greater and more thoughtful
attention as a way to evaluate the democratic responsiveness of government officials.

THE POLITICAL CYCLE OF JOURNALISTIC SOURCES   Two predictable
patterns emerge from our analysis of the media's sources in health reporting since the 1970s. First, the press disproportionately used, as
its sources, authoritative government officials and others influential in
health care whose institutional position provided them with the capacity to affect or determine future events. The dominant sources during
divisive health policy debates were the president, administration officials, and members of Congress. Variations over time in the selection

of these sources (as opposed to others) reflected developments in the lawmaking process. On generic, nonreform issues related to the state of health care, journalists were more likely to cite health experts as well as representatives of health providers, insurers, and businesses than government officials.

It is important to distinguish between the domains of institutional power. Our analysis suggests that the nature of the issues that the press covers affects what set of institutions are most likely to determine their outcome, and this influences the selection of sources by the press.

Second, press coverage of contentious health reform debates produced an expansion of the range of viewpoints that journalists reported. Members of the opposition party in Congress (e.g., Republicans during the Clinton campaign) and health care providers tended to receive more notice in press accounts during periods of often acrimonious reform debate than otherwise. Despite the efforts of the president and his partisans to dominate media coverage, dissenting voices were still loudly reported (though less extensively).

One notable change over time was the declining use of policy experts in news reports. This may reflect the increasing political polarization and the greater press attention to chronicling the outbreak of conflict among government officials rather than to delving into the substance of the policy issues themselves.

The Acceleration in the 1990s

Perhaps, the most striking feature of media coverage from 1977 to 1994 was the *degree of change* both in the frequency that journalists themselves appeared as sources and, especially, in the media's use of strategic framing during Clinton's first two years in office. Although not unprecedented, strategic framing and journalistic commentary peaked at levels in 1993–94 that significantly exceeded any previous high in the AP reports.

Why did this occur? The dominant account points to a common cast of culprits: the White House's flawed political judgment in locking journalists out of the task force process may have fueled the perception of secrecy and triggered the press's watchdog instincts; the congressional and administration officials who betrayed Clinton by leaking damaging information about internal debates provided journalists with a grisly story that seemed likely to titillate audiences; and Clinton was politically vulnerable to Republican attacks after winning office with a mere 43 percent of the vote. The combination of tactical errors by the president, an unwelcoming political situation, and the media's economic and professional incentives may simply have made 1993–94 a unique period.

We disagree. Although these were obviously contributing factors, the changes in press behavior had already begun before Clinton's first term. The acceleration of strategic framing and journalistic commentary was not simply a product of the unique personalities and immediate situations that weigh so heavily in most accounts of Clinton's health reform effort. Figures 5.3 and 6.4 show that the appearance of strategic frames and journalistic commentary had already dramatically risen by the 1987 reform episode. The escalation of strategic framing, which has been the leading criticism of the press (especially of its handling of the Clinton reform episode), rose dramatically in 1992—one year before Clinton was even inaugurated.

The evolution of media coverage of health care issues only makes sense within the context of changes in the structure of American politics. The usual list of institutional suspects for failed reforms—America's constitutional system and its comparatively weak two-party system—did not dramatically change in a way that would explain the rapid evolution of the media's behavior.

The take-off in strategic framing and journalistic commentary was preceded and, in our view, substantially caused by a cluster of significant changes in the structure of American politics since the 1970s: the expanding independence of individual legislators, the proliferation of national interest groups and their use of money to purchase advertisements, and, especially, the widening political polarization within Congress.

Chapter 2 suggested that ideologically extreme legislators in both parties replaced legislators who had consistently taken more moderate positions on a range of issues. As politicians increasingly perceived benefit from pursuing policy goals favored by themselves and their partisan and interest group supporters, the ideological distance between each party in Congress (especially over the responsibility of government) steadily widened during the late 1970s and then again in the late 1980s and the 1990s (fig. 2.3). By the 1990s, congressional Democrats and Republicans, and national politics in general, were more divided over the government's responsibility than in any period since the Second World War. Politicians who were intent on pursuing policy goals attempted to mitigate the risk of alienating centrist opinion by discouraging voters from monitoring their positions and by crafting their presentations to "win" public support for their desired policies. Debates over health care became one battlefield in a full-scale war among legislators and the major political parties over the responsibility of government.

The increase in strategic framing and incidence of journalists inserting their own commentary was a product of genuine changes in the behavior and strategy of government officials in the executive and legislative branches who wield authority over public policy. The rapid escalation of conflict among authoritative government officials in the Democratic and Republican parties came before and contributed to the acceleration of strategic journalism in AP reports since the 1987 health reform episode. The systemic shift toward polarized policy debates also explains why print and broadcast coverage in 1993–94 cited the advocates and critics of health reform as bickering and promoting their own strategic interests.

It is telling that press reporting on the significant push for national health insurance during Richard Nixon's second term—before the current era of ideological polarization began—was apparently neither extensive nor especially acrimonious.[16] After 1987, however, journalists represented or "indexed" the debate on health care reform by conveying the genuinely wide disagreement among authoritative government officials and the elaborate efforts of government leaders (in collaboration with their supporters) to craft their actions and public presentations.

Representation but Not without Distortion

The media's coverage of health issues has generally represented the changing content and intensity of health policy debate among authoritative government officials, but it has certainly not precisely mirrored what has unfolded. The modern news media are unlikely—for clear and understandable reasons—to simply mirror political events or mimic the words of policymakers. Journalists and editors exercise their own standards of quality and interest (Cook 1998).

A variety of factors explain why journalists do not simply parrot the statements of partisans and political activists. Journalists may discount the statements of political activists as part of a highly orchestrated political strategy in an increasingly polarized environment. With political activists in the 1993–94 reform debate openly plotting elaborate plans to manipulate their public presentations, journalists viewed the political angles of Clinton's actions and those of his opponents as revealing as the content of their actual statements.

Journalists implement the norm of "objectivity" by reporting "both" sides of a story on the assumption that "facts" lie somewhere between competing claims (Tuchman 1972). Clinton's statements, for instance, were never likely to be reported fully because journalists were also covering comments and actions by administration officials, other Democrats, health care providers, and the various opponents of health care reform. News reporting is also influenced by journalists exercising professional judgment regarding the appropriateness of different sources. For instance, journalists chose business representatives, health care providers, and health policy experts more often than President Clinton to comment on health care costs, presumably because they judged them better prepared to evaluate this issue.

In addition, political reality may be distorted because economic pressures to draw audiences create incentives for journalists and editors to emphasize political conflict and strategy as an entertaining way to present an otherwise dull policy debate.

Alternatively, the media may fail to mirror reality because political activists have successfully manipulated them. The calculated strategy of health reform opponents to emphasize government bureaucracy may account for the failure of the press to report fully Clinton's public statements on critical issues such as health care costs. (Chapter 3 indicated that controlling health costs was Clinton's primary motivation for pursuing health reform and that at times he devoted extensive public comments to it against the advice of his political advisers.)

There are ample reasons, then, for not expecting the media to closely mirror political developments. We investigated the precision of media coverage through a fine-grained comparison of the health issues and frames that Clinton used in his public statements (see chapters 3 and 4) with media coverage in the print and broadcast reports in 1993–94. Media coverage in each month was compared with Clinton's statements with regard to five critical issues: his own plan, alternative plans, access to health care services, health care costs, and quality of care. We made three sorts of comparisons between Clinton's statements and press reporting: we examined whether the volume of press coverage reflected the overall attention that Clinton gave to these issues; whether it communicated Clinton's positive or negative tone (i.e., the issue negativity); and whether the press reflected the type of framing that the president posed in his own statements.

Media Representation

We found that the media generally reflected Clinton's statements but departed from them in certain respects. For three of the five most widely reported issues, the media quite closely reported Clinton's selection of issues, the relative emphasis he gave them, and his negative or positive tone. Reporters accurately reported the president's emphasis and positions supporting his own plan, critiquing the alternatives, and emphasizing the need to improve access to care.[17] The media's accuracy, then, was strongest on reform issues for which the president was a central government authority.

Our findings qualify a more general criticism of the news media for neglecting the substance of policy in its rush to cover political conflict and strategy (Jamieson 1992; Cappella and Jamieson 1997). Our analysis of media framing of health policy tracked not only whether the press used a strategy or a national problem frame but also whether it by-passed both in favor of covering specific substantive policy issues. This allowed us to analyze directly whether the press's presentation of a particular frame detracted from its coverage of the substance of policy issues. Figure 6.5 partly confirms the charges of media critics: substantive coverage generally declined during the four reform episodes—1978–79, 1981–82, 1987–89, and 1993–94.

But figure 6.5 reveals that overall the charges are overstated, according to the case of health care reporting. The proportion of press

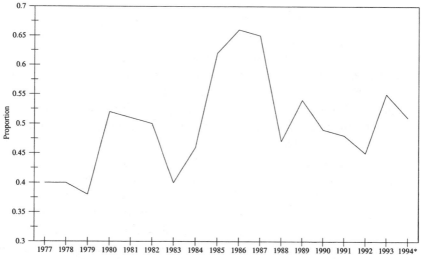

Figure 6.5   Proportion of AP Coverage Focusing on Substance of Health Care Policy, 1977–1994

Source: Compiled by authors; see appendix 3 and text.
Note: The proportions are calculated with mentions of policy substance for each year as the numerator and the total number of mentions per year as the denominator.
* Coverage ends in September 1994.

attention devoted to the substance of health care issues has, in general, risen over time. Proportionately, substantive press coverage was 25 percent greater or more in the 1990s than in the late 1970s: it rose from about 40 percent to over 50 percent (fig. 6.5), even though it declined after the 1987 debate and during the highly partisan debate in 1994. We find no support for the proposition that substantive media reporting has faded or nearly disappeared in the case of health care coverage.

Media Distortion

Clinton initially embraced health reform to lower health care costs; once in office he devoted significant time to discussing the issue against the advice of his political advisers. Yet seasoned observers of the media and health policy criticized the president for failing to address the cost of health reform and how to pay for it (Hamburger, Marmor, and Meacham 1994, 37). They failed to hear the extent of Clinton's public positions on costs (and quality) in part because the press did not extensively report them. We found a positive statistical relationship between Clinton's public statements on the cost and quality of health care and the press's reporting about them, but the correlation was only a weak one.[18]

The reluctance of the press to air fully Clinton's statements is consistent with journalists exercising judgment on the appropriateness or the authority of sources on different issues. As we found earlier, the press devoted only half as much attention to Clinton's comments on such generic health issues as cost and quality as they gave to his statements on proposals for government reform. They were far more likely to turn to health policy experts and representatives of business and health care providers on general health issues than on reform issues. Clinton's authority within government equipped him with significant influence to advance health reform but did not distinguish him in terms of his analytic powers regarding the actual operation of the health care system. Business, providers, and experts were far better positioned here because they regularly administered and studied the system's operations.

In addition, the media did not mirror Clinton's framing of health care issues. Clinton's overall framing of reform issues did not change appreciably, while the media's did.[19] The media's representation of genuine political conflict and strategizing exaggerated its actual proportions. The stunning eightfold jump in strategic framing from 1991 to 1994 overplayed the magnitude of actual political changes (fig. 5.3).

Our findings of media exaggeration are confirmed in previous research.[20]

Explaining Media Exaggeration

The media's exaggeration of political and policy developments stems from several factors. First, the everyday routines of the press—especially its indexing of government debate—make it vulnerable to missing or not extensively covering significant real-world changes that elude the attention of government officials. AIDS was one example, which we discussed earlier. Another was health care costs. After Carter's proposed remedies to growing health care costs, national expenditures as a percentage of gross domestic product continued to rise to a point in the 1990s that was 75 percent higher than that of the late 1970s. Yet, the relative attention that the press devoted to these costs dropped from about 45 percent in the late 1970s to 15 percent during the 1990s. The decline in press coverage of costs corresponded with the decision of prominent policymakers not to make costs their primary focus. Except for Reagan's cuts in 1981, Presidents Reagan and Bush failed to initiate a major proposal to control rising health care costs. Even Clinton's plan, which originated as a means to control costs, ended up making expanded benefits and universal health insurance its primary public objectives.[21]

Precisely because the media do index authoritative policy debates, they are prone to miss real-world events that government officials also neglect. The press selectively exercises its watchdog responsibility; its vigilance is often a function of significant actions or disagreements by authoritative government officials—without them the watchdog may not bark.

Second, the combination of systemic political changes (increased polarization, interest group proliferation, and other factors) and technological developments encouraged media exaggeration. Political polarization occurred at a time when the press had greater capacity for scrutinizing and reporting. Since the Second World War, the previous high in polarization occurred in 1947, when President Harry Truman faced a contentious Republican-dominated Congress in the first return to divided government since Franklin Roosevelt took office. What sets the 1990s apart is that polarization and other political developments have coincided with advances in communication technology and the public's reliance on the press and especially television (and, for some, computers). Advances in media technology since the 1960s created more opportunities for journalists to reach an unprecedented number of Americans with reports on political polarization and other developments when they emerged.

Distortion and Representation

Neither the analysis presented in this chapter nor our earlier comparisons of reform activities and media coverage support the claim that the press distorts reality beyond recognition. We found that press coverage generally represented real changes by increasing the volume of coverage devoted to health care reform, by changing the policy content of its report, and by altering its framing of health issues. There was a clear relationship between Clinton's public statements and the press's reports about them, with the greatest correspondence occurring for three of the most widely covered reform issues.

Nonetheless, journalists magnified or overplayed certain aspects of real-world developments; the crafted presentations of politicians may themselves end up being shaped further by journalists. The efforts of the press to unmask the very real strategic calculations of politicians may magnify the conflict imbedded in the statements of their news sources or lead the press to neglect political developments that are considered to lack strategic potential to succeed. For instance, the press devoted virtually no coverage to the single-payer approach to health care reform despite its large contingent of congressional supporters; its poor prospects for passage may have discouraged coverage by reporters who were concentrating on the fight over the Clinton plan.

Conclusion

Few political observers doubt the overwhelming power of the press to drive American politics and policy debates. The media have been crowned the new leaders of contemporary public affairs. Ample research emphasizes the independent influence of the press in setting the policymaking agenda and in artificially imposing their preoccupation with political conflict and strategy on otherwise substantive policy debates (see chapter 2).

Missing in such media-centered accounts, however, are the powerful and real political and policy-related forces that drive press coverage. Partly because of problems with how the press has been studied, media observers have not given full weight to the original political impetus for media coverage.[22] *Emphasis on the news media's subtle effect in incubating issues has diverted attention from the larger effect of political and policy developments on the press's behavior.*

Our most consistent finding is that the evolution of policy deliberations among authoritative government officials and other influentials
is represented or indexed in the volume and content of press reports.
The periodic surges in health policy debates and the systemic shift toward polarized politics changed first, and these bear substantial and
most likely primary responsibility for parallel changes that occurred in
the news coverage of policy issues, in the strategic as opposed to the
national problem framing of the coverage, and in the selection of
different sources. Bringing politics back into the study of the press is
essential to making sense of the content and character of media coverage and how this coverage feeds back into policy debates.

Our findings suggest two new directions for studying the impact on
press coverage of political and policy developments involving authoritative officials. First, it is important to examine more fully and systematically the nature and development of the political system, and to
connect these systemic changes to variations in the volume and content
of press coverage (Bennett 1990; Alexseev and Bennett 1995). Fundamental historical changes since the 1970s such as increasing ideological polarization, individualization within Congress, and the proliferation of national interest groups and their well-funded campaigns on
behalf of policy positions should be studied for their impact on strategic framing by the press and other aspects of news reporting.

One result of the relative inattention to the nature of political dynamics is the tendency to blur the differences in press reporting on
policy debates as opposed to election campaigns (e.g., Jamieson and
Cappella 1998). Our research on health care reporting between 1977
and 1994 shows, for instance, that political strategy and conflict may
not be chasing out news coverage of substantive policy issues as seems
to be the case in election reporting. In addition, while campaign coverage is often characterized as "negative" because of its focus on the
"horse race" or political battle, we found that health care issues were
portrayed more in positive and constructive terms than negative ones.

Second, as we suggest below, the media represent or (as Bennett
[1990] puts it) index debates among authoritative officials, but press
reports also feed back into the political process. Political polarization
and the maneuvering of the Clinton administration, its supporters, and
the opponents of reform instigated the press's exaggerated focus on
strategy and conflict, which politicians reacted to by intensifying their
efforts to disseminate their "message" and, in the case of the White
House, to install a "war room" in anticipation of further media scrutiny. The media feedback effect suggests that even while political developments drive press coverage, news reports also influence the percep-

tions and evaluations of government officials and other establishment figures.

Journalists themselves are now contributing members to the political cycle of media reporting. In representing politicians' presentations, the press inserts its own interpretations that stress both the strategy of government officials and other influentials and the personal stake of the audience. The ironic result of the media's feedback effect is that the already crafted presentations of politicians are amplified further by the press. The news media's efforts to reveal the genuine calculations of politicians magnify the strategic intentions of their news sources and lead the press to slight policy proposals, like the single-payer plan, that are considered unlikely to produce government action. The media's amplification of already fractious policy debates has important consequences for how the public perceives and reacts to the proposals of government officials.

Our discussion of the formulation of health care reform in chapters 3 and 4 showed that public opinion was not an influential participant but rather the target of politicians and political activists. The next chapter describes how public opinion was affected by the political strategy of crafted talk and press reporting on health care policy.

Chapter Seven

Talking Heads, Cautious Citizens

T he story of public opinion during Clinton's campaign for health care reform may seem anticlimactic at this point. Like the sinking of the *Titanic,* the plot and ending are now familiar.

President Clinton set out on his quest for health reform with public support. Health care reform zoomed to near the top of the public's agenda for government action in the early 1990s. By 1993, Americans' support for rebuilding the health system was at an all-time high and the public seemed poised to accept some (undefined) major plan for reform. After the first nine months of his presidency, the American public expressed substantial support for Clinton's plan, with 59 percent favoring it in one poll.

But in 1994 Clinton's efforts met with fierce political resistance and media reports of the battle. By the end of the year, public opinion had turned in a conservative direction, with support for rebuilding the health system down sharply and majorities opposed to the Clinton plan.

The most common explanation for the public's change of heart by September 1994 was that it had considered the president's plan and found it wanting. Like a deliberating jury, Americans reached a clear and decisive verdict after spending a year weighing the competing arguments regarding Clinton's proposals.

Jury watching was a common practice throughout the health reform debate as political observers waited for the public to reach its verdict. Johnson and Broder staked out the jury room and sifted periodic bulletins on the public's deliberations into their chronology of the health reform debate; at the end they announced that the public failed to reach a "ringing mandate for action" (Johnson and Broder 1996, 371). In the same spirit, the Public Agenda Foundation issued a series of reports that charted the public's tortured efforts to reach a verdict that would give a "full endorsement" to one of the leading proposals (Immerwahr, Johnson, and Kernan-Schloss 1992; Immerwahr and Johnson 1994, 3).

In their post-mortems over the public's failure to return a favorable verdict on health reform, journalists as well as Democratic and Republican leaders all pointed to the innate human tendency to protect one's personal self-interest and concluded that Americans calculated that the costs of reform to them personally were greater than the gains to them (Johnson and Broder 1996, 93, 334, 558). Although the backers of reform insisted that Americans misunderstood how the Clinton plan would serve their interests, they too agreed with their adversaries, as White House aide Harold Ickes put it, that "[y]ou can talk national interest until you're blue in the face, but [Americans] want to know: 'Is it going to help me or hurt me?'" (Johnson and Broder 1996, 264). Indeed, Stan Greenberg (the president's pollster) had repeatedly stressed to the president and his senior advisers that "people are focused above all else at a personal level, on their own well being; . . . That should be our primary communication focus."[1] By the end of 1994, the White House joined others in concluding that the public's protection of its personal stakes and its pocketbook sank health reform.

Legislators, according to this account, simply abided by the jury's verdict when they refused to pass any legislation in 1994. Members of Congress responded to the public's preferences and, in the end, to its opposition to reform. The claim that legislators responded to what Americans' wanted was embraced, as we noted in chapter 4, by a wide assortment of political observers and critics of Clinton's plan such as Newt Gingrich as well as by students of public opinion (Blendon 1994; Blendon, Brodie, Hyams, and Benson 1994; Brodie and Blendon 1995).

The treatment of the public as an idealized jury that deliberates (without outside influence) after both sides make their cases, profoundly misrepresents the nature of the process of public opinion formation and change. In the case of public opinion, the adversarial jousting of advocates and their witnesses and the loud noises outside the "jury room" profoundly affect the audience. Public opinion is in fact the target of intentional strategies by politicians and other political activists as they pursue their own goals and those of their supporters. Politicians and their allies perceive public opinion as a passive object that absorbs the messages that are most effectively crafted, most widely circulated, and most favorably covered in news reports. The behavior and strategies of politicians, in turn, generate predictable patterns of media coverage; chapters 5 and 6 showed that divisive government debates over competing policy proposals created press coverage that magnified the degree of political conflict and strategy on both sides. In short, the content of the information reaching the public about specific policies largely originated in the strategy of policy-oriented politicians to manipulate public opinion.

Although politicians dedicate their resources to moving public attitudes toward specific policies, their actual impact is more complex for three main reasons. First, the public's values and fundamental preferences have been quite stable over long periods of time (Page and Shapiro 1992; Kuklinski and Segura 1995). In particular, basic public preferences toward a range of policies from spending on education and medical care to maintaining Social Security and fighting crime have generally experienced little change since the 1930s. Americans' fundamental policy preferences are resistant, then, to simply following politicians' messages. Second, the public cannot "obey" politicians because the information and political messages they receive are often not uniform. Intense partisan disagreements over specific policies and the media's coverage of the battle produce conflicting messages and information for the public to evaluate; the public is not directed in one clear direction. Third, the public is not a blank slate; the public picks through this flood of information and messages, and it selects, rejects, and ignores the information and messages based on personal experiences and interactions with peers (Gamson 1992; Neuman, Just, and Crigler 1992). Indeed, the reactions of individuals themselves vary depending on their own education, political awareness, and political predispositions and partisanship (Zaller 1992).

The public's basic policy preferences, then, cannot be willfully manufactured by political actors. But its significant (though not exclusive) dependence on the press for information makes the public vulnerable to subtle processes of influence regarding its evaluations of specific policy proposals. After all, public support for specific proposals like Clinton's health plan declined nearly 20 percentage points during a year of intense partisan bickering. Our review of public opinion trends for social welfare issues found a twofold increase in the number of cases of opinion changes from 1984 to 1996 (Jacobs and Shapiro 1997a).[2] Policy debates have been producing changes in public opinion but these changes have generally been in the public's evaluation of specific proposals (rather than fundamental preferences and values). In addition, they have occurred over a relatively short period of time and have usually involved relatively mild shifts (falling in the 10 percentage point range), which suggests some underlying stability (Clinton plan excepted).[3]

The concept of "priming" accounts for public opinion change without falling back to simplistic notions of elite control. The public's evaluations and perceptions, the priming account suggests, are affected by the priority and the weight that individuals assign to particular attitudes and considerations already stored in their memories (Iyengar and Kinder 1987; Iyengar 1991; Neumann, Just, and Crigler 1992; Cappella and Jamieson 1997; Aldrich, Sullivan, and Borgida 1989; Lavine, Sullivan, Borgida, and Thomsen 1992). The pursuit by politicians of policy goals and orchestrated presentations and the resulting media reports of conflict and dueling strategies stimulate the public to put greater emphasis on its ambivalence toward "big government" and on the uncertainty, threat, and risk that policy proposals introduce to its sense of well-being and safety in the status quo (e.g., see Kahneman and Tversky 1984; Quattrone and Tversky 1988; Margolis 1996). Altering the yardsticks that the public uses in its evaluation affects both the public's favorable evaluation of specific policy proposals and its motivations to act based on collective considerations or more narrowly self-interested concerns.

We argue that the conflict among politicians over Clinton's health reform proposal and its coverage by the press soured public opinion on health reform in two ways. First, it depressed the public's preferences for the specific health reform proposals offered by Clinton and other policymakers. Second, the political battling, as conveyed by the press, altered the public's motivations. Although the public was initially motivated to support health reform out of concern for national conditions into 1993, the political firestorm that dominated media coverage in 1994 heightened Americans' personal apprehension about their own interests and pushed them toward opposing the Clinton plan or any reform.

Our analysis is divided into four sections. We begin by reviewing the changes that occurred in public opinion toward health care. In the subsequent two sections, we examine the impact of health policy debates and press coverage of them on public evaluations of reform and on the public's shift from collective to more self-interested motivations. Finally, we consider alternative explanations for opinion change related to the economy and ideology but find them wanting. Although we focus on the 1990s, we draw (when available) on historical evidence of public opinion, media coverage, and policy debates during the four major health reform episodes since 1977: 1978–79, 1981–82, 1987–89, and 1992–94.

Changes in Public Attitudes and Preferences

The Changing Public Agenda

Changes in the public's perception of the health care "problem" as well as its specific policy preferences mirrored changes in the debate over health reform among political activists, as these were conveyed through the media. The debate that consumed President Clinton's promotion of health reform initially prompted a rise in both the public's perceptions of the health system's flaws and the public's support for policy changes. These trends later reversed after 1993 as the opposition to reform intensified. The changes in public opinion toward health policy were evident not only during the health reform initiatives in the 1990s but also during earlier reform periods.

Changing Public Perceptions of the "Problem"

Public perception of the severity of the problems facing the country's health system rose when policymakers' actions and statements (reported in the press) indicated that the country faced dire conditions. Figure 7.1 tracks the percentage of the public from 1982 to 1994 who indicated that the nation's health system was so flawed that "we need to completely rebuild it" rather than make either "minor changes" or even "fundamental changes." (See appendix 2 for wordings of questions.) Public support for rebuilding the system dropped off after the 1981–82 reform episode by 9 percentage points between 1982 and 1987 (from 28 to 19 percent). But as policymakers' discussions of catastrophic insurance and other policy changes intensified in 1987, the public's clamoring for rebuilding the nation's health system rose noticeably by 10 points from 1987 to 1988 (from 19 percent to 29 percent). After receding during the policymaking lull of Bush's presidency, public support for reconstructing the system jumped strikingly by 18 percentage points from 1990 and through September 1993 (from 24 percent to 42 percent; only 6 percent indicated that "only minor changes are necessary," compared to 16 percent in 1990). The take-off in public support for reform followed Harris Wofford's Senate campaign, the

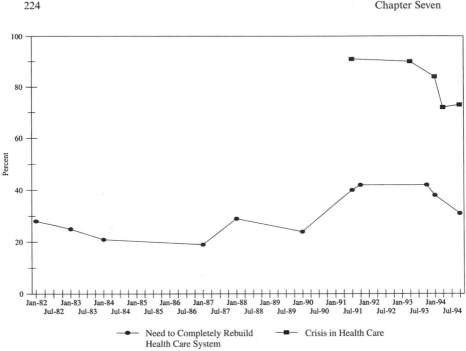

Figure 7.1   Perceptions of Health Care System, 1982–1994

Source: See appendix 2 for question wording and polling organizations.

1992 presidential race, and Clinton's decision to make health care reform a top priority of his presidency. (We discuss below how a sharp
rise in media attention to the national consequences of health issues
between 1990 and 1991 contributed to the rise in reformist sentiments.)

By contrast, the later stages of reform cycles witnessed a decline in
support for rebuilding the health care system. After the reform debates
in the late 1980s, this support fell off 5 percentage points by 1990 (from
29 percent to 24 percent). The public also clearly cooled after September 1993 when critics of Clinton's reform (including Democratic Senator Moynihan and Republican Senator Bob Dole) denied that the
country actually faced a crisis; these denials were widely reported in
press accounts. Just a year after the peak of public support for rebuilding the health system, it quickly dropped 11 percentage points (from
42 percent to 31 percent; support for "minor changes" increased
sharply from 6 percent to 19 percent). A similar pattern is shown in
figure 7.1 for responses to a survey question regarding whether the
public perceived a "crisis" in health care: responses of a "crisis" held
steady at 90 percent in 1991 and May 1993 but then strikingly dropped
fully 18 points in 1994 (from 91 percent to 73 percent).

Enduring Ambivalence toward Government

Americans' attitudes toward health policy are complicated by multiple and competing strands of thought. On the one hand, Americans have historically been conservative when asked to express their philosophy toward activist and expansive government. The role of government in providing for social and economic welfare (including health care and many forms of regulation of business and public safety) has long evoked deep ambivalence (Free and Cantril 1967; McClosky and Zaller 1984; Ladd 1985; Page and Shapiro 1992, 155–59; Nye, Zelikow, and King 1997; Jacobs 1993). The Vietnam War and Watergate crisis aggravated Americans' unease with government by sparking a sharp drop in confidence toward government institutions in the 1970s. On the other hand, these conservative philosophical leanings have existed alongside very strong support for specific government social programs—such as Social Security or Medicare—as well as regulation of business and other means of protecting the public from the ill effects associated with economic development.

Public attitudes toward the general principle of government responsibility for health care have been influenced both by short-term shifts in health policy debates as well as by long-standing beliefs, which have muted the public's overall level of support (Jacobs and Shapiro 1999). Figure 7.2 shows that Americans have been consistently divided when asked whether paying medical bills should be the "responsibility of the government in Washington" or something that "people should take care of . . . themselves." The public's dread of government was most apparent during the lull in health policy debate in the mid-1980s, when President Reagan railed against big government. The upsurge of debate over health reform in 1987, however, coincided with an 11 percentage point increase in support for greater government responsibility (from 46 percent in 1987 to 57 percent in 1991).[4] This support then dropped 9 percentage points between 1991 and 1994 (from 57 percent to 46 percent) in the wake of growing media attention to health care and increasingly shrill warnings from reform opponents beginning in the 1992 presidential campaign that reform would introduce "big government."

Figure 7.2 also presents the opinion trend for a more specific issue: "pay[ing] higher taxes and hav[ing] the government be in charge of the organization and delivery of health care services, or . . . pay[ing] more money out of your pocket directly to private doctors and hospitals, with government involvement only for people who cannot pay for their

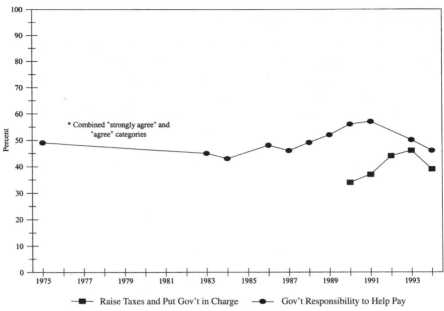

Figure 7.2   Opinion toward Government Role in Health Care, 1975–1994

Source: See appendix 2 for question wording and polling organizations.

own care." As the health reform debate heated up in 1992–93, public support for putting the government in charge peaked, rising 12 percentage points between 1990 and 1993 (from 34 percent to 46 percent).[5] It is a testament, though, to the power of Americans' enduring ambivalence to government that support for putting Washington in charge never reached 50 percent even in 1993. The onset of stiff political opposition to Clinton's reform in 1994 was associated with a clear 7 percentage point drop over the course of one year in support for putting the government in charge (from 46 percent to 39 percent). Reflecting the pullback of public support for government activism amidst the opposition of political leaders to Clinton's reform plan in 1994, public support for an employer mandate also fell 6 percentage points between February and June 1994 (from 53 percent to 47 percent); this contrasts further with responses to an August 1991 poll in which support stood at 57 percent (see fig. 3.1). Americans have also supported specific proposals to expand government involvement in health care during earlier episodes of health reform, though the available data are somewhat limited. During the 1981–82 reform debate, public support for the government to "do more" on "health measures" rose 10 percentage points (from 60 percent to 70 percent).[6] During the debate over extending catastrophic health insurance to the recipients of Medicare, the proportion of Americans who "strongly supported" it increased by 6 percentage points between September 1987 and May 1988 (Jacobs, Shapiro, and Schulman 1993, 430).

Preferences toward Spending on Health Care

Shifts in the debate over health policy also coincided with significant changes in public support for spending on health care. Figure 7.3 presents public beliefs on whether the country is spending too little on health. Public support for spending on health stagnated in the mid-1980s during the lull in policy discussions but rose significantly during the 1987–89 reform debate, jumping 16 percentage points between 1984 and 1989 (from 55 percent to 71 percent). Public support may have fallen a bit (though not beyond normal sampling error) in 1990 before rising again in the face of renewed debate. (The rise in 1993 may have been partly muted by Clinton's emphasis on containing health care spending.) As partisan conflict intensified in 1994, support dropped 9 percentage points from 1993 to 1994 to 61 percent, its lowest level since the mid-1980s.

Three surveys in September and November 1993 and July 1994

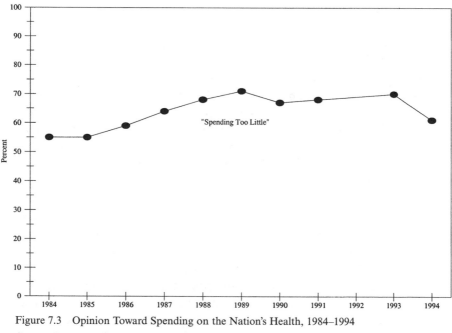

Figure 7.3 Opinion Toward Spending on the Nation's Health, 1984–1994

Source: See appendix 2 for question wording and polling organizations.

found that majorities of Americans were willing to foot the bill for increased government spending when directed at the specific objective of expanding health insurance coverage. During the heyday of Clinton's push for health reform in 1993, the proportion of the public reporting its willingness to pay higher taxes to cover the cost of providing "all Americans [with] health insurance that they can't lose no matter what" ranged from 61 percent to 64 percent. The onset of fierce opposition in 1994, however, undercut this support, which by July 1994 dropped 9 percentage points to 55 percent.

Americans' Change of Heart toward the Clinton Plan

The public's changing evaluations of President Clinton's plan followed the pattern evident in attitudes toward a range of issues (from rebuilding the health system to increased spending on health). The public's receptiveness to Clinton's plan hovered at its peak in 1993 (with perhaps an interlude during Clinton's Whitewater and foreign policy distractions in October or November), followed clearly by growing public uneasiness in 1994.

Figure 7.4 presents the trends in three separate public evaluations of Clinton's plan. The White House's energetic launch of its proposal in September 1993 was the high water mark of public support, though support stayed at the 50 percent range for the rest of 1993 (with a temporary dip in October).[7] Public backing nearly returned to its September high following the president's State of the Union address in January 1994. Increasingly open and fierce opposition to Clinton's plan, however, subsequently coincided with a steady fall in the proportion of Americans who favored his plan; by July 1994, support tumbled nearly 20 percentage points from its September 1993 high. The majorities or pluralities that had supported the Clinton plan in 1993 now opposed it: only 40 percent supported it and opposition to the Clinton plan jumped from 33 percent in September 1993 to 56 percent in July 1994.

The specific criticisms of Clinton's plan that reform opponents emphasized in 1994 also coincided with changes in public opinion. Figure 7.4 shows that Americans who feared too much government involvement stood at 40 percentage or less from Clinton's kickoff in September 1993 until his State of the Union presentation. But the unrelenting charges in 1994 that health alliances and new regulations were ushering in a new regulatory state prompted a 7 percentage point rise in fears of "too much government" (from 40 percent in January to 47 percent

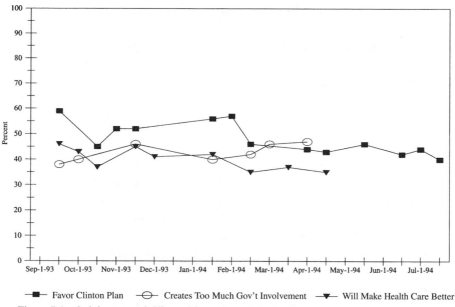

Figure 7.4   Opinion toward Clinton Plan, 1993–1994

Source: See appendix 2 for question wording and polling organizations.

in April) during the three short months after the president's presentation to Congress in January 1994.

A similar pattern is evident in Americans' judgment of whether Clinton's plan would "make health care in the United States better." With the exception of October, from September 1993 to January 1994 40 to 45 percent of the public believed that Clinton's plan would improve care. (In September, more than twice as many Americans believed that Clinton's plan would improve rather than worsen health services.) Once again, though, confidence in the impact of the president's plan dropped in the early months of 1994; it fell 7 percentage points between January and April 1994 (from 42 percent to 35 percent).

Media Coverage and Public Opinion

Changes in public opinion toward health reform mirrored changes in the media's coverage of debates among policymakers and political activists. The media influenced public opinion through the information it provided about the debates over health reform. It was precisely because of the public's dependence on the media for information that political activists concentrated on the press to convey their messages to

Americans (including the use of paid advertisements to communicate directly with the public).

Although we showed in chapters 5 and 6 that press reports on the actions and statements of policymakers were largely representative of health reform debates, the media did not precisely mirror reality. Rather, reporters, news analysts, and commentators accentuated political conflict and strategy through their selection of sources and interjection of interpretations and opinions.

The media's reports, as we have stressed, influence the public's evaluations of policy debates and political candidates through a subtle process of elevating the priority and the weight that the public assigns particular information, standards of judgment, and attitudes or considerations.[8] Studies by social psychologists of individual perception distinguish between the *availability* and the *accessibility* of information and public attitudes. They suggest that individuals have sets of multiple and enduring attitudes stored in their memories; these attitudes influence the judgment of individuals when they are accessed or retrieved from memory (Krosnick and Kinder 1990; Zaller 1992; Iyengar and Kinder 1987; Iyengar 1991; Neumann, Just, and Crigler 1992; Cappella and Jamieson 1997; Aldrich, Sullivan, and Borgida 1989; Lavine, Sullivan, Borgida, and Thomsen 1992; Jacobs and Shapiro 1994). While some attitudes are frequently and consistently activated from memory, others are temporarily accessed because of immediate environmental stimuli.

The mass media are a primary stimulus for accessing attitudes. Studies of individuals have found that the media's emphasis on a particular policy issue or piece of information may prime or temporarily increase the accessibility of attitudes related to this issue. Media coverage influences which attitudes and information individuals retrieve from their memory and incorporate into their judgments. For instance, increased media reports of the attacks on the Clinton plan for creating "big government" boosted the likelihood that many Americans' conservative attitudes toward government—based on underlying values and ideology—were activated and became the standard by which they evaluated health reform.

The media's consistent framing of health policy debates in terms of "issue negativity" and "political negativity" may have been especially influential in priming the public on health care. Issue negativity, however, was an unlikely candidate as a decisive influence on public opinion. News reports on substantive criticism about specific policy issues (such as Clinton health care reform proposal) were relatively stable over time; in addition, they were slanted in a positive direction, with more "pro" than "con" messages, and were therefore unlikely to have prompted the decline in public support for health reform (see figs. 6.1 and 6.2). Indeed, we found no systematic evidence that public opinion toward health care issues was significantly influenced by the media's issue negativity.

By contrast, there are compelling reasons to believe that the media's focus on political conflict and the strategies of politicians and political activists did affect public opinion. First, in chapter 5 we found that the media's use of strategic frames (as opposed to national problem frames) changed dramatically since the 1980s and especially in 1994 (see fig. 5.3).

In addition, an impressive set of studies have found that the media's use of strategic frames has major influences on individuals and the public at large. Joseph Cappella and Kathleen Hall Jamieson (1997) report that the media's focus on political conflict and strategy elevates the prominence of political wheeling-dealing in individual's evaluations of political candidates and policy proposals. The result of the media's strategic framing of recent political campaigns that Cappella and Jamieson examined and of the health reform debate in 1993–94 was to increase the public's cynicism.

The media's emphasis on political conflict and strategy may influence public opinion through two psychological mechanisms. First, the strategic framing of genuinely contentious policy debates may prime the public's cynicism as a standard of judgment in evaluating Clinton's health care reform plan, particularly in conjunction with attacks by Republicans and other opponents that emphasized fears of big government. Second, the strategic framing may highlight the risk of altering the status quo; this framing led individuals to become more risk averse toward their own health care as well as that of the rest of the nation. In general, the public's low trust in the political system may make Americans especially susceptible to adopting cynicism or uncertainty as criteria or yardsticks for evaluating major new government initiatives (Hetherington 1998).

Here we emphasize the impact of the media's framing on public opinion as we trace the changes in public opinion during debates about health care reform. We specifically weigh the relative influence of the media's national problem frame (its presentation of the national consequences of health reform) as well as its strategic frame. Although we did not directly study the impact of the media's national and strategic frames on individuals as Shanto Iyengar and Cappella and Jamieson have ably done, the shifts in aggregate public opinion do track changes in news framing. The media's framing of health care as a collective national concern (most notably in the latter half of the 1980s) provided Americans with a salient standard—the circumstances faced by country as a whole—for favorably evaluating the nation's need for health reform. By contrast, the shift in media coverage from national to strategic frames especially after 1993 elevated cynicism, confusion, and uncertainty as salient considerations in the public's mind. The result was to evoke doubts about government effectiveness and the personal threat or risks of health care reform.

Public Perception of Health Care Problems

Changes in the sheer volume of media coverage as policymakers devoted more attention to health reform raised the public's awareness of the health system's problems. There is a close relationship between the overall level of media reporting in figure 5.1 and Americans' ranking of the most important problems facing the country.[9] Prior to the mid-1980s Americans rarely ranked health care as among the nation's most pressing problems.[10] But with the sharp increase in media reporting on health care after the late 1980s, the public pushed it to near the top of its policymaking agenda; only pressing economic concerns ranked higher (Smith 1980, 1985a, and 1985b). By 1993, health care stood out as the public's first or second most important noneconomic problem (along with crime).[11]

The Impact of Strategic and National Problem Frames

The salience of health care as an issue in the press is just part of the story. Public opinion is influenced not only by the absolute *level* of press reports on health care but also by the *content* of media coverage and especially, as we argue, the media's attention to the political game as opposed to the national consequences of health reform (figs. 5.3 and 5.4). The impact of media framing is evident in three types of public opinion data.

First, the public's support for rebuilding the health system varied in tandem with changes in media framing as the press reacted to shifts in elite behavior. Figure 7.5 shows that greater media attention to the national consequences of health care in 1987–88 and especially in 1990–91 coincided with an increase in public support for rebuilding the health system, which we discussed earlier. The media's reports magnified genuine shifts in policy debates that were connected with Harris

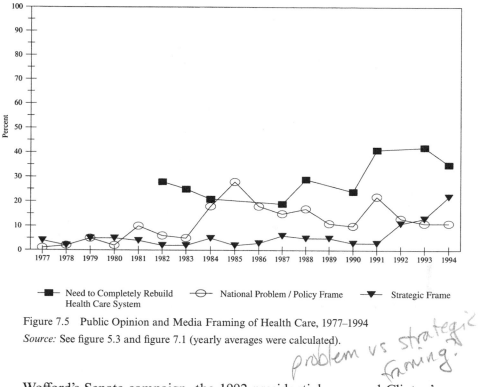

Figure 7.5   Public Opinion and Media Framing of Health Care, 1977–1994
Source: See figure 5.3 and figure 7.1 (yearly averages were calculated).

Wofford's Senate campaign, the 1992 presidential race, and Clinton's presidency. By contrast, the decline in national problem frames in 1981–83 and 1988–90 was associated with drops in support for a major overhaul of the health care system. The public's backing for systemic reform also fell off between the fall of 1993 and September 1994, which was precisely the same period that print and broadcast coverage elevated strategic framing to a series of new highs and dropped national problem framing to new lows (fig. 5.4). (Our analysis here was restricted by the unavailability of public opinion data on support for overhauling the health care system in 1985 and in the nearly two-year period from November 1991 to September 1993.)

Second, the media's presentation of health reform also affected the public's political evaluations. The media's deemphasis on national considerations and increased focus on political conflict and strategy in 1994 (fig. 5.4) coincided with a marked drop, as shown in figure 7.6, in the public's confidence that Congress would pass health reform. In addition, surveys in April 1992, October 1993, and April 1994 reveal a sharp rise during the turmoil of 1994 in the proportion of Americans who concluded that *neither* political party would do a better job in

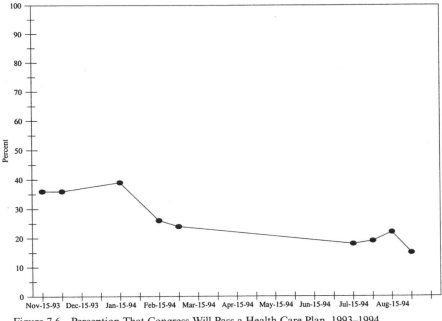

Figure 7.6   Perception That Congress Will Pass a Health Care Plan, 1993–1994

Source: See appendix 2 for question wording and polling organizations.

addressing health care problems. The Democrats were the major losers
from the media's reporting of the political fighting; the public's confidence in them fell 22 percentage points (from 48 percent to 26 percent)
while the proportion trusting neither political party jumped 22 percentage points (from 16 percent to 38 percent).[12]

Third, changes in the content of media coverage also corresponded
with the increased opposition to the Clinton plan. Figure 7.7 indicates
that the media's attention to the national policy significance of health
care showed increases four times in 1993 before falling off to its lowest
levels in 1994, though strategic frames also peaked in September 1993
and January 1994. The increases in the prominence of the national
policy frame preceded the public's highest levels of support for the
Clinton plan in September 1993 and January 1994. Due to changes,
however, in the debate at the elite level that the press magnified, the
media's strategic framing reached new highs in 1994 and national problem framing dropped to new lows in 1994. As press coverage changed,
the public's opposition to the Clinton plan increased.

In short, the media's shift from national policy to strategic frames
presented the public with a steady flow of reports about political pos-

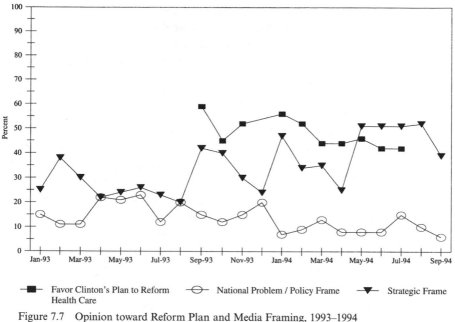

Figure 7.7   Opinion toward Reform Plan and Media Framing, 1993–1994

Source: See figure 7.4, chapter 5, and appendix 3 (monthly averages were calculated).

turing, fierce bickering, and uncertainty about the outcome of health reform. In the wake of this visibly intense partisanship and the media's spotlighting of the ensuing political conflict, there was a noticeable drop in the public's confidence in the Democratic Party to improve health care and in its support for the Clinton plan and for rebuilding the nation's care health system.

Collective versus Self-Interest

The impact on public opinion of changes in the political debate and media coverage are evident not only in the shifts in the public's attitudes already discussed but also in the evolution of Americans' basic motivations as they weighed the prospects of health care reform and the Clinton plan.

Simple intuition as well as theories of economists predict that individuals are motivated by self-interest (Downs 1957). As often claimed, it is only human nature for "pocketbook" concerns and personal circumstances to determine people's attitudes and behavior. For instance, Americans who are financially secure and confident in their ability to pay for medical care for themselves and their family should express unwavering opposition to paying higher taxes for greater government involvement in health care; they would bear the cost of new programs and receive minimal personal gains at best. Indeed, public opinion surveys on health care (and other social welfare issues) often find that the most affluent and least in need are, on average, less supportive of government assistance than the poor. Self-interest would also suggest that Americans who are highly satisfied with the medical treatment that they and their families received would not be very concerned about the experiences of others, and they would tend to resist government reforms that might interfere with their *own* care.

Such selfish-sounding motivations, however, are not innate attributes of human nature. Rather, the extent to which individuals draw on them can depend on particular circumstances and contexts. When it comes to their opinions on policy issues, elite debate and media coverage can influence the relative weight that individuals place on protecting their self-interest and promoting collective or national interests. Indeed, most studies of these influences have concluded that collective considerations are typically more evident than personal self-interest.[13] The decisions of voters, for instance, have repeatedly been found to result as much—or more—from evaluations of national conditions such as the state of the national economy as from their evaluation of their personal income or economic well-being; simple "pocketbook" voting, as a dominant influence, is largely a myth.

Collective considerations and self-interest are not, however, mutually exclusive motivations; Americans are likely to be affected by both. The relative balance of these influences can change as new conditions and circumstances develop, and new information communicated through and by the media can influence which motivations gain the upper hand.

Public opinion toward health reform and the Clinton plan were characterized by complex motivations that changed over time—shifting from collective to self-interested considerations over the course of the 1990s, as well as during earlier episode of reform. From 1990 to 1993, Americans consistently looked beyond their own personal situation to focus on national and collective benefits such as easing the burden of health expenditures on the country's economy and making altruistic efforts to provide others with quality care. During this period of public-spiritedness, the influence of personal costs on the public's preferences for reform were relatively weak, while expectations toward the potentially positive consequences of national reform were comparatively strong. The result was that Americans backed health care reform and the Clinton plan, even though many thought they themselves might be affected adversely as the health care for others improved. In late 1993 and 1994, however, collective and national considerations slipped as self-interest apparently became more important. As the media conveyed the genuinely fractious nature of policy debates, the public became increasingly fearful, if not just uncertain, of the personal costs of higher taxes and lower quality care, and many people switched from supporters (or fence-sitters) to opponents of the Clinton plan or any reform.

Although the relative weight of self-interest and collective considerations shifted, both influences remained evident; Americans were at no point either saints or scrooges. Even during periods of greatest national concern, the public harbored understandable apprehension regarding the cost and availability of health insurance and medical care for themselves and their families.

Public Satisfaction

Perhaps Americans' most deeply felt personal interest in health reform is to protect the medical treatment that they and their families receive. The personal satisfaction of Americans with their current medical care and general treatment has been extraordinarily high and stable over time. Figure 7.8 shows, quite strikingly, that since 1978 between 80

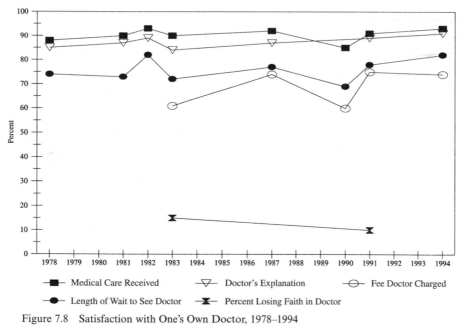

Figure 7.8   Satisfaction with One's Own Doctor, 1978–1994

Source: See appendix 2 for question wording and polling organizations.

percent and 90 percent of survey respondents expressed satisfaction
with their medical care, the explanations offered by doctors, and a host
of other aspects of their experience. (No comparable data are available
for 1993.)

The public's high satisfaction with its personal medical experience
highlights two critical tendencies, both of which suggest that Americans also harbor concerns about others. First, there is an unmistakable
gap between the public's personal contentment with its own medical
care and its dissatisfaction with the treatment that it perceives other
Americans receiving. In contrast to the enormous personal satisfaction
shown in figure 7.8, figure 7.9 reveals that a large percentage perceive
that others do not enjoy the same level of medical attention and satisfaction as they do. Specifically, the proportion of survey respondents
who perceived that other people's doctors are too interested in making
money hovered in the 60 percent range, rising to 69 percent in 1993;
the proportion of the public believing that doctors' fees are generally
reasonable averaged about a third but fell to nearly a quarter in 1994.
This level of suspicion about the financial pressures that doctors place
on their patients is two to three times greater than what respondents
reported about the conduct of their own doctors (though this comparison is not based on the same question wording). In addition, a steady

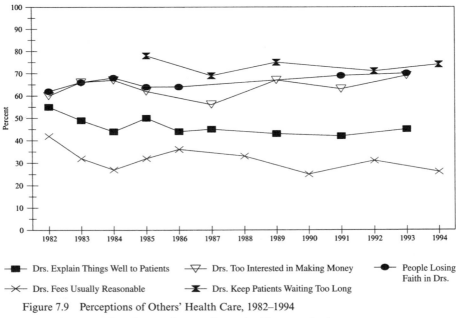

Figure 7.9   Perceptions of Others' Health Care, 1982–1994

Source: See appendix 2 for question wording and polling organizations.

60 to 70 percent also perceived that the faith of other people in physicians has been shaken, while just 10 percent or so consistently reported losing faith in their own doctor. What we find overall, then, is that the public has looked beyond its own personal experiences; Americans are neither uninterested in, nor inattentive to, the conditions and experiences of others.

Second, Americans supported health care reform *despite* their own personal satisfaction. While personal satisfaction has remained remarkably high and stable, Americans rallied behind the idea of government health reforms in 1981–82, 1987–88, and the 1990s. There is no evidence that low or noticeably slipping personal satisfaction was associated with rising support for health reform, which might indicate that Americans were motivated by narrow self-interest. The trends are apparently just the opposite: personal satisfaction was stable or even slightly rising during each episode of health reform. In the 1990s, for instance, Americans shifted toward greater support for rebuilding the health system, spending more on health, and passing Clinton's plan just as satisfaction inched upwards.

Although the evidence on the public's personal satisfaction is consistent with our argument about the significance of national considerations, individuals' perceptions of their own personal ability to pay for medical care indicate that self-interest was also evident. Figure 7.10 presents evidence of the public's confidence in meeting personal expenses for usual medical costs, major illnesses, and long-term care. The severity of medical care affects the overall level of personal financial confidence: Americans' sense of security in meeting usual medical costs has hovered around 70 percent, while their confidence is substantially lower for major illnesses and lower still for long-term care. Americans have been acutely aware of the personal cost of medical treatment, especially extensive and long-term care.

The public's confidence in paying for medical care changed during episodes of reform. Figure 7.10 indicates that there was a decline from 1990 to 1993 in the proportion of Americans who were confident they could pay for usual medical costs (from 77 percent to 72–73 percent), a major illness (from 65 percent to 54 percent), and long-term care (from 46 percent to 36 percent). We infer from these changes that the public, in the aggregate, was partly drawn to health reform efforts in the early 1990s by personal concern for alleviating the threat of financial pressures to pay medical bills.

Figure 7.10 also indicates that confidence in paying the costs of usual care, major illness, and long-term treatment rose as the reform campaigns heated up in 1981–82 and 1993–94 and the public soured on reform. (The significant exception to this pattern was the drop in confidence regarding usual care in 1978–79.) Between 1993 and 1994, the public became more confident that it would be able to pay for usual medical costs (from 73 percent to 75 percent), a major illness (from 54 percent to 58 percent), and long-term care (from 36 percent to 44 percent). This increase in confidence as reform debates escalated is consistent with growing personal concerns: faced with increasingly acrimonious debate in 1994 and media coverage of it, more Americans may well have concluded that the status quo was preferable to what might happen to them personally if the health care system was dramatically changed.

Public Concern for Others

The public's attitudes toward the national health system as well as the medical care of the poor and elderly also provide evidence that Americans were motivated by concerns about others up through 1993 before becoming more fearful of their personal stakes. This shift in the public's motivation may explain our earlier finding that changes in Ameri-

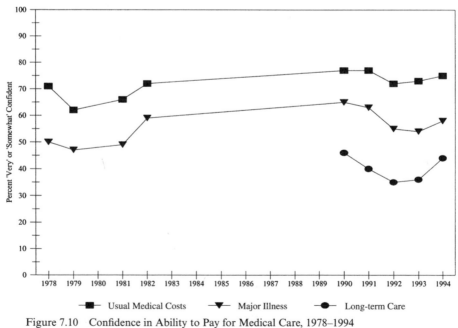

Figure 7.10   Confidence in Ability to Pay for Medical Care, 1978–1994

Source: See appendix 2 for question wording and polling organizations.

cans' support for rebuilding the health system paralleled the media's shift from national to strategic frames.

The increases in public support for rebuilding the country's health system during the 1987–88 and 1991–93 reform periods, which we showed earlier, coincided with a brief rise in support for catastrophic health insurance in the late 1980s and health care reform in the 1990s. This relationship provides circumstantial evidence, then, that the increase in support for changes in policy was connected to the public's concern with the overall health care system, not simply with its own directly personal needs. By contrast, the decline in support for reform during the end stage of the 1991–94 period corresponded with the declining popularity of the Clinton plan. Along with this was a waning concern for meeting a broad national need.

The public receptiveness to rebuilding the country's health system was echoed in its evaluations of whether the elderly and poor received needed medical care—a persuasive indicator of the public's concern for others who are most vulnerable to being excluded from the current health care system. Figure 7.11 indicates that the onset of the reform episodes in 1987 and 1993 coincided with increased public concern about people other than themselves. Public confidence that the elderly received needed medical care dropped 16 percentage points between 1985 and 1987 (from 52 percent to 36 percent) and 12 points between 1988 and 1989 (42 percent to 30 percent); it was still down 7 points in 1991 (34 percent) from its previous 1988 high. Similarly, the public's satisfaction with the treatment of the poor fell 10 percentage points between 1985 and 1988 (from 44 percent to 34 percent) and 9 points between 1990 and 1991 (from 34 percent to 25 percent).

The increases in concern for the poor and the elderly corresponded with increased support for health reform. The jump in public concern also overlapped with changes in media coverage. This was evident during the reform episodes in the mid-1980s, when the media's use of national problem frames increased to an historic peak in 1985 and trailed off 1987 still at a level that exceeded any high prior to the mid-1980s (fig. 5.3). The association between Americans' concern for the vulnerable and their support for reform during a period of the media's heavy national problem framing provides additional evidence that the public's support for reform was boosted by national considerations that were prominent in the press.

By contrast, the later stages of health reform witnessed declining concern for the poor and elderly. Public confidence that the elderly *do* receive needed medical treatment rose 6 percentage points between

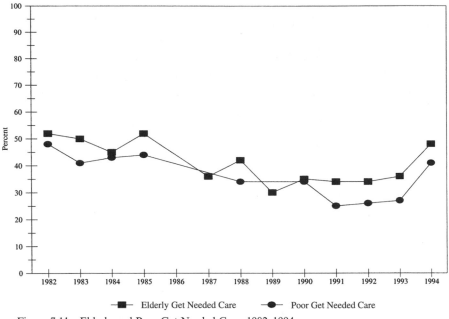

—■— Elderly Get Needed Care   —●— Poor Get Needed Care

Figure 7.11   Elderly and Poor Get Needed Care, 1982–1994

Source: See appendix 2 for question wording and polling organizations.

1987 and 1988 (from 36 percent to 42 percent) when legislation passed
to establish catastrophic insurance for Medicare's recipients. Changes
in public perceptions were especially noticeable from 1993 to 1994: the
public's belief that the elderly get needed medical care rose 12 percentage points (from 36 percent to 48 percent), and its confidence that the
poor would receive it increased 14 percentage points (from 27 percent
to 41 percent). This easing of concern during 1994 for the medical
treatment of those who were most vulnerable corresponded with falling support for health reform and increased media attention to the
political battle instead of the national consequences of health reform.
We infer from these patterns that the public's concern for others receded.

The Attractive and Unattractive Clinton Plan

There are two sets of evidence that link Americans' national concerns
to the peaks in public support for the Clinton health plan during from
the fall of 1993 to January 1994 (fig. 7.4) First, at the height of Americans' support for Clinton's proposal, their evaluation of the reform
plan's impact on them personally was negative. Figure 7.12 indicates

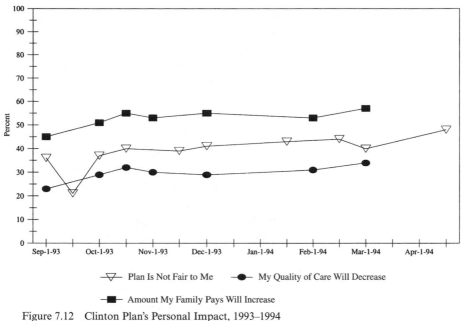

Figure 7.12   Clinton Plan's Personal Impact, 1993–1994

Source: See appendix 2 for question wording and polling organizations.

that during the peak of the Clinton plan's popularity during 1993 and January 1994, a fairly stable majority expected it to increase the amount they paid for health care and health insurance; sizeable proportions and even pluralities of Americans concluded that the administration's reform was not fair to them personally and would decrease the quality of their health care. Although a large percentage of the public expected their personal interests to be hurt, millions of Americans backed the Clinton plan, at least initially. This is not consistent with a public that consists of individuals who only think of themselves.

Second, responses to survey questions that asked people about the impact of the Clinton plan on the country as a whole reveal that in 1993 the public was much more optimistic about the effect of reform on others than on themselves. The proportion of survey respondents who expected reform to improve the health system and quality of care others received was twice as great as the proportion responding that reform would positively affect them personally. For instance, two ABC News surveys in September 1993 found that while 19 percent expected the Clinton plan to make the quality of their personal care better, 36 percent anticipated that the quality of care for "most Americans" would get better. A similar pair of Gallup surveys in October reported

that 28 percent of respondents believed they personally would be better off under the Clinton plan compared to fully 57 percent who expected a better outcome for the "country as a whole."[14] In short, the
public's expectation that other people would be helped by the Clinton
plan seems to have been an important consideration in its evaluation
of health care reform in 1993.

The fierce political conflict that erupted after January 1994 coincided, however, with a sharp increase in Americans' trepidation about
the impact of the Clinton plan on them personally. Figure 7.12 shows
that Americans' fear that the Clinton plan would boost what their family paid rose 12 percentage points in just the six months between September 1993 and March 1994 (from 45 percent to 57 percent).[15] In
addition, the public's anxiety that their family's quality of care would
deteriorate under the Clinton plan rose 11 percentage points after the
president's launch of his plan (from 23 percent to 34 percent).[16]

Finally, figure 7.12 also shows that by April 1994 there had been
a 12 percentage point increase in the proportion of Americans who
concluded that the Clinton plan was unfair to people like themselves
(from 36 percent to 48 percent). A solid core of the public that had
been optimistic about the fairness of the president's proposal was con-
verted into a clear plurality who feared that the plan would not be fair
to them personally. As this concern rose, support fell for the Clinton
plan in particular and also for the idea of rebuilding the health care
system.

Differences among Individuals and Groups

Our analysis up to this point has focused on the attitudes of the public
as a whole. Pinpointing Americans' motivations and the changes in
them require examining the attitudes of different segments of the public. Our examination of pertinent subgroups confirmed what we found
in investigating aggregate public opinion: in the lead-up to Clinton's
reform initiative from 1991 to 1993, the increased support for further
government involvement in health care appeared to be influenced less
by self-interest than by a concern for the health care of Americans as
a whole. By 1994, when the public reversed direction toward health
reform, the influence of national considerations fell off and self-interest
grew. The shift in the motivations of individuals and subgroups in 1994
showed the effects of the increased polarization of political activists
and the media's rising coverage of political conflict and strategy. Individuals reconsidered health care reform and apparently reflected upon
the impact of specific reform proposals on their own health care.

Figures 7.13 through 7.16 present evidence regarding the motivations of subgroups of Americans. Here we make further use of the data reported in figures 7.2, 7.10, and 7.11. Specifically, these figures track public attitudes toward putting the government in charge and paying more taxes based on how people evaluate the elderly's medical care and their own perceived ability to pay for long-term care, major illnesses, and usual medical costs.

Three patterns are evident in figures 7.13 through 7.16. First, the data *within* any one year present patterns consistent with the effects of self-interest. Comparing the *levels* of support in figures 7.13 through 7.15, we see that people who are most confident in their ability to pay for medical care show lower levels of support for the government providing medical services. Specifically, those who are very confident in being able to pay are, on average, about 20 percentage points less supportive of government intervention than those who are not at all confident.

We can also see a pattern of altruism or compassion, in figure 7.16, regarding the impact of the elderly's medical needs on support for reform. In all four surveys from 1991 to 1994, people who disagree that the elderly are able to get needed medical care report more support

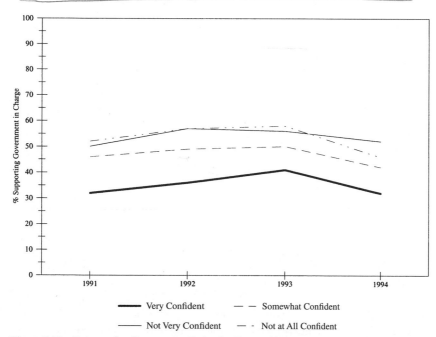

Figure 7.13   Support for Government Being in Charge of Health Care Services by Confidence in Paying Usual Medical Costs, 1991–1994

Source: See text and appendix 2 for question wording and polling organizations.

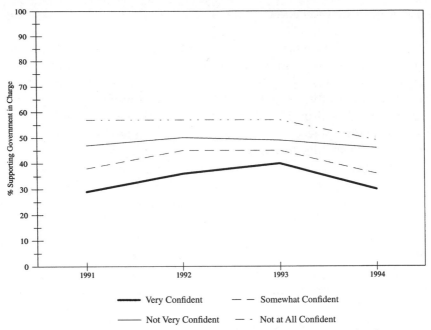

Figure 7.14   Support for Government Being in Charge of Health Care Services by Confidence in Paying for Major Illness, 1991–1994

Source: See text and appendix 2 for question wording and polling organizations.

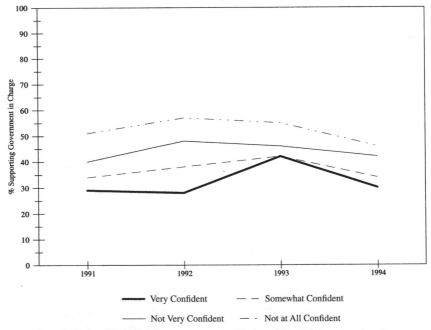

Figure 7.15   Support for Government Being in Charge of Health Care Services by Confidence in Paying for Long-Term Care, 1991–1994

Source: See text and appendix 2 for question wording and polling organizations.

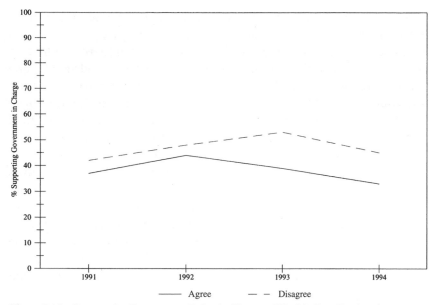

Figure 7.16   Support for Government Being in Charge of Health Care Services by
Perceived Ability of Elderly to Get Care, 1991–1994

Source: See text and appendix 2 for question wording and polling organizations.

for government provision of medical care than those who agree—on
average, a difference of about eight points. In short, the differences in
levels of support regarding financial confidence and appraisal of the
elderly's care reveal that self-interest and, to less of an extent, altruism
are persistently at work.

Second, although public opinion changed in a substantially parallel
fashion for the different subgroups in figures 7.13 to 7.16, the particular patterns of change are also indicative of how media coverage and
the political debate affected the motivations of different subgroups.
Figures 7.13 through 7.15 show that among survey respondents with
differing levels of confidence in paying for medical care, support for
putting the government in charge rose steadily from 1991 to 1993 before declining in 1994. What is striking is that nearly *all* the different
groups—from the very confident to the least confident—moved in the
same direction. For instance, in the trend for confidence in paying
usual medical costs (fig. 7.13), both the most and least confident became more supportive of government intervention up to 1993 and then
became less supportive in 1994.

The pattern of "parallel publics" results from everyone being moved
by the same influences, especially new information provided by the

media (see Page and Shapiro 1992, chap. 7). In the case of health reform, the general pattern of subgroup change in figures 7.13 to 7.15 is
consistent with the argument that the media's framing of health care
as a collective national concern from 1991 to 1993 provided everyone
with a common and highly salient standard for favorably evaluating
the country's need for health reform. When the media deemphasized
the nation's health care needs in 1994 and highlighted the political
battle, all segments of the public saw the issue differently and the threat
to one's self-interest became more apparent to everyone. Although we
find these patterns persuasive, we cannot directly analyze how changes
in the media's framing of health care affected individuals.

The third pattern in figures 7.13 through 7.16 solidifies our interpretation; it provides strong evidence that national concerns motivated
the shift in a liberal direction by 1993 and self-interest propelled the
conservative shift in 1994. Here we are especially interested in the *degree of change* across the different subgroups—that is, how much each
subgroup changed.

Increases in support for government providing health care services
from 1991 to 1993 were greater among those who were *more confident*
in their ability to pay for medical costs than among those who were
less confident in their ability to pay. For instance, as we see in figure
7.14, support for putting the government in charge rose 11 percentage
points among those most confident in paying for major illness (from 29
percent to 40 percent) and 7 percentage points among the "somewhat"
confident (from 38 percent to 45 percent); it remained unchanged (at
57 percent) among those who lacked any confidence, and it rose only
slightly among those who were "not very" confident (from 47 percent
to 49–50 percent).

The differences across the subgroups support the proposition of
public-spiritedness. The individuals who were most confident and who
changed the most were also motivated by self-interest to express the
least overall support for putting the government in charge. But these
same individuals who were personally confident in their own individual
circumstances must apparently have taken into account the needs of
the country and other Americans when they increased their support
for reform in 1993 more sharply than those less confident. Self-interest
could not have led to this disproportionate change in a liberal direction
among respondents who were most confident in their ability to pay for
their medical needs.

Public attitudes toward the elderly's medical care provide further
evidence that concern for others was at work in boosting support for

putting the government in charge from 1991 to 1993. Figure 7.16 indicates that those who thought that the elderly were not able to get needed medical care showed a greater increase in support for government provision of medical services (11 percentage points, from 42 to 53 percent, from 1991 to 1993) than did their opposites (7 points, from 37 percent in 1991 to 44 percent in 1992, but dropping back 5 percentage points to 39 percent in 1993). Americans were apparently motivated to shift their preferences in a liberal direction by their concerns about others—in this case, the vulnerable population of elderly.

The change in opinion from 1993 to 1994 is less clear but is still consistent with a shift toward self-interest during this conflict-ridden stage of the policy debate and media coverage. Although the changes in subgroup support for government activism in figures 7.13 to 7.15 are modest during 1993–94, they nonetheless indicate that those most confident in being able to pay for medical care reversed course a bit more that those less confident. For instance, in figure 7.14 support for putting the government in charge fell 10 percentage points among the most confident in paying for a major illness (from 40 to 30 percent) and 9 percentage points among the "somewhat" confident (from 45 percent to 36 percent); it declined by 8 percentage points among those not confident at all (from 57 percent to 49 percent) and 3 percentage points among those who were "not very" confident (from 49 percent to 46 percent).

Another Look at the Data

We have presented a diverse set of data from a large number of separate surveys to support our argument that the policy debate and press coverage produced a change during 1994 in the public's basic motivations—from the public's concern for the health care of others nationwide to a greater focus on self-interest. Our evidence, though, has been limited to two types. First, we have examined overall public opinion trends based on individual survey questions (e.g., figure 7.1 shows the total percentage perceiving a crisis in health care). Second, we have explored the influences on public opinion at the individual level by examining how two different opinions or perceptions are related to each other (e.g., figure 7.16 examines perceptions that the elderly were not getting needed medical care and support for government provision of medical services). What is needed, however, to confirm our findings and conclusions about the influences on public opinion is analysis that incorporates a *number* of possible influences on individuals and examines them *over time;* in other words, multivariate as well as longitudinal analysis.

The multivariate regression analysis that we and others have conducted converge on a conclusion that confirms our earlier interpretations (especially of figures 7.13 to 7.16). Prior to 1994, the perception of how others fared in the health care system was a strong and increasing consideration in the public's opinions toward health care policy, whereas self-interest was less important. In contrast, by 1994 the effect of self-interest became more apparent. (It is important to note that in the analyses we and others conducted, limitations with the data prevent direct and complete comparisons of collective versus self-interest considerations, taking into account all other relevant influences on public opinion.)

The survey data we used in table 7.1 to analyze the influences on public support for the government taking charge of health care services from 1991 to 1994 provided the best available measures of self-interest and collective concerns. To improve the reliability and validity of some of these measures, we constructed scales of the three separate measures of confidence in the ability to pay for medical care as well as the measures of satisfaction with one's own doctor and with doctors more generally, which taps the perceived experiences of other people. We focus here on the main variables in table 7.1 that bear on the influence of self-interest and collective concerns.[17]

We measured self-interest in five ways: whether individuals had a personal doctor; whether they were insured; whether they were satisfied with their own doctor's care; whether they had *not* visited a doctor recently; and whether they were confident in paying for their own medical care. These people had less to gain from government intervention and we would expect them to be less supportive of government provision of health care services. In contrast, we relied on three measures of collective considerations: evaluations of the health care provided by doctors, and the elderly's and the poor's ability to get needed care. Concern for others was inferred from individuals' unfavorable evaluations of doctor care and from perceptions of seniors and the poor as lacking needed care.

Two trends emerge between 1993 and 1994 (table 7.1). First, the magnitudes of coefficients for three of the five measures of self-interest increased in the expected direction from 1993 to 1994, suggesting a greater influence of self-interest. While no data were available for doctor satisfaction in the 1992 and 1993 surveys, its coefficient increased from 1991 to 1994 in the expected direction. Having health insurance

Table 7.1 Multivariate Analysis of Support for Government Being in Charge of Health Care Services, 1991–1994 (AMA/Gallup Surveys)

Independent Variables	Regression coefficients			
	1994	1993	1992	1991

	Dependent Variable, 1 = Support for government in charge, 0 = oppose			
Race (nonwhite)	.12**	−.01	.01	−.03
Sex (Female)	.06*	−.02	−.02	−.08*
Community (base = suburb)				
City	.05#	−.03	.05#	.03
Small town	−.01	−.02	−.00	.02
Rural area	−.03	−.07#	.05#	.10#
Age (base = 25−64)				
Age 18–24	.06#	−.02	.06#	−.02
Age > 65	.02	−.00	.00	−.01
Education	−.02#	−.01	.00	−.04#
Household income	−.01#	−.03*	−.00	−.01
Unemployed	−.01	.07#	.08#	.17*
Self-interest				
Have personal doctor	−.08#	−.05#	−.06#	
Insured	.05#	.04	.12*	−.00
Short time since last doctor visit	.02#	.01#	−.00	−.01
Satisfaction with own doctor care (scale)	−.05			−.02
Not confident—to pay for medical care (scale)	.05*	.04*	.10**	.07**
Collective concern				
Gen. unfavorable evaluation of doctors' care (scale)	.03	.07#	.13*	.10#
Perceive elderly not able to get care	.05#	.09*	−.04#	.03
Perceive poor not able to get care	.07*	.01	.06#	.04
Constant	.33	.45	.16	.21
R^2	.08	.06	.07	.08
N	1,081	1,102	1,110	677

Note: Omitted coefficients due to measures not included in that year's survey. Other variables controlled, but not shown, are region dummy variables for Pacific (base category): northeast, mid-Atlantic, south Atlantic, east south central, west south central, east north central, west north central, mountain.
#magnitude of the t (coefficient/standard error) is greater than 1.0, p > .05
*p < .05   **p < .01
Independent variables: sex, female = 1, male = 0; age, two dummy (0–1) variables for age 18–24 and age > 65 (base = 25–64); race, nonwhite = 1, white = 0; education, coded 1–6 (from less than high school graduate to some graduate work or degree); household income, coded 1–8 (from under $15,000 to over $100,000); community, three dummy variables for city, small town, and rural (base = suburb); region, eight dummy variables for northeast, mid-Atlantic, south Atlantic, east south central, west south central, east north central, west north central, mountain (base = Pacific); insured, have health insurance = 1, not insured = 0; have a personal doctor, have = 1, do not have = 0; short time since last doctor visit, five categories (from more than two years to less than six months); satisfaction with own doctor—scale based on five items (see appendix 2); not confident to pay for medical care, scale (based on the three items in figure 7.10); perceive elderly not able to get medical care (see figure 7.11, not able = 1, able = 0), perceive poor not able to get medical care (see figure 7.11, not able = 1, able = 0); general unfavorable evaluation of doctors' care, scale (based on five items in figure 7.9).

did not have the expected effect. (These results occur after demo-graphic and other variables are statistically controlled, as shown.) Second, the influence of two of our three measures of collective considerations declined from 1993 to 1994, with the exception being the perception of the poor's access to medical care.

The public's motivations prior to 1994, however, affected support for government activism in health care in two quite different ways. First, there is evidence that the effect of self-interest declined through 1993. Most notably there was a fall-off in the effect of confidence in paying for one's own medical care (especially from 1992 to 1993) and a slight (though statistically insignificant) drop in the effect of having a personal doctor. There was no effect of having recently been to the doctor, but from 1991 to 1992 those with health insurance became *more* supportive of government activism. However, the self-interest of the insured became more apparent in 1993 as the coefficient then dropped off.

Second, collective considerations boosted support for the government being in charge of health care prior to 1994. Individuals who perceived the elderly as needing care expressed much greater support for government activism in 1993 than in prior years. Increased support for government intervention also occurred in 1992 for those who evaluated doctors in general unfavorably and for those who perceived the poor as not able to get care.

The highly partisan debate and media emphasis on political conflict and strategy during 1993–94 influenced public support for government activism in health care not only by changing public motivations but also by increasing the prominence of partisanship and liberal and conservative ideology. While the surveys in table 7.1 did not include direct measures of these, we might consider race, gender, and community of residence as proxies for ideology and partisanship: nonwhites, women, and urban residents are typically more Democratic and liberal than whites, men, and noncity dwellers (Abramson, Aldrich, and Rohde 1999). The results suggest that ideology and partisanship became more influential: being a Democrat and liberal played a greater role after 1993 in boosting support for government activism, while identifying with the Republican Party and conservatism were more influential in 1994 in decreasing support. We cite more direct evidence for this interpretation below.

The multivariate results in table 7.1 are consistent with our earlier interpretation of the changing influences on public opinion of the health care reform debate, even though limitations in the data prevented a stronger test. Different methods and data sets converge on a similar conclusion: by 1994 personal interest appeared to matter more than it had earlier, whereas concern for the plight of others and the nation mattered less. These findings on the influences on public opinion toward health care policy are confirmed in research by other scholars.[18]

A study by Koch (1998), in particular, provides a compelling survey analysis of the effect of self-interest and ideological partisanship based on the 1984, 1988, 1992, and 1994 American National Election Studies (NES). He measured self-interest by studying the impact of an individual's disability and health insurance status on support for government as opposed to private provision of health insurance: the *un*-insured and disabled were expected to be more supportive of government-provided health insurance and less supportive of private health insurance.[19]

Table 7.2, taken from Koch's study, persuasively shows the increasing effect of self-interest in 1994 on support for *private* in contrast to nationally provided health insurance. (His dependent variable is support for private insurance.) Individuals who had *no* disability and those who had insurance were less supportive of government health insurance in 1994 than in 1984–1988 and 1992, suggesting the rising influence of self-interest.

Koch's analysis also confirms another impact on public opinion of the media's emphasis on political conflict and strategy. He shows that the effects of political partisanship and ideology were high or increasing (in the case of liberal-conservative ideology) in 1994, when the public became less supportive of government activism. Koch also found that the overall changes in and structure of preferences occurred most strikingly for the low and medium politically aware—not the most highly politically aware (data not shown in table 7.2).

Although the available data prevent a full analysis of what influenced public opinion toward health care policy over time, we are persuaded that the preferences and motivations of the public were determined by the policy debate and media coverage. The impact of politics and the press on public opinion is especially persuasive because evidence for it emerges both from our varied analyses of a large number of different surveys and from the independent research of other scholars.

Alternative Explanations

We have argued that political debate and conflict as well as the media's (exaggerated) coverage of it ultimately drove public opinion to oppose

Table 7.2   Determinants of Preferences on National Health Insurance Policy, 1984/88 to 1994

Independent Variables	Regression Coefficients		
	1984/88	1992	1994
	Dependent Variable = support for private insurance		
Equality	.11*	.25***	.30***
	(1.86)	(4.03)	(4.28)
Guaranteed job	.22***	.27**	.24**
	(7.99)	(9.43)	(7.76)
Services versus taxes	.26***	.14***	.22***
	(8.23)	(4.40)	(6.71)
Income	.18***	.04	.036
	(4.02)	(1.10)	(.959)
Own insurance	N.A.	.37***	.60***
		(2.90)	(4.11)
Partisanship	.12***	.18***	.15**
	(4.46)	(6.46)	(5.38)
Ideology	.02	.05	.10**
	(.73)	(1.52)	(2.92)
Female	.015	−.13	−.04
	(.172)	(1.48)	(.494)
Black	.48***	.30*	.08
	(3.13)	(1.97)	(.546)
Single	.08	−.02	−.16*
	(.82)	(.216)	(1.64)
Disabled	−.21	−.15	−.61**
	(.671)	(.681)	(2.65)
Constant	.54***	.02	−.062
	(2.16)	(.076)	(.150)
$R2$	.19	.26	.34
N	1,604	1,361	1,295

Source: Koch 1998, 222.
Note: Entries are unstandardized regression coefficients. *T*-statistics are shown in parentheses. Significance tests are two-tailed. N.A. = not available.
* p < .10   ** p < .05   *** p < .01.

health reform and to spotlight self-interest as their primary motivation. But there are also reasonable alternative explanations. The most credible alternative accounts emphasize the impact of economic cycles and the public's general ideological shift against Clinton (rather than health reform in particular). Close examination finds each of these accounts relevant but unpersuasive.

Economic Cycles

Economic downturns and recoveries no doubt affect public opinion. Americans cannot ignore the pain inflicted by economic recessions on themselves or others; indeed, this pain may well boost support for health care reform. By the same token, economic recoveries may ease public anxiety and remove the urgency of government action.

There is scattered evidence for the economy's impact on public opinion. The economic recessions in 1981–82 and 1987–91 coincided with some vivid cases of increased support for health care reform. As we noted above, the public's backing for the government to "do more" on "health measures" rose 10 percentage points in 1981–82 and support for rebuilding the health system in figure 7.1 rose 13 percentage points in 1987–91. By contrast, the economic recoveries following these economic downturns were marked by periods of declining support for health reform. The sentiment for rebuilding the health system fell 9 percentage points after the recession ended in 1982, and the public's personal satisfaction with their medical care also rose after the recession in the early 1990s (fig. 7.8).

Although economic swings clearly affected public thinking, they did not on their own dictate public opinion. Patterns that point to the economy's influence are offset by contradictory evidence. For instance, the increase in personal satisfaction during the recession of 1981–82 (fig. 7.8) contradicts the expectation of rising personal alarm during periods of economic duress.

Equally troubling is whether the public has fully and accurately perceived economic conditions. Although economic indicators suggested that an economic recovery was in full swing by 1994, it may not have been noticeable to Americans in their day-to-day lives. It was neither substantial enough nor sufficiently acknowledged to be the single most important force in public thinking. Indeed, had it been, we might have expected the Democrats not to have taken the beating they did in the 1994 congressional elections; incumbents are generally rewarded for economic recovery (see Kramer 1971; Tufte 1975, 1978).

The dominating influence on public opinion in 1993–94 and other periods of health reform was the full-fledged national debate about changing health care policy and the media's coverage of it. The evidence across a large number of surveys points to a strong and consistent association between the behavior of policymakers, the press, and public opinion. We want to reiterate, though, that while the economy did not drive public opinion, it no doubt augmented or offset trends that arose from media reports on policy debates. Indeed, the economy's greatest influence may have been indirect; the economic upturn in 1993–94, for instance, may have influenced public opinion by prompting the media to devote less attention to the national consequences of health reform for the economy and everyday life.

The Limits of Ideology

The changes in public opinion toward health could conceivably have
resulted from a general ideological reaction against Clinton's liberalism. An impressive body of research shows that the public's "thermostat" reacts when policymakers pursue a strong ideological agenda of
policy changes that move beyond the more centrist approach that most
Americans support. The public's reaction is to swing from supporting
policymakers' initiatives to favoring a cooling-off period of ideologically moderate policies and slower change (see Wlezien 1995; Durr
1993; Erikson, MacKuen, and Stimson, forthcoming). Americans react not only against actual changes in policy but also against *perceptions* of how policymakers and political parties may overstep what the
public wants. The public's expectations regarding the behavior of
Democratic and Republican presidents make them prone to anticipate
that each party will move toward their ideological extremes.[20]

The thermostat hypothesis is illustrated by the last two instances in
which Democratic or Republican control of the White House shifted
to the other party—Ronald Reagan and Bill Clinton. Reagan, who
was helped into office in 1980 by a conservative shift in opinion, took
immediate action as president to enact in 1981 unequivocally conservative changes in economic and welfare policy. By the end of Reagan's
first year in office, the public perceived the president as taking the
country in too conservative a direction and began to move in a liberal
direction (Page and Shapiro 1992; Mayer 1993; Stimson 1991).

The public's reaction to Clinton was seemingly quite similar. His
election campaign benefited from a liberal shift in public opinion as
Americans looked to the government to actively work at solving domestic problems, especially economic ones. Despite his claims of being a "New Democrat," Clinton took some highly visible liberal actions upon taking office in 1993, such as loosening the ban on gays
and lesbians in the military and revoking the "gag order" on doctors
at public clinics that provided information on abortion. As Clinton
entered his second year, the public evidently saw Clinton and the
Democrat-controlled Congress as pursuing policies that were too liberal and reversed course in a conservative direction. Scores of public
opinion surveys between 1992 and 1994 show a widespread shift
against funding for welfare, establishing affirmative action on racial
matters, expanding immigration, protecting the environment, and government activism to assist those in need (Weaver, Shapiro, and Jacobs
1995a; Times Mirror Center 1994). The "thermostat" thesis suggests,

then, that Americans turned against Clinton's reform effort because of a sweeping ideological backlash rather than a specific reaction to the health reform debate.

The thermostat thesis, however, does not clearly fit the story of health care reform for three reasons. First, it confuses the causal ordering: Americans' reaction against health reform in particular and the highly partisan debate over it drove the general ideological shift in public opinion rather than the other way around. Health reform dominated the public's attention in 1993–94 and fed into long-standing public assumptions about the Democratic Party's ideological inclination to expand government. The Clinton administration assured health care reform's dominance by elevating it above nearly all other issues—including welfare reform, environmental protection, and affirmative action. By making health reform its defining issue in 1993–94, the administration kept other issues off the policy agenda for immediate action.

The dominance of health reform in Washington and in the public's mind meant that as the public became disenchanted with health reform, it also came to reconsider and reject government action in other policy areas, which it assumed Democrats would favor. The press also contributed to the public's reevaluation of a range of social policies by its close coverage of the political battle over whether Democrats were promoting "another big government bureaucracy." Although we cannot show directly that the health reform debate affected public opinion toward social policies across the board, its visible and highly partisan politics clearly singled it out as the standard by which Americans would judge the Clinton presidency and other issues traditionally linked to the Democratic Party.

Second, the recent cycles of public opinion change during health reform episodes occurred without clear ideological shifts. In particular, during the 1987–89 debate over health reform, the cycle of public support amidst national concern followed by disillusionment and rising personal considerations occurred when Reagan's ideological aspirations were smothered by the Iran-Contra scandal and George Bush distanced himself from strident ideological positions. During the falloff of support for major systemic reform, the public continued to move in a liberal direction on other economic issues (Stimson 1991; Mayer 1993; Page and Shapiro 1992; Weaver, Shapiro, and Jacobs 1995a).

Third, and central to this book, the emphasis on a thermostatic process that focuses on public opinion and policy outputs neglects the political campaign aimed at manipulating the public's evaluations of health care reform proposals. The reality was that in the 1990s the public was the target of orchestrated attacks by opponents of health care reform, which the media readily conveyed. It was actual political efforts to influence public opinion that produced the public's move toward health reform and liberalism by 1993, and that reversed the course in 1994. The shift in opinion was driven by political opposition to an historic effort to expand the scope of government policymaking in a particular area. Comparing public opinion changes to the mechanistic adjustments of a thermostat does not give due weight to politics and the determined interventions of goal-oriented political actors to move public opinion.

Overall, alternative explanations for the public's turn against health care reform are less persuasive and convincing than they might first appear. The public's rejection of health care reform by 1994 was the result of powerful political dynamics associated with a specific policy, which overshadowed any ostensibly automatic effects of economic conditions or ideology.

Conclusion

The public responded to the political debate and news coverage of health care by moving toward support for major reform by 1993, if not earlier, and then against reform in 1994. In particular, the level of support for reform and public-spiritedness throughout the 1992 election into 1993 faded as the bitter conflict, risks, and uncertainty over the Clinton health plan dominated both the debate and the media's coverage of the episode. The political cycle of rising and then falling support for reform was echoed in earlier periods of health reform, most clearly in 1987–89.

Health reform debates, as shown in chapters 3 and 4, revealed that political observers and the Democratic and Republican leaders who worked to shape public thinking harbored an idealized image of public opinion. This idealized model of public opinion rests on two false assumptions.

First, political elites presume that public opinion will quickly reach a decision for or against a specific policy once it is proposed and the proposers quickly make their case. Public opinion, however, is invariably shaped over some period of time by the political debate and the information conveyed by the media; if the debate is conflictual and polarized, the press will magnify it (as chapters 5 and 6 showed).

Public opinion during the 1993–94 health reform debate was influenced by politicians and news reports through a subtle process that defied the kind of outright manipulation attempted by political elites. In the end, what mattered was the relative balance of the standards of judgment that the public used in reaching its final decision on health reform in 1994. The public's concern for health care as a collective national problem was overshadowed by the media's coverage and magnification of partisan strategy and fierce bickering. The combination of the media's stress on political conflict and strategy and antireformers' continuous warnings about the danger of "big government" primed the public to focus on the ineffectiveness and uncertainty associated with major government policy reform as it evaluated the Clinton plan. The result was a drop in public support for the Clinton plan and a turn toward concern about personal well-being and away from what benefited the nation as a whole.

It is telling that when Congress in 1965 passed Medicare, which remains the most significant health reform legislation in American history, the public was not unified despite extraordinarily favorable political conditions. Washington and the public had swung in a decidedly liberal direction; the 1964 elections handed Lyndon Johnson a landslide victory over Barry Goldwater and returned huge Democratic majorities in the House and Senate. Yet, on the eve of Medicare's passage and under ideal political conditions, Americans were split—with 46 percent favoring Medicare and 36 percent backing private health insurance. The fierce and quite vocal opposition of Republicans, the American Medical Association, and other interest groups highlighted the risks of health reform and stoked the public's apprehension (Jacobs 1993).

The lesson is clear: political conflict invariably breeds media scrutiny and public divisions. Do not expect the public to offer a quick and resounding verdict when faced with fierce and highly public partisan conflict. No campaign for policy reform can concoct a "game plan" to beat that rule.

Political activists operate under a second false assumption: the personal "pocketbook" consequence of health reform is not always the main issue for Americans. Human nature does not necessarily dictate that self-interest must be what people truly care about. Of course, the impact of policy changes on oneself or one's family will be a significant concern, but it is not the only nor necessarily the most decisive consideration. The evidence concerning public opinion on health care reform suggests that other competing frames for understanding the issue can offset or diminish the significance of self-interest.

In the case of Clinton's health care plan, Americans were not moti-

vated by some innate pursuit of personal interests; rather, the public
reacted to what it learned through the political process. In particular,
the media's presentation of national health care problems, policies, and
political debate alternately raised the importance of national considerations and then later (intentionally or not) increased the public's attention to self-interest.

The assumption of political elites that the public always reached its
verdict based on self-interest profoundly misunderstood public opinion; this also produced significant political miscalculations.[21] Chapter
3 showed that the Clinton White House based its elaborate campaign
to build public support for health care reform on persuading Americans that they would personally gain from it and on avoiding any appeal to their concern about the overall national payoff. Pitching reform
to the public's self-interest was a persistent theme in the reports prepared by the president's pollster, Stan Greenberg.[22] President Clinton's
own statements emphasized the implications for individuals—how
they would gain financially and retain the same quality of care.

The White House's decision to frame its proposal in terms of the
benefits to individuals ignored the public's concern about the implication of health reform for the whole society—helping people who
lacked coverage and bolstering the overall economic performance of
the country. Ironically, such national considerations, which had propelled the rising support for health reform in 1991 and 1992, were
deliberately avoided by the White House when it actually campaigned
for its health care proposal. The White House's decision to rest its case
for health reform on the public's personal self-interest not only tossed
away an important basis for rallying support, it also unwittingly played
into the hands of reform opponents by highlighting personal (rather
than collective) considerations. The experience of the Clinton White
House illustrates the cycle of crafted talk and the perverse consequences of adapting to it.

We have focused to this point on the dynamics of policymaking,
media reporting, and public opinion with regard to health care issues.
What remains unclear is whether our findings, especially regarding
critical elite mobilization strategies toward policymaking, are merely
a unique feature of this one policy area. This is not the case—and
increasingly so, as we have argued. The next chapter turns to the Republican Congress in 1995–96 and its pursuit of the Contract with
America.

Part Four

The Cycle of Crafted Talk

Chapter Eight

Dissolution of the Republican Revolution

Changes in the political and institutional conditions during 1995 and 1996 clearly affected the political motivations of Republicans in Congress and President Clinton regarding electoral and policy goals. The stunning elections of November 1994 catapulted the Republicans into control of both chambers of the 104th Congress, and House Speaker Newt Gingrich proclaimed a "revolution" against the established social policy of the federal government.

Although congressional Republicans (especially in the House) and the Clinton White House championed dramatically different policies, they shared a strikingly similar motivation until the fall of 1996: they pursued the policy goals that they and their supporters wanted to achieve, and they discounted the fact that many of these desired policies were not supported by a majority of the public. Republican leaders in 1995–96 pursued a political strategy that paralleled the Clinton White House's strategy of crafted talk in its health reform campaign—of using polls and focus groups to pinpoint the words, arguments, and symbols to move centrist public opinion to support their desired policies. "Winning" public opinion was expected to lessen the electoral risk of discounting centrist public opinion and to increase the pressure on Clinton and moderate legislators to follow their lead.

The policy debates of 1996, however, departed from the Clinton health reform campaign in one important respect: the approach of the 1996 elections greatly increased the incentives of both congressional Republicans and the White House to alter their behavior by responding to public opinion and absorbing the costs of compromising their policy goals. Clinton and, ultimately, the Republicans pursued a "median voter" strategy: the competition for independent or swing voters, who would determine the presidential contest and competitive congressional races, motivated both Clinton and the Republicans to adopt positions that were closer than they had been to the midpoint of public opinion and to work together to pass legislation enjoying strong public support, such as the minimum wage law, the Kennedy-Kassebaum reform of private health insurance operations, and, arguably, welfare reform.

The Gingrich House not only made calculations that were similar to those that Clinton made earlier on health reform, but this also precipitated a similar cycle of interactions with political opponents, the press, and public opinion. Convinced that the press was prone to distortion, Gingrich and other Republican leaders concentrated on managing the press to gain favorable coverage and public support. Democrats countered with their own messages. For its part, the public reacted to the intense political disagreements by opposing the Republicans' proposals and questioning their judgment. Policy debates, then, were influenced by feedback effects: the political behavior and strategy of Republicans affected the press and public opinion, which in turn fed back into the political process—first by further fueling politicians' efforts to manipulate the press and the public, and then (as the elections approached) by pressuring them to converge on policies that enjoyed the support of centrist opinion.

Our discussion is divided in four sections. The first compares the policy proposals of Republicans and centrist public opinion prior to the fall of 1996. The second analyzes their political strategy as they attempted to change public opinion using crafted talk. The third section tracks Clinton's strategy to counter the Republican initiatives in response to centrist opinion and the Republican retreat back to the center as the 1996 election approached. We conclude by discussing why the Republicans failed to move public opinion to support their policy goals. Our evidence is based on secondary sources, data on public opinion, previously confidential private records from President Clinton's private strategy meetings published by Dick Morris as an appendix (1999), and interviews with a sample of fifty-two senior legislative staff during 1995 and 1996 regarding the connection of public opinion to policy decisions and political strategy.[1]

The Republican Revolution against Centrist Opinion

The social policy proposals and legislation that congressional Republican leaders pursued during 1995 and the first half of 1996 generally diverged from what most Americans supported.

Republican Positions versus Public Opinion

The great bulk of the congressional Republican's initial agenda—from tax cuts and increased defense spending to capping punitive damages in liability and malpractice cases—was not ranked by most Americans as among the country's major problems in 1995 and the first half of 1996. At the outset of the 104th Congress in January 1995, a *New York Times*/CBS News poll identified eight issues that respondents volunteered as the most important national problems. Only two of these eight issues were listed in the "Contract with America"—crime and the federal budget deficit.

Although the Republicans' agenda was largely disconnected from what concerned Americans most at the outset of the 104th Congress, the Republicans' policy proposals and the ensuing contentious debate (as conveyed in the press) soon changed the public's agenda (cf. Iyengar and Kinder 1987). The federal budget deficit was surpassed by general economic concerns and unemployment as one of the public's top concerns during Clinton's first two years, but the Republican initiatives for a balanced budget and the subsequent acrimonious debate over fiscal priorities propelled it to a top ranked issue by January 1996. Welfare reform had been a prominent campaign issue in 1992, but it slipped from public prominence in 1993 and 1994, and then regained the public's attention after Republicans aggressively pursued it following the 1994 elections.

The connection between the policies Republicans proposed and centrist opinion was also decidedly mixed. The responsiveness of their welfare proposal was especially ambiguous. The Republicans were in step with the public's philosophical commitment to individual self-reliance and its strong distaste for government programs labeled "welfare," which had strengthened during the 1990s. Americans, however, did not support either the sharp cuts in government spending for poor people or the punitive approach to children and the poor that the House proposed. Despite shifts in a conservative directions, majorities of nearly 60 percent of Americans continued to support government assistance for "poor" people and over 80 percent believed that the government was spending too little or about the right amount on "assistance to the poor" and "poor children" (Weaver, Shapiro, and Jacobs 1995).

For most other policies, the Republicans echoed the public's broad objectives and philosophical leanings toward individualism and limited government, but their specific proposals contradicted the public's specific preferences. On the one hand, many of the Republicans' broad positions followed the general contours of public opinion. A Gallup poll in late November 1994 revealed that supermajorities of more than 70 percent favored balancing the budget, cutting taxes, establishing a presidential line-item veto, and passing term limits (Public Perspective 1995, 28). Moreover, the Republicans did respond to public opinion by not proposing to reform some programs like Social Security, which enjoyed strong support. In addition, Republican conservatism regarding individualism versus government responsibility matched public opinion. The *New York Times*/CBS News polls during the 104th Congress confirmed previous evidence that about two-thirds of Americans believed that the government does too many things that are better left to business and individuals and that a smaller government providing fewer services would be preferable (*New York Times*/CBS News poll, 22–24 February 1996; Weaver, Shapiro, and Jacobs 1995; McClosky and Zaller 1984).

On the other hand, the Republicans' specific proposals to achieve these broad objectives did not reflect public opinion. They ran counter to the long-standing public preferences supporting Medicare and Medicaid, health and safety regulation, school lunches, student loans, Americorps volunteers, education and training, and other policy areas (Cook and Barrett 1992; Page and Shapiro 1992). Nearly 80 percent agreed in a 1995 Princeton Survey that the government should play an active role in improving health care, housing, and education for middle income families.[2]

Republican positions toward environmental protection exemplified the party's distance from centrist opinion. Although the public did shift a bit away from backing environmental protection at all costs, Republican proposals for relaxing regulations contradicted strong public support for protection and regulation. A February 1996 *New York Times*/CBS News survey reported that 55 percent supported the federal government doing more to regulate the environmental and safety practices of business (23 percent felt the government was doing enough; 17 percent favored it doing less). House Majority Whip Tom DeLay was clearly far from centrist opinion when he compared the EPA to the Gestapo and insisted, "I can't think of one [regulation I would keep]" (Morgan 1996).

Political reform issues and defense spending further illustrate the Republicans' disregard for what most Americans supported: the 104th Congress failed to act on term limits (though many Republicans had campaigned on them) and on lobbying regulations despite their popularity, and they proposed increased defense spending even though the public's support for defense spending remained at a near all-time low. The same pattern occurred for other issues we discuss in more detail below, including Medicare and budgetary policy. In short, even though the relationship between Republicans positions and centrist opinion was more ambiguous on some policies such as welfare reform, many of the Republicans' proposals during the 104th Congress were at odds with public opinion.

Explaining Republicans' Distance from Centrist Opinion

The Republicans' meager responsiveness to the public during the period prior to the fall of 1996 was the product of at least three factors. First, the Republicans' information about public opinion may have been faulty because they distrusted public opinion surveys and overvalued focus groups. Congressional staff persistently asserted in our interviews that polls were easily manipulated and therefore could neither be trusted nor used regularly to monitor public opinion for the purposes of policymaking. As one Republican staffer insisted, "we discount any polling—it all depends on how questions are asked, who is asked. Who designs [a poll] can make it say what they want. We trust direct contact with constituents instead." Sixty-two percent (32 of 52) reported that their offices did not commission surveys. (Not surprisingly, nearly three-quarters [38 of 52] indicated that no one in their office had special responsibility for analyzing them.) There was no significant difference here between Democrats and Republicans.

In place of polls, political activists (namely, social conservatives and interest groups representing business) and, especially, Republicans turned to focus groups, which are unstructured conversations with a dozen or so "ordinary" Americans. Although the findings from focus groups are not (by design) representative of the views of the entire country, they have nonetheless been treated as such by political activists.

A second factor contributing to the Republicans' relatively low responsiveness to the public's substantive preferences was the wide-

spread conviction among legislators that information about public
opinion was an inappropriate consideration in formulating policy.
When we pushed our staff respondents on the usefulness of public
opinion information in policymaking, a common response was that it
was not directly considered: when we asked whether existing opinion
today or anticipated future opinion influenced decisions, three-
quarters (18 of 24) *volunteered* spontaneously that public opinion was
of no use. A plurality (9 of 25, 36 percent) responded to a separate
question about how public opinion influences their legislator's decisions about specific policies like health care or welfare reform by again
spontaneously challenging the question's premise and insisting that
their legislator's decisions were not guided by public opinion.

The third and most significant explanation for Republicans' low responsiveness to public opinion was the importance that legislators
attached to their own policy goals—what they considered "good public policy" as well as the objectives of supportive party activists and
interest groups. The policy decisions of many House Republicans were
driven by the fact that—in the words of House Republican Whip Tom
DeLay—they were "ideologues [with] an agenda [and] philosophy"
(Drew 1996, 116). House Republican Sam Brownback, who was a
leader of legislators who first entered Congress in 1994, agreed that
"most of my colleagues are very ideologically driven" and came to
Washington committed to making good on a "very aggressive, very
ideological campaign [to] reduce the size of the federal government"
(124–25).

The views of DeLay and Brownback were repeated in our interviews
with staffers who emphasized their legislators' determination to "do
what's best" according their personal values. One Republican respondent explained: "On policy, beliefs are more important than public
opinion." Another explained that the member of Congress "just does
what he feels he needs to do. Public opinion is not at all useful in day-
to-day policymaking." Eighty-eight percent (46 out of 52) acknowledged that public opinion information was used to lobby their offices
but argued that it had no influence on the member; their member
"stuck" to his or her beliefs and distrusted the results because the
"numbers are so easy to manipulate" to serve the interests of the lobbyist—whether it was an interest group, another legislator, or the White
House. The persistent and unequivocal downplaying of public opinion
by the staff we interviewed is consistent with the gap between public
opinion and Republican positions as well as with previous research
(reviewed in chapter 2) that the preferences of a member's constituents

has only a modest and highly contingent effect on the legislator's voting decisions and electoral prospects.

The policy goals of Republicans were the product not only of legislators' own beliefs but also the preferences of the Republican Party activists and interest groups who supported them—especially the Christian Coalition, the National Rifle Association, and the National Association of Small Businesses (Drew 1996). The standing of the Republicans' allies was reflected in the dramatic increase during the 104th Congress in testimony before congressional committees by conservative advocacy groups, business groups, and others sympathetic to the party's goals (Gormley 1998).

As Republican leaders would discover, legislative proposals that compromised the party's policy goals and responded to centrist opinion faced a potential revolt by rank-and-file legislators as well as party supporters. Conservative Republicans (especially in the House) were vigilant in protesting what they saw as backsliding on key elements of their agenda, equating "compromise" and "split[ting] the difference" with the abdication of principle (Drew 1996, 310). The Christian Coalition and other supporters pressured Republicans to enact their preferred legislation and ominously warned (in one mailing) of retribution for failing to follow its policy goals: "we'll throw you out. We mean it" (Schneider 1995).

The Republican Bully Pulpit

The Congressional Connection to Public Opinion

Republican Leaders Take Their Message to the Nation

Members of past congresses did not see national opinion leadership as their primary responsibility (Herbst 1993). Congressional leaders like Speaker Tom Foley or Minority Leader Robert Michel avoided routine and conspicuous appeals to the public; they certainly lacked the personal skill, temperament, and capacity to conduct effective public relations campaigns.

Below the ranks of leaders, individual legislators have generally not conducted national appeals for public support and that has not changed. The staff we interviewed consistently emphasized that the legislator they worked for had not become either more sensitive to public opinion or more intent on tracking it through polls. Of the members who served ten years or more, 68 percent (17 of 25) of their staff reported that the member's sensitivity to tracking public opinion had decreased or remained unchanged. Staff reported that their members conduct little opinion polling of their own, and that the surveys they conducted were largely limited to district or state election campaigns. Instead, individual legislators still rely on the traditional contacts with their constituents—face-to-face meetings, mail, and phone calls.[3]

What changed most conspicuously in the 104th Congress was the unprecedented efforts of the Republican leadership to manage public opinion. Senate Majority Leader Bob Dole and, especially, Speaker Gingrich set out to rally public support by using the kind of direct bully-pulpit appeals that had previously been reserved for presidents (Harris 1998). Challenging Clinton for the visibility that is usually bestowed on presidents, Gingrich attempted to make congressional Republicans the primary source of policy initiative and news reports: he increased the frequency of his appearances on news programs; initiated daily press conferences; focused national attention—as have presidents since Roosevelt—on the House's first hundred days; and delivered a nationally televised address on the House's accomplishments after one hundred days. To handle his new responsibility of directing public opinion, Gingrich delegated to others the Speaker's traditional responsibility over the day-to-day management of the House floor and administration of the House and the Capitol.

Acting Presidential

Not only did congressional leaders sound like presidents on their bully pulpits, but their two central calculations were also presidential in nature (Maltzman and Sigelman 1996). First, congressional leaders calculated that changing public opinion allowed them to minimize the electoral risk of discounting centrist opinion even as they pursued the policy goals favored by a majority of their party's legislative caucus or conference within each chamber. Congressional leaders have greater incentives than rank-and-file members to satisfy both the policy goals favored by most legislators in their party and the electoral goal of winning the White House and majority party status in Congress. Electoral success and policy coherence are collective goals that enhance the institutional and personal interests of leaders (Arnold 1990; Jacobs, Lawrence, Shapiro, and Smith 1998). Their motivation to move public opinion is enhanced by their capacity to sell the party position more quickly and cheaply to national opinion than individual legislators who use the retail approach of reassuring voters constituency-by-constituency.

Congressional leaders were confident that they could change public opinion to support their policy goals; the public's preferences were considered uncertain and susceptible to change if presented with the "right" message. During 1995, Gingrich and Haley Barbour (leader of the Republican National Committee [RNC]) repeatedly pointed to the experience of Republican Governor John Engler as evidence that Republican legislators could defy existing public opinion to pursue their policy goals and—in Gingrich's words—still "survive low poll numbers": "Our polls would come back when the people see that we kept our promises." (This calculation rested on a mistaken anecdote: Engler's low poll ratings early in his term were actually based on a loaded question in a private poll [Drew 1996, 82, 380].)

Second, congressional leaders calculated that moving public opinion not only lowered the electoral risk of pursuing their caucus's policy goals but also expanded their political leverage over President Clinton and congressional moderates who would be sensitive to centrist opinion. The House leadership, for instance, widely circulated to its members pollster Richard Wirthlin's analysis of public opinion that showed public support (using slanted questions) for changing the school-lunch program in order to reassure and solidify wavering Republicans (Weisskopf and Maraniss 1995). As one congressional aide explained to us in an interview, demonstrating public support was politically important in "being able to sell [a policy] in Congress."

Gingrich was particularly eager to rally Americans because of his political vulnerability; his political incentives were reinforced by his personal comfort with making public presentations from his new vantage point. Gingrich presided over a House majority that was the narrowest in four decades and was continually threatened by divisions between the ideologically committed and the small but critical number of moderates.

The New Craft of Politics

Republican leaders relied, like the Clinton White House, on the strategy of crafted talk to move public opinion. They utilized public opinion research and an elaborate institutional apparatus to hone the presentation of their proposals in order to rally public support for the policies they desired. "It's not what you're doing," House leader John Boehner explained, "but the perceptions that are so important" (Maraniss and Weisskopf 1996, 142). Finding the most effective "message" was considered decisive in shaping the public's perceptions and in enacting legislation. In effect, Republican leaders pursued a priming strategy: they identified the information and messages that portrayed their proposals in a favorable light and raised the salience of these considerations to Americans as standards for evaluating the proposals.

Polling the Message

Republican leaders received a constant stream of information and public opinion analysis in order to identify the language and arguments that would maximize the appeal of their proposals (Drew 1996, 204; DeParle 1996). Republican leaders and rank-and-file legislators as well as the party's pollsters agreed with the staff we interviewed that polls were "useful in terms of framing what you were going to do anyway."

Information on public opinion was "not the source of decisions on policy," one Republican staffer commented. Rather, Republican staff repeatedly emphasized that polls and focus groups were a "tool to shape our message," "educate the citizens," and to "learn what messages we need to get across." The results of polls and focus groups were likened by one Republican staffer to "intelligence gathering in war," except the battlefield was Washington and the targets were civilians. Sixty percent of congressional staff (31 of 52) indicated that public opinion information had been used to frame already decided policy decisions. More of those we interviewed indicated that public opinion information was useful for leading or educating Americans (42 percent, 22 of 52) than for responding to them (35 percent, 18 of 52). (Of the 52 staffers we interviewed, 9 argued that both were important and 3 others pointed to other uses of public opinion.) Republicans, in particular, tended to see this information as more important for leading (47 percent, 14 of 30) than responding (30 percent, 9 of 30) while Democrats were nearly evenly split. In addition, more than a majority of the staffers (35 of 52, 67 percent)—drawn equally from both parties— viewed public opinion as an opportunity that enhanced their political resources and ability to lead rather than as a constraint.[4]

Republican leaders regularly commissioned Frank Luntz, Bill McInturff, Linda DiVall, and other pollsters to adapt the techniques of test marketing—common in election campaigns, commercial advertising, and White House operations—to the business of crafting the most "salable language" for presenting their policy goals (Kelly 1994; Weisskopf 1994). According to Gingrich, political success went to those who "test [words], deliver them and repeat them in ways that devastate the opposition or provide the best protection against enemy attack" (Weisskopf and Maraniss 1995). The Republican research was geared to finding the words or arguments that highlighted the benefits of the GOP proposals to individuals and minimized the costs. For instance, Luntz conducted research on the wording of the Contract with America in order to satisfy Americans' longing for freedom, opportunity, and security. (The Contract was not intended to mobilize centrist voters and, in fact, was not very salient to most Americans before the 1994 elections. Rather, its planks echoed the goals of Republican activists and supporters.) After the 1994 elections, Luntz tracked the reactions of focus groups—captured on electronic dials—in order to tailor Gingrich's speeches to evoke support (DeParle 1996). Indeed, Gingrich brought in additional pollsters to prepare his nationally televised speech commemorating the Republicans first hundred days in office (Drew 1996, 187).

Using the Media to Spread the Message

The first step in the Republicans' recipe for political success was to identify a poll-crafted message; two steps followed—disciplining their team to use them and making sure that the press followed their lead. Only by saturating the country with their message could Republicans hope to prime Americans to evaluate their proposals favorably.

"The key," Barbour insisted, was to "get everybody saying the same thing." Barbour worked closely with Gingrich and other leaders to create a "unified approach" to communications (Maraniss and Weisskopf 1996, 133). They assembled a "vast communications army" by expanding the outreach capacity in the offices of congressional leaders and the Republican National Committee. The purpose was to create the institutional capacity to settle on a common message for legislators, the RNC, and their allies, and then to distribute it, check up on its delivery, and help members react to attacks from political opponents in their districts (Maraniss and Weisskopf 1996, 138; Harris 1998). "CommStrat," which was staffed by congressional and party staff and supervised by the Speaker's office, was especially important in designing and distributing the Republicans' "message for the day" (Weisskopf and Maraniss 1995).

Like a string of presidents since the 1960s, congressional Republicans concluded that "punch[ing] through the establishment media" to reach the public with their carefully crafted message was key to swaying public opinion (Bruck 1995). They pursued three tactics to promote their message through the press. First, Republican leaders

launched a campaign to saturate the country with their message by
flooding reporters with the same pitch. Barbour's motto at the RNC
was "Repeat it until you vomit": "The only way you can get market
penetration is through repetition, repetition, repetition" (Maraniss
and Weisskopf 1996, 131–32; Weisskopf and Maraniss 1995). The purpose of the communications operation—according to its director in
the House (Robert Istook)—was to "make sure radio talk-show hosts,
political pundits, editorial writers all receive the same information . . .
with the same parts accented" (Bruck 1995).

Second, Gingrich and other Republican leaders worked hard to
lobby the press to adopt their preferred language. Third, the Republicans carefully monitored the media's interpretation of public opinion
itself because they were concerned this would shape the perceptions of
lawmakers and the public itself. For instance, Republicans attempted
to champion the Contract with America by insisting to journalists that
its ten main proposals enjoyed the support of at least 60 percent of
Americans in polls by Luntz. The claims of public support were un-
true; they were concocted—one Republican figure explained—to "get
across [the point] that this wasn't something drawn up by politicos"
but had "the support of the American people" (Drew 1996, 29; Ferguson 1996). (The American Association for Public Opinion Research
subsequently censured Luntz for misleading public statements about
his research on the Contract [Greve 1995]. For earlier cases of ques-
tionable professional conduct by pollsters including Louis Harris, see
Jacobs and Shapiro 1996a.)

When not promoting the popularity of their policy goals, Republican leaders attacked press reports that highlighted public doubts that
might sway moderate legislators or the president. One of the most dramatic efforts to undermine unfavorable reports on public opinion was
Gingrich's October 1995 attack on the *New York Times* for devoting
its lead column—on the morning of a critical House vote—to its own
poll that found public opposition to Republican proposals. Gingrich
accused the *Times* of using "deliberately rigged questions that are totally phony"; he denounced the story as "a disgraceful example of dis-
information" (Fisher 1995).

The Republican Sales Pitch on Medicare and the Federal Budget

The proposals of House Republicans to balance the budget and reform
Medicare precipitated two of the biggest battles over social policy in
the 104th Congress, and they illustrate the Republicans' deployment
of crafted talk as a strategy to promote policy goals. From their own

public opinion research, Gingrich and his advisers appreciated that Americans opposed their budget and Medicare proposals; their reaction was not to reconsider their policy positions but rather to craft their presentation to sway public opinion.

Independent polls showed that while Americans supported the objective of a balanced budget as much as ever, they did not support the Republicans' policies for achieving it. Americans consistently opposed the objective of balanced budget if it required significant cuts in popular existing programs like college loans, school lunch programs, Social Security, and Medicare or if it was primarily aimed at cutting taxes.

The Republicans understood the existing state of public preferences toward a balanced budget and decided to discount them in order to fulfill their overriding goals of reducing government and ensuring that Democrats, as Gingrich explained, "cannot sustain the old welfare state" (DeParle 1996). Gingrich's spokesman Tony Blankley emphasized that "[o]ur objective isn't just to balance the budget, it's to transform the government" and (in the words of influential Republican adviser Bill Kristol) "force a number of budget-cut versus tax-increases fights . . . that's good for us" and "hurts the Democratic Party" (Drew 1996, 119).

On the budget—as well as on Medicare—the Republicans defied what most Americans preferred not out of a disregard for elections but rather based on a conviction that their carefully crafted message would win public support for their desired policy. Luntz's advice to the House Republican caucus was to communicate the "moral force for balancing the budget" by "turning the issue of 'fairness' against the Democrats" and "focusing the general rhetorical attack on the 'Washington bureaucracy'" (Luntz 1995). Republican leaders and advisers were confident that steadfast insistence on balancing the budget to cut wasteful bureaucracy—even if it meant closing the government—would win public support, rally moderate legislators, and make Clinton cave in.

On Medicare, Republican leaders actually debated whether to defy centrist opinion before deciding to plough ahead. Barbour and other prominent Republicans argued strenuously against tackling Medicare reform before the 1996 elections because it enjoyed strong support from large majorities of Americans as well as from seniors, who pay attention to Medicare policy and vote (DeParle 1996). Public opinion experts had forcefully argued that it would take two years to get the public to accept major changes in Medicare (Maraniss and Weisskopf 1996, 131). Gingrich himself confessed that "every day" in 1995 he worried that Medicare "could kill us" (DeParle 1996).

Independent polls confirmed the concerns of Republican leaders and advisers about public opposition to their proposals for reforming Medicare. A number of surveys in the fall of 1995 and early 1996 showed that large majorities opposed reducing the growth of Medicare expenditures in order to balance the budget or deliver tax cuts. Two polls (a *Time*/CNN poll in May 1995 and a CNN poll in January 1996) showed that lopsided majorities of about 65 percent preferred a budget-balancing plan that made smaller reductions in the growth of Medicare and abandoned a larger tax cut. In addition, the public opposed the Republicans' proposals to scale back the role of government and expand individual "choice" in Medicare through Medical Savings Accounts and vouchers. A September 1995 *Los Angeles Times* poll revealed that 51 percent opposed Medical Savings accounts (38 percent supported them, with 11 percent offering no opinion).[5] An August 1995 NBC/*Wall Street Journal* survey reported that 55 percent opposed reforming Medicare by introducing vouchers (whereas 32 percent supported this and 13 percent were not sure).[6]

Gingrich and others decided, however, that balancing the budget was the "glue" that bonded Republicans together and achieving this policy goal required Medicare reform. "If we're going to successfully balance the budget," the chair of the Republican caucus John Boehner explained, "we've got to deal with Medicare" (DeParle 1996). In other words, the Republicans were primarily motivated by the larger goal of reducing government rather than by the problems of Medicare per se. Medical Savings Accounts and vouchers were consistent with Republicans' overriding interest in reducing government and in expanding individual self-reliance.

The Republicans' confidence in their ability to move public opinion offset their political trepidation about reforming Medicare and created confidence (at that time) that they could defy current public preferences to pursue their policy goals. Gingrich and other leaders were convinced they could use public opinion research to select the words and arguments that would manipulate the public into thinking that they were responding to centrist opinion.

John Boehner, who chaired the House Republican caucus, explained that Republican leaders "tested [Medicare] and found out that if you talked about balancing the budget and Medicare in the same sentence, you were asking for [b]ig trouble" (DeParle 1996). The Republican polls showed that a whopping 70 percent of Americans opposed cutting Medicare to balance the budget (which was the Republicans' intent), but 70 percent also favored cutting Medicare to "save" its trust fund (Drew 1996, 204). Gingrich followed the advice of Republican pollsters and decided to "tal[k] about 'preserving' and 'protecting' Medicare": the Republicans would publicly present their proposed changes in Medicare as essential to "saving" the program from financial insolvency (DeParle 1996; Bruck 1995). DiVall and McInturff cheered Republicans on, concluding from an extensive survey in the spring of 1995 that the Republicans should describe their efforts as intended to "protect, improve and preserve Medicare . . . not transform, reform or change it" (Maraniss and Weisskopf 1996, 134). Indeed, independent surveys confirmed that the Republicans' presentation enjoyed public support: 54 percent reported in a September 1995 Harris survey that they favored cutting future Medicare costs to save the program from bankruptcy.[7]

RNC Chairman Barbour took charge in coordinating the party's message on Medicare. He kept Republicans in touch with the leadership's approved "power phrases" and saturated journalists with faxes (Drew 1996, 204, 206). When the press refused to adopt the Republicans' preferred language, Gingrich, Barbour, and other party leaders vigorously pressed journalists to present their plan as merely "slowing the rate of growth" in the program rather than "cutting" it (Weisskopf and Maraniss 1995).

Many of the Republicans' most prominent policy initiatives from Medicare to environmental legislation were at odds with the specific preferences of centrist opinion, though welfare reform was more ambiguous. Moving public opinion seemed to promise both reelection and the achievement of their policy goals: they championed their desired policies with the expectation that Americans would follow them, and they would secure reelection and the cooperation of moderate legislators and President Clinton. Much like Clinton's experience on health reform, however, they would witness how political competition, the media's portrayal of policy disagreements, and enduring public preferences would interfere with and dampen their efforts to obtain public support for their desired policy goals.

The Clinton Phoenix: Attacking from the Center

Following the Republicans' dramatic gains in the 1994 elections and the resulting threat to his reelection in 1996, Clinton adopted positions and reacted to Republican proposals based on his pollsters' analysis of centrist opinion. Shifting their calculus from the 1993–94 health reform campaign, Clinton and his political advisers increased their responsiveness to the specific policy preferences of centrist opinion and compromised their own policy goals as well as those of many Democratic legislators, activists, and allies. As we discuss below, they pursued strategies both to appeal to the policy preferences of the median voter and to prime Americans to focus on popular aspects of Clinton's words, strategies, and gestures.

The strategy of "triangulation," which Dick Morris promoted in 1995–96, was the label attached to Clinton's adjustment of his positions toward centrist opinion and, if necessary, away not only from his political rivals in the Republican ranks but also from the policy goals of his Democratic allies. Morris and a new crop of political consultants argued that Clinton's policy goals during his first two years in office had become "too oriented toward traditional Democrats," who "applau[d] moves that attack Republicans and defend Democratic values." Instead, Clinton's political advisers recommended that the president respond to what most Americans preferred and, as Morris noted, the "20 percent [of the] vote that is up for grabs." The key to Clinton's victory would be "go[ing] after [the] marginal voter, not after [the] base." The political downside of pursuing the policy goals that were embraced in 1993–94 was that they "come back to haunt you in ratings" (Morris 1999, appendix of materials for private meeting with the president, 361, 369, 500).

Responding to centrist opinion required Clinton to absorb the costs of compromising the policy goals favored by traditional Democrats (and an earlier incarnation of Bill Clinton). These compromises created resentment and opposition within the Democratic Party, opened him up to Republican charges of "flip-flopping," and, to some extent, aroused anguish for the president himself as he reversed what he had once considered good public policy (Solomon 1995).

Clinton Responds to Public Opinion

Clinton started his term in 1993 by carrying over his 1992 campaign pollster, Stanley Greenberg. Following the Republican gains in the 1994 elections, Clinton, the First Lady, and the vice president decided that the president needed new political advisers and pollsters and invited in Dick Morris, Mark Penn, and Douglas Schoen to reposition him toward centrist opinion in preparing for his 1996 reelection campaign (Drew 1996, 61). (Morris had navigated Clinton back from defeat as Arkansas governor in 1980 by similarly counseling him to respond to centrist opinion.) In 1995 and 1996, opinion surveys were conducted every week and, in some periods such as during the government shutdown and the 1996 campaign, every day at a cost of about $1.25 million a year. For most of this period, Morris and the other political consultants regularly met with Clinton and a small group of his close aides and presented a weekly analysis of the approval ratings for Clinton, the First Lady, the vice president and Mrs. Gore, as well as pairings with possible opponents and the public's attitudes on policies and values (Frisby 1996; Clines 1996; Mitchell 1997; Stengel and Pooley 1996).

Clinton's heightened sensitivity to centrist opinion influenced both the new policy positions he promoted and the words, strategy, and symbols he used in 1995 and 1996.

Substantive Responsiveness to Public Opinion

Clinton's decisions on whether to publicly support or oppose the Republicans' far-reaching initiatives in 1995 and 1996 were guided by the public opinion research of his advisers, who assiduously tracked Americans' preferences about the broad direction of government policy as well as their evaluations of specific proposals. The president in effect pursued a median voter strategy of adopting positions on salient issues that were closest to the midpoint of public opinion in order to show most voters that they would benefit from his reelection. But Clinton was not free to chart his own independent course based on polls; the Republicans' initiatives influenced what issues were on the agenda of Congress, the press, and the White House's pollsters, and the cost of compromising on some issues (like affirmative action) proved too costly in terms of alienating a major party constituency (African Americans).

CLINTON SUPPORT FOR REPUBLICAN PROPOSALS POPULAR WITH AMERICANS   Clinton's attentiveness to perceived public opinion prompted him to change his policy on welfare reform in the direction favored by Republicans. Although Clinton campaigned on "ending welfare as we know it," his 1994 plan for welfare reform proposed to *add* about $10 billion more in spending on the poor (Weaver, 2000). By 1996, though, Clinton had agreed to abolish Aid to Families with Dependent Children as an entitlement (a program that originated in Franklin Roosevelt's 1935 legislation) and to *cut* about $55 billion in assistance for the poor over the next six years. Morris and his other political consultants had persuaded Clinton (as they explained in their private memos to the president) that he should follow the large majority of Americans, who preferred by a 58 percent to 35 percent margin the "end of [the] entitlement" (Morris 1999, appendix, 384–85).

Morris and his team carefully tracked public preferences toward specific aspects of welfare reform and did not assume that the public only cared about the symbol of "ending welfare." Their research and recommendations to the president identified the specific policy changes that the public would support.

Three policy issues stand out as areas where Clinton reversed earlier positions in favor of those recommended by his analysts' investigation of public opinion. First, Clinton reversed his 1994 position and accepted in 1996 a hard five-year limit on the amount of time individuals could receive public assistance (Weaver 2000). His decision reflected the consistent advice of his polling analysts that by a 55 percent to 39 percent margin Americans "want welfare reform" that imposed time limits (Morris 1999, appendix, 384–85, 466–67).

Second, Clinton altered his earlier position by signing into law legislation that imposed stricter work requirements. Morris and other consultants repeated that "stiffer work requirements" had to be a "main objective" in order to respond to the supermajority of Americans (73 percent) who favored "throw[ing] [welfare recipients] off if [they] won't work" (Morris 1999, appendix, 384–85, 466–67). Finally, Clinton signed legislation that imposed massive cuts in benefits for immigrants after his polling experts reported that a "cutoff to legal immigrants" was one of the "things we like" (Morris 1999, appendix, 384–85).

After the administration negotiated some of its differences with Republicans, Clinton's polling experts strenuously argued in the summer of 1996 leading up to the election that "nothing [is] more important than bi-partisan passage." From the perspective of wooing centrist voters, another veto (they told Clinton) would be a nearly unrivaled "disaster" (only Colin Powell's selection as Dole's vice president matched it); they predicted a precipitous 8 percentage point drop in his lead against Dole (Harris 1998; Purdum 1996; Morris 1999, appendix, 451, 465, 593).

Clinton followed, in effect, a median voter strategy. He compromised the policy goals that he and his allies had supported in order to move him closer to the midpoint of public opinion and deny Republicans the opportunity to capture swing voters by "accept[ing] defeat [in order] to blame [it] on you." Clinton's consultants warned that Republicans would be given more "credit" by Americans for welfare reform than he; the GOP was perceived as "more committed" to it (Morris 1999, 466–67; Groseclose and McCarty 1996). Signing the 1996 legislation, however, signaled to Americans, as the *New York Times* reported, that Clinton's "sympathies lie with more moderate swing voters, not with liberals who have no alternative but to back him for reelection" (Berke 1996).

Clinton's decision, as Senator Daniel Patrick Moynihan observed, to side with his "pollsters" even though his "Cabinet is against the bill" inflicted real political costs. Compromising the policy positions that the president and his allies had favored required him to overrule senior administration officials (his chief of staff, Leon Panetta, and Health and Human Services Secretary Donna Shalala), to provoke the opposition of a host of Democratic legislators (half of all House Democrats— including two of their top leaders—voted against Clinton's position), and to alienate a slew of party loyalists including civil rights advocates, organized labor, and religious organizations. Following his "political advisers' urg[ing] to sign the bill to show he was in step with public opinion" also opened the president to political attacks for "flip-flopping" and thrusted him into the position of feeling, in the words of one Democratic legislator, "genuinely torn" between conflicting impulses (Pear 1996). The motivation to win reelection prodded the president to respond to centrist opinion and discount the policy goals favored by his allies and, at one time, himself.

Clinton's stand toward balancing the budget followed much the same pattern as his handling of welfare reform. His pursuit of centrist opinion in the face of Republican demands for a balanced budget over seven years prompted him in 1995 to reverse the budget he had announced only a few months earlier, which envisioned successive annual deficits of $200 billion. Morris, Penn, and Schoen repeatedly reported that approving a balanced budget was a "[m]ost important thing," enjoying the support of 80 percent of Americans and the backing of independent voters who had supported Ross Perot in 1992 (Morris 1999, appendix, 451; Drew 1996, 217; Stengel and Pooley 1996).

Following the reports of his pollsters, Clinton agreed to the Republicans' objective of a balanced budget but avoided making the cuts in domestic programs they recommended (Morris 1999, appendix, 456). Clinton's reactions to Republican proposals were consistent with the public's specific policy preferences: he acknowledged that Americans supported the objective of a balanced budget while he selectively resisted Republican proposals for cuts. Clinton's public opinion specialists recommended that Clinton embrace the popular objective of a balanced budget while "contrast[ing]" the Republican "extreme" approach of "cutting everything in sight" with his efforts to "bring down

[the] deficit more gradually so as not to cut children and education investments" (Morris 1999, appendix, 399, 431–32).

Clinton's embrace of a balanced budget, however, sparked a fierce debate filled with "fury and fire" within the White House and the Democratic Party. Siding with the balanced budget required him to reject the strong advice of senior White House officials (Panetta, George Stephanopoulos, and Harold Ickes), Democratic legislators, and party loyalists (Morris 1999, 439).

Clinton absorbed these costs, though, because he perceived—as his political consultants argued—greater benefits in being able to claim "credit for fiscal conservatism" and to "counter [the Republicans'] fiscal issue." "[R]eaching a deal with Republicans in Congress [to balance the budget would]," Morris argued, "get th[e] issu[e] off the American Agenda" and "take away the fiscal issue" from Republicans, forcing them to distinguish themselves on other (less popular) grounds (Morris 1999, appendix, 435–36).

There are several important caveats to add to the story of Clinton's pursuit of centrist opinion. First, his policy positions were rarely a simple by-product of what the polls said Americans wanted. The Republicans' proposals helped set the legislative agenda, which in turn influenced what issues White House pollsters explored and how they framed them in their survey questions. The result was that the White House's strategic interaction with Republicans influenced how Clinton and his advisers defined and perceived centrist opinion. For instance, Clinton and his advisers focused on Americans' opposition to "welfare" reform but apparently did not seriously explore the public's continuing support for government "assistance for the poor" (Smith 1987); the Republicans' initiatives focused attention on welfare and precluded a genuine discussion of government steps to reduce poverty, which was an aspect of the administration's own 1994 welfare reform plan. Clinton responded to one aspect of centrist opinion without taking full stock of the public's preferences.

Second, although the president put aside his policy goals on the budget and welfare reform in deference to centrist opinion, administration officials used evidence of public support as leverage for promoting their favored policies. Economic advisers like Treasury Secretary Robert Rubin welcomed the influence of centrist opinion in persuading Clinton to reverse field on the balanced budget and adopt their preferred policy. Similarly, liberal Labor Secretary Robert Reich calculated as the 1996 elections approached that the most effective means for advancing his favorite issues (e.g., boosting the minimum wage) was to encourage Morris to "poll on the proposals, and [then to] use the favorable results as leverage" when the pollster reported that it was an "unbelievably strong issue [that was m]uch more important than any issue now in play" (Morris 1999, appendix, 525, 528; Harris 1997a,b).

Third, despite the influence of public opinion, Clinton never uniformly followed it. He refused to compromise some policy positions (such as by pulling back fully on affirmative action and reversing his opposition to school prayer) that Morris and his other polling analysts recommended (Balz 1996; Mitchell 1996b). The president continued to weigh his personal preferences as well as the intense concerns of critical Democratic constituencies.

CLINTON OPPOSED REPUBLICAN PROPOSALS UNPOPULAR WITH AMERICANS   Clinton's willingness to reach agreement with Republicans on policies areas that enjoyed public support—the budget and welfare—was motivated by a strategy to "neutralize" those issues and force the GOP to run on unpopular issues that would "ghettoize its appeal and keep marginal or swing voters away" (Morris 1999, appendix, 431, 433).

Clinton's pollsters targeted Medicare as an important issue to tarnish Republicans as "extremists" who were out of step with centrist opinion. Initially, Clinton was reportedly reluctant to challenge Republicans on Medicare out of concern that swing voters would perceive him as defending a "special interest" (Frisby 1996). But Morris and other political consultants produced evidence that Republican legislation that reduced spending on Medicare was "not a special interest issue" but provoked "opposition by all voters." Probing Americans on "almost any argumentation" found "solid opposition" from two-thirds of survey respondents to Republican actions on Medicare. The strategic calculation in 1995 and into the presidential campaign was that "Medicare cuts derail Republicans" and drove up "Dole Negatives" (Morris 1999, appendix, 462, 505, 511, 516–17). "Dole's move to the center" and away from unpopular issues should be countered, the consultants argued, by "remind[ing] [voters] of the record" of Republicans' "Medicare cuts"; they cited their poll results indicating that this strategy made two-thirds of respondents "less likely" to vote for Dole (Morris 1999, appendix, 571).

Clinton's research on public opinion overcame his initial hesitancy to join forces with congressional Democrats to warn Americans that Republicans' Medicare policy would produce draconian cost hikes and disruption in care (Harris and Pianin 1995). Clinton's pollsters cheered on the president's attacks on the unpopular Republican position, reporting that "[w]e are winning the rhetoric on Medicare" and are now perceived by a 52 percent–31 percent margin as "more likely to protect Medicare and insure that it exists for future generations" (Morris 1999, appendix, 473–74).

Symbolic Responsiveness to Public Opinion

Clinton responded to public opinion (as characterized by his polling consultants) not only by selecting his policy positions but also by crafting what he said and did to convey his affinity with what most Americans were feeling and thinking. Illustrating the feedback of previous policy debates on politicians, Clinton concluded that his initiatives on health care reform and other policies during his first two years in office had failed because, as he explained to an aide in early 1995, "I was totally absorbed in getting legislation passed [and] totally neglected how to get the public informed." Clinton's lesson was that "I have to get more involved in *crafting my message*—in getting across my core concerns" (Drew 1996, 66, our emphasis). In effect, Clinton and his advisers deployed a strategy to prime the public by using poll-selected language, arguments, and gestures to retrieve attitudes and information already stored in the public's mind, which cast the president in favorable light, and to prompt Americans to adopt them as their standard of judgment for evaluating him and his policies.

Clinton's pollsters counseled the president on how to "get the message right" by constantly testing different words and arguments to predict their likely impact on what the "public perceives" *even if it is misleading* (Morris 1999, appendix, 473–74). In August 1995, for instance, they counseled the president on how to present his "differences" with Republicans on Medicare, noting that polling respondents were more receptive to the statement that "Republicans want to cut Medicare" than the claim that "Republicans want to cut Medicare so that they can pay for a $245 billion tax cut for the wealthy" (Stengel and Pooley 1996).

Clinton also used analysis of public opinion to calibrate his strategy toward cooperating with Republican. During the first half of 1995, the administration "recoiled in horror" at the "trainwreck" of a government shutdown and assumed (for political and other reasons) that the president would have to reach budgetary agreement with Republicans. But research by Penn and Schoen on different outcomes of the administration's battles with Republicans over the budget—including the "trainwreck" scenario—showed that most Americans "blame the Republicans rather than Clinton" and "focus national anger at the [Republican] cuts." As the White House and Republicans inched toward a shutdown in the fall of 1995, Clinton's pollsters urged the president not to "give an inch" because "the public wants a veto" of the Republicans' budget; a large majority of 61 percent believed that "important issues were at stake" rather than "normal political bickering" (Morris 1999, appendix, 455, 459, 485, 489–91).

The president and his most senior advisers came to see a budgetary showdown with Republicans as the "way for Clinton to recover from the defeats of 1994." Vice President Al Gore rebuked Republican threats during negotiations to "shut down the government" by warning that the White House would not abandon its own budgetary priorities because "[o]ur polls show you guys lose if the government shuts down" (Maraniss and Weisskopf 1996, 146).

By the summer of 1996 when the election was within sight, Clinton's political consultants reported that the president was "overcom[ing]" the "perception of weakness" after the budget showdown, and they recommended cooperating with Republicans to enact welfare reform and other legislation backed by majorities of Americans (including the Kennedy-Kassebaum health insurance plan and the increase in the minimum wage). In July 1996, they persuasively advised the president that legislative accomplishment was the "only way" to "move head to head [pairings with Dole] over 55 percent on a sustained and stable basis" (Morris 1999, appendix, 592).

White House polling also contributed to a variety of smaller actions by Clinton to signal Americans about his commitments and "public values." The reports by the political consultants contributed to a range of disparate gestures from supporting a crack-down on "deadbeat dads" and embracing school uniforms to Clinton's meeting with the families of the victims of TWA flight 800 and his selection of speakers at the 1996 Democratic National Convention (Christopher Reeves was chosen after outpolling Walter Cronkite and John F. Kennedy Jr.) (Harris 1998; Morris 1999).

Clinton's Media Strategy and Tactics for Reaching Americans

The grave concern of Clinton and his closest advisers about winning reelection in 1996 motivated them to use public opinion analysis to select the president's policy positions as well as his words, strategies, and gestures. Deciding what the president should say or do, however, was but the first step; it was equally important to ensure that his actions and statements were noticed by Americans. Breaking through to voters was critical for guiding them to use the White House's carefully selected indicators of the president's "public values" as the "more relevant indicators of his character than the allegations of personal prior conduct." Clinton and his advisers were acutely aware of the potential political damage from the charges of financial improprieties and sexual transgressions. They agreed that centrist voters would turn against Clinton if his campaign failed to "offset private scandal" in their minds. The Clinton team adopted two tactics to receive "credit" from median voters for Clinton's positions and to prime Americans to evaluate him favorably (Morris 1999, appendix, 515–17).

Controlling the Agenda

A recurrent concern among Clinton's advisers was to control the agenda of public debate and, especially, the topics that the press reported in order to focus the public's attention on the aspects of presidential actions and statements that they intended. The president's political consultants repeatedly warned against "dilut[ing] the focus." If Clinton's speeches serve the "press a smorgasbord, they'll choose the wrong issue." Their analysis of press coverage revealed that a series of Clinton public announcements had received little or "no coverage at all" (Morris, appendix, 356, 414, 445).

The remedy, they counseled, was to "discipline speeches to showcase only one push at a time" and to select "one subject per speech" based on its popularity with most Americans. On major speeches—the president's 1996 State of the Union message and his address to the Democratic Convention—he cited more issues but the list was carefully limited in size and based on each issue's "rank[ing] by their likelihood of making people vote for Clinton" (Morris 1999, appendix, 370, 616, 626).

Taming the Temptation to Criticize

Clinton's advisers warned that their ability to control the public's "focus" on political debate was also affected by the media's inclination to cover political conflict. "Anytime we offer an attack on Republicans mixed with anything else, it's the attack that will get covered"; it "takes over" "like a drop of ink in water" (Morris 1999, appendix, 398, 414). They concluded that when Clinton emphasizes the differences between Republicans and his own "New Covenant" approach, "the press will ignore [his remarks on the] New Covenant and only cover [his] attacks on Republicans" (Morris 1999, appendix, 370). The consequence, the political consultants reported, was that the "new Clinton positions are receiving short shrift and getting submerged in a two-way Democrat vs. Republican fight." Despite all their efforts to select popular actions and statements, "Clinton's centrist accomplishments are getting no attention [in the press because they are] drowned out by partisan rhetoric" (Morris 1999, appendix, 406–7).

The remedy for this problem was to reach deliberate decisions about when and on what issues to criticize Republican initiatives. Much of the advice that Clinton received from his political consultants concentrated on what issues to "stay out of" and leave to others in the administration to "work quietly" on. The president was advised to adopt a "publicly high profile" against Republican initiatives only when it was in his political interest for this difference to "dominate [the] media" (Morris 1999, appendix, 355).

Buying Access to Americans

Clinton and his advisers hoped to influence media coverage by narrowing the president's public presentations to a few issues and by carefully regulating his public criticism of Republicans. They also persuaded Clinton that buying advertisements was an important supplement to their efforts to influence the "free media."

The consultants' monitoring of free media coverage convinced them that it was dominated by "anti-Clinton" messages and was inadequate as the sole vehicle for delivering the president's carefully honed message (Morris 1999, appendix, 553). Some twenty months from election day, Clinton's political consultants argued that the president's team "need[ed] to get [the] basic messages out to the public . . . before [the] political season is too far along," while it still had the opportunity to reach "people's minds [when they are] open to new centrist information" (Morris 1999, appendix, 444, 451).

By the summer of 1995, Clinton had accepted his consultants' unprecedented recommendation for heavy media advertising more than eighteen months from election day and overruled Harold Ickes and other senior advisers who echoed the conventional wisdom that it would be ineffective (Morris 1999, appendix, 352, 449). Clinton's decision once again demonstrates the feedback effect of previous policy debates on political strategy: he agreed to the early media buys in reaction to the earlier success of "Republicans [in] beat[ing] him on health care with $13 million in advertising" (Morris 1999, appendix, 358; Stengel and Pooley 1996.)

Paid media offered two advantages in the eyes of Clinton and his advisers. First, it greatly enhanced their ability to reach Americans with messages that they controlled. Gaining credit from centrist voters and successfully priming their evaluations required "get[ting] the president's issues before the public." "Punch[ing] the message through over the paid media" would produce the kind of "repetition and simplicity" that would be necessary to "ge[t] credit" and "set up the battle in the public's mind. Second, the paid media allowed the president's team to pinpoint the audience who received specific messages and to concentrate on the most important "media market[s]" based both on the "chances of carrying [the] electoral vote of [the] state, [and on the] cost" (Morris 1999, appendix, 438, 439, 475).

The Republicans Retreat to the Center

Gingrich and his brigade of enthusiasts began the 104th Congress confident that they could "win" public support for their self-proclaimed "revolution" in government policy. The Republicans, however, failed to win this support; instead, the reaction of Democrats and, especially, Clinton to the GOP's policy positions and strategies produced political dividends for the Democrats and hurt the GOP's national reputation.

Democrats Rebound at Republicans' Expense

The effectiveness of Democratic leaders in countering the Republicans' positions and strategies was evident in two ways: changes in aggregate opinion that corresponded with Clinton's pursuit of the median voters' policy preferences, and results from an experiment that confirmed the likely effectiveness of a priming strategy.

POLITICAL DEBATE AND NATIONAL OPINION   First, aggregate changes in public opinion paralleled Clinton's poll-calibrated decisions to seize policy positions favored by the median voter and to "ghettoize" the Republicans with their unpopular policies and strategies. Clinton's reactions to three of the Republicans most prominent initiatives—their proposals on the budget, Medicare, and welfare—elevated the political standing of himself and his party at the expense of Republicans.

Clinton's counter-strategy to the Republicans' drive for a balanced budget convinced majorities of Americans, according to a series of independent surveys, that the Republicans were to "blame" for the government shutdown and that Clinton (who had been reviled a year earlier) had "acted more responsibly" and "really tr[ied]" to find a compromise to resolve the impasse.[8] Policy areas that Republicans had traditionally enjoyed sizeable advantages in public confidence were neutralized: Gallup polls showed that the 15-percentage point Republican advantages on taxes and the federal budget deficit had been eliminated following the government shutdowns.[9]

On Medicare, Gallup polls revealed that Clinton's intensified public defense of Medicare in reaction to Republican initiatives produced an 11-percentage point rise in the public's approval of the president's handing of Medicare (from 47 percent in October 1995 to 58 percent in mid-January 1996). The Democratic Party's handling of Medicare also rose sharply in the public's confidence from 33 percent in June 1995 to 50 percent in January 1996.[10] In addition, a series of Gallup survey showed the damage to the Republicans' national reputation: in December 1994, a plurality of Americans (46 percent to 41 percent) expressed greater confidence in Republican leaders' handling of health care than Clintons'; by mid-April 1996, a clear majority preferred Clinton (56 percent–34 percent). Following the intervention of Clinton and congressional Democrats, the Republicans simply lost credibility with the public; 57 percent in a *Los Angeles Times* survey sided with the Democrats in questioning the Republican claims that Medicare proposal was simply intended to save the program.[11]

A similar reversal in public confidence occurred on welfare. The majority siding with Republicans in a December 1994 Gallup survey (52 percent–37 percent) switched their allegiance to Clinton in April 1996 (50 percent–37 percent).

The public's turn against the policy initiatives of Republicans following the intervention of Clinton and congressional Democrats was echoed in a series of polls that revealed a sharp erosion in the public's confidence in the GOP. Between the summer of 1995 and February 1996, the public's approval of Clinton's performance rose 9 percentage points (from 43 percent to 52 percent) while Congress's dropped 10 percentage points (from 31 percent to 21 percent).[12] Gallup polls showed that the public welcomed Republican leaders into office in November 1994 with 55 percent believing that they were moving the country in the "right direction" as opposed to 27 percent who worried that it was heading in the "wrong direction." By April 1996, only 45 percent still saw the country moving in the "right direction" and 41 percent worried that it was heading in the "wrong direction." *New York Times* polls indicated that more registered voters considered Clinton a moderate in mid-1996 than had in mid-1993.

THE IMPACT OF A POLITICAL PRIMING STRATEGY: AN EXPERIMENT
Our second approach to evaluating the possible impact of Clinton's political strategy was to conduct a survey experiment in December 1994 to explore the impact of priming on the evaluations of individuals (Lock, Shapiro, and Jacobs 1999). As noted earlier, Clinton attempted to use his statements and actions (and their coverage in the free and paid media) to influence public evaluations by highlighting what the public pays attention to—what standards of judgment, criteria, or considerations rank foremost in its mind when it evaluates politicians and policies. For instance, "focusing" public attention on "Medicare cuts" might stimulate individuals to bring their attitudes about the elderly and Medicare to the forefront, with the effect—Morris, Penn, and Schoen reported—of elevating the "negatives" of Republicans and Dole.

We included a "split ballot" experiment in a national telephone survey of just over eight hundred adults between late December 1994 and mid-January 1995. One half of the survey sample was first asked about their *general confidence* in the national government's ability to carry out its programs; these respondents were then asked about their confidence in the federal government in the *specific* policy areas of national defense, medical care, social security, the environment, and "welfare." In contrast, the other half of the sample was asked first about confidence in specific government programs, and then about the government more generally. Comparing the responses to the two formats reveals the extent to which respondents evaluated government more positively if they were first reminded in even a subtle way about specific policies for which the national government was responsible (much as Clinton's consultants attempted to accomplish with Medicare).

Respondents who were first asked about specific policies were somewhat more confident in government overall (by 8 percentage points) than the respondents to the first ballot. The most striking finding, however, involved an important set of subgroup differences: the politically knowledgeable and self-identified Republicans were most affected by being reminded of specific government policies—they were greater than 20 percentage points more confident in government overall than their counterparts in the first ballot.[13]

These results indicate that when Clinton's strategy in 1995–96 succeeded in focusing on specific programs and government accomplishments such as Medicare, attentive voters (including some Republicans) became more likely to evaluate government favorably. By implication, the Republican strategy in 1993–94 to divert discussion from very specific government activities toward overall government performance in the abstract (through emphasis on "big" bureaucracy and stultifying "red tape") prompted Americans to reach a less favorable evaluation of government because they typically paid less attention to government policies that are quietly effective.

Republicans Pursue Centrist Opinion

The constraints on Republican efforts to gain the support of centrist opinion for their policy goals and the political risks of failing to change course began to dawn on Gingrich and other GOP leaders during the government shutdown. Their limited tactical decision to reopen the government would evolve into a full-scale retreat by the fall of 1996.

Senate Republicans and, especially, Bob Dole (who was running for president) became increasingly vocal in late 1995 in warning that the pursuit of policy goals by their House counterparts were alienating (rather than wooing) centrist opinion. Dole publicly split with House Republicans in December 1995 because he was "worried about the public perception out there . . . that we're the ones shutting down the government" (Maraniss and Weisskopf 1996, 165).

Gingrich had also spotted the impending political train wreck in December 1995 and the likely damage to the party's national reputation. Having failed to rally public opinion behind the GOP, Gingrich worked feverishly from the end of December 1995 to early January 1996 to reconcile the divergent impulses of GOP legislators and to attempt to restore the public's confidence in the party. The public's turn against the Republicans spooked about 25 to 54 House Republicans to consider voting for Democratic proposals to reopen the government. But allowing moderate Republicans to dictate his decision risked losing the bulk of House Republicans who continued to favor the standoff with Clinton. Gingrich confided in Clinton that if he moved to reopen the government in mid-December "you'll be dealing with Speaker Armey" (174). Adjusting his caucus's strategy to reflect the sentiment of centrist opinion required several frantic weeks of tempering the ideological convictions of his rank and file—especially sophomore and freshmen House members—and winning the support of his own leadership team, which had unanimously voted in late December against reopening the government. Even with his strongest pleas to recognize that the government shutdown had been a "failed strategy" and the political importance of "get[ting] the shutdown off the front page," Gingrich only garnered a bare majority for an interim spending bill (fifteen Republicans voted against Gingrich, including twelve freshmen members) (Weisskopf and Maraniss 1996; Deparle 1996; Drew 1996, 365–79).

By the fall of 1996, the approaching elections and the risk of facing the wrath of voters persuaded many Republicans to accept a full-scale retreat. Polls in June 1996 showed Republicans lagging in national election campaigns and possibly losing control of the House. Republican Senator John McCain of Arizona summarized the consensus among many Republicans—including the ideologically driven House—that they had pushed "too far, too fast." McCain warned, "If we don't compromise, we risk losing everything." Most Republicans agreed during the summer to compromise their policy goals and to move toward the center of public opinion; they adopted the motto, "Get things done, retain the majority and then be able to do more" (Dewar and Pianin 1996a,b).

The Republicans' retreat in late 1996 produced a stream of compromise legislation in which Republicans abandoned earlier proposals to cut or abolish established programs and signed off on policies identified with the Democrats. The surge of congressional action produced new money for education (including the largest increase in maximum Pell Grant awards in twenty years), wider access to health insurance, a higher minimum wage, and important environmental legislation (including the reauthorization of the Safe Drinking Water Act and a rewriting of federal pesticide laws). In addition, Republicans abandoned their campaign for a major tax cut—the "crown jewel" of the Contract with America—and a constitutional amendment to balance the budget. On one policy after another, Republicans conceded, as Gingrich did on the environment, that they had "mishandled" the issue and had to reverse course to close their distance from centrist opinion (Morgan 1996).

Between Clinton's inauguration in 1993 and the 1996 elections, competing political leaders changed their strategies toward centrist opinion. Both Clinton and the Republicans in the 104th Congress began their terms by attempting to move public opinion to support their desired policy goals. But concern within the White House and among congressional Democrats and Republicans about the 1996 elections motivated them to compromise their policy goals and to cooperate to pass legislation that responded to centrist public opinion.

The interactions of political actions, press coverage, and public opinion produced influential feedback effects on politicians. Their evaluation of past media coverage and public reactions reinforced and guided their dependence on strategies for manipulating public opinion. But the failure of political leaders to control press coverage and public opinion induced politicians (as elections approached) to move toward centrist opinion. Clinton's previous experience (particularly his struggle for health care reform and his repudiation by voters in the 1994 elections) prompted him in 1995–96 to become increasingly attentive to centrist opinion and to getting his message out by using both the free and the paid media. Gingrich and congressional Republicans similarly compromised their policy goals in response to centrist opinion in 1996.

False Hopes, Damaging Consequences

The strategy of crafted talk deployed by Republican leaders—attempting to sway centrist opinion to favor their desired policy goals—was enticing. It held out the promise of satisfying both their policy and political goals. Despite its seductiveness, however, the strategy was perilous for three reasons. First, championing policy initiatives favored by most Republican legislators (especially in the House) isolated them from most Americans. Their unresponsiveness, conservative commentator Kevin Phillips observed, exiled them to "fringe positions" and abandoned "centrist issues which Clinton has preempted" (Berke 1996).

Second, Republicans promoted policies that overreached what Americans were willing to accept because of an exaggerated confidence in their ability to move public opinion. The sophistication of public opinion research and the strategic attraction of obtaining public support for strongly held policy goals seduced the Republicans (and Clinton before them) to abandon their seasoned instincts of caution.

Third, the Republicans' efforts to sway public opinion were vulnerable to counterattacks by political rivals and media coverage of political conflict and strategy. The Democrats, led by Bill Clinton, capitalized on Republicans' inflated confidence and political miscalculations by aligning their own policy positions with the median voters and by priming Americans to see the president and other Democrats in favorable terms and Republicans in an unfavorable light.

The political failure of Republican actions and statements cannot simply be attributed, though, to faulty personal judgment or the peculiar conditions of 1995–96 (e.g., the historically narrow Republican congressional majority). Rather, the behavior and strategy of Republicans was the product of the political system and its reliance on public communications: partisan polarization and other political developments, media amplification of acrimonious policy debates, and the public's inclination to have second thoughts about major policy initiatives.

There are formidable barriers facing orchestrated campaigns to move public opinion toward supporting the enactment of partisan goals. Both Clinton's policy initiatives in 1993–94 and the Republicans' proposals after the 1994 elections were cases in which opponents successfully activated the public's doubts and mobilized opinion against new policy initiatives.

The lesson is not that more skilled political leaders or a better "message" could have won the day. Rather, the cycle of American politics and political communication nearly ensures that the pursuit of contentious policy goals and orchestrated presentations in a polarized environment will depress aggregate public support for the proposed reforms.

Chapter Nine

Dilemmas of Democracy

The representation of citizens in the American policymaking process is inseparably linked to mass communication and the formation of public opinion. The behavior and strategies of political leaders affect the mass media and public opinion in ways that have fundamental implications for democratic responsiveness to the concerns of citizens and, at a practical level, the stable operation of liberal democratic government.

We begin this chapter by reviewing our evidence for the connectedness of politics and public communications as well as the challenges these links pose for future research. We then devote most of the chapter to exploring the implications of our findings for our normative standards about democracy and for the operation of government. Is the muted responsiveness to centrist public opinion that we have found a boon or bane for representative democracy? What are the implications of our findings for promoting an informed citizenry and a stable and effective political order?

We challenge the long-standing bias among elites against government responsiveness to public opinion. It is the failure of politicians, we argue, to attend to the public's preferences and to encourage public deliberation that is threatening America's democratic system. We devote the final chapter to suggesting ways to improve democratic governance and the quality of public opinion.

Variations in Responsiveness and the Rise of Crafted Talk

Politics in the 1990s

We have outlined a theory that treats politicians' responsiveness to centrist opinion as a function of political and institutional dynamics. Without the immediate threat of elections, we expect politicians to perceive benefits in pursuing policy goals and discounting centrist opinion under conditions of rising partisan polarization, incumbency advantage, interest group proliferation, individualization of power within Congress, and intensified interbranch conflict. Politicians attempt to achieve their political goals by adopting a poll-driven strategy of crafted talk to rally public support and minimize their risks of electoral punishment by centrist voters. In fact, these five conditions were observed during the two episodes we studied—the Clinton health reform episode and Gingrich's efforts to lead a Republican revolution in Congress—and policy goals and crafted talk trumped responsiveness to centrist opinion. (We have defined "centrist opinion" as the *midpoint* in the distribution of public opinion and not as a partisan term referring to a particular group, such as the "Democratic Leadership Council.") Polls and public opinion analysis were not used to mold government policy but rather—according to Bill Clinton's pollster Dick Morris—to determine "how [the president] could convince people of his point of view" (Morris 1999, 338–39).

Although the responsiveness of politicians to centrist opinion has been diminishing since 1980, there are also short-term cycles. The approach of elections (especially, presidential races) prompts politicians both to adjust their calculations toward responsiveness and to absorb (at least temporarily) the costs of compromising policy goals. Indeed, we found that as the 1996 elections grew nearer, Republicans and Democrats yielded on their strong policy goals and responded to public support for an increase in the minimum wage, some minimal health insurance reform, and an overhaul of the welfare system.

The Clinton and Gingrich episodes provide evidence for our argument that responsiveness to centrist opinion is not a uniform feature of government decision-making. Rather, it varies over time under identifiable conditions. In the 1990s, political polarization and other conditions induced long periods of muted responsiveness punctuated by brief intervals of responsiveness preceding elections. It is worth stressing, however, that the ebbing of polarization and changes in other prominent features of today's political system could well produce a rise in responsiveness back to the levels prior to 1980.

Politicians' reliance on crafted talk to promote their desired policy goals during the health reform debate in 1993–94 and most of the first Gingrich Congress was conditioned by and influenced the large-scale processes of public communications, which encompasses press coverage and public opinion. The polarization of American politics and other changes that produced dueling political strategies to achieve policy goals and move public opinion were represented or "indexed" in the volume, sources, and content of press reports. Although the media's notable focus on political strategy and conflict clearly reflected genuine political conditions, professional journalistic norms and market considerations increased pressures on journalists to accentuate, overplay, or magnify political developments, which in turn feed back into the political process and reinforce leaders' strategies aimed at manipulating the press and the public.

Political strategies to move public opinion to support opposing policy goals and the media's (somewhat exaggerated) depictions of the battle create conditions that heighten the public's sense of uncertainty and risk and increase the public's inclination to pull back its support for proposed policy reforms. In turn, the public's evaluations influence political dynamics and media coverage.

Politics is public communications. The actions of politicians, journalists and editors, and ordinary Americans create a cycle of crafted messages and recriminations. The incentives of each set of actors invite conflict rather than cooperation, extremism rather than compromise, and a sense of uncertainty and risk that primes self-interest rather than concern for the whole society.

Theory and Future Research

A small but growing body of evidence confirms the pattern we found in the Clinton and Gingrich case of policy goals trumping responsiveness to centrist opinion (Monroe 1998; Ansolabehere, Snyder, and Stewart 1998a; Jacobs and Shapiro 1997a). Additional research is, however, critical on three fronts. First, more analysis of politics in the United States and other industrialized nations is needed to further confirm the decline in responsiveness since 1980 that we and others have reported. Indeed, European countries are increasingly debating the "democratic deficit" (Dahl 1999 and 1994). The most persuasive studies will need to combine quantitative and qualitative analysis, including interviews and archival research to investigate changes over time in institutions, political processes, the mass media, and public opinion.

Second, additional research is required to uncover the causal mechanisms that explain the variations in responsiveness over time. Focusing on archival evidence concerning the behavior of authoritative government officials like U.S. presidents offers a promising approach to explaining changes in political behavior and strategy.

Third, research on variations in responsiveness must be integrated directly with analysis of political strategies to manipulate public opinion. Studying both political responsiveness to public opinion and efforts by political elites to move public opinion is critical for distinguishing politicians who respond to manipulated public opinion (what we call "simulated responsiveness") from politicians who follow public preferences that are more autonomous or shaped in more constructive ways.

The Trustee Model: Elite Independence and Public Incompetence

Evidence that politicians discount centrist opinion invites sharply different reactions by defenders of divergent models of democracy. Whether such muted responsiveness is applauded or condemned depends on the normative interpretation of two aspects of democratic governance. The first involves the vertical relationship between the governed and governors and it rests on the degree to which government decisions respond to the will of a popular majority or attempt to influence or direct it. The definition of responsiveness to public opinion and elite direction is behavioral: the public's preferences point the decisions of government officials in specific directions, or government officials induce citizens to modify their preferences to follow and support their desired policy goals (Blondel 1987).

Models of liberal democracy are often described as posing diametrically opposed and inversely related claims about officeholders' *responsiveness* to public opinion versus their *direction* of public opinion (Sartori 1987; Campbell 1987 and 1988; Rockman 1984). The "trustee" model advocates low responsiveness and decisive, independent leadership, while the "delegate" paradigm champions minimal leadership and strong responsiveness (Wahlke, Eulau, Buchanan, and Ferguson 1962). Framing the issue of representative democracy, however, as a choice of either responsiveness or direction is a false one; we propose a model of "responsive leadership" as an alternative.

The second trait of democratic governance regards the quality of public opinion. "Democracy," Robert Dahl (1994) argues, "cannot be justified merely as a system for translating the raw, uninformed will of a popular majority into public policy" (30–31). Models of democracy differ over whether popular majorities possess the innate competence to participate as informed and engaged citizens in government decisions. The justification for political independence and muted responsiveness to public opinion often rests on conclusions about the minimal competence of the public. Alternatively, the argument for greater government responsiveness typically rests on the expectation that citizens are or can become informed and enlightened through education and deliberation. We suggest below that the quality of public opinion is the product of both vertical and horizontal relations—the behavior and strategy of politicians (as conveyed by the press) and the interactions among private citizens.

Vertical Dimension: The Independent Trustee

Muted responsiveness by contemporary government officials to centrist opinion would be applauded by a diverse set of political theorists as creating the potential for politicians to act as trustees, independent of public opinion and committed to advancing the national interest (Weber 1968; Schumpeter 1976; Sartori 1987).[1] "Your representative owes you," Edmund Burke announced to the electors of Bristol in 1774, "his judgment; and he betrays, instead of serving you, if he sacrifices it to your opinion." The core dilemma of representative democracy, Burke and others have claimed, is to generate strong political leadership that exerts its "mature judgment [and] enlightened conscience," or face the prospect of ungovernability as individuals and groups pursue their particularistic interests (Burke 1949, 114–16).

The framers of the American Constitution would certainly not recoil at evidence showing diminished responsiveness to public opinion. One of their fundamental objectives was to expand the discretion of elites and limit the influence of the mass public.

The Philadelphia Constitutional Convention convened in 1787 after a decade of intensive public participation in legislative politics (Wood 1969). The concern of James Madison and other framers of the U.S. Constitution was to avoid democracy and, in particular, to guard against "government by the people" or government guided by the popular will. Madison (1966) argued in Federalist Papers No. 63 and No. 10 for "the total exclusion of the people in their collective capacity" from government and for the adoption of a "scheme of representation" to select officeholders and moderate the influence of constituents. The aim of the framers was to ensure the "partial autonomy of representatives" from the preferences of citizens (Manin 1997, 161–63, 195; Ball 1987). "[T]he paradox," Bernard Manin observes, is that "the relationship between representatives and those they represent is today perceived as democratic, whereas it was originally seen as undemocratic" (1997, 236).

More recent commentators have continued to insist that elected representatives act in accordance with their judgment of the "broader community interest" and "good public policy" and exercise independence from their constituents' preferences (Huntington 1975; Maas 1983). Anthony Lewis (1993), David Broder (1997), and other prominent contemporary observers urge that policymakers must "apply their best judgment" rather than "doing what the public . . . want" and "yielding to instant public opinion" (Kosterlitz 1993). "[S]afeguarding our freedom and our form of government requires us," Broder (1995) insists, "to protect the Constitution against . . . pandering to public opinion." The independence of political leaders is extolled in both domestic and foreign policy (Alterman 1998).

Reasoning Elites, Unenlightened Citizens

The trustee model of democracy rests on the presumption that viable government requires the superior knowledge, skill, and temperament of elites. This model asserts that the mass public is prone to contradiction, misinformation, and wild fluctuations as it is whipped along by winds of "passion," as Madison put it. By contrast, elites are better able to reach consistent decisions based on objective knowledge regarding the most effective means for furthering the country's well-being (e.g., Sartori 1987). "[G]overnment and legislation," Burke insisted, "are matters of reason and judgment, and not of inclination" (1949, 114–16). Madison (1966) also expected representatives to "refine and enlarge" the mass public's base considerations; he explained in Federalist Paper No. 10 that "the public voice, pronounced by the representatives of the people, will be more consonant to the public good than if pronounced by the people themselves." To attract the individuals whom they expected to naturally exhibit reasoned judgment, the Constitution's framers encouraged the selection of representatives who possessed the most wealth, talent, and virtue (Manin 1997, chap. 3).

Contemporary policymakers share their predecessor's dismal evaluation of the public's competence for reasoned consideration of government matters; this deficiency is regularly trotted out to justify not responding to opinion polls (Althaus et al. 1996). Our interviews with officials in the Clinton administration as well as staff to Republican and Democratic members of Congress revealed a strong and consistent disdain for the public's competence to understand policy and offer reasoned input into policymaking. Our findings are echoed by other surveys of legislative and executive branch officials, which revealed that two-thirds or more of government officials doubted that the public was sufficiently informed, long-sighted, and emotionally detached to provide sound guidance for government decisions (Pew 1998; Kull 1999; Kull and Destler 1999). (This dismal view of citizens is rejected, perhaps not surprisingly, by large majorities of Americans, as we discuss below.)

Elections, as the institutional foundation for representative democracy, are interpreted by advocates of trusteeship as a procedural instrument or "method" by which voters decide on the deciders and then leave policymaking to this chosen (small) set of political elites (Schumpeter 1950). The key test of democratic governance is formalistic—adherence to the formal procedural requirements that elected officials face reelection or removal at the end of their term. The procedure of competitive elections provides a stamp of legitimacy for elites to use government power to make independent judgments and pursue goals that they choose.

Democracy and Deliberation

Warnings about the dangers of responding to public opinion are a familiar refrain to students of American history. Politicians who exhibit signs of attending to the mass public's wishes have over the course of American history been singled out for scorn. A century ago, Woodrow Wilson (1952) observed, in his scholarly writings, "When we are angry with public men nowadays we charge them with subserving instead of forming and directing public opinion" (40). More recent political observers continue to warn about the danger of "hyperdemocracy" and "too much democracy" (Heclo 1999; Brittan 1975). Samuel Huntington (1975) warned in the mid-1970s that "the strength of democracy poses a problem for the governability of democracy" (115). The risk, he cautioned, is that citizens are "progressively demanding and receiving more benefits from their government" and this "excess of democracy" is "overloading" the capacity of government to function and sapping its authority (64).

The warning against responsiveness has remained a common refrain among policymakers and political observers in the 1990s. The pitfalls of following public opinion were loud and clear messages from the government officials we interviewed. It was also eloquently articulated by House Republicans during their attempt to impeach and remove President Clinton from office in order to defend the "rule of law" and uphold their "constitutional duty."

The trepidation about responsiveness was a common criticism of President Clinton, who was chided (as one Democratic senator put it) for "poll[ing] the daylights out of everything" at the high cost of "inhibit[ing] good judgments and replac[ing] instincts" (Drew 1996, 103). Clinton's advisers were sufficiently concerned about allaying elite griping about his responsiveness that Dick Morris outlined in a June 1996 memo the "unpopular actions you have taken despite polls," which the president and his aide could cite to dismiss charges that "you govern by polls" (Morris 1999, appendix, 583). (The irony is that Morris compiled his list in a memo devoted to reviewing poll results, during a period when Clinton was unusually responsive to public opinion.)

We disagree with this long-standing bias against government responsiveness to public opinion and the presumption that responsiveness presents a dire threat to stable government. It is the failure of politicians to attend to the public's preferences that is threatening America's democratic system. The health of democracy rests, we argue, on responsive policymakers and an informed and knowledgeable citizenry that is engaged in rational and critical discussions about government.

Substantive Democracy

Government Responsiveness

An impressive tradition in political theory[2] and empirical research[3] associates popular sovereignty with "responsiveness by governing elites to the needs and preferences of the citizenry" (Verba 1996, 1). "Responsiveness" means that the public's substantive preferences point government officials in specific policy directions (what we call "substantive democracy"); it is recognized by this tradition as a realistic, workable, and normatively desirable standard for evaluating whether the authority to govern has in fact been grounded in the consent of the governed. Public opinion is expected not only to point the decisions by government officials in specific directions but also to influence the formation of agendas and policy choices. Without the ability to structure the choices addressed during political debate, the democratic process will be biased by the exclusion of issues that concern citizens (Dahl 1989; Schattschneider 1960b; Bachrach and Baratz 1962).

The expectation that elected officeholders respond to the wishes of citizens provides a standard for analyzing the substantive content of government actions between elections and for moving beyond the formalistic tendency to equate democracy merely with elections. *Democracy does not begin and end with exercising the right to vote.*

In short, a large, diverse body of political theorists, empirical researchers, and others hold responsiveness as the operative standard for evaluating most government actions. They ask: Do government decisions regularly respond to the public's wishes? When policies are habitually at odds with public opinion, the government is acting in a "nondemocratic" manner (Manin 1997, 170; Pitkin 1967).

Responsive Leadership

Critics of the trustee model of democracy typically offer the delegate model as an alternative. While the trustee model recommends low responsiveness to centrist opinion and decisive, independent initiatives by governing elites, the delegate perspective emphasizes that elected representatives serve as comparatively passive agents who mirror the public's wishes in policymaking (Wahlke, Eulau, Buchanan, and Ferguson 1962; Gallup 1940; Crespi 1989).

Although the delegate model helpfully stresses the importance of policymakers responding to the public's wishes between elections, this responsiveness requires some degree of initiative by government officials. We agree with Hanna Pitkin (1967) that representative democracy requires both responsiveness to the public's substantive wishes and independent initiative.

Two reasons stand out why representatives must, in practice, exercise some degree of independence, discretion, and judgment as they respond to public preferences.

GOVERNMENT OFFICIALS ARE THE ONES WHO MUST ACT   First, government officials are the ones who must "act" to formulate and implement specific government decisions. The requirement of initiative from policymakers rests on the nature of formulating and implementing government programs and on the character of public opinion. Although public opinion can point government policy in particular directions, it cannot "rule" itself. By definition, constituents are not literally the ones who govern in a representative democracy; they can neither directly make nor propose detailed policies. Only administrators and elected representatives can translate public opinion into proposals and authoritative decisions.

In addition, the very character of public opinion typically prevents it from imparting detailed instructions to government officials. Even if public opinion is informed and enlightened along the lines we suggest below, the mass public will generally articulate preferences regarding principles and directions (such as support for universal health insurance). The public rarely forms opinions toward detailed policy issues, which serve as roadmaps for representatives and administrators who formulate, enact, and implement new government programs. In the early 1990s, for instance, Americans never offered a loud and clear message in support of a detailed proposal for reforming health care; large majorities of Americans agreed that the current system was fundamentally flawed (a "negative consensus") and supported expanding access to health insurance and controlling the personal costs of health services.

THE SPECIAL CHARACTER OF CERTAIN ISSUES   The second reason that representatives must exercise some freedom from public opinion is that the character of certain policy issues requires independent action to further the needs and interests of the nation and its citizens. This is necessary for three reasons.

First, the public neither cares nor knows about the vast majority of government decisions regarding noncontroversial and politically settled issues connected with routine services. In these situations, representatives have a duty to do what they believe is in the best interests of their constituents (Warren 1996). For example, adjustments in Medicare's formulas for reimbursing doctors and hospitals involve relatively clear data, and experts are well-equipped to provide recommendations. The routine exercise of discretion to handle settled issues allows the public to focus its scarce time, energy, knowledge, and attention on issues that matter to it. This does not, however, give representatives free rein to keep hidden from the public potentially controversial issues or seemingly settled matters that change and raise larger political questions.

Second, representatives have a special responsibility to reconcile responsiveness to the preferences of majorities with the rights of minorities to dissent and to conduct their political, economic, social, and personal lives free of unwanted interference. The tension between individual liberties and majority preferences may be mitigated by the kind of responsible public deliberation that we discuss below (Benhabib 1996, 74–79). Americans' strong support for the Constitution can be translated (through relatively informed and reasoned public debate) into public support for protecting the civil and political rights of even disliked or feared groups and individuals (at one time or another) like Communists and homosexuals. The Constitution and its institutional framework, however, remain as a backup when public deliberations break down. The independent authority of the judiciary provides formal procedures for protecting the basic civil and political rights guaranteed by the Bill of Rights against the responsiveness of the lawmaking branches to majority views. The protection of minority rights, however, should not translate into a routine veto on the preferences of the majority (cf. Calhoun 1992, 1–48; Dahl 1985).

Third, officeholders may need to take actions that conflict with the public's current preferences in order to advance the country's overall collective interests in emergencies or other critical situations. For example, prior to America's formal entry into the Second World War, FDR challenged public support for isolationism by initiating (without a declaration of war) a modest military build-up in reaction to the threat that he believed Germany and Japan posed to American interests. Another example was Richard Nixon's effort to ease tensions between the United States and China. The president's efforts led to China's admission to the United Nations, which the public had opposed in the past.

There are two standards for identifying genuine and necessary government actions in the "national interest" that defy public preferences. First, the policy actions should be perceived by independent political observers and politicians from both political parties as credibly fostering the long-term interests of the community rather than merely augmenting the political power of the government officials and their supporters who initiate the actions. Second, the process for evaluating the claims should be based on reasoned and critical debate that persuades citizens (and independent political observers) that they would have supported the government policy if they possessed all the information at the disposal of representatives (Pitkin 1967).

The persistent and routine disregarding of the public's wishes in the name of the "national interest" deserve especially careful scrutiny for two reasons. First, "expert answers" on most policy issues rarely establish one position as the only avenue for advancing the "national interest." As a general proposition, policy decisions typically involve weighing risks, assessing uncertainties, and trading off the relative desirability of competing moral values (Dahl 1989).[4] In addition, claiming to represent the "national interest" is a common tactic to promote narrow interests and to marginalize the claims of other individuals and groups. Rather than knowledge and information dictating policy, it is more common for politicians' policy goals to determine what information and evidence is selected (Peterson 1997).

The polarization of elected officials provides a second reason for scrutinizing recurrent claims to represent the national interest in defiance of centrist opinion. Divergent policy goals and divisive political strategies based on crafted talk encourage relatively extreme policy initiatives and undermine the conditions for reasoned agreement (rather than political bickering) on common interests. For instance, the "national interest" was invoked by the White House during its drive for health care reform and by the Republicans during their campaign for the Contract with America; their political rivals understandably dismissed these claims of promoting the common interest as merely a cover for special interests, party activists, and personal ideology.

Deliberation and the Quality of Public Opinion

There is agreement among researchers on democratic governance and political theorists that the basis for democratic society and government responsiveness is a public that is informed, exercises critical reasoning, and engages in open and fair discussion.[5] This growing but quite diverse school of "deliberationists" has challenged the sweeping indictment of the public's competence by the advocates of the trustee model of democracy; they agree that ordinary citizens possess the innate temperament and cognitive skill to be reliable partners in governing—a view shared by large majorities of Americans.

The focus of deliberationists is on whether the process and conditions of public communications produce an informed, reasoning, and deliberative public. They tend to focus on two distinct dimensions of public communications that form public opinion—*vertical* and *horizontal* communications. Vertical communications concerns the process by which the public obtains, interprets, and comes to understand the information it receives from elites either directly or through press coverage (Lazarsfeld, Berelson, and Gaudet 1994; Popkin 1991; Zaller 1992; Gamson 1992; Neuman, Just, and Crigler 1992; Page 1996; Page and Shapiro 1992; Graber 1984). Horizontal communications occur between citizens. Individuals discuss their point of view (often spontaneously and anonymously) in dialogues with family and friends as well as in associations, networks, and organizations spanning political parties, citizen initiatives, voluntary associations, and organized social movements (Berelson, Lazarsfeld, and McPhee 1954; Huckfeldt and Sprague 1995; Popkin 1991; Gamson 1992; Neuman, Just, and Crigler 1992; Benhabib 1996, 68, 72–74).[6]

Vertical and horizontal communications provide the basis for the public as a collectivity to react in explicable and sensible ways to events and information experienced directly or conveyed by the press (Page and Shapiro 1992; Zaller 1992; Popkin 1991; Downs 1957). Consider, for instance, the apparent contradiction in public opinion during the Republican "revolution": Americans both supported a balanced budget and opposed cuts in specific social welfare programs. Interpreting this as evidence of public confusion ignores the fact that the public supported approaches to deficit reduction that avoided cuts in social welfare program; polls suggested that the public favored reducing defense spending, forgoing tax reduction, limiting net benefits received by the rich (including Medicare and Social Security), and raising taxes on the rich and on tobacco and alcohol. The problem is that the public's preferred approach was ruled out by its elected officials who favored different policy goals. In addition, the public's evaluation echoed the political information conveyed by the press; journalists covered the implausible claims by Clinton and the Republicans that the budget could be balanced without identifying specific programs for cuts.

The formation of public opinion is not a process comparable to an idealized version of a sequestered jury that reaches judgment in isolation. Nor does the mass public develop the elaborate and refined knowledge of policy specialists. Nonetheless the public reacts sensibly to events and available information, and it approaches a kind of "equivalent enlightenment" with specialists on the basic contours of reality and reasonable principles and directions for new policy (Lasswell 1948, 51).

The *quality* of public opinion, which forms the basis for responsive policymaking, has been threatened and diminished, however, by severe limitations with contemporary public deliberations (Bartels 1996; Althaus 1998; Austen-Smith and Banks 1996). This book has shown that public communications about policy issues are distorted by both the persistent strategies of government officials to use crafted talk to move public opinion and the tendency of the press to represent and amplify the actions and statements of authoritative government. We found that the public reacted by shifting from strong support for the Clin ton health plan to strong opposition within one year as the result of the uncertainty and perceptions of risk created by politicians' policy choices and strategies as well as the media's coverage of them.

Research and theorizing about public deliberation have identified three broad standards for evaluating the nature and content of political competition over national government policy: establishing a "public sphere" for discussion; relying on rational and critical debate; and fending off government domination. Defining these standards enable us to identify distortions in political communications and to justify our case for expanding substantive responsiveness.

The Public Sphere

High-quality public opinion forms in a "public sphere" where private citizens can discuss and scrutinize government actions in an open and critical manner (Habermas 1989). Private citizens are entitled, deliberationists argue, to discuss and consider public matters (in person or through modern technology) in a sphere that is conceptually distinct from the government and market relations. The arena in which private citizens debate in public should not simply be an extension of the battle by government officials for power or the drive of business leaders for money. The deliberationists' aim is to recreate the original effect of constitutional protections for freedom of speech and assembly—citizens who are free from the interference of government as they form and express their political opinions.

In the 1990s, however, government provision of information and politicians' attempts to promote their own policy goals (as well as those of privileged private interests) have encroached on the independence of the public sphere. Today's polarized politicians view public criticism as a political threat and attempt to shape public opinion as an integral component of their campaigns to enact the policies they want. Clinton reacted to the near-defeat of his budget and other political setbacks during his first six months in office by elevating the influence of his "political communications" staff, reestablishing his "war room," and treating the public sphere as another arena for struggle. One of Gingrich's first acts after the November 1994 elections was to establish a communications "team" to disseminate the Republicans' crafted "message" among their partisans and to blitz the press with it.

The strategies of today's politicians to stifle criticism represent an interference in the efforts of private citizens to monitor their elected representatives, to scrutinize and criticize government actions, and to form freely their own opinions. The intended effect of these strategies is to invade public communications and to disrupt the formation of public opinion of higher quality.

Rational and Critical Debate

Deliberationists argue that public communications should be characterized by rational and critical debate. Government actions, they argue, should be subject not only to open and public communications but to *"critical publicity"*—the "use of reason" to scrutinize government in public (Habermas 1989, 195). The defining feature of "critical publicity" is to rely on the conscious cognitive process of private citizens to initiate questions of government officials, to identify the interests advanced by each proposed policy, and to articulate the pro and con arguments for choosing one option over another.

Deliberationists expect a public process of rational and critical debate to deliver two practical payoffs (Benhabib 1996, 71–72). First, it should prompt citizens to assemble and think about a large volume and diversity of information relevant to evaluating government actions (Fishkin 1991, 1995; Dewey 1916). Second, rational and critical debate should encourage citizens to weigh the reasons for competing positions and to revise their own initial opinions as they become aware of the views of others. Articulating what others would consider a "good reason" for one's position in a public debate forces speakers to think about how other individuals reason about an issue and perhaps to revise one's own initial position. For instance, public discussion in the American northwest concerning the divisive issue of lumber harvesting produced notable revisions in the way alternatives were defined and in how local citizens viewed the issue (Reich 1991).

Deliberationists warn, however, that public debate over the merits of government actions is threatened by "publicity . . . for manipulative ends" (Habermas 1989, 232–33). Politicians prepare poll-honed messages to move the public to embrace views and offer acclaim that it would not express if it were better informed and engaged in critical public debate. Deception replaces reason and the public is treated as an object to be manipulated. *The problem, then, is not publicity but rather the shift in public communications from critical publicity to manipulative publicity* and a mindset that asks, as *New York Times* columnist William Safire (1996) put it, "How can I avoid responding to distracting questions and shape my answers to stay on message?"

Manipulation and deception were routine in the 1990s. The Clinton

White House staged public appeals in 1993–94 that deliberately obscured the new costs and government regulations inherent in their health reform plan in order to best "sell" it in a country uneasy with government; its regret in hindsight, as one official put it, was not being more aggressive in countering "the attack on big regulatory, mandatory bureaucracy." Clinton aides later conceded that the White House's claims about costs and government regulation failed to "level with people" and to be "honest up front." Similarly, Republicans attempted to obscure the reductions in Medicare spending and its use to fund a tax cut.

Deception by Clinton and Republicans extended from the presentation of their own policy initiatives to their treatment of their opponent's proposals. Although Republican leaders publicly welcomed Clinton's health reform proposal in the fall of 1993 with promises to work with him to pass legislation, Gingrich had already been plotting its defeat for nearly a year in order to boost Republican fortunes in the 1994 elections (Johnson and Broder 1996). For his part, Clinton attacked the Republicans' cuts in Medicare in 1995 and 1996 to improve Democratic chances in the 1996 elections, though he accepted the need for cuts (as evident by his later agreements to balance the federal budget). Clinton's and Gingrich's deception and mutual recriminations in 1998 prompted David Broder (1998) to lash out at both for "degrad[ing] and diminish[ing] the high offices they hold" and "damag[ing] the credibility of the government they head."[7]

Public Deliberation without Government Domination

The nature of leadership by government officials, deliberationists suggest, should be to facilitate public deliberation by equipping citizens with the necessary information to sort out competing interests and to engage in rational and critical debate. Reasoned public deliberation is threatened, though, when government officials attempt to dominate public debate and to overrun the efforts of private citizens to scrutinize government actions. Indeed, we have amply documented the repeated efforts by the Clinton White House and Republican leaders to interfere with debate among private citizens by "saturating" the country with partisan messages and priming individuals to focus on their claims and ignore criticisms and alternative arguments. Their determined drive to dominate public debate was evident in Jay Rockefeller's memorable plea to Mrs. Clinton to establish a "crafted information flow," in Dick Morris' advice to Clinton to fully capitalize on the "amplified bully pulpit [by exerting s]ustained presidential leadership," and in the Republicans' conclusion that "we'll get killed [if] we lose the public relations goals" (Morris 1999, 340; Drew 1996, 135).

Political success, politicians calculate, goes to the faction that most completely suffocates criticisms and sets the terms of public debate. The presumption of scholars like Doug Arnold (1990) that politicians and the mass public base their behavior on evaluating the objective costs and benefits of government policy gives too little attention to the pervasive and sophisticated attempts to manipulate public perceptions of policy attributes.

Public Deliberation and the Mass Media

The press is torn in two directions. On the one hand, its representation of authoritative government actions makes it susceptible to being used by one political faction as a tool for distributing its messages. Our analysis of press coverage demonstrated its fidelity to the actions and statements of authoritative government officials. In addition, special interests like the Health Insurance Association of America flooded millions of dollars into paid advertisements (such as "Harry and Louise") during Clinton's health care reform initiative in order to inundate the country with its misleading claims and shape the nature of public discussion (West and Loomis 1999; West, Heith, and Goodwin 1994). The press is, in effect, a gate through which government officials and privileged private interests can disproportionately communicate their crafted presentations.

On the other hand, however, the range and accessibility of the press endow it with unparalleled potential to make the actions of government plainly visible, to create a space for private individuals to converge, and to provide the basis for public deliberations and criticism (even if they fall short of idealized standards). The press can aid public deliberation by supplementing its coverage of authoritative government actions with attention to nonestablishment sources (e.g., private citizen initiatives and experts) and by expanding coverage that exposes government officials' efforts to manipulate public opinion.

Responsive Leaders of a Deliberative Public

The choice between the trustee model of independent political leadership and the delegate model of slavishly responsive government officials is a false one.

The claims for trustee democracy turn their back on long-standing norms of popular sovereignty and rest on often contestable claims to represent the national interest. What is heralded as principled independent leadership in the current polarized political environment is often merely a cover for crafted talk aimed at bending public opinion and claiming to be responsive to it.

On the other hand, the kind of subservient responsiveness to public opinion assumed by naive models of delegate democracy neglects the significance of quality public opinion and the importance of guarding against "simulated responsiveness"—a strategy that usurps the normative claims of popular sovereignty to justify responsiveness to manipulated public opinion. In addition, the delegate model ignores the practical need for initiative by administrators and elected officials. The operation of government requires its officials to take the initiative in formulating the details of legislation, providing information, and implementing noncontroversial "settled" issues.

In contrast to the delegate and trustee models, responsive leadership incorporates popular sovereignty and political leadership that facilitates reasoned public discussion. Government officials should, as a general rule, respond to the strong and sustained preferences of informed and well-reasoned public opinion, while exercising restrained initiative.

Threats to the Stable Operation of Government

The case for government responsiveness to informed public opinion rests not only on a normative commitment but also on its practical necessity for inducing the consent and trust of the mass public and maintaining the stable operation of government (Key 1961, 3–4; Ginsberg 1986). The competition among elites to dominate public communication with their manipulative messages comes at a high cost: it checks policy initiatives but also publicizes muted responsiveness and erodes the legitimacy of the political system as representative of the popular will.

Competition among government officials and other activists in the policy process is credited by political observers and scholars with producing two outcomes. First, the existence of multiple and competing individuals and groups has been lauded since the Constitution's framing as producing a countervailing dynamic that checks autocratic government and large-scale policy change (Madison [1966], Federalist Papers Nos. 10 and 51; Bentley 1908; Truman 1951; Dahl 1956). Although the extent and outcome of political competition face significant limitations,[8] the Clinton health plan and much of Gingrich's Contract with America were defeated by the counteracting effect of opposition by Democrats, Republicans, and other political activists. Their use of crafted talk as an oppositional strategy continues and intensifies the long-standing difficulties of political leaders to move public opinion through their orchestrated appeals to the nation (Tulis 1987).

Second, competition among political elites is credited with generating (through press coverage) diverse interpretations about policy and politics (Zaller 1992; Brody 1991). Although the political and economic establishment are disproportionately covered in press reports (Danielian and Page 1994), our study of the 1993–96 period found that oppositional elites were able to publicize—through press coverage—their opponents' deceptive claims, political overreaching, and departures from public preferences. The public received sufficiently diverse information that the contending claims of elites were, at least partially, counteracted.[9]

Elite competition in an age of ubiquitous public communications not only checks formal government decisions but also dramatically raises the visibility of government officials' diminished responsiveness and their deceptiveness in courting public support. The very success of dueling campaigns of manipulation erodes the legitimacy of the political system by highlighting the failure and ineffectiveness of high-profile policy initiatives. Attempts to dominate public debate with deceptive claims also erode the legitimacy of the political system as democratic: they raise questions in the public's mind about whether American government is responsive to its citizens or a vehicle for privileged private interests and promoters of narrow policy goals.

Thwarted policy initiatives, muted responsiveness, and dueling strategies of manipulation can produce two effects: they can sour public trust and foment overreaching and manipulation by government leaders.

Souring Public Trust

There is an apparent paradox in American politics: political leaders devote more attention to tracking public opinion than their predecessors, and yet ordinary Americans have increasingly perceived policymakers as unresponsive and out of touch with them (especially on domestic policy issues). The intense and highly visible efforts by Clinton and the Republicans to mold the policy preferences of Americans to their liking have—along with other social and economic factors— fed the public's distrust of government and its perception that policymakers do not listen to them.

There is ample evidence of the public's strong and growing sense of detachment from government since the 1970s. One of the most striking trends has been the fall-off in Americans' confidence in the government's ability to solve problems and in their sense of political efficacy—that their political activities influence government actions (Nye, Zelikow, and King 1997). The decline in the public's perception that Washington policymakers listen to them and can be trusted began in earnest during the 1970s and reached its all-time low in 1980; it improved a bit but then fell after the late 1980s to its all-time low in the mid-1990s. The proportion of Americans who reported "trust[ing] the government in Washington to do what is right" "just about always" or "most of the time" fell to 19 percent in January 1999, the lowest level ever recorded in nearly four decades of surveys.[10]

In addition, changes in the public's low sense of efficacy have paralleled the trend of rising government distrust—it accelerated in the 1970s and peaked in the 1990s. Responses to a variety of survey question-wordings found that Americans' perceptions that they do not have "much say" in government and that officials do not "care much" about their views rose from about 25 percent in 1960 to nearly 60 percent in the second half of the 1990s.[11] A participant in a citizen study group in Minnesota captured the rage felt by many Americans: "The politicians always talk like they want citizen input but like a lot of other things politicians say, they don't really mean it" (Blake 1993).

Americans increasingly concluded that political institutions are unresponsive to them and that they do not see the clear payoffs for participating in politics and trusting the government. The critical (though daunting) challenge is to explain why this has occurred.

Two prominent and reasonable explanations for this puzzle—politicians devoting more attention to public opinion and Americans perceiving less responsiveness and less reason to trust government—have emphasized the public's expectations, wants, and community orientations. The first explanation, associated with Lipset and Schneider (1987) and Robert Samuelson (1995), suggests that the extraordinary growth of the economy immediately after the Second World War elevated Americans' sense of well-being, their hopes for their children, and their confidence in the government's ability to deliver an ever-improving quality of life. America's successes in foreign policy—the end of the Cold War and the victory in the Gulf War—may have further raised expectations on the domestic front. Yet the crises of Vietnam and Watergate in the 1970s powerfully illustrated the real limitations of American government. It only became clearer during the 1980s that the government faced more intractable problems than before in managing the domestic economy in the international economic environment, in translating economic growth and productivity into increased personal income, and in generally improving Americans' standard of living and sense of security.

In short, the public has come to expect government to solve the country's problems, and when the problems are not settled Americans conclude that officeholders are inattentive, do not listen to them, and cannot be trusted.

The second explanation, most closely associated with Robert Putnam (1995), traces rising political distrust and alienation to the erosion of social connectedness and civic engagement. The breakdown of voluntary associations, which had once linked activities at the local, state, and national levels, removed a set of experiences that gave citizens a sense of participating in decision making.

Rising expectations in the face of limited government capacity and declining "social capital" most likely contribute to the public's frustration with Washington. But these explanations place an overly one-sided emphasis on the nature of Americans' attitudes and behavior—what they expect, request, and do.

What must be incorporated into the existing accounts of political alienation are the behavior and strategy of government officials themselves. The decision of polarized politicians to discount centrist opinion in favor of their preferred policy goals and then attempt to manipulate the public into supporting those goals can affect the public's perception of policymakers' responsiveness, its trust in government, and its interest in participating in the political process.

Muted Responsiveness, Weak Citizens, and Government Distrust

Two quite different bodies of evidence suggest that trust in government is related to the public's sense that it exerts influence on government. The first comes from public opinion surveys; the second involves the experience of city governments that have expanded public engagement in their activities.

THE POPULIST PUBLIC   Our own public opinion survey as well as a report by the Center on Policy Attitudes (Kull 1999) provide evidence that the decline in trust we reported earlier is associated with large majorities who reject the trustee model of government by independent representatives, prefer strong government responsiveness, but conclude that today's government is captured by privileged private interests.

The public's perception that government officials do not listen to or
care much about their views accelerated in the 1970s and peaked in
the 1990s. Paralleling this trend, polls by Gallup, the Pew Center, and
the Center on Policy Attitudes during the second half of the 1990s
consistently found that large majorities doubted the founding premise
of American government—popular sovereignty and consent of the
governed. Over 60 percent of the public (according to responses to a
diverse set of survey questions) believed that elected officials in Washington and members of Congress "lose touch" or are "out of touch"
with average Americans" and do not understand what "most Americans" or "people like you" think (Kull 1999, 7).

What is especially telling for our purposes is that Americans do not
contentedly accept their marginal role in government; they believe that
they deserve to influence government and that they should exercise
greater sway. In contrast to the dismal evaluation of the public's competence by government officials, 64 percent of Americans in a September
1997 Pew Center poll reported having a "good" or "great deal" of
"trust and confidence . . . in the wisdom of the American people when it
comes to making political decisions." Seventy-six percent in a January
1999 survey believed that the public as a whole (rather than either Democratic or Republican officials) was "most likely to show the greatest
wisdom on questions of what the government should do" (Kull 1999, 5).

Large majorities also demanded greater influence over government.
Polls by the Center on Policy Attitudes in 1999 and the Pew Center in
1996 found that 80 percent or more of Americans believed that "the
public should have more . . . influence on Congress [than] now" and
that the country would be better off if its leaders followed the public's
views more closely (Kull 1999, 3, 9, 11). Given a choice between detached trustees and responsive delegates, Americans overwhelmingly
preferred the latter: two-thirds or more of respondents in surveys by
the Center on Policy Attitudes in January 1999 and *Time*/CNN in February 1993 agreed that a member of Congress should consider his constituent's feelings "more important" in the member's vote than his or
her "own principles and judgment about what is best for the country"
(4, 9–11).[12]

Americans gave a similar endorsement of responsive government
during the impeachment of President Clinton. Sixty-three percent in
a September 1998 Gallup survey believed that "members of Congress
should stick closely to American public opinion" on impeachment
rather than "do what they think is best" (Kull 1999, 6).

Demanding greater influence on government but convinced that
they were denied it, Americans increasingly concluded that the privi-

leged were shaping policy. The proportion of Americans who believed that government was run by a "few big interests looking out for themselves" rather than "for the benefit of all the people" rose from 29 percent in 1964 to 53 percent in 1972 to 70 percent or more during the 1990s (Kull 1999, 9).[13] (Questions that asked respondents about the influence of the wealthy or special interest groups also found trends of acceleration in the 1970s with peaks in the 1990s.) A survey we conducted with Ronald Hinckley in May 1999 echoed these results: respondents ranked public opinion as clearly less influential in policymaking in the cases of Medicare and the war against Serbia than government officials' judgment of the national interest or the pressure of special interests or lobbyists (Jacobs, Hinckley, and Shapiro 1999).[14]

The combination of these survey results indicate that the legitimacy of American government as representative of the public will is eroding. The message is that a large and growing number of Americans are questioning whether American government rests on popular sovereignty and the consent of the governed; instead, they are concluding that it represents the privileged.

Government officials, in the view of Americans, not only fail to listen and attend to the public's wishes, they also attempt to deceive them. Widespread polling by politicians and the press is interpreted by Americans as evidence of policymakers' efforts to move (rather than to follow) public opinion. Seventy-one percent of respondents in our May 1999 survey reported that government officials tracked public opinion to "sound as if they were listening to the public's wishes" rather than actually "respond[ing] to the public's wishes" (Jacobs, Hinckley, and Shapiro 1999, 1).

In short, evidence from public opinion surveys of a strong and growing belief among Americans that government officials do not listen to them is associated with two trends. First, the public's declining sense of its own influence on government, which accelerated in the 1970s and peaked in the 1990s, corresponds with a decline in the actual responsiveness of government and a rise in ideological polarization (chaps. 1 and 2). Second, the public's strong and growing perception of government officials as detached and distant is associated with a similar trend of declining confidence and trust in government. Americans are unlikely to trust government when they perceive it as unresponsive to them and beholden to privileged private groups.

RESPONSIVE CITY GOVERNMENT AND HIGH PUBLIC TRUST   Over the last three decades, there has been a revolution among public administration scholars and practitioners in state and city government regarding the importance of incorporating citizens in running government programs—from crime prevention to city planning. The "new public administration" counsels public administrators to abandon exclusive reliance on "professional expertise" in favor of citizens' "lived experiences" and to elevate citizens (especially at the local level) to "governors of the community instead of its customers" (Kramer 1999, 90; Box 1998, 4; Thomas 1999). Indeed, citizen participation in such activities as administering public programs increased 10–20 percentage points from 1967 to 1987 (Verba et al. 1995, 72–73).

A fundamental precept of the "new public administration" is that engaging citizens as active participants in administering government programs will win back the public's trust in government (Kramer 1999; Thomas 1999). Research on city government offers some confirmation that distrust and cynicism are related to unsatisfied citizen wishes. Public alienation dropped in localities where public officials adopted vigorous outreach efforts and welcomed extensive public participation in decision making. In addition to public hearings and open meetings, cities with high levels of trust used voter referenda, citizen panels, and surveys to identify public preferences, which were reported (along with accomplishments) in mass mailings. Even when controlling for economic and social conditions, more responsive cities enjoyed higher citizen trust than those that shied away from building a climate of public trust. The implication is that government responsiveness to citizens increases their perception that they can influence decision making and that public officials listen to them and can be trusted (Berman 1997).

Crafted Talk and Declining Participation

Government officials' use of crafted talk to offset the political risk of discounting centrist opinion has occurred simultaneously with falling levels of political participation. It is tempting to infer a very strong causal connection. The turnout of eligible voters for presidential elections fell from its post-war peak of 62 percent in 1960 to a bare majority in 1988 and slightly below that in 1996. Turnout for midterm elections showed the same pattern: a decline from a high of 48 percent in 1966 to barely a third in 1990. Indeed, even the implementation of the "motor voter" law, which requires registration at motor vehicle and public assistance agencies, has not increased actual voter turnout. In addition, the number of people who work as volunteers for political parties and candidates has dwindled from 5.5 percent in 1960 to 3.7

percent during the 1980s. The same pattern of shrinking activism in governmental and electoral politics since the 1960s is evident in the declining numbers that turn out for rallies or speeches, attend local meetings on town or school affairs, write members of Congress, and sign petitions (Rosenstone and Hansen 1993; Verba, Schlozman, and Brady 1995).

The decline in participation reflects a dramatic change in the strategy of elected officials and other political activists (Rosenstone and Hansen 1993). Prior to the 1960s, politicians, political parties and other political organizations equated their success with mobilizing the electorate by offering transportation, absentee ballots, and voter registration forms as well as by mounting elaborate parades, mass demonstrations, and rallies to distribute information about their tickets. For voters, relatively little time and energy was necessary to become interested, informed, and engaged in politics, and they reaped the psychological and social rewards of friendships and strengthened ethnic, religious, and class identities. In effect, elites lowered the costs of participation and boosted its benefits.

The decline since the 1960s in voting and participation more generally is connected to the strategic choice of political leaders to abandon the tactic of mobilizing the mass public. Political activists replaced labor-intensive tactics with capital-intensive approaches, which relied on blanketing the country with their crafted presentations through television advertisements, direct mail, and the management of the news media. The consequence of the strategic shift toward moving public opinion was to alter the costs and benefits to citizens who commit time and energy to participation.

Americans participated less, then, because political activism became more costly and less attractive: they needed to devote more time to becoming informed, and the unmistakable strategic focus on manipulating their opinions rather than responding to them, depressed their interest in becoming engaged in politics. By extension, voters would be more likely to turn out and participate in politics if elected officials paid more attention to fulfilling their wishes (Abramson and Aldrich 1982).

In short, the trend since the 1980s of declining government responsiveness to centrist opinion and increased reliance on poll-driven manipulation of public opinion (as evident in the activities of President Clinton and Republican leaders in the 1990s) contributed—along with the public's rising expectations and eroding community bonds—to undermining Americans' confidence in their ability to influence government and in government itself. The effect was to erode the foundation for the stable operation of government—the belief that the political order is representative of the popular will.

Political Pathologies: Overreaching and Manipulation

Political polarization, the widening number and activities of interest groups, and other factors lured officeholders into pursuing policy goals that overreached their political resources and prompted them to attempt to dominate public debate with manipulative and deceptive claims. The result was to imperil the effective operation and credibility of political institutions.

Political Overshooting

Clinton and Republican leaders pursued a strategy of mobilizing public opinion that was at once enticing and yet perilous. The confidence of Clinton and the Republicans that political leaders could dominate public debate and move public opinion lured them into championing proposals that overreached what Americans or Washington moderates were willing to accept. The strategy of crafted talk failed to manipulate the public as expected for two reasons.

First, political leaders were unable to saturate the public debate with clear or nearly uniform messages regarding the direction in which to head. Promoters of policy reform found it maddeningly difficult to control their message from unexpected events, leaks, or interference from the opposition. For instance, in the late spring of 1993 a panic-stricken Clinton White House resuscitated the war room from the 1992 presidential campaign in a concerted effort to control its message over the budget. White House officials found themselves helpless, though, to stop leaks from warring factions within the administration, which were snapped up by journalists, jumped on by reform opponents, and turned into a "potent force" that contaminated budget negotiations to the point of nearly "killing" them.[15] In addition, both the Clinton White House and Republican leaders found their best laid plans countered by opponents who capitalized on their authoritative positions in the American system of divided authority to publicize alternative messages. Moreover, the media's tendency to represent or "index" acrimonious policy discussions further amplified conflicting messages from authoritative government officials. No single message was likely to dominate because rival political leaders used public presentations to underscore policy differences and journalists seized on the ensuing conflict.

The second factor that hindered political efforts at manipulation was public opinion itself. Americans were not blank slates passively waiting to receive information. Instead, they came to public debates harboring complex values and attitudes, which made even well-orchestrated propaganda campaigns susceptible to effective counterattacks that primed Americans to weigh conflicting values and attitudes.

In short, elites operated on the basis of inflated expectations about the power of their orchestrated presentations and the susceptibility of the mass public to their leadership. The result during the 1990s was a regular pattern in which alternating groups of leaders overreached their political resources and the opposition capitalized on the political miscalculation. Echoing Gingrich's own confession, Clinton conceded in 1996 that he "overestimated" his political resources when he proposed his health reform initiative (Mitchell 1996a).

Manipulation and Deception

The reliance on crafted presentations to move public opinion not only backfires on politicians who fail to achieve their policy goals and suffer political retribution for overextending their resources, but it also corrupts public communications and the public debate by making manipulation and deception the currency of political discourse. Within the Clinton White House, aides openly discussed the fact that "the priorities of the policymakers and the policy communicators [may be] at odds" but (like their Republican counterparts) settled for deception as a pragmatic adaptation to the reality of contemporary American politics.[16]

It is a telling irony that deceit arose from orchestrated campaigns that promised just the opposite—rational and critical deliberation over policy substance. Outwardly, Clinton and Gingrich promised a transparent debate: it would be open to all and in full public view, with policy decision based on the merits. Each invited the public to raise questions about the logic of their initiatives, introduce new evidence, and evaluate their proposals using what were presented as objective standards for promoting the nation's interests. Public debate based on critical and reasoned discussion would, it was promised, identify the "common good" that transcends initial public reactions and the demands of sectional interests. The Clinton White House was especially earnest (as one official put it) in trumpeting its commitment to creating a public debate based on "engaging in an honest, intellectual debate about what should be done."

In reality, Clinton and Republican leaders were engaged in a kind of double deception: they crafted misleading claims and they used the cover of promoting rational and critical discussion about the "national interest" to dominate public debate on their terms. Indeed, Clinton's proclaimed openness to revising his health reform plan in the face of compelling evidence and argument was itself a front: his aides privately urged him to "call for a serious, deliberative process that makes the right kind of changes" even while confidentially ruling out the possibility that their plan would "fundamentally change." [17]

Adding still another dimension to the deception, Clinton and the Republicans framed their proposals as part of an honest discussion of the "national interest" in order to obscure the play of special interests behind the scenes. While hyping the common good served by their proposals, political leaders promoted decisions that reflected the preferences of special interests, party activists, and ideologues. Chapter 3 peeled back the Clinton administration's deliberations on health reform, revealing its concessions to Democratic party constituencies, large and small businesses, older Americans, and others. The Republicans' initiatives after the 1994 elections openly acknowledged their receptiveness to pressure from conservative activists, business interests, and the affluent.

The drive to dominate public debate was insatiable. Americans' refusal to follow politicians' lead was interpreted by the Clinton White House and Republican leaders as confirmation of their suspicion that citizens were hobbled by faulty cognitive capacity and that promotional campaigns had to be intensified. Public doubts about aspects of the Clinton health reform plan were met within the White House and Congress, as a senior health policy aide explained, by the suspicion that "people are changing their minds based on . . . misleading information." Public dissensus was used, then, to justify intensified efforts at further deception.

The deceptive practices of the Clinton White House and the Republicans spawned complaints within Congress itself. Democrat Robert Byrd complained on the Senate floor that "cool, reasoned study and debate" had been replaced by deliberate "oversimplification and gross politicization" (Johnson and Broder 1996, 468). A senior aide to Senate Minority Leader Robert Dole similarly protested that ideological polarization meant that "you can't debate substance . . . in a bipartisan environment [that would allow] reasonable people [to] do the reasonable thing" (386).

Misleading political rhetoric has of course always been a part of public life. The rhetoric of today's politicians and journalists does not represent a new corrupting force that has been imposed on an otherwise pristine realm that once allowed open communication. New, however, is the heightened political motivation to manipulate public opinion and the advances in the technology and scope of mass communications, which have expanded politicians' capability to invade and attempt to dominate public discussion.

Politicians' efforts to dominate public communications not only degrade the credibility of government officials but also inhibit the internal deliberations of policymakers, as the Clinton administration discovered. When the president's proposed federal budget strayed perilously close to congressional defeat in the summer of 1993, the administration felt compelled by the perceived need to control public communication to close down its private discussions of health reform out of fear that leaks would disrupt their "message" on the budget. Even after the health reform debate, Clinton conducted fewer private debates, according to his advisers, and aides withheld their views, producing "bizarre . . . meetings where you know the meeting doesn't mean anything because nobody's saying what they really think, because they think it's going to be in the newspaper the next day."

Politicians Should Respond to Centrist Opinion

While the prevailing wisdom among policymakers, journalists, and many other political observers is that politicians are too responsive to centrist opinion, we would argue that government officials should be both more responsive to public opinion and less disruptive of the kind of rational and critical debate that forms those opinions. Our claim for greater responsiveness to reasoned public opinion rests on normative *and* practical considerations. Although responsible politicians may be justified in not responding to public opinion when faced with emergencies or nonsalient, settled issues, the principle of popular sovereignty and consent of the governed suggests that they should normally respond to centrist opinion. We agree with Professor Woodrow Wilson (1952), who challenged criticism of responsive government for "[allowing] our standards of judgment to lag behind our politics [and]

the principle that public opinion must be truckled to:" "[I]t is a digni-
fied proposition with us—is it not?—that as is the majority so ought
the government to be" (40).

The case for greater responsiveness also rests on a pragmatic consideration: the stable operation of government is best served by restoring
the legitimacy and effective performance of the political order. Greater
responsiveness to a reasoned public opinion would remove a direct
drag on public trust and moderate some of the exaggerated political
strategies to manipulate public preferences, which too often deadlock
the performance of government functions (even to the point of forcing
them to shutdown).

The objections to government responsiveness to public opinion cannot be justified by evidence and logic. The dire warnings about the
innate limitations of the public are not persuasive in the face of evidence that the preferences of the mass public react in an understandable and, in this sense, rational fashion to new information and events.
More than the public, it is the elite class that has violated the standards
of reasoned public debate by subverting it with manipulative and deceptive claims.

Equally untenable is the claim that the viability of representative
democracy rests on allowing only some abstract "national interest" to
drive government policy. In an era of polarized politics, competing
political leaders routinely wrap their promotion of partisan policy
goals or narrow private interests in claims about national interests,
thereby degrading its credibility and inviting skepticism.

After stripping aside the normative and practical charges against
democratic responsiveness, we are faced with the stark possibility that
the objections to public influence on policy stems from a deep-seated
prejudice and not from the usual tests of evidence and logic. Complaints against government responsiveness may simply be a front for
shackling democracy and further limiting the influence of citizens.

Chapter Ten

Disrupting the Cycle

Disagreement and conflict are unavoidable and necessary in politics. The cure for the ailments of Americans politics—the public's alienation and political leaders who discount centrist public opinion, overshoot their political resources, and rely on manipulation—lies not in ending or even muting conflict over major government policies but in altering the incentives that drive it and modifying its content and character.

Achieving a deliberative and responsive democracy requires two changes. First, the focus of political competition needs to be shifted from pursuing policy goals favored by a relatively narrow group of partisans and private interests toward responding to centrist opinion. The current system, which politically rewards government officials for discounting what most Americans prefer, undermines the founding creed of popular sovereignty and invites political recklessness.

Second, the quality of public opinion needs to be improved by extending and defending rational and critical debate regarding government. The primary threat to public communications lies in the content and character of highly polarized policy debates rather than press coverage; the media largely represent disputes between authoritative government officials.

We begin by examining the durability of the current system and whether reform is necessary. We argue that change is critical and propose using the process of public communication to achieve it.

The Durability of Current Political Patterns

It is, of course, conceivable that no reform is necessary because government will become more responsive as a result of the system of electoral and legislative competition. There are two mechanisms that might prompt political leaders to increase government responsiveness; we argue that neither is sufficient.

Throw the Bums Out

The institutional bedrock of democratic accountability is competitive and inclusive elections that allow voters to remove officeholders. Accountability requires that voters be able to assign responsibility and then drive from power those whom they consider responsible for undesired policy or conditions.

The use of competitive elections to remove or punish unresponsive officeholders has been well-illustrated during the 1990s. Congressional Democrats took a beating in 1994 following Clinton's promotion of a health reform plan that defied important aspects of public preferences. The congressional majorities of Republicans were narrowed in the 1996 and 1998 elections after they pursued unpopular policies. Patricia Hurley (1991) suggests that the Republicans failed to sustain the realignment process during the 1980s because they too were unresponsive to the policy preferences of key voting groups—namely, independents, disaffected Democrats, and some of those identified with the GOP.

Elections matter, but we are not sanguine that they provide the cure to depressed responsiveness. The tendency of politicians during the 1990s to discount centrist opinion has persisted during the course of two decades of elections; historical trends show similar periods in which responsiveness remained at low levels across a number of elections and, at times, decades (Shapiro 1982; Ansolabehere, Snyder, and Stewart 1998a). Elections appear to require a considerable period of time to restore overall government responsiveness to centrist opinion.

Three factors explain sustained periods of unresponsiveness amidst competitive elections. First, when motivated, officeholders can exercise wide discretion to pursue policy goals unpopular with centrist opinion. Public disapproval of specific policies (in contrast to actual outcomes and government performance) rarely results in electoral punishment because of the multitude of considerations that enter into voters' choices among candidates (including personal image), the public's incomplete knowledge of most officeholders' positions, and elected officials' strategic packaging of their decisions to obscure otherwise unpopular positions and responsibility for policy changes (Page 1978; Arnold 1990). The significance of multiple voter considerations and incomplete knowledge may explain why Clinton and Republican leaders were largely rewarded for passing welfare reform in 1996: although it did respond to Americans' dislike of welfare, the cuts in spending and other reductions in benefits contradicted the public's continued strong support for helping the poor.

Second, discounting centrist opinion is electorally necessary for most members of Congress from ideologically homogeneous districts. Because majorities of party members in each legislative chamber control the party's positions, congressional parties face strong pressure to pursue policy goals backed by supporters of the party rather than by centrist opinion.

Third, both the Democratic and Republican parties have relied on crafted talk to obscure their actual policy goals and avoid openly embracing their *true* positions. In 1993 and 1994, Republicans launched an orchestrated campaign against Clinton's health plan that criticized its excessive reliance on government while acknowledging the need for health care reform to expand access and control national health expenditures and professing a commitment to "get it done right" rather than simply "rushing" to "get it done fast" (Devroy, 1994b). (The record of subsequent Republican-controlled Congresses exposed the insincerity of these commitments.) Clinton and the Democrats similarly used poll-honed presentations in 1995 and 1996 to attack the Republicans' budget cuts while professing a newfound devotion to balanced budgets and tax reductions. The problem is that each party used crafted talk to prevent competitive elections that were clearly policy focused, with each party adopting divergent positions and voters choosing among them (American Political Science Association 1950). While the true policy goals of each party have diverged, the public *rhetoric* of Democrats and Republicans has converged as each professes support for what the public favors and the news media focus on the political charges and countercharges.

Elections matter, but we are not optimistic that they are sufficient to raise responsiveness (in a timely manner) to consistently higher levels throughout the period between elections. The ineffectiveness of elections in strengthening government responsiveness to centrist opinion prompted Bernard Manin to conclude recently that "representative government appears to have ceased its progress toward popular self-government" (1997, 233, 235).

Political Adjustments by Incumbents

It is, of course, conceivable that the legislative defeats of prominent
policy initiatives by Clinton and the Republicans will prompt political
leaders and other incumbents to respond to centrist opinion in anticipation of electoral defeat. After all, reliance on the strategy of poll-
driven crafted talk delivered neither Clinton's health plan nor the Republicans' Contract with America, and each set of political leaders
witnessed the electoral defeats of fellow partisans.

In reality, however, the political pain inflicted on Clinton and the
Republicans is unlikely—without intervention or new political developments—to lead future politicians to compromise consistently their
policy goals in light of centrist opinion and to scale back their attempts
to manipulate public opinion. Two reasons stand out.

"Manipulation Pays," or at Least It Seems To

First, neither Democrats nor Republicans are likely to view their previous deployments of crafted talk as a complete failure. It did, after all,
work quite effectively as a strategy in opposition; the Republicans
drowned out Clinton on health care reform and the administration
defined the policy debate in 1995 and 1996.

It is telling that both Clinton and the Republicans blamed their defeats on the same problem—tactical errors in executing their strategies
for "winning" public opinion. From the perspective of Clinton and his
aides, their failure to win public support for the president's health plan
resulted from "poor presentation" and the late timing of their public
campaign (Bennet 1997). They could have more effectively dominated
public debate, White House officials concluded in hindsight, by taking
"prophylactic" action that anticipated the charges of their opponents
and "innoculat[ed] people up front against the attacks that were to
come." Indeed, after the 1996 election, Clinton and his advisers continued (according to his own aides) to equate political success with securing public acclaim by dominating public debate: they remained convinced that "if he keeps his approval ratings up and sells his message
as he did during the campaign, there will be greater acceptability for
his program within Washington." And the Clinton team openly acknowledged that it still relied on the familiar tactics of poll-honed presentations to control public communications: polls continued to be
used to "test and craft language for his speeches" that "resonat[e] with
the public" in order to be "as persuasive as possible" in "marshalling
public opinion" (Mitchell 1997).

In terms nearly identical to those used by the White House, Gingrich and other GOP leaders blamed the Republicans' troubles since the 1994 elections on "communication disaster after communication disaster," which allowed Clinton to move public opinion as he desired. Their mistake was being "late in communicating" and failing to effectively counter Democratic messages (Dewar and Pianin 1996a; Clymer 1996). In 1998, Frank Luntz continued to plot a "comprehensive national communications strategy" and to identify "language that works" in selling the GOP's policies (Connolly 1997; Dewar and Ellperin 1998).

In short, Democrats and Republicans attributed their various defeats to the tactics they used to manipulate public opinion and not to the strategy itself. What persisted was the presumption that public support for policy proposals could be "won" and that crafted talk offered the most feasible basis for building a supportive coalition of elites.

Enduring Incentives to Discount Centrist Opinion

A second factor that fuels unresponsiveness and a dependence on crafted talk is that politicians continue to face strong incentives to tailor their decisions to policy goals rather than to the preferences of centrist opinion. Political polarization, individualization within Congress, the bias toward incumbents, interest group proliferation, and intensified conflict among the lawmaking branches create a predisposition toward policy goals and crafted talk. Responding to centrist opinion and compromising the policy goals near and dear to the hearts of party activists and campaign contributors may be more politically threatening to many legislators than defying the median voter. The source of political behavior and strategies lies in the structure of American politics and not in individuals or unique situations.

Muted responsiveness and emphasis on crafted talk persisted after changes in the individuals and situations we studied from 1993 to 1996 because the enduring set of incentives remained. Ideological polarization within Congress has continued and politicians motivated by policy goals continue to remain "fed up with cooperation" and resistant to compromising these goals.[1] The revolt against Gingrich's reign as Speaker of the House was sparked by conservatives' frustration that he compromised or failed to achieve their policy goals (Connolly, Broder, and Balz 1997; Dewar and Ellperin 1998).

Without changes in the system of public communications and politics, there is little reason to expect a sustained increase in government responsiveness to centrist public opinion and a significant diminution of politicians' reliance on the strategy and tactics of crafted talk.

Toward a New Philosophy of Public Governance

Reversing Americans' cynicism toward government and the erosion of popular sovereignty requires a change in the behavior of politicians and in our expectations about politics. Politicians need to be held to two high and very clear standards in order to restore the health of American democracy: they should be responsive to centrist opinion when making major policy decisions throughout the governing process *or* offer a credible explanation for their independence; and private citizens are entitled to criticize government in public without facing a government-backed onslaught of deceptive and manipulative claims.

The List of Well-Known Reforms

It is not difficult to list changes in the political system that would, in the abstract, diminish the attractiveness to politicians of pursuing policy goals instead of centrist opinion and spewing out government-backed deception. Campaign finance reform holds out the promise of diminishing the influence of wealthy individuals and proliferating interest groups who are rewarding politicians who advance their preferred policy goals.

Party reform is a golden oldie among political observers. "Responsible political parties" have long been hailed as a mechanism for imposing the popular will on government officials: parties are expected to propose clear and distinct election platforms that allow voters to choose the direction of government; members of the winning party are rewarded or punished based on whether they enact their platforms and improve conditions (American Political Science Association 1950). Indeed, today's relatively high party unity of congressional Democrats and Republicans has been hailed as a form of "conditional party government" (Rohde 1991; Aldrich 1995).

Reforms of American parties that aimed at reducing the perceived political benefit of manipulating public opinion to support policy goals might focus on curtailing the influence of party activists in the selection of candidates (perhaps through reducing the importance of election primaries and caucuses).

The enduring problem of American parties, however, is that they do not link the legislative and executive branches. In addition, they rely on manipulating public opinion to support their policy goals. The result is to sharpen political conflicts that the news media convey and magnify, which in turn short-circuits the process of reasoned decision-making by voters and makes it difficult for Americans to fully identify and evaluate the distinct policy positions of the parties. Moreover, politicians' overconfidence in their ability to manipulate public opinion between elections hinders the governing process by encouraging political overshooting and policy deadlock.

Party reform and new campaign finance regulations could help to reduce both the political benefits of pursuing policy goals in place of centrist opinion and the ability to circulate manipulative messages, but they are not likely to be sufficient to elevate responsiveness and deter rampant crafted talk. After all, historical analyses suggest that muted responsiveness existed during periods (such as prior to the 1930s) that lacked ballooning campaign spending and the current party system that empowers ideologically extreme activists.

Reforming the Process of Public Communications

We propose an alternative direction for reform—namely, altering the process of public communications. We propose to capitalize on already existing institutions as the basis for encouraging new directions that increase the incentives for politicians to respond to centrist opinion and to refrain from rampant manipulation of the public sphere. Reforming the process of public communications should proceed on a dual track that involves both the processes of opinion formation of private citizens at a physical distance from government and the constellation of institutions and individuals clustering around government policymaking.

The Public Communication of Private Citizens

A critical dimension of public communication about government must involve the processes of private citizens forming and disseminating opinions far from government. The participation of private citizens in associations, networks, and organizations create opportunities for individuals to engage in free and spontaneous communications that impart information about government and teach skills in argumentation and compromise. This world of private communications is evident within churches and neighborhood organizations, as well as within political parties, interest groups, consumer associations, and new social movements on such issues as the environment (Habermas 1989; Benhabib 1996; Fraser 1992).

These arenas where private citizens congregate in public to trade arguments and ideas exhibit three important traits. First, they are geared to forming opinions but exist outside the formal government structure. Second, participants speak as anonymous citizens and their arguments are evaluated based on whether they make sense rather than on the status or official position of the individual. Third, these diverse sites of public discussion are dispersed and loosely organized rather than concentrated and tightly controlled.

The private life of public discussion should be protected and expanded. The formation of informed and balanced public opinion is degraded to the extent that deceptive campaigns (propelled by the authority and administrative power of government) interfere with the process of private citizens criticizing government proposals and actions in public. *Promoting public deliberation requires an informal but widely accepted new corollary to the Bill of Rights: citizens have a right to debate and form critical views of government without facing poll-honed campaigns to manipulate their evaluations.* The commitment of government power to dominating public debate is inappropriate and is in as much need of scrutiny as the exercise of formal government authority.

Generating and protecting the kind of active public debate among private citizens that produces informed and reasoned public opinion is a difficult, long-term project.[2] Pinning the hopes of deliberative democracy on a flowering of citizen organizations alone runs a very high risk of failure and contributes little to the task of designing practical solutions in today's complex world. The challenge is to capitalize on existing tendencies to design workable improvements in citizen deliberation today.

One direction is to rethink the role of the public opinion survey as a common device for prompting citizens to form attitudes and for measuring them. The quality of public opinion gleaned from surveys is far from ideal; it largely relies on private choices that preclude actual discussion and on limited choices (between, say, favoring or opposing the Clinton plan) that fail to capture the complexity of public thinking (Herbst 1993). Whatever the limitations of surveys they are one of our few widely and routinely used methods for eliciting public attitudes and values.

Dissatisfactions with survey research has, over the past several decades, led to a flowering of imaginative approaches to stimulating individual thinking and group discussions in order to improve the quality of the public's opinions toward government actions (Price and Neijens 1998). One set of innovations has focused on reforming the way surveys themselves are constructed in order to capture the opinions of an informed set of respondents: these initiatives "educate" respondents by providing them with information on multiple policy options and the possible consequences of their opinions (Kay, Henderson, Steeper, and Lake 1994; Kay 1998; Neijens 1987; Neijens, Ridder, and Saris 1992).

Another approach has focused on convening groups of citizens (often selected to be representative of the population as a whole) for the purpose of both stimulating face-to-face discussions of prepared informational materials on policy issues and directing the dialogue toward identifying desirable solutions for national and local problems. These groups have included "deliberative polls" and "planning cells," as well as citizen "panels," "juries," or "advisory councils" (Alterman 1998, 168–80; Dahl 1970, 149–50; Price and Neijens 1998; Cook and Jacobs 1999).

Despite their own limitations (which we note below), these innovations hold out the promise of stimulating better-informed public opinion than captured in the standard survey. Even so, they do not replace the need and importance of expanding and protecting the private world of citizen engagement. Innovations in surveys and public deliberation forums offer an incremental improvement in stimulating individual and group reasoning, measuring public opinion, and enhancing our collective understanding of the views of a better informed and thoughtful public.

Revitalizing Democratic Processes

The second front in revitalizing the process of public communications and democracy is the world of government policymaking and the surrounding constellation of institutions and individuals. The combination of developments within journalism and innovations in stimulating and measuring public attitudes provide readily available means to raise the visibility of informed public opinion and to increase the incentives for politicians to weigh public preferences in reaching decisions between elections (and not just immediately prior to them). We should turn up the lights on government officials who persistently discount centrist opinion.

The process of public communication can be used in two related ways to increase public attention on officials who disregard what most Americans prefer and turn instead to manipulation for political advantage. The first involves scrutinizing the media's performance in distributing coherent information about public opinion, and the second entails using media coverage and other devices to publicize government officials' distance from what most Americans prefer.

MEDIA MONITORING OF PUBLIC OPINION   David Broder and other media watchers (Patterson 1994) have criticized the press for over-reporting polls and "reduc[ing] every issue to public referendum, ignoring the special responsibilities that elected officials hold in a republic like ours" (Broder 1997).

We disagree. The problem today is not that the press solicits the public's views too often and hunts down politicians who wander away from the public. Rather, the problem is that the press distorts public opinion and fails to chronicle politicians' distance from the public. Our findings in previous chapters as well as research by others suggest that the press does not often file *coherent* reports on patterns and trends in public opinion toward a wide range of issues, nor confront office-holders with their defiance of centrist opinion (Bennett 1990).

The press should spend more time, rather than less, on high quality reporting about public opinion. If the press devoted more and better attention to the public's preferences toward substantive policy issues, it would reinvigorate discussions about the quality of public opinion and its appropriate role in democratic government and raise the visibility and therefore the political costs of diverging from what most Americans prefer.

A growing reform movement within the news media, called "civic journalism," has created an unusually receptive environment for raising the critical publicity of public opinion and its connection to government. The aim of civic journalism is to reinvigorate public deliberation by incorporating the public's preferences and concerns into news coverage. Civic journalism has received a serious hearing in newsrooms and journalism schools across the country because of the crisis that has enveloped news reporting due to intense economic pressure, uncertainty over the future of journalism as reflected in record levels of discontent among reporters, and the public's cynicism toward the press, government and other institutions (Rosen 1994; *Civic Catalyst* 1997; Bennet 1996).

Civic journalism and other developments have created opportunities for innovation. One innovation is the "pollwatch," which builds on the "adwatch" that journalists and press critics use to scrutinize political advertising (Jamieson 1992). The pollwatch monitors *reporting* about public opinion and polling (Jacobs and Shapiro 1996b, 1997b). The media's reporting on public opinion often misrepresents and distorts the public's thinking (Frankovic 1998). The purpose of a pollwatch would be to scrutinize the media's often misleading portrayals of public opinion and voter preferences. Much like the adwatch, media reporting on polls could be evaluated by independent critics (including survey researchers) as well as by the growing number of media watchers who work for newspapers and television.

Our pollwatches during the 1996 election and the debate over social welfare entitlements in 1997 found that journalists loaded their stories with shallow allusions to public opinion and polls as a quick frame of reference—the journalistic equivalent of a drive-by shooting. Nearly 40 percent of references to public opinion and polls in the coverage of entitlement issues did not report actual data or evidence. Only a quarter of the references discussed survey results in an in-depth manner as the main focus of a story; the overwhelming majority of references cited polls in passing. Polls were briefly cited in a rapid-fire delivery. Over 80 percent of the references to them consumed the equivalent of ten lines of newspaper text or less; half of the references were five lines or less. It was rare for poll results to receive much genuine substantive discussion concerning the public's policy preferences and the considerations and values underlying them (Jacobs and Shapiro 1996b, 1997b).

Journalists have too often settled for vacuous references to "poll after poll" and to "strong" or "weak" public attitudes, which leaves the audience helpless to evaluate the public's preferences on its own. When the media have covered polls during elections, they largely focus on the results for horse-race pairings of the candidates. Journalists ought to present far more fully the multiple and competing concerns that Americans bring to their evaluations of politics *and* government policy.

The single most constructive change in media reporting would be to report poll results from sets of identically worded questions over a period of time and, of course, report the exact wordings. One major problem is that poll results are extremely sensitive question wordings; as is well known, survey responses can be an artifact of how poll questions are phrased. Comparing identically worded questions and examining the effects on responses to different wordings provide a powerful method for identifying clear patterns and trends in public opinion (Page and Shapiro 1992; Zaller 1992).

PUBLICIZING POLITICIANS' DEFIANCE OF PUBLIC OPINION   One of the most unusual features of the impeachment of Bill Clinton was the attention within the press and among private citizens to the Republicans' defiance of public opinion. What made this striking was the infrequency with which the press and the American public talk about and critically debate whether and to what degree government officials should respond to public opinion. (Americans are clear on their strong preference for greater responsiveness.)

As it is, the press, philanthropic and research foundations, and public-spirited organizations devote millions of dollars to opinion polling in the often futile hope that it will inform policy decisions and invigorate wider discussion about democratic governance within the media and the public more generally. The Public Agenda Foundation, for instance, released a report on public opinion at the outset of Clinton's health reform initiative with the hopeful assumption that "surveys are an enormously useful means for giving the public a voice in the public policy process" (Immerwahr and Johnson 1994, 3). The Kaiser Family Foundation, the Robert Wood Johnson Foundation, and others invested millions of dollars in polling on health reform in 1993–94 on the basis of the same hopeful assumption—that their efforts would (through media coverage of poll results) influence policymaking and stimulate wider public debate.

Our study has shown, however, that when policymakers reached decisions they were neither persuaded nor even attentive to polling results (even by well-meaning foundations), and the press did not use them to scrutinize policymakers who ignored public preferences. In nearly two decades of press reports on health care, polls and public opinion were a relatively rare source for media reports and were infrequently used to confront politicians with their distance from the public (chap. 6).

There are several means for creating and encouraging routines within the processes of public communication that would increase the visibility of whether politicians respond to public opinion. One possibility is for the press to expand its presentation of legislative roll call votes, which originated in an earlier attempt to widen public awareness of the actions of elected officials. In particular, the roll-call listing could be expanded to compare congressional votes and presidential recommendations with the public's responses to opinion surveys on the same issues. Publicly, comparing these summaries of government decisions and survey results would both pressure elected officials to be responsive and encourage them to explain their decisions in public, thereby adding to constructive debate.

Another possibility would combine press coverage with innovations in public deliberation to increase the scrutiny of politicians. During the 1996 presidential primaries, James Fishkin brought a national sample of Americans to Austin, Texas for several days of face-to-face discussions about policy issues among themselves, policy experts, and candidates for office. (This kind of "deliberative poll" was also conducted during the last two British elections.) The purpose was to use widespread media reporting to confront politicians and political parties with the participants' "informed" preferences (as measured by surveys before and after the discussions). The execution of Fishkin's experiment in American and British elections sparked criticism, including the charge that putting respondents in a fishbowl distorts their views and depreciates the preferences of people immersed in their everyday lives (*Public Perspective* 1996; Merkle 1996).

The critics of deliberative polls, however, missed one of the polls' fundamental purposes—to elevate politicians' responsiveness to reasoned public opinion.[3] Although press coverage of Fishkin's deliberative polls did not galvanize national attention on politicians and informed public opinion, the coverage it did attract shows the potential for using innovations in public deliberation to publicize democratic governance.[4]

The rise of civic journalism and its interest in "citizen juries" could well feed into a widening use of deliberative polls in cities and towns across the country. From 1997 to 1999, the Pew Charitable Trusts launched an ambitious program of forums in five medium-sized cities and a ten-city teleconference on the issue of Social Security, which was also linked to ongoing national surveys. Newspapers and television stations in a number localities sponsored citizen juries and surveys to identify the issues that most mattered to the public in order to determine which issues these news outlets should cover (*Civic Catalyst* 1997; Cook and Jacobs 1999; Cook, Jacobs, Barahas 1999).

The unfurling of these diverse efforts to track the public's views and then incorporate them into public debate can raise the perceived political costs to politicians of discounting centrist opinion while improving the quality of public opinion itself.

Revitalizing the Debate about Democratic Responsiveness

Increasing the attention to public opinion and its connection to government policy does not offer, we would argue, a technocratic solution. George Gallup (1940), a pioneer in polling, hoped that the technology of public opinion research would in itself create an objective and nonpartisan means for making policy that follows the popular will. But social science measurement of public attitudes cannot deliver an unambiguous report that politicians, the press, and the public could (or would want to) follow mechanically. The ambivalence of public opinion (and its measurement) combined with the diversity of media reporting and politicians' political orientation prevent any single, monolithic view of public opinion from being established, communicated, and accepted.

It is not necessary, though, for the press to attain idealized standards for it to stimulate deliberation about the nature of democratic governance. What is critical is creating the expectation that substantial government responsiveness to public opinion is appropriate and necessary, and then widening the media's reporting about public opinion and government responsiveness. The commentaries of prominent journalists like David Broder and William Safire as well as the paucity of coherent public opinion analysis in the press suggest that this expectation is far from being widely accepted.

The purpose of widening press coverage of public opinion on policy issues (not horse-race pairings of election candidates) is to fuel diverse and competing interpretations of public opinion by journalists and political elites (Page 1996). The relative silence today about the substance of the public's policy preferences must be replaced with a vigorous debate about these preferences and the government's reactions to them.

In short, strengthening American democracy requires fundamental changes in the behavior of the press and political elites. The political calculus that counts on mobilizing public opinion in order to unify a fractured elite is nearly backwards: only significant elite agreement can mobilize public opinion. Public opinion cannot be reasonably expected to unify divided elites in a polarized environment that is polluted by the efforts of elites to manipulate public opinion. Press reports of competing efforts to move public opinion only reinforce or deepen the public's ambivalence and elite conflict. The end result is that poll-driven crafted talk encourages just the developments it hopes to escape—fractious and ideologically divided elites.

Reclaiming Democracy

Increasing political responsiveness to centrist opinion would not produce neutral changes in government policy but ones that can have profound political implications. Politicians who respond to public opinion would enact policies that defied today's calcified political categories of liberal and conservative. The public, on balance, is more conservative on social issues than Democrats; it is less liberal, for instance, toward homosexuality and criminal behavior. On the other hand, the public is supportive of proposals for political reforms and progressive economic, health, and environmental programs, which Republicans reject. More responsive government might well pursue more conservative social policies and more progressive economic and political ones.

The most important implication of raising responsiveness is to re-affirm the spirit and content of democracy in America. The continued slippage in government responsiveness threatens the foundation of our democratic order and the meaning of rule by and for the people. Whether *democratic* government survives is not foreordained or guaranteed; it is the challenge of each generation to be vigilant and reassert its importance. Insisting that politicians follow the popular will and allow citizens to engage in unfettered public debate is central to that struggle.

Appendixes

Appendix 1: Approaches to Studying Representation (Appendix to Chapter 1 and Chapter 2)

Scholars have taken different approaches to studying the political representation of mass publics and other constituencies. In this book, we investigate responsiveness to public opinion on specific policy issues rather than global shifts in American liberal-conservative ideology. We also focus on collective representation of the national public as a whole, in contrast to representation of congressional or state-level constituencies (cf. Weissberg 1978; Erikson, Wright, and McIver 1993).

Studying Specific Policy Issues

James Stimson, Michael MacKuen, and Robert Erikson (1994, 1995), for example, study political representation by examining highly aggregated or global measures of ideology. Collective policy decisions by each branch of government (legislative, executive, and judicial) are examined through a single dimension of ideological conservatism and liberalism; the national public's preferences toward domestic policy issues are also reduced to a single ideological continuum. These authors compare overarching policy measures to the public's liberal-conservative "mood" on the assumption that the attitudes of policymakers and the public are closely connected to one another. It is more realistic, they argue, to assume that typical citizens form highly generalizable policy attitudes and "usually fail" to develop specific preferences; "it is the general public disposition, the mood, which policymakers must monitor" to reliably identify the public's thinking (Stimson, Mackuen, and Erikson 1994, 30–31).

In contrast, we argue that the public can and does develop preferences regarding specific policy issues and that the policymakers and the press typically track these separate opinions and incorporate them into their actions. Our policy-specific approach to studying political representation goes beyond the more sweeping ideological approach in two important ways, which then lead to a somewhat different conclusion.

First, while the use of global ideological measures offers the possibility of providing system-wide evidence (see especially Erikson, MacKuen, and Stimson [forthcoming]), this approach also limits the data and other evidence concerning public opinion and government policy in systematic ways. Most notably, important distinctions that the public makes among different policies do not fit along a single ideological continuum. Americans' thinking about social welfare policies is quite different than their evaluation of social policies (abortion, capital punishment, law and order issues, and different racial issues) and cannot be accurately reduced to a single ideological dimension (cf. Page and Shapiro 1992). While Stimson (1991) can account for some of these differences by allowing for a small number of additional dimensions, there are important and often nuanced differences in social welfare issues (e.g., past conflictual "welfare" policy issues versus more consensual issues like Social Security and Medicare; cf. Page and Shapiro 1992). (Foreign policy issues, by design, are excluded from the analysis of strictly ideological shifts in public opinion and national policy.) By contrast, we focus on tracking the level of public support for specific policies, changes in these preferences over time, and subgroup differences in opinion on specific issues. Moreover, our in-depth analysis of politicians' calculations, behavior, and strategy reveals that they (and journalists) were not content to rely upon global indications of public opinion. Instead, they devoted enormous time, money, and organizational resources to tracking public preferences and reactions toward specific policy issues.

Second, the efforts of Erikson, MacKuen, and Stimson (forthcoming) to track global shifts in public opinion and policymaking (and aggregate partisan and economic influences on both) leaves open questions about the *processes* leading up to congressional action (voting) and presidential decisions. The political processes of formulating policies and balancing policy and electoral goals are often highly-charged. For this reason, we study the policymakers' attentiveness to public opinion early in the policy-making process before votes are taken; this pre-vote process includes the setting of agenda, the formulation of the details of policies, and the attempts to construct supportive coalitions. This prevote process is especially important because of the efforts during it to manipulate public opinion.

These two differences lead to a somewhat different conclusion. Our analysis (and those of others, cited in chapter 1) indicates that public opinion toward specific proposals moved in different directions since the 1980s and that policymakers' responsiveness on some issues cancelled out unresponsiveness on others through important micro-level processes. The complex behavior and strategies of politicians to manipulate public opinion is beyond the scope of an approach that analyzes highly aggregated liberal-conservative trends in public mood and national policy. *The study of global ideological trends may overstate the actual level of government responsiveness to public opinion since 1980. Indeed, this approach may mistakenly include in its estimation of responsiveness what we refer to as "simulated responsiveness"*—cases in which politicians (with the inadvertent aid of the media) change public opinion in order to create the *appearance* of responsiveness to public opinion. (See the feedback cycles shown in figure 2.6 that allow for opinion manipulation by politicians on specific policies.)

Studying Collective Representation

Political representation in the United States can involve both the national relationships that we focus on and also relationships for congressional constituencies or individual states. The latter case refers to "dyadic" representation: the representation by a single officeholder of the voters residing in the district (or state) from which that official is elected. Some research on dyadic representation has usefully shown that electoral arrangements affect political behavior: the larger and more diverse state-wide constituencies of U.S. senators generally produce more responsiveness than the narrower districts of members of the House of Representatives (Hurley 1991, 7–8).

This dyadic approach, however, is not well-suited to evaluate the responsiveness of government as a whole. Studying members in the House in isolation from the positions of senators, the president, and national opinion has obvious limitations (given the American separation of powers system) in the analysis of the overall government responsiveness. The legislative process in the House is controlled by ideologically extreme and safe incumbents who use the caucus system and leadership positions to block or promote legislation that depresses the constituent responsiveness by House members who come from "mixed" or unsafe districts and by senators and the president who must negotiate with the House.

The motivation behind this book is to study whether, at the end of the day, government follows the preferences of its citizens. What matters most is whether the decisions of the national government reflect what Americans as a whole want. For this reason we focus on the collective representation of the public nationwide: whether the decisions of the executive and legislative branches of government as separate institutions respond to the distribution of national public opinion.

Appendix 2: Survey Question Wordings for Figures and Tables

Figure 3.1

EMPLOYER MANDATE   (variations as noted, CBS News/*New York Times* [CBS/*NYT*]): "Do you think the (federal) government should require employers (companies) to make (provide) health insurance (for all) available to all their workers, or (don't you think the government should require all employers to do this) is this something that should be left to the individual employer (company)? Survey dates: October 1988, June 1991, August 1991; (CBS/*NYT*): "Do you think the federal government should require companies to provide health insurance for all their workers, including temporary and part-time employees, or should companies be allowed to decide themselves whether or not to provide workers' health insurance?" Survey dates: February 1994, June 1994; (Yankelovich Partners): "Do you think that all employers, including small businesses which employ few workers, should be required to pay for health insurance to every full-time employee, or don't you think so?" Survey dates: September 1993, February 1994, May 1994, June 1994, July 1994.

UNIVERSAL HEALTH CARE   (Yankelovich Partners): "Do you think the federal government should guarantee health care for all Americans, or don't you think so?" Survey dates: September 1993, February 1994, March 1994, May 1994, June 1994.

Figure 3.2

SINGLE-PAYER   (Louis Harris and Associates [Harris], *Los Angeles Times* [*LAT*, variation as noted]: "In the Canadian system of National

Health Insurance, the government pays most of the cost of health care for everyone out of taxes, and the government sets all fees charged by doctors and hospitals. Under the Canadian system (which costs the taxpayer less than the American system) people can choose their own doctors and hospitals. On balance, would you prefer the Canadian system or the system we have here?" November 1988, January 1990 (*LAT*), November 1991.

NATIONAL HEALTH INSURANCE   (CBS/*NYT*): "Do you favor or oppose national health insurance, which would be financed by tax money, paying for most forms of health care?" Survey dates: October 1990, June 1991, August 1991, January 1992, July 1992, January 1993.

Figure 7.1

HEALTH SYSTEM NEEDS REBUILDING   (Harris, CBS/*NYT*): "Which of the following statements comes closest to expressing your overall view of the health care system in this country? 'On the whole, the health care system works pretty well, only minor changes are necessary to make it work better'; 'there are some good things in our health care system, but fundamental changes are needed to make it work better'; 'the American health care system has so much wrong with it that we need to completely rebuild it.' Survey dates: 1982, 1983, 1984, 1987, 1988, 1990, August 1991 (CBS/*NYT*), 1991, September 1993 (CBS/*NYT*), January 1994 (CBS/*NYT*), September 1994 (CBS/*NYT*).

CRISIS IN HEALTH CARE   (Gallup, *NYT,* CBS/*NYT*): "In your opinion, is there a crisis in health care in this country today, or not?" Survey dates: June 1991 (Gallup), May 1993 and January 1994 (Gallup for Cable News Network [CNN]/*USA Today*), March 1994 (*NYT*), September 1994 (CBS/*NYT*).

Figure 7.2

GOVERNMENT RESPONSIBILITY   (National Opinion Research Center-General Social Surveys [NORC-GSS]): "In general, some people think that it is the responsibility of the government in Washington to see to it that people have help paying in paying for doctors and hospital bills. Others think that these matters are not the responsibility of the federal government and that people should take care of these things themselves. Where would you place yourself on this scale or haven't you made up your mind on this?" (Scale goes from "1," strongly agree it is responsibility of the government ["2" is located on the "agree" side] to "5," strongly agree people should take care of themselves.) Survey dates: March 1975, March 1983, March 1984, March 1986, March 1987. March 1988, March 1989, March 1990, March 1991, March 1993, March 1994.

HIGHER TAXES AND GOVERNMENT IN CHARGE   (Gallup/American Medical Association): "Would you rather pay higher taxes and have the government be in charge of the organization and delivery of health care services, or would you rather pay more money out of your pocket directly to private doctors and hospitals, with government involvement only for people who cannot pay for their own care?" Survey dates: 1990, 1991, 1992, 1993, 1994.

Figure 7.3

OPINION TOWARD SPENDING   (NORC-GSS): "We are faced with many problems in this country, none of which can be solved easily or inexpensively. I'm going to name some of these problems, and for each one I'd like you to tell me whether you think we're spending too much money on it, too little money, or about the right amount. . . . Are we spending too much, too little, or about the right amount on . . . Health." Survey dates: March 1984, March 1985, March 1986, March 1987. March 1988, March 1989, March 1990, March 1991, March 1993, March 1994. *Note:* This is part of a "split ballot" that the NORC-GSS uses in which the other ballot asks about spending on "improving and protecting the nation's health" instead of "health"; the trends in responses to both questions track each other closely (e.g., see Jacobs, Shapiro, and Schulman 1993, 405).

Figure 7.4

FAVOR CLINTON PLAN   (Gallup): "From everything you have read or heard about the plan so far, do you favor or oppose President Clinton's plan to reform health care?" Survey dates: September 1993, October 1993, early November 1993, later November 1993, mid-January 1994, late January 1994, late February 1994, late March 1994, April 1994, May 1994, early June 1994, late June 1994, July 1994.

CREATES TOO MUCH GOVERNMENT INVOLVEMENT   (ABC News/ *Washington Post* [ABC/*WP*]): Do you think the Clinton plan creates too much government involvement in the nation's health care system, not enough government involvement, or about the right amount?" Survey dates: September 1993, October 1993, November 1993, January 1994, February 1994, early March 1994, late March 1994.

MAKE HEALTH CARE BETTER (CBS/*NYT*): "In the next few years, if the Clinton health care reform plan is adopted, do you think it will make health care in the United States better, make health care worse, or won't it have much impact one way or the other?" Survey dates: September 1993, early October 1993, later October 1993, November 1993, December 1993, January 1994, February 1994, March 1994, April 1994.

Figure 7.5

See figure 7.1.

Figure 7.6

CONGRESS WILL PASS HEALTH CARE PLAN (CBS/*NYT*): "Congress will spend several months considering the President's health care proposals. Do you think Congress will pass some sort of health care plan before the end of this year or do you think Congress will be unable to agree on a health care plan?" Survey dates: November 1993, December 1993, January 1994, February 1994, March 1994, July 1994, early August 1994 (one-day poll), later August 1994 (two-day poll), September 1994.

Figure 7.7

See figure 7.4.

Figure 7.8

LOSING FAITH IN DOCTOR (Gallup/AMA): "Now I am going to read you several statements. For each one, please tell me if you agree or disagree: . . . 'I am beginning to lose faith in my doctor.'" Survey dates: 1983, 1991. The remaining items graphed are responses of "very satisfied" or "somewhat satisfied" to a subset of the following battery of questions (Gallup/AMA): "Thinking about your most recent visit to a medical doctor, would you say you were very satisfied, somewhat satisfied, somewhat dissatisfied very dissatisfied with: . . . **The medical care you received? . . . The way the doctor treated you? . . . The way the doctor explained things to you? . . . The amount of time you had to wait** to get an appointment? . . . **The amount of time you had to wait before seeing the doctor? . . . The fee the doctor charged? . . . Overall,** how satisfied or dissatisfied were you with this **most recent visit?**" Survey dates: 1978, 1981, 1982, 1983, 1987, 1990, 1991, 1994.

Figure 7.9

PERCEPTIONS OF OTHERS' HEALTH CARE   Shown are responses to a subset of the following battery of questions (roughly divided into two sets asked in alternative years; Gallup/AMA): "(Now) Please tell me if you agree or disagree with each of the following statements: . . . Doctors usually explain things well to patients? . . . **Doctors are too interested in making money? . . . Doctors act like they are better than other people? . . . Most doctors spend enough time with their patients? . . . People are beginning to lose faith in doctors? . . .** Doctors are usually up-to-date on the latest advances in medicine? . . . Most doctors take a genuine interest in their patients? . . . Doctors fees are usually reasonable? . . . Doctors keep patients waiting too long in their waiting rooms? . . . Doctors do not involve patients enough in deciding on treatment? . . . Doctors don't care about people as much as they used to?" Survey dates: 1982, 1983, 1984, 1985, 1986, 1987, 1988, 1989, 1990, 1991, 1992, 1993, 1994.

Figure 7.10

CONFIDENCE IN ABILITY TO PAY FOR MEDICAL CARE   Responses of "very confident" or "somewhat confident" to the following questions (Gallup/AMA): "How confident are you that you have enough money or health insurance to pay for each of the following? Are you very confident, somewhat confident, not very confident, or not at all confident that you have enough money or insurance to pay for . . . **Usual medical costs? . . . A major illness? . . . Long-term care if you became unable to take care of yourself?**" Survey dates: 1978, 1979, 1981, 1982, 1990, 1991, 1992, 1993, 1994.

Figure 7.11

ELDERLY AND POOR GET NEEDED CARE   Question (Gallup/AMA): "Please tell me if you agree or disagree with each of the following statements: . . . **The elderly are able to get needed medical care? . . . Poor people are able to get needed medical care?**" Survey dates: 1982, 1983, 1984, 1985, 1987, 1988, 1989, 1990, 1991, 1992, 1993, 1994.

Figure 7.12

PLAN IS NOT FAIR   (CBS/*NYT*): "Do you think the health care reform plan Bill Clinton is proposing is fair to people like you, or not?" Survey dates: mid-September 1993, late September 1993, early October 1993, later October 1993, November 1993, December 1993, January 1994, February 1994, March 1994, April 1994.

QUALITY OF CARE   (CBS/*NYT*): "From what you have heard, if the Clinton health care plan is adopted, do you think the quality of the health care you and your family receive will increase, decrease, or stay about the same?" Survey dates: September 1993, early October 1993, later October 1993, November 1993, December 1993, February 1994, March 1994.

AMOUNT PAID FOR HEALTH CARE   (CBS/*NYT*): "From what you have heard, if the Clinton health care plan is adopted, do you think the amount you pay for the health care you and your family receive will increase, decrease, or stay about the same?" Survey dates: September 1993, early October 1993, later October 1993, November 1993, December 1993, February 1994, March 1994.

Figure 7.13

See figures 7.2 and 7.10.

Figure 7.14

See figures 7.2 and 7.10.

Figure 7.15

See figures 7.2 and 7.10.

Figure 7.16

See figures 7.2 and 7.11.

Table 7.1

For the question wording for the dependent variable, see figure 7.2; for the questions used in the scale for confidence in paying for medical care, see figure 7.10; for questions used in the scale for satisfaction with one's own doctor, see figure 7.8; for questions used in the scale for the general evaluation of doctors' care, see figure 7.9; for perceptions of care available to the elderly and the poor, see figure 7.11.

The survey questions used for the remaining variables were: "Do you have a personal doctor you usually go to when you are sick?" (yes, no); "Approximately, how long has it been since you last went to a medical doctor?" (coded as less than six months, six to nine months, more than nine months but less than twelve months, one to two years, more than two years); "As of today, are you covered by a health insurance plan?" (yes, no). The demographic questions included: "What is your race? Are you white, African American, or some other race?" (recoded as white, nonwhite); "What is the highest level of education you received?" (recoded as less than high school graduate, high school graduate, some college or trade/technical training, college graduate, post-graduate work); "Are you currently employed, unemployed, or looking for work, or not in the labor force?" (recoded as unemployed, employed/not in labor force); "Is your total annual household income, before taxes, over $30,000? Is it over or under . . ." (coded as under $15,000, $15,000–$24,999; $25,000–$29,999, $30,000–$44,999, $45,000–$54,999, $55,000–$74,999, $75,000–$99,999, $100,000 or over); "Would you describe the community where you live as a city, a suburb, a small town, or a rural area?" (city, suburb, small town, rural area); region was coded based on the respondent's area code location; sex (male, female) was coded by the interviewer after asking to speak with the "youngest male" or, if unavailable, "oldest female"; "Please tell me your age, are you under 18 (not eligible, return to introduction/terminate interview), 18–24, 25–34, 35–44, 45–54, 55–64, 65 or over?"

Table 7.2

For question wordings and measures, see Koch 1998.

Appendix 3: Content Analysis of News Media Reports and Presidential Statements, Coauthored by Greg M. Shaw

Chapters 3, 5, and 6 rely on a systematic content analysis of a large collection of White House Press Office releases and published presidential documents, as well as news stories from a variety of print and broadcast news outlets. The White House documents and public statements by President Clinton were first assembled from a diverse set of online archives during the 1993–1994 period (103d Congress). In terms of the media, we studied two sets of news stories: one longitudinal covering the years 1977 through 1994, and an additional set for the 1993–1994 period. These data sets enabled us to compare patterns of press coverage with political developments and with trends in public opinion over nearly two decades. The 1977–1994 set of news stories comprised an extensive sampling of Associated Press (AP) accounts mentioning health care. The additional 1993–1994 stories represented a sampling of television news accounts, articles from daily newspapers, and national news magazine stories. We describe below the collection of text material, procedures used in the content analysis, and our evaluations of coding reliability.

Collection of Text

Presidential Statements

President Clinton's public statements from January 1993 through December 1994 were tracked through various online archives that contained transcripts of presidential speeches, remarks at photo-opportunities and public meetings, formal statements, and press releases attributed to the president. None of these archives contained a comprehensive collection of White House Documents, but by capturing every Clinton message available containing the term "health" during the two-year period from every known archive, a substantial start was made on assembling a complete inventory of presidential health care rhetoric. To complete the search, the *Public Papers of the President* and the *Weekly Compilation of Presidential Documents* (Washington, D.C.: Government Printing Office) were consulted (see Shaw, Shapiro, and Jacobs 1996, for further discussion of the inclusiveness of various sources). Press releases and other messages not directly attributable to President Clinton were excluded. Our intent was to focus on public statements by the president, not messages from other administration officials. Just under five hundred documents were collected and included in the analysis.

News Stories

News stories used both in our longitudinal analysis of 1977 through 1994 and our examination for the 1993–1994 period were obtained from the NEXIS news archive. Both collections of news stories represented extensive random sampling of all the stories related to health care available in NEXIS's news archives. In order to identify stories relating to health care, the search was broad but within limits. The search included stories containing at least two keywords. One was *health* or any of the permutations of *hospital, medical,* or *nursing.* The second term was a permutation of one of the following terms: *alliance, benefit, bill, care, cost, coverage, crisis, debate, financial, group, insurance, legislate, mandate, package, panel, plan, policy, priority, program, proposal, reform, security,* or *spend.* We coded news reports through September 1994 when President Clinton and Democratic congressional leaders abandoned health care reform.

For the longitudinal collection of AP stories, once all of the stories mentioning these terms were identified, a sample of stories was randomly selected (using a random number generator). To ensure a distribution of stories across years that accurately reflected the rise and fall of total news coverage, the sample was stratified within five periods (1977–79; 1980–84; 1985–88; 1989–92; and 1993–94). Despite the filters placed on the search, many stories were captured that mentioned health care only in passing and were, therefore, not appropriate for content coding. Approximately 40 percent of the AP stories initially captured were ultimately determined to be relevant for further analysis. In the end, we coded the content of 3,092 Associated Press stories.

For the 1993–1994 period, we collected a sample of print and broadcast stories from among all such stories mentioning the key terms indicated above (health, medical, etc.). We did not stratify the sample across time because this period was much shorter, covering from January 1993 through September 1994. Instead, this sample was stratified by news medium: television, magazines, national newspapers, and regional newspapers. In the end, 1,625 news stories focusing on health care and appearing during 1993 and 1994 were collected and coded from the following print and broadcast news outlets: *USA Today* (229 stories), *New York Times* (170), *Washington Post* (129), *Atlanta Journal-Constitution* (86), *Dallas Morning News* (83), *Sacramento Bee* (83), *Minneapolis Star Tribune* (84), Cable News Network (206), ABC News (218), *Newsweek* (223), and *Fortune* (114). The overall distribution of these data for the entire 1993–1994 period by type of news medium was the following: 32 percent from television, 25 percent magazines, and 43 percent newspapers. The relative prominence of each medium in health care coverage changed over time: the proportion from television rose from 1993 to 1994 from 24 percent to 41 percent, while the magazine and newspaper proportions fell—from 30 percent to 19 percent for magazines and from 47 percent to 40 percent for newspapers.

Content Coding

Coding the news stories was more complicated than the content analysis of President Clinton's public statements. Two research assistants at the University of Minnesota read and separated news story into small segments with each segment comprising a specific "message." Each message consisted of an *issue, source* (cited or implicit), *directional content* regarding the issue, and *frame.* Because we sought substantial detail in our coding, we used this message from a particular news source regarding a specific issue as the unit of analysis rather than using the story or paragraph as the unit of analysis (Page, Shapiro, and Dempsey 1987; Jacobs, Watts, and Shapiro 1995; Cook and Jacobs 1999). In other words, each message received a single record of coded data in our analysis. The typical segment of a news story made up only a few lines of newspaper text (on average, just under six lines). For the 1993–94 period's stories there were a total of 9,740 messages and 10,640 in the 1977–94 period's Associated Press stories.

We coded each message's substantive issue content, each source the journalists relied upon for their information, the directional thrust toward the issue conveyed by the source, and the way in which the issue was framed. A list of 228 issue codes was developed, covering highly specific aspects of health care. (The list is available from the authors.) We collapsed the issue codes into two broad categories—"generic" and "reform." Under "reform" we included topics having to do with government policy or proposed policies and the political processes associated with such reforms. Discussions of support or opposition to the Clinton plan, of course, fell into this category. In contrast, generic issues were those having to do with the general state of affairs regarding health care. These issues included, for instance, the performance of and problems with the health care delivery system and discussions of the high costs of health care. The classification of our many issue codes as reform versus generic issues was accomplished through discussions between one of the authors and a research assistant; the validity and reliability of these decisions was confirmed by independent coding judgments by the other author.

Drawing on the insights of Iyengar (1991), Patterson (1993), and Cappella and Jamieson (1997), we analyzed the ways in which each segment of news text was framed. Four framing variables were conceptualized and coded (allowing us to distinguish the several categories of frames that follow: "substantive" versus "strategy and conflict" (the "strategy and conflict" frame distinguishes messages about political conflict from messages about substantive policy issues, versus neither of these); "national problem frame" (broad societal impact of events versus narrower group-specific consequences); "threat frame" (content that describes a potential "threat" to an average individual); and "episodic" versus "thematic" coverage. Each message was typically assigned a single frame code. A minority of passages (20 percent) involved the use of multiple frames, and a relative few embodied no discernible frame in the above categories (7 percent of messages coded).

The directionality of media messages was analyzed using a five-point scale, ranging from explicitly support/agree to neutral to explicitly oppose/disagree. To gauge the prevalence and extent of this "issue negativity" (discussed in chapter 6) we returned to the original 228 substantive issue codes to identify those that embodied what we took to imply negative comments about either generic issues relating to the provision of health care (such as "health care access is insufficient") or about reform proposals (such as "oppose the Clinton plan because it is too bureaucratic"). Comments conveying constructive messages regarding government health policy (such as "support expansion of Medicaid") were coded as positive ones, although they implicitly identified a problem. Mentions of issues receiving a neutral direction code were effectively omitted from the analysis of issue negativity. Neutral mentions made up 9 percent of the 1977–1994 data and 11 percent of the 1993–1994 data. (A check of intercoder reliability for this step found near perfect agreement: of the 228 substantive issue codes, on only one coding decision was there disagreement between the two coders—this involved one coder being unsure as to whether it was negative or positive.)

Our coding of the sources cited (or implied) by journalists included forty-five different sources, including public official and private persons. For officials, we identified their institutional affiliation and partisanship. These sources were identified both by explicitly attributed quotations and by less direct but clear attribution. In a minority of cases the source was not clearly identifiable. Such cases constituted 15 percent of the 1977–1994 Associated Press data and 6 percent of the 1993–94 data. When journalists offered (directly or by implication) their own assessments or analyses, we coded the journalist as the source.

We measured the magnitude or volume of the messages by coding the number of lines of text and the number of mentions. We focused

for the most part on the simple numbers or proportions of mentions—
that is, the number or proportions of mentions of a particular issue or
source. The correlations (Pearson r's) between trends over time in the
measures of mentions and the corresponding measures using the numbers of lines (e.g., the number of lines devoted to an issue or source)
consistently was .9 or better. In short, analyzing the number of mentions for the messages leads to similar findings and substantive conclusions.

Coding the content of the Clinton statements was somewhat less
complicated than the coding of the news stories. We employed a rather
fine-grained coding method. We used messages regarding different issues addressed by the president as the units of analysis in our coding,
instead of sweepingly treating entire speeches as single message. Comparable to the media coding, the average message in our Clinton public
statements data represents just under six lines of actual text concerning
an issue. This data set contained 4,695 messages.

Two research assistants at Columbia University read and coded
each of the nearly five hundred statements, finely coding the messages
in each statement according to substantive issues and our five-point
scale of directionality. With only very slight modifications (all of which
involved adding topic categories to address specific points in Clinton's
statements), the same list of issue codes used in the media analysis was
applied to analyzing the presidential statements. We also coded the
type of audience to whom Clinton addressed his remarks (we developed a list of twenty-four categories of audiences). Because the president was the source for all these messages, no other source identification was necessary. In our analysis of framing, we coded a sample of
Clinton's public statements. Finally, we used the number of lines of text
to measure the magnitude or volume of presidential statements.

Coding Reliability

The four main content coding decisions for each message—its substantive issue, source, directionality, and frame—were sufficiently
complex that they offered opportunity for disagreement in coding.
Even with this complexity, however, the four coders agreed substantially in the coding decisions they made. Where there were disagreements, they were generally resolved by a partial collapsing of
categories within the variables coded, eliminating some of the very
fine-grained detail originally built into the coding instrument but still
preserving substantial differentiation across categories. The most sig-

nificant collapsing occurred in the substantive issue list; the 228 highly specific topics were combined into 30 broader ones. We did less substantial collapsing of our categories of sources, reducing them to 32 categories from the initial 45. For instance, we combined all House Democrats into a single category instead of attempting to distinguish among those holding various House leadership positions. In addition, our list of presidential audiences was collapsed from 44 categories to 4.

We describe here the reliability of our coding of media content and the president's public statements. Once the news stories had been coded, a sample of 74 stories was drawn for duplicate coding by two assistants who had not previously been involved in this research. Their reading and coding of these stories produced strikingly similar data. Of the 554 messages in the sample, the second team of coders agreed with the original coders on 78 percent of the issue codes. Collapsing the issue codes from 228 categories to 30 improved the rate of reliability to 82 percent.

The second team of coders tended to agree with the first team's coding of the other variables as well. There was perfect or nearly perfect agreement on the direction code (within one point on the five-point scale) 73 percent of the time; significant disagreements (codes on opposite sides of the midpoint) occurred in only 9 percent of the cases. Cross-tabulating the two teams' directional codes produced a correlation (gamma) of .65, based on the 432 cases in which there was agreement on the issue codes. The identification of various frames was also quite similar across coders. Among these 432 cases the two teams agreed on the use of the strategy and conflict frame in 77 percent of the cases (273 of 353), on the national problem frame 92 percent of the time (36 of 39 cases), and in 95 percent of cases on the episodic/thematic frame (21 of 22 cases).

While identifying sources in news stories was a simple task, classifying them into very specific categories, and defining the categories themselves, was somewhat more difficult. The rate of agreement in coding sources into 32 categories across the two teams was 57 percent. This rate of agreement does not imply as much random error as might initially appear. Of the cases of disagreement, most of them (59 percent) involved one team of coders attributing the passage to the journalist as the source while the other team assigned it to a different person or group. That this single category accounts for such a large portion of the source code disagreements means that among the other nonjournalistic sources the rate of agreement was a good deal higher. In fact, setting aside the cases involving the use of this problematic category boosts the agreement rate to 75 percent. Further, in our original development of the coding rules, we intentionally wanted coders to limit carefully the use of the "journalist" category, so that we would be conservative in our conclusions about messages that we were most confident came from journalists themselves. We took great care in making sure that our main coders were attentive to this, with regular discussions occurring as the coding proceeded. In contrast, the new coders did not have the same extensive training in this regard.

Estimating the intercoder reliability for the coding of Clinton's public statements involved the same approach as the news media coding. Based on the coding by a second person of a sample of fifteen of Clinton's statements scattered across the two-year period, we found agreement on the specific issues coded in 51 percent of the cases (involving 309 message segments). Some of these disagreements were eliminated by collapsing issue codes, bringing the agreement rate to 61 percent. The two coders were substantially in agreement regarding the directional content of the message, with only minor disagreements in magnitude, not in direction (a correlation [gamma] of .66 based on 158 cases).

The identification of audiences was a straightforward task. While it was not possible to know among which type of listener the president sought to have his messages resonate most strongly, identifying the groups and individuals to whom he spoke was apparent from the headings on the White House Press Office transcripts.

Final Notes

The above discussion summarizes the coding reliability at the level of the individual messages. In our analysis, however, we *aggregated* these data into large issue and source categories (e.g., health care reform; administration officials and members of the president's party) for years in the analysis of the AP data for 1977 to 1994, and into months in the study of health care reform from 1993 to 1994. The process of aggregating the messages in these ways reduces the measurement error in our data of media reports and the president's public statements (e.g., Nacos et al. 1991).

Notes

Preface and Acknowledgments

1. Hyde 1999; Barr 1999; Rogan quoted in Gugliotta and Eilperin 1999; Rosenbaum 1998.

2. The *Oxford English Dictionary* (1989) mostly clearly traces the term "pander" to the 16th century when it was used in two quite negative ways: as a description of a pimp and as a characterization of an individual who "ministers to the baser passions or evil designs of others." While the reference to pimps has remained consistent, the second meaning has been expanded. In *Thesaurus of English Words and Phrases by Peter Roget* (1860, 1909, 1994), the synonyms for pander widen from "pimp" and "indulge" in its 1860 edition to "flatter" in the 1909 edition and "toady to, truckle to, cater to" in the 1994 edition. The 1973 edition of *Webster's New Collegiate Dictionary* connects it with "someone who caters to or exploits the weaknesses of others."

The evolution of pandering as a disparaging description of politicians who respond to public opinion is not entirely clear but its use was common by the early 1970s. Politicians used the term to undercut rivals who sided with public opinion and to fortify their unpopular positions. On 27 March 1971, for instance, the *New York Times* reported that Robert Dole (Senator and Chairman of the Republican National Committee) lashed out at Democratic politicians who had sided with the growing opposition to the Vietnam War for "pander[ing] to the war-weariness [of Americans.]"

3. We treat the terms "poll" and "survey" as synonyms, recognizing that the quality of research associated with them can vary.

Chapter One

1. Perry 1994; Drew 1994; Berke 1993; Center for Public Integrity 1994; A. King 1997; Harris 1997a and 1997b; Bennet and Pear 1997; Henry Hyde quoted in Clines 1999.

2. Stimson 1991; Stimson, MacKuen, and Erikson 1994; Stimson, MacKuen,

and Erikson 1995. For a review of research on public opinion and policymaking, see Jacobs and Shapiro 1994b; Jacobs 1993; Burstein 1998; Glynn, Herbst, O'Keefe, and Shapiro 1999, chap. 9. Our previous research pointed to the influence of public opinion on policymaking, but it also emphasized that policymakers' responsiveness to public opinion was conditioned by political and institutional dynamics as evident in the variations across policy issues, time periods, and political environment (Jacobs 1993 and 1992b; Shapiro 1982; Page and Shapiro 1983, especially note 17).

3. In addition to the aggregate studies we review, there have also been studies of single issues. For instance, Richard Sobel (1998) finds that political discussion (and media coverage) were at odds with public opinion on the issue of U.S. intervention in Bosnia (also see Page 1995). For a relevant study of state politics, see Herbst 1998.

4. The most dramatic drop in opinion-policy consistency was on social welfare, economic and labor issues, and, especially, political reform (Monroe 1998).

5. Focusing on four social policies (welfare, crime, social security, and health care), we found that congruent changes in opinion and policy fell from 67 percent during Reagan's second term (1984–87) to 40 percent during the Bush administration (1988–91) and 36 percent during half of Clinton's first term (1992–94) (Jacobs and Shapiro 1997a). Further analysis is necessary because this research is at its early stages and is not yet as exhaustive as Monroe's (1998) or Page and Shapiro's (1983).

6. As we note below, scholars have become more attentive to the interconnections within the political system (Zaller 1992; Page and Shapiro 1992; Rosenstone and Hansen 1993). This has been most evident in research on public opinion, which is increasingly treated as endogenous to the political process (Kuklinski and Segura 1995; Gerber and Jackson 1993). We build on this growing body of research by investigating the interconnection of politicians' behavior and strategy, press coverage, and public opinion.

7. We interviewed staff in congressional offices, officials in the Clinton White House and executive branch departments, as well as administration advisers who worked outside government. A handful of individuals were interviewed on more than one occasion. Most of the interviews were conducted in person in Washington, D.C.; a few were continued by phone. The interviews ranged from thirty minutes to two hours, depending on time constraints, and were based on a common set of structured questions (which were taped and transcribed). We granted anonymity to encourage candor, as most interviews occurred during policy debates, and assigned a random number to most interviews to help us track them.

8. Although research such as Ansolabehere's project examines representation in terms of an officeholder's responsiveness to his or her particular constituents (e.g., a congressional district), our general approach concentrates on the collective responsiveness of an institution (e.g., Congress) or the national government as a whole. Our view is that the multiple and competing systems of political representation (e.g., the representation of narrow districts by members of the House of Representatives as opposed to the president's representation of the nation) should largely offset each other and produce policies that correspond with the national distribution of public opinion (for a review see Jacobs and Shapiro 1994b; Shapiro and Jacobs 1988; Burstein 1998). We discuss this issue of political representation in appendix 1.

9. Previous research would suggest that Clinton and Gingrich should have responded to public opinion because they headlined policy issues that ignited strong party divisions and became highly salient to centrist opinion and to policymakers (Hill and Hurley 1999); they focused on social welfare issues; and large majorities favored policy positions (which Clinton and then Gingrich discounted; see Monroe 1979; Hill and Hurley 1999; Page and Shapiro 1983; Kingdon 1989; Kuklinski and Elling 1977). It is possible, however, that the attempt by Clinton and Gingrich to significantly change the status quo depressed responsiveness (Page and Shapiro 1983; Monroe 1979).

10. We largely draw on the American case; for discussion of policy and political goals in a comparative context of multiparty elections, see Adams and Merrill 1999 and Iversen 1994.

11. In contrast to what is often considered Downsian analysis, Downs himself focused on the behavior of political parties rather than on individual candidates. He assumed that candidates would act as teams with all candidates and legislators adopting a common platform of positions. Another important issue is the size of the electoral majority: Downs suggested that politicians sought to maximize their number of votes, while Riker (1962) and others (Mayhew 1974a, 46–48) argue that a comfortable winning majority is the most attractive strategically.

12. Research has uncovered a number of limitations with the median voter account including the following: the existence of multiple issue dimensions defies any officeseeker's attempt to locate a position that will appeal to the median voter in all directions (but cf. Davis, Hinich, and Ordeshook 1970); candidates are uncertain about their information concerning the electorate's preferences and their own ideal positions in relation to those preferences (Erikson and Romero 1990); in this environment of uncertainty, candidates that announce definitive policy positions on conflictual issues risk alienating centrist voters; candidates are constrained in their position-taking by ideologically oriented activists within the political parties, which explains persistent ideological differences among candidates that do not reflect the view of median voters; and American candidates rarely sublimate their own policy convictions and career interests in order to run as part of a team committed to a joint party platform (Wittman 1990 and 1983; Page 1978; Kessel 1992; Ginsberg 1976; Poole and Rosenthal 1984, 1991).

13. Mayhew (1991) argues that significant public policy enactments were just as frequent during divided government as during unified government. The enduring weakness of parties to control politicians made them equally ineffectual during divided and unified government. More recent research finds evidence that unified government is more effective at enacting new legislation and perhaps also at producing "great" presidents (Coleman 1997; Quirk and Nemith 1995; Cameron 2000a,b).

Chapter Two

1. While we agree that political motivations change and produce routine adjustments of politicians' policy actions, we supplement the account offered by Stimson, MacKuen, and Erikson in several ways. First, we more fully specify the set of factors that produce policy goals; they are not simply the product of the politicians' personal attitudes. Second, Stimson, MacKuen, and Erikson suggest that policymakers adjust their positions in response to the "anticipated future consequence of the sensed change in public opinion." Politicians' positions, they claim,

are a function of public opinion movement (that is, moving toward politicians' preferred policy positions when public opinion shifts in that direction and away from their preferred positions when opinion moves in other direction). This account does not allow for the possibility that policy goals have a value of their own and are not simply the toy of public opinion. As the party voting and strategic shirking models suggest, compromising policy can produce costs that outweigh the perceived consequences of changing public opinion. In addition, politicians pursue a number of strategies, including efforts to change public opinion, in order to minimize the costs of discounting opinion. Reelection is not an unambiguous constraint on policy independence that Stimson, MacKuen, and Erikson imply. See appendix 1 for a fuller discussion of this research.

2. Party activists influence the selection of candidates not only by dominating the nomination process but also by recruiting candidates. Many candidates are drawn to politics by their initial experience as activists and by their attraction to the policy positions of the party and their fellow activists (Aldrich 1995, chap. 6).

3. During a period when the country became a bit more conservative, the proportion of Democratic delegates that identified themselves as liberal rose from 40 percent in 1976 (the first year for which the ideology of party delegates was collected) to 47 percent in 1992 before slipping a bit to 43 percent in 1996. The proportion of Republican delegates that identified themselves as conservative rose from 48 percent in 1976 to 70 percent in 1992 and 66 percent in 1996 (Wayne 1997, 118–19).

4. King measures ideological orientation by using thermometer ratings rather than support for ideological positions (D. King 1997, 171–73, 307 n.39).

5. In particular, the Speaker of the House was able to diminish the domination of committees by referring bills to multiple committees instead of one and by setting time limits on each committee's consideration of bills. Enabling the Speaker to extend the number of days during which the House could act under the suspension of rules enhanced his control over floor debate. In addition, the Speaker gained greater sway over the powerful Rules Committee by appointing the chair (with caucus approval) and all the members from his party.

6. Disagreements among scholars stem from difficulties in measuring the preferences and contributions of different groups (Domhoff 1996; Sorauf 1988) and disputes over whether money is dispersed to reflect the distribution of influence in American politics (Sorauf 1988) or concentrated in the hands of blocs of business investors to advance (at least since the 1970s) conservative interests (Ferguson 1995). One challenge (requiring additional research) is to link variations in campaign finance to the rises and falls of responsiveness before 1980.

7. Another factor was the need to win Senate Republican votes to overcome the threat of a filibuster; the shrinking number of moderates removed a critical pool of potential converts for presidents of the opposite party.

One limitation of Bond and Fleisher's analysis is that it omits legislation such as health reform that was not voted up or down on the House and Senate floors. As we discussed above, the caucus system identified significant opposition within Democratic ranks, which contributed to the decision of leaders to withdraw it from consideration.

8. Some of the more important interactions include the combination of incumbency and partisan polarization. Incumbency without polarization produces the nonprogrammatic orientation to casework and noncontroversial legislation that

Fiorina emphasized in the early 1970s (Fiorina 1977). The combination of polarization and incumbency, however, created the partisan pressure to pursue policy goals and discount centrist opinion that emerged since the 1970s. In addition, polarization interacted with interest group proliferation and the individualization within Congress. Narrow interest groups found a combustible environment to launch advertisements that fanned ideological fault lines that divided the parties (e.g., the "Harry and Louise" ads aimed at Republican antipathy toward government). Moreover, the fact that individual officeholders were responsible for their own fund raising made them more dependent on securing campaign contributions based on their policy positions.

9. Election studies from 1952 to 1964 consistently found that approximately 75 percent of the electorate identified themselves as either Democrats or Republicans; by 1992, this had shrunk to 60 percent.

10. Surveys of voters indicate that as many as 26 percent of Democrats have defected in their presidential vote since 1976, and at least 8 percent of Republicans have done the same. In addition, split-ticket voting has more than doubled since 1952; normally, 20 percent or more have chosen different parties when selecting congressional and presidential candidates.

11. Many of these factors are highly interrelated, which makes it difficult to isolate the particular influence of each (controlling for the others).

12. Our interviews with White House officials between 1993 and 1995 and surveys of congressional staff from 1994 to 1998 indicate a widespread presumption that public opinion is unstable and considerable confidence in their ability to change it.

13. Cook's (1998) important point about the interaction of politics and media coverage does not fully consider the constraints on politicians: officeholders and candidates may set conditions on access to them and plan events, but the competing efforts of rivals generally prevent them from achieving their objectives on the terms they desire.

14. Quote by Susan Neely, HIAA's senior VP for public affairs.

15. Memo to First Lady from Jay Rockefeller, 26 May 1993, regarding "Health Care Reform Communications," Confidential; "A Winning Strategy for Health Care Reform," Presentation to First Lady by Magaziner, Boorstin, July 1993; Memo to First Lady from Mike Lux, regarding "Positioning Ourselves on Health Care," 3 May 1993.

16. The "Harry and Louise" spots were aired in only a few parts of the country. But the White House's reaction to them, and then the press coverage of this reaction and its (*free*) rerunning of the ads themselves boosted their impact beyond the narrow audience that HIAA originally targeted (West, Heith, and Goodwin 1996).

17. National opinion research using polling emerged in the 1930s but Franklin Roosevelt chose not to expand his relatively informal contacts with the pollster Hadley Cantril; Harry Truman and Dwight Eisenhower also had informal channels to pollsters, but they apparently made little use of them and chose not to institutionalize public opinion analysis as a routine part of White House operations. In addition the U.S. State Department conducted polls (unapproved by Congress) (Eisinger 1993 and 1994; Foster 1983).

18. Kennedy viewed polling and public relations activities as a potential political liability. Criticism of him as "slick" and willing to use government funds for

polling prompted him to store his polls in his brother's safe in the Justice Department (Jacobs 1993, chap. 2).

19. Although the Clinton and Kennedy proposals were not comparable in terms of their scale (Clinton's was more comprehensive), they both evoked fierce partisan divisions. The original Medicare legislation inaugurated government into expanding access to health insurance and ignited the kind of ideological disagreement over the role of government that resurfaced in the 1990s (Jacobs 1993).

20. McCombs and Shaw 1972 and 1993; Erbring, Goldenberg, and Miller 1980; Cook et al. 1983; Brosius and Kepplinger 1990; Rogers, Dearing, and Bregman 1993; Rogers, Hart and Dearing 1997; Iyengar and Kinder 1985 and 1987; Iyengar, Peters, and Kinder 1982; for a review see Rogers and Dearing 1988.

21. Timothy Cook makes a similar point about disentangling the causal connections between media coverage, journalistic behavior, and government actions (Cook 1998, 8, 194 n.15).

22. We supplement Bennett's account by incorporating political changes into explaining oscillations in the volume and content of press reports.

23. Americans became more educated (measured in terms of years of schooling) during the past three decades. After 1960, Americans with a high school diploma rose from 40 percent to over 75 percent, and the proportion who finished college climbed from 7 percent to 20 percent.

24. We simplified figure 2.6 by not examining many possible interactions nor additional reciprocal relationships. For instance, political and institutional conditions not only influence political behavior and strategy but are also influenced by them (Rosenstone and Hansen 1993). Although we recognize such reciprocal relationships, we focus here mainly on particular one-way causal relationships in order to simplify our presentation and to limit our discussion to the relationships that are most theoretically important to our analysis. We also do not elaborate here on the direct impact of politicians' actions on interest group behavior.

Chapter Three

1. In actuality, the disagreement was not nearly as clear cut as the media portrayed it. Hillary Clinton's argument for comprehensiveness was backed by a number of other officials, including the White House's political advisers and the Secretaries of Labor and Health and Human Services.

2. The phrase "task force process" refers to the large advisory component of the White House's health reform organization. Formally, the "task force" was chaired by Mrs. Clinton and consisted of twelve senior administration officials (the National Economic Council plus Health and Human Services Secretary Donna Shalala). The task force was advised by a group of policy and political experts directed by Ira Magaziner, who organized the policy advisers into thirty-four working groups. Journalists and political observers associated the White House's task force with Magaziner's policy advisory group; we continue this practice.

3. Interviews; Memo to Clinton Administration Health Team from Chris Jennings and Steve Edelstein, regarding "Meetings and Outreach Report," 24 January 1993.

4. For an explanation of Clinton's placement of health care high on his agenda and his adoption of a managed competition approach, see Hacker 1997.

5. Memo to Mrs. Clinton from Magaziner, 3 May 1993, regarding "The Policy"; "Preliminary Work Plan for the Interagency Health Care Task Force," by Maga-

ziner, 26 January 1993, notes; Memo to Mrs. Clinton from Lynn Magherio regarding "Waste in Current System," 18 September 1993; Memo to the president and First Lady from Magaziner, 8 March 1993, regarding "Health Care Reform and the Budget Process"; Interviews.

6. Interviews; Johnson and Broder 1996.

7. Memo to the president and Mrs. Clinton from Magaziner, Walter Zelman, and Lynn Margherio regarding "Positioning of September Health Reform Introduction," 30 August 1993.

8. Memo from Magaziner to Bill Clinton, George Stephanopoulos, and Albert Gore, 15 August 1992, regarding "Health Care—Next Steps."

9. Interview; Johnson and Broder 1996, 452.

10. Memo to president and Mrs. Clinton from Magaziner and Zelman regarding "Positioning of September Health Reform Introduction," 30 August 1993; Interviews; Letter to McLarty from Paster, 11 December 1993.

11. Interviews; Memo to Clinton Administration Health Team from Chris Jennings and Steve Edelstein, regarding "Meetings and Outreach Report," 24 January 1993; Starr 1995 and 1994.

12. "Health Care Reform: Communications Strategy," fall briefing material, handwritten date, 17 December 1993; Interviews.

13. Memo to the president and First Lady from Magaziner regarding "Where We Are Positioned," 1 October 1993; Memo to Clinton Administration Health Team from Chris Jennings and Steve Edelstein, regarding "Meetings and Outreach Report," 24 January 1993.

14. "Passing Health Reform," by Magaziner, Mike Lux, Bob Boorstin, and staff, prepared for briefing Pat Griffin and Harold Ickes, 9 December 1993. The White House targeted fourteen moderate Republican senators: John Chafee, Richard Cohen, Alfonse D'Amato, John Danforth, David Durenberger, Mark Hatfield, James Jeffords, Nancy Kassebaum, Robert Packwood; the most difficult were expected to be Christopher Bond, Conrad Burns, Connie Mack, William Roth, and Arlen Specter. The White House also targeted twenty-three moderate or conservative Democratic senators: Max Baucus, Bill Bradley, John Breaux, Richard Bryan, Christopher Dodd, William Ford, Bob Graham, Ernest Hollings, Bob Kerrey, Herbert Kohl, Robert Krueger, Frank Lautenberg, Joseph Lieberman, Daniel Patrick Moynihan, Harry Reid, and Charles Robb; they expected David Boren, Dennis DeConcini, Jim Exon, Howell Heflin, Bennett Johnston, Sam Nunn, and Richard Shelby to be the most difficult votes to get. Aides optimistically predicted the support of fifteen or twenty House Representatives out of a pool of fifty-three moderate Republicans or conservative Democrats. Memo to Mrs Clinton from Jennings, regarding "Senate Republicans to Target as Possible Supporters and Senate Democrats to Attract and Keep on Board," 22 March 1993, attached to the following: Memo to Distribution from Jennings and Steve Ricchetti, 14 April 1993, regarding "Congressional Update and Strategy for Health Reform"; "Congressional Strategy," marked "confidential," fall briefing material, probably by Ricchetti, probably December 1993.

15. Hacker (1997) argues that managed competition (and specifically Clinton's liberal variant) emerged from relative obscurity because of the policy ideas developed by its advocates, the political struggles with Bush and within Clinton's circle of advisers, and the support from powerful private interests within the business community and medical industry. Hacker suggests that public opinion toward

managed competition was simply not a concern in its formulation during the election campaign (138–42). Once politics and policy ideas had pushed managed competition onto the campaign's agenda, Clinton latched onto it because it reflected his philosophy, his policy preferences, and his political judgments.

16. Memo from Judy Feder to Bruce Fried, regarding "Tsongas Plan and Clinton Campaign," 12 March 1992.

17. Interview; Johnson and Broder 1996.

18. Interviews; Memo to the president and First Lady from Magaziner regarding "Where We Are Positioned," 1 October 1993; "Major Attacks on Our Bill," fall briefing material, handwritten, 17 December 1993.

19. "Financing Health Reform: The Tradeoffs," by Magaziner and aides for president, National Economic Council, and Shalala, 31 August 1993; Memo to president and First Lady from Magaziner, regarding "Health Care Reform and Economic Package," 7 March 1993.

20. Memo to Mrs. Clinton from Magaziner, 3 May 1993, regarding "What Is Ahead and How to Organize for It"; Interviews. For discussion of the split among health policy specialists, see Glied 1997.

21. Interviews; Memo to the president and First Lady from Magaziner, Walter Zelman, and Lynn Margherio regarding "Positioning of September Health Reform Introduction," 30 August 1993. One of Magaziner's major efforts to battle the divisions among Democratic health policy experts involved a large and fractious meeting in Washington during August 1992.

22. Memo to Magaziner from Jennings, regarding "Congressional Strategy for Health Reform," 5 February 1993 (copies sent to Howard Paster and Steve Ricchetti).

23. Memo from Stanley Greenberg to president, vice president, First Lady, Mack McLarty, and David Gergen, 30 July 1993, regarding "Issue Priorities NAFTA, Health Care, and Reinventing Government"; Memo from Greenberg, Mandy Grunwald, Paul Begala, and James Carville to president, vice president, Mrs. Clinton, McLarty, Stephanopoulos, and Gergen, 2 August 1993, regarding "Issue Priorities: Timing."

24. Interviews; Memo to the president and First Lady from Magaziner, 8 March 1993, regarding "Health Care Reform and the Budget Process."

25. Interviews. Clinton's hostility toward the Health Care Financing Administration, which administers federal participation in health care, originated from his bitter experiences as governor with what he saw as HCFA's excessively regulatory and bureaucratic handling of Medicaid.

26. Report by Magaziner, "Preliminary Work Plan for the Interagency Health Care Taskforce," 26 January 1993.

27. Interviews. One well-placed administration official explained that the relatively infrequent instances when Magaziner omitted information from his presentation to the president probably stemmed from his failure to understand the arguments (such as on tax policy) or from Clinton's harsh criticism for slowness, which led Magaziner to relay the majority view rather than the minority positions.

28. Interviews; White House records of briefing materials, mid-April 1993 to mid-May 1993; Memo to president and First Lady from Magaziner, regarding "Major Health Care Reform Decisions" (two-page covering memo attached to 126-page listing of issues); "The Major Cost and Financing Questions," 19 April 1993, by Magaziner and aides for the president, National Economic Council, and

Shalala; Memo to Mrs. Clinton from Magaziner, 3 May 1993, regarding "The Policy"; Memo to McLarty, Gergen, and Stephanopoulos from Magaziner, 22 July 1993, regarding "Health Care Reform Timing"; "Presidential Level Health Care Decisions" for the president, National Economic Council, and Shalala by Magaziner and aides, handwritten date 8 August 1993.

29. Memo to First Lady from Senator Jay Rockefeller, 26 May 1993, regarding "Health Care Reform Communications," Confidential.

30. Report by Magaziner, "Preliminary Work Plan for the Interagency Health Care Taskforce," 26 January 1993.

31. Interviews.

32. Interviews; Johnson and Broder 1996, 131–32.

33. Appendix 2 attached to Memo to Distribution from Jennings and Ricchetti, 14 April 1993, regarding "Congressional Update and Strategy for Health Care Reform."

34. Interviews; Johnson and Broder 1996, 161–2.

35. Memo to McLarty, Gergen, and Stephanopoulos from Magaziner, 22 July 1993, regarding "Health Care Reform Timing"; Interviews.

36. Interviews; Memo to McLarty, Gergen, and Stephanopoulos from Magaziner, 22 July 1993, regarding "Health Care Reform Timing."

37. Memo to the president and First Lady from Magaziner, 8 March 1993, regarding "Health Care Reform and the Budget Process."

38. Interviews; "Major Attacks on Our Bill," fall briefing material, handwritten 17 December 1993; Memo to First Lady from Magaziner, 10 May 1993, regarding "Quantitative Analysis" (copy to Carol Rosco).

39. Interviews; Memo to McLarty, Gergen, and Stephanopoulos from Magaziner, 22 July 1993, regarding "Health Care Reform Timing."

40. "A Winning Strategy for Health Care Reform" for First Lady by Magaziner, Jeff Eller, and Bob Boorstin, July 1993; Memo to Magaziner from Lux, 20 July 1993, regarding "The Effect of the Delay of Health Care Reform on the President's Political Base"; Memo to McLarty, Gergen, and Stephanopoulos from Magaziner, 22 July 1993, regarding "Health Care Reform Timing"; Memo to president and First Lady from Magaziner, regarding "Health Care Reform and Economic Package," 7 March 1993; Interviews.

41. Memo to president and First Lady from Magaziner, regarding "Health Care Reform and Economic Package," 7 March 1993.

42. Interviews. The White House blames Byrd for blocking the inclusion of health care reform in the budget process. But the fact is that the reconciliation rules were an obstacle regardless of whether Byrd invoked the rule or not; any senator could invoke the rule (and no doubt one would have volunteered) which would require sixty votes to overcome. The White House would need sixty votes whether they went through the reconciliation or the normal legislative process.

43. Appendix 2 attached to Memo to Distribution from Jennings and Ricchetti, 14 April 1993, regarding "Congressional Update and Strategy for Health Care Reform"; Interviews.

44. "Health Care Reform: Communications Strategy," fall briefing material, handwritten date, 17 December 1993; Memo to McLarty from Paster, 21 December 1993, regarding "Health Care Legislative Strategy."

45. Berke 1993. White House expenditures on polling were paid by the Demo-

cratic National Committee; these appear to have exceeded Bush's expenditures on polls but were in the ballpark of Nixon's. Archival records indicate that Nixon's polls between 1969 and 1972 cost over $5 million in 1994 dollars (Jacobs and Shapiro 1995). During George Bush's presidency, the Republican National Committee claimed to have spent $1.7 million on polling for the president (Cannon 1994).

46. Interviews; White House records.

47. We interviewed twenty-three individuals associated with the Clinton administration, a handful of them on more than one occasion. Most of the interviews were conducted in person; a few were continued by phone. The interviews ranged from thirty minutes to two hours a session, depending on time constraints, and were based on a common set of structured questions (which were taped and transcribed). We granted anonymity to encourage candor, as most interviews occurred during policy debates, and assigned a random number to most interviews to help us track them.

48. Memo to First Lady from Boorstin and David Dreyer (copies to McLarty, Rasco, and Magaziner), 25 January 1993.

49. Interview with Greenberg by LRJ, 26 January 1995.

50. Yankelovich surveys in February, May, and June 1994 indicated that employer mandates were supported by 65 to 68 percent of respondents identifying themselves as Democrats. In addition, *New York Times*/CBS News surveys in January and July 1992 and January 1993 revealed that 71 to 76 percent of Democrats supported "national health insurance, which would be financed by tax money, paying for most forms of health care." Moreover, Yankelovich surveys in September 1993 and February, March, May, June, and July 1994 reported that 72 to 81 percent of Democratic loyalists supported a "federal government . . . guarantee [of] health care for all Americans."

51. Memo from Greenberg to Mr. and Mrs. Clinton, Gore, McLarty, Stephanopoulos and Frank Greer, 30 July 1993, regarding "Issue Priorities."

52. Public opinion toward taxation was more ambiguous and less unequivocally antitax than has been commonly assumed. Polls in 1993, found consistent majority support for tax increases to pay for national universal health insurance. For more discussion see Jacobs and Shapiro 1994c and 1994d; Page and Shapiro 1992.

53. Memo to the president and First Lady from Magaziner regarding "Where We Are Positioned," 1 October 1993; "Long-Term Care: Political Context," 2 June 1993, by Magaziner.

54. Louis Harris and Associates, March 1993; Marttila and Kiley, March 1993 (Jacobs and Shapiro 1994c, 213).

55. The survey question is as follows: "In the Canadian system of National Health Insurance, the government pays most of the cost of health care for everyone out of taxes, and the government sets all fees charged by doctors and hospitals. Under the Canadian system, people can choose their own doctors and hospitals. On balance, would you prefer the Canadian system or the system we have here?"

56. Untitled Memo, 7 April 1993, marked "Privileged & Confidential."

57. Memo to First Lady from Boorstin and Dreyer (copies to McLarty, Rasco and Magaziner), 25 January 1993.

58. Email exchange from Stanley Greenberg to LRJ, 12 February 1999.

59. Ibid.

60. Appendix 2 attached to Memo to Distribution from Jennings and Ricchetti, 14 April 1993, regarding "Congressional Update and Strategy for Health Care

Reform"; "A Winning Strategy for Health Care Reform" for First Lady by Magaziner, Jeff Eller, and Bob Boorstin, July 1993.

61. Memo to the president and First Lady from Magaziner, Walter Zelman, and Lynn Margherio regarding "Positioning of September Health Reform Introduction," 30 August 1993; Memo to the Communications Team from Greenberg, 12 October 1993.

62. Interviews. Jacobs (1993) makes a similar argument with regard to the enactment of the original Medicare program in 1965 and the British National Health Service Act in 1945.

63. Memo to president and First Lady from Magaziner, regarding "Health Care Reform and Economic Package," 7 March 1993.

64. Grunwald quoted in Woodward 1994; Appendix 2 attached to Memo to Distribution from Jennings and Ricchetti, 14 April 1993, regarding "Congressional Update and Strategy for Health Care Reform"; Memo to First Lady from Boorstin and Lois Quam, 6 February 1993, regarding "Health Care Communications 100 Day Strategy"; Memo to First Lady from Senator Jay Rockefeller, 26 May 1993, regarding "Health Care Reform Communications," Confidential.

65. Quoted in Blumenthal 1994; Interviews.

66. Memo from Lux to the president, 15 December 1993.

67. Interviews; Report by Magaziner, "Preliminary Work Plan for the Interagency Health Care Taskforce," 26 January 1993; Memo to First Lady from Magaziner, 3 May 1993, regarding "What Is Ahead and How to Organize for It"; Memo to Distribution from Jennings and Ricchetti, 14 April 1993, regarding "Congressional Update and Strategy for Health Care Reform"; Memo to First Lady from Boorstin and Lois Quam, 6 February 1993, regarding "Health Care Communications 100 Day Strategy."

68. As we mentioned in chapter 2, the concept of "priming" originates in research in social psychology and is widely used by scholars to analyze the impact of the mass media on public opinion. Although the term "priming" is not used by politicians, it accurately describes their strategies and tactics. We extend the application of priming from its original focus—the analysis by social psychologists of how individuals form attitudes and make decisions—to the study of opinion manipulation by government officials and political activists. This new use changes the analytic focus from unintentional priming (i.e. the inadvertent impact of the media's behavior and news coverage on individuals) to intentional priming— namely, the deliberate strategies that politicians pursue to influence the public (Jacobs and Shapiro 1994a; cf. Iyengar and Kinder 1987).

69. Memo to First Lady from Boorstin and Lois Quam, 6 February 1993, regarding "Health Care Communications 100 Day Strategy."

70. Memo from Greenberg to Mr. and Mrs. Clinton, Gore, McLarty, Stephanopoulos, and Greer, 30 July 1993, regarding "Issue Priorities."

71. "A Winning Strategy for Health Care Reform" for First Lady by Magaziner, Jeff Eller, and Bob Boorstin, 7, 1993; Memo to First Lady from Lux, regarding "Positioning Ourselves on Health Care," 3 May 1993.

72. Memo to First Lady from Senator Jay Rockefeller, 26 May 1993, regarding "Health Care Reform Communications," Confidential.

73. "A Winning Strategy for Health Care Reform" for First Lady by Magaziner, Jeff Eller, and Bob Boorstin, July 1993.

74. Memo to First Lady from Boorstin and Lois Quam, 6 February 1993, re-

garding "Health Care Communications 100 Day Strategy"; Memo to First Lady from Senator Jay Rockefeller, 26 May 1993, regarding "Health Care Reform Communications," Confidential; Interviews.

75. Memo to Magaziner from Greenberg, 14 September 1993, regarding "The Health Care Joint Session Speech"; Memo to president and First Lady from Magaziner, Zelman, and Lux regarding "Positioning of September Health Reform Introduction," 30 August 1993.

76. The number of interviews reported varies because time constraints prevented some staff from finishing the interviews.

77. Memo from Greenberg to Mr. and Mrs. Clinton, Gore, McLarty, Stephanopoulos, and Greer, 30 July 1993, regarding "Issue Priorities."

78. Memo to Magaziner from Greenberg, 14 September 1993, regarding "The Health Care Joint Session Speech."

79. Memo from Greenberg to Mr. and Mrs. Clinton, Gore, McLarty, Stephanopoulos and Greer, 30 July 1993, regarding "Issue Priorities."

80. Memo to Magaziner from Greenberg, 14 September 1993, regarding "The Health Care Joint Session Speech"; Memo to president and First Lady from Magaziner, Zelman, and Lux regarding "Positioning of September Health Reform Introduction," 30 August 1993.

81. Memo to Magaziner from Greenberg, 14 September 1993, regarding "The Health Care Joint Session Speech"; Memo to Magaziner from Greenberg, 14 September 1993, regarding "The Health Care Joint Session Speech"; "A Winning Strategy for Health Care Reform" for First Lady by Magaziner, Jeff Eller, and Bob Boorstin, July 1993; Memo to the president and First Lady from Magaziner, Walter Zelman, and Lynn Margherio regarding "Positioning of September Health Reform Introduction," 30 August 1993; Interviews.

82. We compiled a complete set of Clinton's recorded statements from *The Public Papers of the Presidents*, the *Weekly Compilation of Presidential Documents*, as well the online archives at the University of California at Irvine, Northwestern University, and the University of Michigan. We only coded documents that were directly attributable to the president, yielding 4,695 discrete statements by Clinton about identifiable health policy issues.

83. Twenty-three percent of the president's time promoting health reform was devoted to championing the "Clinton plan." The other top issues were controlling costs (21 percent) and expanding access (16 percent).

84. As we observed in the previous note, Clinton devoted 16 percent of his time to the issue of supporting universal access for all; he committed 23 percent to promoting the Clinton plan and 21 percent to cost.

85. Interviews; Memo to Magaziner from Joe Goode, 4 June 1993, regarding "Greenberg's Focus Groups Discussion of Funding Proposals."

86. Thirty percent of Clinton's statements mentioned a specific case or event rather than the general or abstract context.

87. Interviews; Memo to Boorstin and Magaziner from Gatz, 16 May 1993, regarding "Message about Health Alliances."

88. Memo to First Lady from Boorstin and Lois Quam, 6 February 1993, regarding "Health Care Communications 100 Day Strategy"; Memo to First Lady from Senator Jay Rockefeller, 26 May 1993, regarding "Health Care Reform Communications," Confidential; Interviews.

89. Our analysis of Clinton's public statements indicates that he devoted just

over 17 percent of his time solely to addresses to citizen gatherings. His discussion of health reform was directed to a variety of other audiences: 39 percent of his presentations were divided among a range of interest groups including organizations representing business, labor, public interests, and professionals; 38 percent of his discussions were directed to national audiences in the form of town meetings, speeches and exchanges with reporters; 11 percent were White House press releases; and 9 percent of his comments were made to gatherings of government or party leaders like the Democratic National Committee and the National Governors' Association.

90. Interviews; "A Winning Strategy for Health Care Reform" for First Lady by Magaziner, Jeff Eller, and Bob Boorstin, July 1993.

91. Yankelovich reported that 57 percent favored the Clinton plan (in a one-day survey), Gallup found 59 percent (two-day survey).

92. Memo to David Wilhelm from Greenberg Research regarding "Survey Research on President's Address to Congress on Health Care," 23 September 1993.

93. Interviews; Memo from Greenberg to president, vice president, First Lady, Mack McLarty, and David Gergen, 30 July 1993, regarding "Issue Priorities NAFTA, Health Care, and Reinventing Government"; "New Health Care System," handwritten date, 26 March 1993; "Economic Dilemmas for Health Care Reform," 25 March 1993, for National Economic Council and Shalala from Magaziner; "The Problem" by Magaziner and staff to First Lady in preparation for health care university, handwritten 12 September 1993.

94. "A Winning Strategy for Health Care Reform" for First Lady by Magaziner, Jeff Eller, and Bob Boorstin, July 1993.

95. Interview with President Clinton, *New York Times,* 28 July 1996, 11.

96. Interviews; Memo to Stephanopoulos and Boorstin from Magaziner regarding "Health Care Press Strategy", 4 February 1993; Memo to First Lady from Senator Jay Rockefeller, 26 May 1993, regarding "Health Care Reform Communications," Confidential.

97. Memo to First Lady from Boorstin and Lois Quam, 6 February 1993, regarding "Health Care Communications 100 Day Strategy."

98. Memo to Stephanopoulos and Boorstin from Magaziner regarding "Health Care Press Strategy," 4 February 1993; "A Winning Strategy for Health Care Reform" for First Lady by Magaziner, Jeff Eller, and Bob Boorstin, July 1993; Interviews; Johnson and Broder 1996, 140.

99. Interviews; "A Winning Strategy for Health Care Reform" for First Lady by Magaziner, Jeff Eller, and Bob Boorstin, July 1993; "War Room: White House Strategies to Counter Negative Media Coverage," from Lux, 2 March 1994.

100. From a diverse set of documents, we selected a sample of three hundred instances in which Clinton discussed health issues in 1993 and 1994. The sample was evenly split between 1993 and 1994.

101. Memo to Magaziner from Greenberg, 14 September 1993, regarding "The Health Care Joint Session Speech"; Memo to president and First Lady from Magaziner, Zelman, and Lux regarding "Positioning of September Health Reform Introduction," 30 August 1993.

102. Memo to the president and First Lady from Magaziner, Walter Zelman, and Lynn Margherio regarding "Positioning of September Health Reform Introduction," 30 August 1993.

103. Memo to the president and First Lady from Magaziner regarding "Where We Are Positioned," 1 October 1993.

Chapter Four

1. When Clinton was inaugurated in 1993, the Democrats held a 258–176 edge in the House (with one Independent) and a 57–43 edge in the Senate.

2. "A Winning Strategy for Health Care Reform" for First Lady by Magaziner, Jeff Eller, and Bob Boorstin, July 1993.

3. Interviews.

4. Interviews; interview with President Clinton, *New York Times,* 28 July 1996, 11.

5. Our interviews were conducted during the summer of 1994 and were mostly held with top aides (administrative assistants or chiefs of staff), though we also interviewed several legislative assistants, legislative directors, and committee staff members, depending upon who appeared to be best informed about a member's thoughts concerning health care reform. Most of the interviews were conducted by telephone; a few were done in person. The interviews ranged from fifteen minutes to ninety minutes, depending on the time constraints, and were based on a common set of structured questions.

6. The following question was asked: "Some people suggest that polls and other public opinion information are important for responding to public opinion; others suggest that this information is a tool to test and enhance the **MEMBER's** ability to lead or educate public opinion. What do you think is the primary purpose of gathering information on public opinion?" Fourteen congressional staff (36 percent) reported that public opinion information was used to lead or educate and twelve (31 percent) indicated using it to both lead and respond.

7. See Allard 1941. Allard's survey was based on fifty-six completed surveys that had been mailed to 106 members of Congress. A random sample was drawn by selecting every fifth name from an alphabetical list. Caution should be exercised in concluding that the two sets of interviews have identified a trend of declining responsiveness; the contrast in the results from our interviews and those in the 1940s may stem from differences in question wordings and differences in samples.

8. On financing arrangements, 34 percent (12 of 35) characterized their constituents as supporting a payroll tax, value-added tax or employer mandate, and 37 percent (13 of 35) predicted opposition; 27 percent (9 of 33) indicated no opinion among their constituents. On cost control, 51 percent (19 of 37) believed that their constituents supported controls and 14 percent (5 of 37) estimated opposition; 35 percent (13 of 37) did not think their constituents had an opinion or that there was an even split in the constituency. (The number of interviews reported are less than 39 because time constraints prevented some staff from finishing the interview.)

9. Interviews; Brady and Buckley 1995.

10. The following five congressional committees were largely responsible for handling health care reform: House Education and Labor Committee, House Ways and Means Committee, House Energy and Commerce Committee, Senate Labor and Human Resources, and the Senate Finance Committee.

11. The following question was asked: "After a **MEMBER** has taken a position on an issue, has he/she ever justified his/her position on an issue by referring to polls, focus groups, or other public opinion information?"

12. The following question was asked: "Has information on public opinion been used by **MEMBER** in deciding how to frame policy decisions in statements or speeches?"

13. Our discussion of Republican leaders and their efforts to lead public opinion draws on Jacobs, Lawrence, Shapiro, and Smith 1998.

14. That members deferred to leaders to manage public relations is confirmed by research by Sinclair (1995) and Harris (1998) and reflects the reality of modern communications where Americans hear the messages of leaders sooner and more frequently (through the national media) than the explanations of individual senators and representatives (Carmines and Kuklinski 1990). Indeed, actual media coverage of individual members of Congress suggests that the top leaders are the most common sources for journalists (Hess 1986).

15. "Health Care Reform and the Congress," probably July/August 1993; "Our Challenge," by Magaziner for briefing the president, 2 September 1993.

16. "Paying for Health Coverage," handwritten, 2 September 1993.

17. Gingrich, Trent Lott, Phil Gramm, Dan Coats, and Robert Smith led the faction that supported outright opposition to any health reform well before Clinton's speech in September 1993 (Johnson and Broder 1996, xi, 304).

18. Memo to Republican Leaders from William Kristol, 2 December 1993.

19. We tracked legislators' positions using the *National Journal, Congressional Quarterly Weekly Report,* and the *Washington Post.* Using these media reports to track congressional position-taking runs the risk of distortion; journalists' selection and interpretation of events can color the presentation of leaders and influence how the public perceives their behavior. These media, however, are especially geared to tracking legislative developments.

20. Memo to Magaziner from Greenberg, 14 September 1993, regarding "The President's Speech to a Joint Session of Congress."

21. Memo to David Wilhelm from Greenberg Research regarding "Survey Research on the President's Address to Congress on Health Care," 23 September 1993.

22. Appendix 4: Memo to Mrs Clinton from Jennings, regarding "Senate Republicans to Target as Possible Supporters and Senate Democrats to Attract and Keep on Board," 22 March 1993, attached to the following: Memo to Distribution from Jennings and Steve Ricchetti, 14 April 1993, regarding "Congressional Update and Strategy for Health Reform"; Interviews.

23. Memo to the president and First Lady from Magaziner regarding "Where We Are Positioned," 1 October 1993; Interviews with Magaziner.

24. Memo to the president, vice president, First Lady, McLarty, Stephanopoulos, and Gergen from Greenberg, Grunwald, Begala, and Carville, 2 August 1993, regarding "Issue Priorities: Timing"; "A Winning Strategy for Health Care Reform" for First Lady by Magaziner, Jeff Eller, and Bob Boorstin, July 1993; Memo from Greenberg to president, vice president, First Lady, McLarty, and Gergen, 30 July 1993, regarding "Issue Priorities NAFTA, Health Care, and Reinventing Government"; Memo to First Lady from Greenberg and Grunwald, 28 October 1993, regarding "Planning forHealth Care"; Memo to First Lady from Greenberg, Grunwald, Magaziner, Celeste, 31 October 1993, regarding "Planning for Health Care."

25. Memo to president and First Lady from Magaziner, Zelman, and Margherio, regarding "Positioning of September Health Care Reform Introduction," 30 August 1993.

26. See note 24 above.

27. Memo to the Communications Team from Greenberg, 12 October 1993.

28. In March 1993, a Republican task force chaired by Gingrich and Michel produced a legislative proposal to achieve incremental reform (Gingrich 1993).

29. Memo to the Communications Team from Greenberg, 12 October 1993.

30. Memo to First Lady from Greenberg and Grunwald, 28 October 1993, regarding "Planning for Health Care."

31. Memo to the Communications Team from Greenberg, 12 October 1993.

32. Memo to First Lady from Greenberg, Grunwald, Magaziner, and Celeste, 31 October 1993, regarding "Planning for Health Care."

33. Memo to the Communications Team from Greenberg, 12 October 1993.

34. Memo to First Lady from Greenberg, Grunwald, Magaziner, and Celeste, 31 October 1993, regarding "Planning for Health Care."

35. "Passing Health Reform," by Magaziner, Lux, Boorstin, and staff, prepared for briefing Pat Griffin and Harold Ickes, 9 December 1993; Memo from Lux to the president, 15 December 1993.

36. Memo by William Kristol to Republican leaders, 2 December 1993, "Defeating President Clinton's Health Care Proposal," Project for the Republican Future; *National Journal* 1994.

37. Memo to Republican Leaders from William Kristol, 2 December 1993.

38. Ibid.

39. The perception that Harry and Louise's influence on public opinion resulted from the attention that elites and journalists gave it, is confirmed by Cappella and Jamieson (1997).

40. Memo to McLarty from Paster, 21 December 1993, regarding "Health Care Legislative Strategy."

41. Interviews.

42. Memo to First Lady from Lux, 29 October 1993; Interviews.

43. "Health Care Reform: Communications Strategy," fall briefing material, handwritten date, 17 December 1993; Memo from Lux to the president, 15 December 1993; Interviews.

44. "Health Care Reform: Communications Strategy," fall briefing material, handwritten date, 17 December 1993; Interviews.

45. "Congressional Strategy," marked "confidential," fall briefing material, probably by Ricchetti, probably December 1993.

46. Interviews; Johnson and Broder 1996, 270.

47. Interviews.

48. Memo from Lux to First Lady, Harold Ickes, Gordon Li, Alexis Herman, Ricki Seidmanm, Boorstin, Dick Celeste, 21 February 1994, regarding "Mobilizing the Base"; Interviews.

49. In July, Clinton aimed 61 percent of his public statements on health reform at elite forums.

50. Memo to Fisher from Lux, 22 March 1993; Interview.

Chapter Five

1. McCombs and Shaw 1972 and 1993; Erbring et al. 1980; Cook et al. 1983; Brosius and Kepplinger 1990; Rogers, Dearing, and Bregman 1993; Rogers, Hart and Dearing 1997; Iyengar and Kinder 1985 and 1987; Iyengar, Peters, and Kinder

1982; for a review see Rogers and Dearing 1988. Chapter 2 briefly reviews this literature.

2. An example of the selective focus of the AP stories is the failure to report on the possibility of controlling costs by establishing government authority over national health care spending; other industrialized countries have used government financial authority to control expenditures and then allow doctors and hospitals to operate with wide clinical autonomy (Brown 1992; Jacobs 1995).

3. Our argument expands on the growing appreciation of the two-way causal relationships between media coverage and the political process. Cook (1998, 8 and 194 n.15) stresses the importance of disentangling the causal connections of media coverage, journalistic behavior, and government actions. Cappella and Jamieson (1997) acknowledge political dynamics in their introductory and concluding sections, though they concentrate on studying the impact of media coverage on public opinion.

4. Popular studies of the media often zero in on a few stories as anecdotes to support their arguments. Fallows's (1996) widely read critique of journalists did just this. But anecdotes alone do not reveal reliable information about the general pattern; it is speculation whether they illustrate a dominant pattern. The more rigorous approach used by Kathleen Hall Jamieson and Joseph Cappella (1995), the Kaiser Foundation (Times Mirror Center et al. 1995), and others in their studies of media coverage of Clinton's health reform efforts focuses on the dominant messages found in entire stories. The limitation of this approach is that each story typically contains a host of different messages from different sources.

By contrast, our tracking of individual statements or "messages" in news stories enabled us to provide an exceptionally detailed picture of media coverage (Page, Shapiro, and Dempsey 1987; Jacobs, Watts, and Shapiro 1995; Cook and Jacobs 1999; Fan 1988).

We conducted a broad search of stories relating to health policy. We used the NEXIS database to identify stories that contained the word "health," any permutation of "hospital," "medical," and "nursing," as well as two dozen other key terms. (See appendix 3 for further discussion.) We next measured the space devoted to each issue by counting both the number of mentions of each issue *and* the number of lines of text devoted to it. The counts were then totaled for each specific time period that we examined (months or years). These two measures of space (mentions and lines) were highly correlated and therefore very similar. We chose to focus on the number of mentions because it made more intuitive sense.

5. These figures include the elderly. Data on the nonelderly uninsurance rate show an increase from 15 percent in 1980 to estimates between 15 percent and 18 percent in 1991 (*Statistical Abstract of the United States* [various years]; *Health Care Financing Review* 1992; Thorpe 1997).

6. Our search for health care stories did not specifically target abortion coverage per se; it was picked up in the context of discussions of health or health care issues. See appendix 3.

7. While 11 percent of television's coverage of health care issues was devoted to cost, newspapers committed 14 percent and magazines 18 percent. The press as a whole reduced its coverage of cost by approximately 50 percent between 1993 and 1994, with television showing the greatest absolute and proportional decline. In terms of the issue of access, TV and newspapers committed 16 percent and 19

percent of their overall coverage to cost, respectively, compared to 10 percent for magazines. There was a modest increase in total press coverage of access from 1993 to 1994.

8. Another approach would be to compare media coverage with actual statistics such as the rate at which health care costs rose. As we suggest above and below, the content and rising volume of press coverage did generally reflect the rise in health care costs. Although there is a general correspondence of health care developments and press reports, it probably resulted from the attention that authoritative government officials devoted to health. It is unrealistic to expect that the press would closely cover changes in health care in the absence of authoritative government actions. As we have noted, there are strong theoretical reasons to expect the press to cover the actions of authoritative government officials. But economic pressures and professional norms do not create overriding incentives for the press to treat long-term trends in health care expenditures themselves as comparably "newsworthy" as presidential proposals and congressional debates.

9. As a relative proportion of all health care coverage, public health received less attention during the 1991–94 period than it had during its 1990 peak.

10. As a proportion of the media's total coverage of health care, news reports on comprehensive government health reform exceeded its previous highs (except for 1978 when Kennedy and Carter dueled over national health reform); but the proportional increase in coverage of the comprehensive reform topic did not match the fivefold jump in total coverage.

11. The attention to access as proportion of total health care news rose since 1992 but did not surpass its peaks in the late 1980s.

12. The proportional attention to access fell slightly as total health care coverage surged.

13. The greatest proportional attention to abortion came in January 1993 followed by April 1993 and then January 1994.

14. For a review of media "framing," see Cappella and Jamieson 1997, chap. 3, as well as Neuman, Just, and Crigler 1992; Iyengar 1991.

15. Our analysis of media coverage tracked additional frames discussed in the appendix. These additional frames received much less individual attention than the strategic and national frames. The percentages for the two major frames shown in the figures do not add up to 100 percent due to the use of these other frames.

16. Jamieson 1992; Patterson 1994; Cappella and Jamieson 1997; Interviews with Clinton administration and congressional officials.

17. For instance, a story might contain the following: a report on the opposition facing the White House's efforts to expand access to health insurance; a discussion of the realization by both political parties that rising health care costs threatens the country's economic performance; and a conclusion that the Clinton health plan seemed unlikely to pass as Republicans looked to use the president's overly bureaucratic scheme as a political advantage against the Democrats in the upcoming 1994 elections. This story would be coded as containing a strategic frame (first and last sections) and a national frame (middle section); we would measure the volume associated with each frame by recording the number of mentions of each frame (this story contained two mentions of the strategic frame and one mention of the national frame), and the total number of lines of text devoted to the frames. Our analysis focuses on the number of mentions, as we noted earlier.

18. Statistical analysis of these data indicates that the media's use of strategic frames came at the expense of national frames. After 1985, strategic frames in AP coverage are negatively correlated with national frames ($-.56$, $p < .10$). The coverage of print and broadcast media followed a similar pattern from January 1993 to December 1994 ($-.59$, $p < .01$).

We distinguish the period after 1985 because the political polarization discussed in chapter 2 (fig. 2.3) reached a level where government consideration of health care issues were especially prone to become the focus of fierce partisan sniping.

19. Statistical analysis of the correlation of generic issues (using a variable coded 1 for generic and 0 for reform) and strategic framing confirms that news reports on generic issues shied away from strategic frames. The bivariate correlation for AP coverage indicate that strategic frames were negatively correlated over time with generic issues ($-.52$, $p < .05$). Print and broadcast journalists exhibited a similar and stronger tendency during the period from January 1993 to December 1994 ($-.72$, $p < .001$). By contrast, journalists who reported on reform issues were drawn to strategic frames.

20. For other pertinent analyses of media coverage of health care reform and other health care and related issues, see Media Monitor 1994; Times Mirror Center et al. 1995; Dorfman et al. 1996; Chard and Ling 1999; Huebner, Fan, and Finnegan 1996; Fan and Norem 1992; and Lawrence 1998. Oxley (1998) reports findings that are very similar to ours regarding the increasing attention to strategy and conflict (and the relative balance of strategy versus substantive policy statements and messages) and how this influenced public opinion toward the Clinton reform plan.

21. During the period 1993–94, print and broadcast media used strategic frames in 37 percent of their messages as compared to 13 percent for national frames; for AP coverage during the same period, the figures were 21 percent and 9 percent, respectively.

Chapter Six

1. The interesting analysis of Brodie, Brady, and Altman 1998 does not distinguish between these two different forms of negativity nor does it differentiate the media's handling of reform issues as compared to generic issues. In addition, they use the story as the unit of analysis, which (as we suggested in chapter 5) omits potentially important information and is more difficult to code accurately because coders have to make judgments about how to weigh conflicting message from different sources.

2. In a separate analysis not presented, we compared the news frames (strategic and national) and the negativity of news reports on reform and generic issues in order to investigate a standard critique of news coverage—that its focus on political gamesmanship provides another means for criticizing or denigrating politicians and their proposals for reform. We found, however, that news reports often opted for a positive tone even when a strategic frame was used to report on reform issues. For instance, CNN's story of Clinton's September 1993 address to black leaders noted the president's strategic motivations—he was "caught up in the campaign for his health care plan"—but it did not cite criticism of his health reform plan; it settled instead for a reminder that the caucus represented a potential pool of supporters. Reporting on the political gamesmanship in debates over

health reform issues conveyed on average more "pro" messages than "con" messages.

3. AP citations of Clinton constituted over 9 percent of its sources, while previous Democratic candidates never received more than half that and Republicans not even 2 percent.

4. As mentioned above, the president accounted for 6 percent of AP reports (9 percent during 1993–94) and 7 percent of print and broadcast coverage.

5. Democratic legislators accounted for 11 percent of television's sources, 8 percent for newspapers, and 5 percent for magazines; congressional Republicans comprised 10 percent of television sources, 3 percent for newspapers, and 2 percent for magazines.

6. There is some quantitative evidence of the capacity of the president and his party to draw media attention away from other sources. Statistical analysis suggests that greater attention to the president and his party, which includes administration officials, depresses the media's use of advocates, providers, and experts. For the entire period of the AP coverage, the yearly citations of the president and his party are negatively related to those of advocates ($-.61$, $p < .05$), providers ($-.51$, $p < .05$), and experts ($-.79$, $p < .001$). The one exception is journalists themselves: increases in attention to the president and his team after 1985 were associated with a rise in the tendency of AP journalists to insert their own interpretation and commentary ($.68$, $p < .05$ for the period after 1985).

Journalists who used national frames shied away from citing the president and his partisans but the press was drawn to citing them when focusing on political strategy and conflict (after 1985). For the entire period of the AP coverage, the yearly use of national frames are negatively correlated (using the variable coded 1 for national frames, 0 for other) with the references to the president and his partisans ($-.59$, $p < .01$). By contrast, the president and his team were positively correlated with strategic frames for the period from 1985 to 1994 ($.79$, $p < .01$). The increased intensity of the legislative process, however, produced a different pattern for the print and broadcast coverage in 1994: these reports focusing on political strategy and conflict cited executive officials less frequently ($-.52$, $p < .1$).

7. Journalists focusing on political strategy and conflict shied away from citing providers. For the entire period of the AP coverage, the use of strategic frames is negatively correlated with citing providers ($-.40$, $p < .10$); the negative correlation increased after 1985 to $-.64$ ($p < .05$). The coverage by print and broadcast media in 1993–94 followed a similar pattern ($-.41$, $p < .05$); the negative correlations was stronger during 1993 ($-.59$, $p < .05$).

8. Both the AP and print and broadcast reports indicate that journalists who concentrated on political strategy and conflict shied away from advocates. For the entire period of the AP coverage, the use of strategic frames is negatively correlated with citing advocates ($-.56$, $p < .10$). Print and broadcast coverage in 1994 followed a similar pattern ($-.57$, $p < .10$).

In contrast, AP journalists who focused on national consequences were drawn to advocates. For the entire period of AP coverage, the use of national frames is positively correlated with advocates ($.42$, $p < .10$). Print and broadcast journalists during 1993–94, though, behaved differently: those who used national frames shied away from advocates ($-.48$, $p < .05$), more so during 1993 ($-.57$, $p < .10$).

9. Executive branch officials included White House aides as well as officials

from departments and agencies. These officials were folded into our measure for the president and his party in figure 6.4 because executive branch officials were formally under the direction of the president.

10. Statistical analysis indicates that journalists who focused on the national consequences of health issues were inclined to cite experts. For the entire period of AP coverage, the use of national frames is positively correlated with citing experts (.54, p < .05).

11. Statistical analysis indicates that journalists' use of administration officials came at the expense of experts and advocates who were cited less frequently. For the entire period of the AP coverage, the use of executive officials as sources is negatively correlated with the use of experts (−.72, p < .01) and advocates (−.49, p < .05).

12. The patterns in print and broadcast reports were not uniform: journalists as sources were far more common in print reports and declined sharply after May 1994, while they started at a lower level in broadcast but rose rapidly in 1994 to a point comparable to those in print media.

13. Statistical analysis indicates that the tendency of AP journalists to insert their own interpretations after 1985 depressed their use of providers as sources (−.74, p < .05, for after 1985). In addition, the tendency of print and broadcast journalists to insert their own interpretations came at the expense of advocates. For the entire period of 1993–94, citings of advocates were negatively correlated with journalists (−.38, p < .10).

14. Statistical analysis indicates that journalists who focused on political strategy and conflict were inclined to insert their own interpretations and commentary. For the entire period of AP coverage, journalist sources and the use of strategic framing are positively correlated (.71, p < .01).

15. In particular, we examined the yearly average space devoted to sources in AP reports (i.e., the total number of lines as a proportion of the number of mentions each year). The general pattern between 1977 and 1994 shows that the average space devoted to journalists' opinions rose and that given to other political sources fell. Nonetheless, by 1993–94, the average space given to providers, experts, executive branch officials, and advocates significantly exceeded that devoted to commentary by journalists.

16. National Health Insurance reform probably had a better shot at enactment in 1974 than at any time in American history, but did not receive extensive coverage. An earlier draft of Flint Wainess's (1999 and conversations with the author) analysis reviewed news reports on health care reform in the *New York Times, Washington Post, Atlantic Monthly, New Republic,* and *Newsweek* during 1974 but did not find extensive coverage; what was reported focused on the substance of policy. This coincided with a policy debate that was surprisingly consensual.

17. Our statistical analysis showed significant correlations between media coverage and Clinton's statements on his own plan, the alternatives, and access to health care in the .5 to .7 range. The correlations are not perfect (1.0), but this might reflect random sampling errors by the press as well as the imperfect reliability of our content analyses of Clinton's public statements and the media's coverage of them as well as the economic, political, and professional factors we just discussed.

18. The correlations for both issues are in the .2 to .3 range (and not statistically significant), which are weaker than the .5 to .7 range for Clinton's plan, the alternatives, and access.

19. As noted in chapter 4, we analyzed Clinton's framing by examining a random sample of Clinton's actual statements for 1993 and 1994.

20. For instance, Althaus et al. (1996) compared press coverage with legislative debate recorded in the *Congressional Record* over the U.S.-Libya crisis in 1985 and 1986, and concluded that the press portrayed legislators as more opposed to the use of force and engaged in a more simplified debate than is evident in the *Record* (415–16). See also Zaller and Chiu 1996.

21. Clinton's public comments on costs declined rapidly from 1993 to 1994, and antireformers stressed the erosion of health care quality and the threat of bureaucratic red tape.

22. For example, the results of the agenda-setting studies may be partly a function of the cases selected for examination. Selecting issues that were dormant and then highly salient and targets of intense policy attention naturally produce a pattern that supports the causal role of early media coverage. By contrast, we tracked a much more diverse set of issues, which represented regulatory, redistributive, and distributive issues and exhibited the full range of political choices from enactment, to repeal and nonaction (e.g., the failure to pass national health insurance legislation). Many of the health issues that the press covered since 1977 were well-established and long-standing possibilities for the policy agenda; the media's influence in incubating issues was less evident than suggested by the agenda-setting literature. New national policy issues like AIDS, which pop on to the agenda for the first time, were quite rare over this period.

The agenda-setting literature can also be questioned because it has often relied on counting the total number of stories in the *Readers' Guide* or another index. Baumgartner and Jones claim that "media attention tends to focus for some periods of time on the positives associated with an issue, but later may shift to consider almost exclusively the negatives" (1993, 104). Their coding of full stories based on listings in the *Readers' Guide,* though, prevents detecting multiple and competing sources, and both positive and negative messages within a given story. By contrast, our detailed content analysis used each policy-specific message as the unit of analysis (rather than the story). We found complex combinations, as we showed earlier.

These limitations are not restricted to studies on agenda setting. For instance, Putnam's (1995) claim that the media have eroded social capital rests on the unsupported assumption that press coverage is uniform, uninformative, and unengaging. Evaluating this claim would require (at a minimum) a representative and reasonably detailed analysis of the content of media reports.

Chapter Seven

1. Memo to the Communications Team from Greenberg, 12 October 1993; Interview with Greenberg by LRJ, 28 June 1994, in person in Washington, D.C.

2. We cannot rule out the possibility that increased opinion change since 1981 was due to more polling over time.

3. We are studying relatively short-term changes in public opinion, while Page and Shapiro looked at longer trends. In addition, we are analyzing moderate

changes in public opinion compared to the larger ones that Page and Shapiro tracked (Page and Shapiro 1992, chap.1–2).

4. Respondents chose from a five-point scale from strongly agreeing with government responsibility to help to strongly agreeing with people taking care of themselves, which normally attracted 15 to 20 percent of respondents. The middle category was agreeing with both positions; this generally accounted for about a third of respondents. See appendix 2 for question wording.

5. The proportion in favor of paying more out of pocket dropped from 60 percent in 1990 to 49 percent in 1993; the don't knows were 6 percent and 5 percent, respectively.

6. The rise in public support for government activism is evident in seven surveys conducted by Trendex between January 1981 when 60 percent supported the government doing more on health and July 1982 when 70 percent favored more government action; the survey for January 1982 showed a drop back down to 60 percent, which might be attributed to the acrimonious debate over President Reagan's budget cuts in health care. The question asked: "I would like to get your opinion on several areas of important government activities. As I read each one, please tell me if you would like to see the government do more, do less or do about the same amount as they have been on . . . Health measures" (Shapiro and Young 1986, 422).

7. The Gallup Poll and Yankelovich Partners most consistently surveyed Americans about their support for the Clinton plan. Gallup asked: "From everything you have heard or read about the plan so far, do you favor or oppose President Clinton's plan to reform health care?" Yankelovich Partners asked: "In general, do you favor or oppose President Clinton's health care reform plan?" Although differences in question wording produced some slight differences in their results, Gallup and Yankelovich generally reported a similar pattern of changes in Americans' attitudes. We focus on the more numerous Gallup surveys; Yankelovich did not ask questions regarding attitudes toward the Clinton plan during certain critical periods such as January 1994.

8. Zaller (1992) emphasizes that Americans harbor varying "considerations," but not true attitudes. We would argue, though, that the central tendency of these considerations constitute something sufficiently close to genuine attitudes that we can talk meaningfully about public attitudes and opinions as a normatively central part of democratic politics and policymaking (see Page and Shapiro 1992, 1999; Shapiro 1998).

9. The public's ranking of the nation's problems is based on the Gallup question: "What do you think is the most important problem facing this country today?" (Up to three mentions were recorded.)

10. According to Tom Smith's extensive studies of the Gallup "most important problem" question, prior to the mid-1980s medical care and health only received a passing mention as "miscellaneous issues"—typically receiving but one or two percentage points, at most. When questions asked about "family" or "personal problems," then "health" was more frequently cited and was reported by Gallup as a distinctive response. But these responses focused on illness and well-being and not on access, quality, or other policy aspects of health care (Smith 1980; Smith 1985a; Smith 1985b).

11. Gallup Polls, January 1993 to September 1994.

12. The question asked in the survey conducted by Hart and Teeter was: "When it comes to dealing with the problem of health are, which party do you think will do a better job—the Democratic Party, the Republican Party, both about the same, or neither?"

13. Kinder and Kiewiet 1979; Rosenstone, Hansen, and Kinder 1986; Sears, Lau, Tyler, and Allen 1980; Citrin and Green 1990; Sears and Funk 1990.

14. The ABC News questions were worded as follows (16–19 September 1993): "Under (President Bill) Clinton's plan, do you think the quality of the health care you receive will get better, get worse, or stay the same?" (19 percent reported better, 31 percent worse, 46 percent the same, and 4 percent had no opinion.) "Do you think the quality of health care (under President Bill Clinton's plan) for most Americans will get better, worse, or stay the same?" (36 percent better, 29 percent worse, 31 percent same, and 4 percent no opinion.)

The Gallup questions (28–30 October 1993) asked: "(I'd like to ask you about a series of things that might happen under President (Bill) Clinton's health care (reform) plan, if it is passed.) . . . Under the Clinton health care reform plan, do you think you, yourself, would be—a lot better off, a little better off, a little worse off, or a lot worse off—or will the plan have no effect on you?" (8 percent a lot better, 20 percent a little better, 22 percent a little worse, 15 percent a lot worse, 31 percent no effect, 4 percent other.) ". . . . Under the Clinton health care reform plan, do you think the country as a whole would be—a lot better off, a little better off, a little worse off, or a lot worse off—or will the plan have no effect on the country?" (22 percent a lot better, 35 percent a little better, 17 percent a little worse, 17 percent a lot worse, 5 percent no effect, 4 percent other.)

15. In September, respondents' evaluation of the impact of the Clinton plan was split, with 45 percent predicting an increase in their costs and 47 percent a decrease or that their costs would remain the same.

16. The issue of quality was one of the areas, as reported in chapter 6 (see "Media Distortion"), in which the press failed to reflect the emphasis that Clinton had placed on it.

17. Shapiro, Jacobs, and Harvey (1994) and Jacobs, Shapiro, and Harvey (1998) offer a fuller discussion of these and other multivariate analyses that we conducted.

18. Heldman and Lau 1997; Stoker 1994; Zinni and Stanton 1994; Mutz's research on self-interest and public opinion toward health care reform cited in Mutz 1998, 7; on the effects of negative versus positive messages on health care reform and responses to risk, see Cobb and Kuklinski 1995.

19. The different analyses of the influences on public opinion were not able to include the same variables. Koch was not able to directly contrast self-interest versus collective concern specifically with regard to health care. The increasing effects that he reported for attitudes toward equality and government providing jobs might be interpreted as proxies for the increasing effect from 1984 to 1992 of people's concern for others with regard to health care policy.

20. For example, public preferences regarding whether we are spending too much on welfare is apparently influenced not only by changes in government spending but also by the presence of a Democratic or a Republican president (above and beyond the effect of actual spending). If a Democrat comes into office, more of the public responds that we are spending "too much" on welfare; if a Republican enters office, a smaller percentage of survey respondents leap to this conclusion (Weaver, Shapiro, and Jacobs 1995b, 146 n.162).

21. Mutz (1998) studies how perceptions and misperceptions of public opinion affect political attitudes.

22. Memo to the Communications Team from Greenberg, 12 October 1993; Interview with Greenberg by LRJ, 28 June 1994, in person in Washington, D.C.

Chapter Eight

1. The material from Morris' book, *Behind the Oval Office* (1999), include not only his recollections of his White House experiences but also (more valuably) the documents that Morris and the other consultants distributed at the private strategy sessions that Clinton convened in 1995 and 1996. When supplemented with other material, these briefing materials for each specific meeting during this two-year period are a useful body of evidence on internal White House deliberations.

Our interviews were conducted on a confidential basis and used a preset questionnaire in order to facilitate comparisons across the interviews. Twenty-one of the interviews were completed during the summer and early fall of 1995; thirty-one were conducted in 1996, with most concluded in June and July. The response rate was approximately 40 percent; nonresponse was due to some staff simply lacking the time to give to a detailed and time-consuming interviews. To reflect the partisan balance in Congress and the larger size of the House of Representatives, we oversampled both Republicans and House members. Of our fifty-two interviews, forty-one were with House staff (eleven with Senate staff) and thirty with Republicans (twenty-two with Democrats). (The number of interviews reported below is at times less than fifty-two because time constraints prevented some staff from answering all of our questions.)

2. Princeton Survey Research Associates poll, 25–30 October 1995, for the Times Mirror Center for the People and the Press.

3. When given the opportunity to identify all the ways they monitor public opinion, five of fifty-two staffers (10 percent) reported private polls being conducted (all in the 1996 election year), fifty (96 percent) mentioned that their offices monitored public opinion by relying on letters or phone calls; twenty-two (42 percent) pointed to personal encounters.

4. Only two respondents of the fifty-two identified it as a pure constraint. (Eight [15 percent] identified public opinion as neither a constraint nor an opportunity; seven [13 percent] classified it as both.)

5. *Los Angeles Times* poll, 16–18 September 1995.

6. NBC News/*Wall Street Journal* poll, 29 July–1 August 1995.

7. Louis Harris and Associates poll, 28 September–1 October 1995.

8. A February 1996 *New York Times*/CBS News poll show that a majority blamed the Republicans in Congress more than Clinton for the budget impasse. Fifty percent blamed Republicans, 31 percent attributed the standoff to Clinton, 14 percent blamed them both equally, and 6 offered don't know/no answer. *New York Times*/CBS News poll, 22–24 February 1996. According to two separate questions in a January 1996 *NYT*/CBS survey, 62 percent concluded that Clinton was "really trying" to find a solution while only 42 percent felt the same about the Republicans. In addition, a series of four polls from December 1995 to late February 1996 showed that the Democrats opened a fairly stable 10 percentage point advantage over Republicans in the public's evaluation of whether Clinton or Republican leaders in Congress have "acted more responsibly in the negotiations over the budget."

9. In December 1994, the public had greater confidence in Republican leaders than Clinton by a 55 percent–33 percent margin on taxes and a 50 percent–34 percent margin on the federal budget deficit; in April 1996, the public was evenly split (42 percent–42 percent) on the budget deficit and slightly favored Clinton (44 percent–41 percent) on taxes.

10. Louis Harris and Associates poll, 18–22 January 1996; NBC News/*Wall Street Journal* poll, 2–6 June 1995.

11. *Los Angeles Times* poll, 16–18 September 1995.

12. *New York Times*/CBS News poll, 18–20 January 1996.

13. Political knowledge was determined by correct answers to factual questions about politics (Zaller 1992; Carpini and Ketter 1996).

Chapter Nine

1. Despite differences, Weber, Schumpeter, and Sartori share a view of democracy as "competitive elitism" in which the role of citizens is largely limited to choosing the deciders who were then to be guided by their independent judgment (Held 1987, chap. 5).

2. Pitkin 1967; Manin 1997; Held 1987.

3. Key 1961; Stimson et al. 1994 and 1995; Page and Shapiro 1992; Kuklinski and Segura 1995, 4; for a review see Jacobs and Shapiro 1994b.

4. Claims to serving the "national interest" are especially prominent in international relations. See Katzenstein 1996; Lebow and Kappen 1995; Finnemore 1996; and Weldes 1999 for analyses of why these claims are not "objective."

5. See, for empirical research, Keeter and Delli Carpini 1996; Page 1996; and Page and Shapiro 1992. Important works of political theory here include Habermas 1989 and 1996; Benhabib 1996; Fraser 1992; Offe 1992; Dryzek 1990; Calhoun 1992a,b.

For the sake of simplicity and conciseness, we group together the variants of deliberative democracy, emphasizing their common themes and neglecting critical differences. The political theorists of deliberation ground their model of democracy in the rational and critical discussions among citizens—a "public of private people engaged in rational-critical debate" in Jurgen Habermas's (1989) infamous phrase. Deliberation theorists contrast the public opinion formed through active debate among people in the eighteenth and nineteenth centuries with the "public opinion" today, which is "merely" the aggregation (through survey research and polls) of individual opinions that are unformed and manufactured by powerful elites (Habermas 1989 and 1996; Benhabib 1996; Offe 1992; Dryzek 1990; Calhoun 1992a, 1992b). The vertical division between governors and the governed is rejected as a model because it reduces democracy to a relationship between masses and elites, and then further reduces this to elites responding to a contentless "public opinion" (Habermas 1989).

Habermas's (1996) later work acknowledges the reality of a vertical organization between public opinion formation, political elections, and administrative and legislative actions. He notes that "the public opinion that is worked up via democratic procedures . . . cannot 'rule' of itself, but can only point the use of administrative power in specific directions." After the public "react[s] to the pressure of society-wide problematics" "in the first place," it is left "only [to] the administrative system itself [to] 'act' [and reach] collectively binding decisions" (Habermas 1996, 29).

Other deliberationists concede that the notion of a modern society organizing itself in a "mass assembly [that] carr[ies] out its deliberations in public and collectively" is a "fiction" and they dismiss it as a vestige of an "early history of democratic theory" (Benhabib 1996, 73–74).

The limitations, however, of the full-blown deliberationist theory cannot be rectified by adjustment; its critique of public opinion, the media, and the state of existing public deliberation are empirically inaccurate and its remedies a utopian distraction.

First the inaccuracies. Habermas (1989) claims that contemporary public opinion is a "fiction"; it suffers from "social psychological liquidation" and therefore "lack[s] the attribute of rationality" and "merely supplies acclamation" to elite initiatives (219, 238). Research based upon diverse methodologies as well as the findings presented in this study provide evidence of thoughtful and stable public deliberations: individuals balance multiple and competing considerations as they follow and sensibly react to information (substantially conveyed through the press) about policy debates and real-world events (Page and Shapiro 1992; Popkin 1991; Hochschild 1981; Gamson 1992; cf. Zaller 1992). The mass public can only rarely provide the "acclaim" to initiatives that Habermas imagines because intense partisan disagreement and the media's portrayal of them prevent the public from being inundated with information that is uniform or dictated by one individual or group. In short, Habermas neglects the tension in the communication process and press coverage between attempts at domination and the provision of substantive information for genuine public deliberation (Page 1996; Zaller 1999; Benhabib 1992; Boyte 1992).

Deliberation theorists ground their model in a utopian model that has never and will likely never be realized in practice (Fraser 1992). Holding the search for an all-encompassing "consensus" on the common good as a standard for public deliberation ignores the enduring strategic context of policy debates and the competing claims of politicians, interest groups, and individuals. The standards for public deliberation must incorporate a realistic respect for the context and power relations of actual politics.

6. Political theorists have been especially prominent in promoting this horizontal form of communication between free and equal citizens as an alternative to the vertical communications from elites to citizens, which are portrayed as resting on an inevitable hierarchy and severe inequalities in the capability to articulate competing perspective publicly. Survey research and analysis of small group dynamics have also shown that individuals draw information and interpretations from their interactions with peers as well as from their personal experiences.

7. Broder was specifically criticizing their comments in spring 1998 over investigations of the president and his 1996 campaign.

8. There is a large body of research that identifies the presence of elite control due to cooperation (rather than competition) among groups and individuals and the restriction of the policymaking agenda to "safe" issues (e.g., Lowi 1979; Schattschneider 1960b; Bachrach and Baratz 1962).

9. Our interpretation offers a corrective to Habermas's (1989) overly one-sided interpretation of the triumphal impact of elite efforts at manipulating public opinion. Habermas does not assign sufficient analytic weight to the ineffectiveness of

manipulation (given the character of public opinion and the limitations of opinion-molding techniques) and the countervailing effect of contending elite efforts at manipulation.

10. The American National Election Studies (NES) have asked this question since the 1950s; the Center on Policy Attitudes asked the NES question in January 1999 (Kull 1999, 7).

11. A January 1999 survey conducted by the Center on Policy Attitudes used identically worded questions that NES has fielded since the 1950s (Kull 1999, 7). The proportion convinced that "people like me don't have any say about what the government does" increased from 27 percent in 1960 to 56 percent in 1999. Similarly, the proportion of Americans who agreed that "public officials don't care much what people like me think" has risen from 25 percent in 1960 to 58 percent in 1999 (Kull 1999, 9–10).

12. Even when survey questions invited respondents to welcome independent action by policymakers because they were well-informed, thoughtful, and objective in contrast to an "emotional, volatile, and uninformed" public, only a quarter preferred the trustee model (Kull 1999, 4).

13. In January 1999 the Center on Policy Attitudes asked a question that NES had posed since the 1950s.

14. A novel finding in our survey was that the particular policy area affected whether respondents perceived the national interest or special interests as the most influential: 55 percent of respondents believed that interest group pressures were the primary consideration in Medicare policy while 57 percent cited the national interest with regard to the war with Serbia. We included our questions in a survey conducted by Research/Strategy/Management, Inc.

15. Interviews.

16. Memo to First Lady from Boorstin and David Dreyer, 25 January 1993.

17. Memo to the president and First Lady from Magaziner regarding "Where We Are Positioned," 1 October 1993; Memo to president and First Lady from Magaziner, Zelman, and Magherio regarding "Positioning of September Health Reform Introduction," 30 August 1993; Memo to Magaziner from Greenberg, 14 September 1993 regarding "The Health Care Joint Session Speech."

Chapter Ten

1. Greenblatt 1998; Cohen 1998, *Congressional Quarterly* 1998; Doherty 1998; *National Journal* 1998; Nitschke 1998.

2. See Public Perspective 1996b for a debate both on whether and to what degree public engagement in community activities has broken down—as captured by the image of individuals "bowling alone"—and on realistic and appropriate remedial actions.

3. We disagree with Fishkin's (1991) presumption that public opinion is already substantially driving public policy decisions and that the analytic challenge is simply improving the quality of that public input.

4. Although the New Hampshire primary received far more coverage than the 1996 deliberative polls in Austin, the coverage that this experiment received was nonetheless striking. As Merkle (1996) notes, there is significant potential for expanding on this initial media coverage in the future.

References and
Additional Sources

Abramowitz, Alan. 1989. Viability, electability, and candidate choice in a presidential primary election: A test of competing models. *Journal of Politics* 51 (November): 977–92.

Abramson, Paul, and John Aldrich. 1982. The decline of electoral participation in America. *American Political Science Review* 76 (September): 502–21.

Abramson, Paul R., John H. Aldrich, and David W. Rohde. 1999. *Change and continuity in the 1996 and 1998 elections.* Washington, D.C.: CQ Press.

Adams, James, and Samuel Merrill. 1999. Modeling party strategies and policy representation in multiparty elections: Why are strategies so extreme? *Journal of American Political Science* 43 (July): 765–91.

Aldrich, John H. 1995. *Why parties: The origin and transformation of political parties in America.* Chicago: University of Chicago Press.

Aldrich, John H., John Sullivan, and Eugene Borgida. 1989. Foreign affairs and issue voting: Do presidential candidates waltz before a blind audience? *American Political Science Review* 83 (March): 123–41.

Alexseev, M. A., and W. L. Bennett. 1995. For whom the gates open: Journalistic norms and political source patterns in the United States, Great Britain, and Russia. *Political Communication* 12 (4): 395–412.

Alford, John R., and David W. Brady. 1989. Personal and partisan advantage in U.S. congressional elections, 1846–1986. In *Congress reconsidered,* 4th ed., edited by Lawrence C. Dodd and Bruce I. Oppenheimer, 153–69. New York: Praeger.

Allard, Winston. 1941. Congressional attitudes toward public opinion polls. *Journalism Quarterly* 18 (March): 47–50.

Alterman, Eric. 1998. *Who speaks for America? Why democracy matters in foreign policy.* Ithaca: Cornell University Press.

Althaus, Scott L. 1998. Information effects in collective preferences. *American Political Science Review* 92 (September): 545–58.

Althaus, Scott L., Jill A. Edy, Robert M. Entman, and Patricia Phalen. 1996. Revising the indexing hypotheses: Officials, media, and the Libya crisis. *Political Communication* 13 (4): 407–21.

Amacher, Ryan G., and William J. Boyes. 1978. Cycles in senatorial voting behavior: Implications for the optimal frequency of elections. *Public Choice* 33 (3): 5–13.

American Political Science Association. 1950. Toward a more responsible government: A report on the committee on political parties. *American Political Science Review Supplement* 44 (September), part 2.

Ansolabehere, Stephen D., and James M. Snyder Jr. 1997. Party platform choice in single-member-district and party list systems. Working paper, Spring. Department of Political Science, Massachusetts Institute of Technology.

Ansolabehere, Stephen D., James M. Snyder Jr., and Charles Stewart III. 1998a. Candidate positioning in U.S. House elections. Working paper, 29 July. Department of Political Science, Massachusetts Institute of Technology.

———. 1998b. Old voters, new voters, and the personal vote: Using redistricting to measure incumbency advantage. Working paper, November. Massachusetts Institute of Technology.

Aranson, Peter H., and Peter C. Ordeshook. 1972. Spatial strategies for sequential elections. In *Probability models of collective decision making,* edited by Richard G. Niemi and Herbert F. Weisberg, 298–331. Columbus, Ohio: Merrill.

Arnold, R. Douglas. 1990. *The logic of congressional action.* New Haven: Yale University Press.

Auletta, Ken. 1996. Inside story: Why did both candidates despise the press? *New Yorker,* 18 November, 44–60.

Austen-Smith, David, and Jeffrey S. Banks. 1996. Information aggregation, rationality, and the condorcet jury theorem. *American Political Science Review* 90 (March): 34–45.

Bachrach, Peter, and Morton S. Baratz. 1962. Two faces of power. *American Political Science Review* 56 (December): 947–52.

Backstrom, Charles, and Leonard Robins. 1998. The media and AIDS: Health elite policy perspectives of coverage. *Journal of Health and Social Policy* 9 (3): 45–69.

Bagdikian, Ben H. 1992. *The media monopoly.* 4th ed. Boston: Beacon.

Ball, Terence. 1987. "A republic—if you can keep it." In *Conceptual change and the constitution,* edited by Terence Ball and J. G. A. Pocock, 137–64. Lawrence: University Press of Kansas.

Balz, Dan. 1994. Dole urges GOP unity on health plan. *Washington Post,* 23 January.

Barnes, James. 1994. Selling ideas. *National Journal,* 13 August, p. 1944.

———. 1995. Privatizing politics. *National Journal,* 3 June.

Barr, Bob. 1999. Closing arguments in senate trial. *Congressional Record,* 8 February.

Bartels, Larry M. 1996. Uninformed votes: Information effects in presidential elections. *American Journal of Political Science* 40 (February): 194–230.

Baumgartner, Frank R., and Bryan D. Jones. 1993. *Agendas and instability in American politics.* Chicago: University of Chicago Press.

Benhabib, Seyla. 1992. Models of public space: Hannah Arendt, the liberal tradition, and Jurgen Habermas. In *Habermas and the public sphere,* edited by Craig Calhoun, 73–98. Cambridge: MIT Press.

———. 1996. Toward a deliberative model of democratic legitimacy. In *Democracy and difference: Contesting the boundaries of the political,* edited by Seyla Ben-habib, 67–94. Princeton: Princeton University Press.

Bennet, James. 1996. North Carolina media try to lead politics to issues. *New York Times,* 24 September.

———. 1997. At retreat, president takes look at the past. *New York Times,* 3 January.

Bennet, James, and Robert Pear. 1997. A presidency largely defined by the many parts of its sum. *New York Times,* 8 December.

Bennett, W. Lance. 1990. Toward a theory of press-state relations in the United States. *Journal of Communication* 40 (spring): 103–25.

———. 1996. *News: The politics of illusion.* 3d ed. White Plains, N.Y.: Longman.

Bennett, W. Lance, and John Klockner. 1994. The psychology of mass-mediated publics. In *The psychology of political communication,* edited by Ann Crigler, 88–109. Ann Arbor: University of Michigan Press.

Bentley, Arthur F. 1908. *The process of government: A study of social pressures.* Chicago: University of Chicago Press.

Berelson, Bernard R., Paul F. Lazarsfeld, and William N. McPhee. 1954. *Voting: A study of opinion formation in a presidential campaign.* Chicago: University of Chicago Press.

Berke, Richard. 1993. Clinton Adviser says polls had a role in health plan. *New York Times,* 9 December.

———. 1996. Master move in campaign. *New York Times,* 1 August.

Berman, Evan. 1997. Dealing with cynical citizens. *Public Administration Review* 57 (March/April): 105–12.

Bianco, William T. 1994. *Trust: Representatives and constituents.* Ann Arbor: University of Michigan Press.

Black, Duncan. 1958. *The theory of committees and elections.* Cambridge: Cambridge University Press.

Blake, Laurie. 1993. Citizen pain. *Minnesota Star Tribune,* 10 May.

Blendon, Robert. 1994. The gridlock is us. *New York Times,* 22 May.

Blendon, Robert, Mollyann Brodie, Tracey Hyams and John Benson. 1994. The American public and the critical choices for health system reform. *Journal of the American Medical Association* 271 (18 May): 1539–44.

Blondel, Jean. 1987. *Political leadership.* Beverly Hills: Sage.

Blumenthal, Sidney. 1994. The education of a president. *New Yorker,* 24 January, 31–43.

Blumler, Herbert. 1948. Public opinion and public opinion polling. *American Sociological Review* 13 (October): 542–54.

Blumler, Jay G., and Michael Gurevitch. 1981. Politicians and the press: An essay in role relationships. In *Handbook of Political Communication,* edited by Dan D. Nimmo and Keith R. Sanders, 467–93. Beverly Hills, Calif.: Sage.

Bond, Jon R., and Richard Fleisher. 1990. *The president in the legislative arena.* Chicago: University of Chicago Press.

Box, Richard. 1998. *Citizen governance: Leading American communities into the 21st century.* Thousand Oaks, Calif.: Sage.

Boyte, Harry C. 1992. The pragmatic ends of popular politics. In *Habermas and the public sphere,* edited by Craig Calhoun, 340–55. Cambridge: MIT Press.

Brace, Paul, and Barbara Hinckley. 1992. *Follow the leader: Opinion polls and the modern presidents.* New York: Basic Books.

Brady, David and Kara Buckley. 1995. Health care reform in the 103d Congress: A predictable failure. *Journal of Health Politics, Policy, and Law* 20 (summer): 447–54.

Brittan, Samuel. 1975. The economic contradictions of democracy. *British Journal of Political Science* 5 (April): 129–59.

Broder, David. 1993a. GOP health care strategy emerging. *Washington Post,* 11 October.

———. 1993b. On divided hill, expectations of action are high. *Washington Post,* 28 October.

———. 1993c. Gingrich takes "no-compromise" stand on health care plan. *Washington Post,* 15 December.

———. 1995. The ghosts of term limits past. *Washington Post,* 28 May.

———. 1997. Where journalists have no place. *Washington Post National Weekly Edition,* 13 January.

———. 1998. Leaders in wretched rhetoric. *Washington Post National Weekly Edition,* 5 May.

Broder, David, and William Claiborne. 1994. Governors call for health reform bill. *Washington Post,* 1 February.

Broder, David, and Spencer Rich. 1993. Route through Congress is strewn with hazards. *Washington Post,* 19 September.

Brodie, Mollyann, and Robert J. Blendon. 1995. The public's contribution to congressional gridlock on health care reform. *Journal of Health Politics, Policy and Law* 20 (summer): 403–10.

Brodie, Mollyann, Lee Ann Brady, and Drew Altman. 1998. Media coverage of managed care: Is there a negative bias? *Health Affairs* 17 (January/February): 10–25.

Brody, Richard A. 1991. *Assessing the president: The media, elite opinion, and public support.* Stanford: Stanford University Press.

Brosius, Hans-Bernd, and Hans M. Kepplinger. 1990. The agenda-setting function of television news. *Communication Research* 17 (April): 183–211.

Brown, Lawrence. 1992. Political evolution of federal health care regulation. *Health Affairs* 11 (winter): 17–37.

———. 1993. Dogmatic slumbers: American business and health policy. *Journal of Health Politics, Policy and Law* 18 (summer): 339–57.

Brown, Jane D., Carl R. Bybee, Stanley T. Weardon, and Dulcie M. Straughan. 1987. Invisible power: Newspaper sources and the limits of diversity. *Journalism Quarterly* 64 (spring): 45–54.

Bruck, Connie. 1994. Hillary the pol. *New Yorker,* 30 May, 58–96.

———. 1995. The politics of perception. *New Yorker,* 9 October, 50–76.

Bruni, Frank. 1999. Lott condemns president over "this sordid saga." *New York Times,* 13 February.

Burke, Edmund. 1949. *Burke's politics: Selected writings and speeches of Edmund Burke on reform, revolution, and war,* edited by Ross J. S. Hoffmann and Paul Levack. New York: A. A. Knopf.

Burstein, Paul. 1998. Bringing the public back in: Should sociologists consider the impact of public opinion on public policy? *Social Forces* 77 (September): 27–62.

Cain, Bruce, John Ferejohn, and Morris Fiorina. 1987. *The personal vote.* Cambridge: Harvard University Press.

Calhoun, Craig, ed. 1992. *Habermas and the public sphere.* Cambridge: MIT Press.

Calhoun, John C. 1953. *A disquisition on government and selections from the discourse.* Indianapolis: Bobbs-Merrill.

Campbell, Colin. 1987. Review article: Administration and politics: The state apparatus and political responsiveness. *Comparative Politics* 19 (July): 481–99.

———. 1988. Review article: The political roles of senior government officials in advanced democracies. *British Journal of Political Science* 18 (April): 243–72.

Cameron, Charles. 2000a. *Veto bargaining.* New York: Cambridge University Press.

———. 2000b. Bargaining and presidential power. In *Presidential power: Forging the presidency for the twenty-first century,* edited by Robert Y. Shapiro, Martha Joynt Kumar, and Lawrence R. Jacobs. New York: Columbia University Press.

Cannon, Angie. 1994. Clinton's pollster busy on issues that can sell. *Detroit Free Press,* 12 April.

Cannon, Carl. 1998. Hooked on polls. *National Journal,* 17 October.

Cappella, Joseph N., and Kathleen H. Jamieson. 1997. *Spiral of cynicism: The press and the public good.* New York: Oxford University Press.

Carmines, Edward G., and James H. Kuklinsi. 1990. Incentives, opportunities, and the logic of public opinion in American political representation. In *Information and democratic processes,* edited by John A. Ferejohn and James H. Kuklinski. Urbana: University of Illinois Press.

Carmines, Edward G., and James A. Stimson. 1989. *Issue evolution: Race and the transformation of American politics.* Princeton: Princeton University Press.

Carpini, Michael Delli, and Scott Keeter. 1996. *What Americans know about politics and why it matters.* New Haven: Yale University Press.

Center for media and public affairs. 1994. Diagnosing health care reform: How TV news has covered President Clinton's Health Security Act. *Media Monitor* 8 (May/June): 1–6.

Center for Public Integrity. 1994. *Well-healed: Inside lobbying for health care reform.* Washington, D.C.: Center for Public Integrity.

Chard, Richard E., and Cristina M. Ling. 1999. Media priming of the health security act: How Harry and Louise affected Presidential vote intention. Presented at the annual meeting of the Midwest Political Science Association, Chicago, Illinois.

Chen, Edwin, and David Lauter. 1993. Clinton unveils health reform. *Los Angeles Times,* 23 September.

Cigler, Allan J., and Burdett A. Loomis. 1983. *Interest group politics.* Washington, D.C.: CQ Press.

Citrin, Jack, and Donald P. Green. 1990. The self-interest motive in American public opinion. In *Research in micropolitics: A research annual,* edited by Samuel Long, 1–27. Greenwich, Conn.: JAI.

Civic Catalyst. 1997. Publication of the Pew Center for Civic Journalism. January.

Clausen, Aage. 1973. *How congressmen decide: A policy focus.* New York: St. Martin's.

Clines, Francis X. 1996. The president's strategist puts his faith in timing and telephone calls. *New York Times,* 9 August.

————. 1999. Searching for a modern Machiavelli. *New York Times,* 20 May.

Clymer, Adam. 1993. Clinton health plan: The overview. *New York Times,* 23 September.

————. 1996. Clinton and Congress: Partnership of self-interest. *New York Times,* 2 October.

Clymer, Adam and Robin Toner. 1994. For health care, time was a killer. *New York Times,* 29 August.

Cobb, Michael D., and James H. Kuklinski. 1995. Changing minds: Political arguments and political persuasion. Working paper #47. The Institute of Government and Public Affairs, University of Illinois, December.

Cohen, Jeffrey E. 1997. *Presidential responsiveness and public policy-making: The public and the policies that presidents choose.* Ann Arbor: University of Michigan Press.

Cohen, Richard E. 1994. Now it's time to play the blame game. *National Journal.* 8 October, 2357.

————. 1998. Business as usual. *National Journal,* 7 March.

Colby, David, Timothy Cook, and Thomas Murray. 1987. Social movements and sickness on the air: Agenda control and television news on AIDS. Paper presented at the annual convention of the American Political Science Association, Chicago.

Coleman, John. 1997. Unified government, divided government, and the production of significant public policy. Paper prepared for the Annual Meeting of the Midwest Political Science Association, April.

Congressional Budget Office. 1993. Trends in health spending: An update. Washington, D.C.: U.S. Government Printing Office. June.

————. 1994. An analysis of the administration's health proposal: A CBO study. Washington, D.C.: U.S. Government Printing Office. February.

Congressional Quarterly Weekly Report. 1998. Guide to CQ's voting analyses. 3 January.

Connolly, Cecil. 1997. Consultant offers GOP a language for the future. *Washington Post,* 4 September.

Connolly, Cecil, David Broder, Dan Balz. 1997. A GOP divided. *Washington Post National Weekly Edition,* 4 August.

Cook, Fay L., and Edith J. Barrett. 1992. *Support for the American welfare state: The views of Congress and the public.* New York: Columbia University Press.

Cook, Fay L., and Lawrence R. Jacobs. 1999. Evaluation of *Americans Discuss Social Security:* Deliberative democracy in action. Report to the Pew Charitable Trusts.

Cook, Fay L., Lawrence R. Jacobs, and Jason Barabas. 1999. Deliberative democracy in action: An analysis of the effects of the Americans Discuss Social Security deliberative forums. Presented at the 1999 Annual Meeting of the American Political Science Association.

Cook, Fay L., Tom R. Tyler, Edward G. Goetz, Margaret T. Gordon, David L. Protess, Donna R. Leff, and Harvey L. Molotch. 1983. Media and agenda-setting: Effects on the public, interest group leaders, policymakers, and policy. *Public Opinion Quarterly* 47 (spring): 16–35.

Cook, Timothy E. 1998. *Governing with the news: The news media as a political institution.* Chicago: University of Chicago Press.

Cox, Gary, and Jonathan Katz. 1996. Why did the incumbency advantage grow? *American Journal of Political Science* 40 (May): 478–97.

Cox, Gary W., and Matthew D. McCubbins. 1993. *Legislative leviathan: Party government in the House.* Berkeley: University of California Press.

Crespi, Irving. 1989. *Public opinion, polls, and democracy.* Boulder, Colo.: Westview.

Cronin, Thomas E. 1980. *The state of the presidency.* 2d ed. Boston: Little Brown.

Dahl, Robert. 1956. *A preface to democratic theory.* Chicago: University of Chicago Press.

———. 1970. *After the revolution: Authority in a good society.* New Haven: Yale University Press.

———. 1985. *A preface to economic democracy.* Cambridge: Polity Press.

———. 1989. *Democracy and its critics.* New Haven: Yale University Press.

———. 1994. A democratic dilemma: System effectiveness versus citizen participation. *Political Science Quarterly* 109 (spring): 23–35.

———. 1999. Democratic deficits and foreign policy. *Dissent* 46 (winter): 110–13.

Danielian, Lucig H., and Benjamin I. Page. 1994. The heavenly chorus: Interest group voices on TV news. *American Journal of Political Science* 38 (November): 1056–78.

Davidson, Roger and Walter Oleszek. 1998. *Congress and its members.* 6th ed. Washington, D.C.: CQ Press.

Davis, Otto, Melvin J. Hinich, and Peter C. Ordershook. 1970. An expository development of a mathematical model of the electoral process. *American Political Science Review* 64 (June): 426–48.

Dearing, James. 1989. Setting the polling agenda for the issue of AIDS. *Public Opinion Quarterly* 53 (fall): 309–29.

DeParle, Jason. 1996. Newt's Endgame. *New York Times Magazine,* 28 January.

Devroy, Ann. 1994. Clinton asks critics to compare his health care plan with alternatives. *Washington Post,* 2 February.

———. 1994b. President signals health flexibility. *Washington Post,* 20 July.

Dewar, Helen and Juliet Ellperin. 1998. From compromise to confrontation. *Washington Post National Weekly Edition,* 25 May.

Dewar, Helen, and Eric Pianin. 1996a. Choosing pragmatism over partisanship. *Washington Post National Weekly Edition,* 12–18 August.

———. 1996b. A switch in time that may have saved the GOP. *Washington Post National Weekly Edition,* 7–13 October.

Dewar, Helen and Dana Priest. 1994. Old Republican fissures feel strain as health care debate grows. *Washington Post,* 20 February.

Dewey, John. 1916. *Democracy and eduction: An introduction to the philosophy of education.* New York: Macmillan.

Dimaggio, Paul, John Evans, and Bethany Bryson. 1996. Have Americans' social attitudes become more polarized? *American Journal of Sociology* 102 (November): 690–755.

Doherty, Carroll. 1998. Clinton finds support on Hill despite GOP's vocal attacks. *Congressional Quarterly Weekly Report,* 3 January.

Domhoff, G. William. 1996. Book review of golden rule: The investment theory of party competition and the logic of money-driven political systems by Thomas Ferguson. *Contemporary Sociology* 25 (March): 197–98.

Donohue, George, Phillip Tichenor, and Clarice Olien. 1995. A guard dog perspective on the role of media. *Journal of Communication* 45 (spring): 115–32.

Dorfman, Lori, Helen H. Schauffler, John Wilkerson, and Judith Feinson. 1996. Local television news coverage of President Clinton's introduction of the Health Security Act. *Journal of the American Medical Association* 275 (April 17): 201–5.

Dowd, Maureen. 1997. Leaders as followers. *New York Times,* 12 January.

Downs, Anthony. 1957. *An economic theory of democracy.* New York: Harper and Row.

Drew, Elizabeth. 1994. *On the edge: The Clinton presidency.* New York: Simon and Schuster.

———. 1996. *Showdown: The struggle between the Gingrich Congress and the Clinton White House.* New York: Touchstone.

Dryzek, John. 1990. *Discursive democracy: Politics, policy and political science.* New York: Cambridge University Press.

Durr, Robert H. 1993. What moves policy sentiment? *American Political Science Review* 87:158–70.

Edwards, George C. 1983. *The public presidency: The pursuit of popular support.* New York: St. Martin's.

———. 1989. *At the margins: Presidential leadership of Congress.* New Haven: Yale University Press.

Eisinger, Robert M. 1993. The president's stethoscope: Franklin Delano Roosevelt and presidential polling. Revised paper presented at the annual meeting of the Social Science History Association, Baltimore, Maryland, 6 November.

———. 1994. Pollster and public relations advisor: Hadley Cantril and the birth of presidential polling. Paper presented at the annual meeting of the American Association of Public Opinion Research.

Elling, Richard C. 1982. Ideological change in the U.S. Senate: Time and electoral responsiveness. *Legislative Studies Quarterly.* 7 February: 75–92.

Enelow, James J., and Melvin J. Hinich. 1984. *The spatial theory of voting: An introduction.* New York: Cambridge University Press.

Entman, Robert and Benjamin Page. 1994. News before the storm: The Iraq War debate and the limits to media independence. In *Taken by storm: The media, public opinion, and U.S. foreign policy in the Gulf War,* edited by W. Lance Bennett and David L. Paletz, 82–101. Chicago: University of Chicago Press.

Erbring, Lutz, Edie N. Goldenberg, and Arthur H. Miller. 1980. Front-page news and real-world cues: A new look at agenda-setting by the media. *American Journal of Political Science* 24 (February) 16–49.

Erikson, Robert S. 1978. Constituency opinion and congressional behavior: A reexamination of the Miller-Stokes data. *American Journal of Political Science* 22 (August): 511–35.

Erikson, Robert S., Michael B. MacKuen, and James A. Stimson. Forthcoming. *The macro polity.* New York: Cambridge University Press.

Erikson, Robert S., and David Romero. 1990. Candidate equilibrium and the behavioral model of the vote. *American Political Science Review* 84 (December): 1103–26.

Erikson, Robert S., Gerald C. Wright, and John P. McIver. 1993. *Statehouse democracy: Public opinion and democracy in American states.* New York: Cambridge University Press.

Fallows, James. 1996. *Breaking the news: How the media undermine American democracy.* New York: Pantheon.

Fan, David P. 1988. *Predictions of public opinion from the mass media: Computer content analysis and mathematical modeling.* New York: Greenwood.

Fan, David P., and Lois Norem. 1992. Medicare Catastrophic Extension Act. *Journal of Health Politics, Policy and Law* 17 (spring): 39–70.

Fearon, James. 1999. Electoral accountability and the control of politicians. In *Democracy, accountability, and representation,* edited by Bernard Manin, Susan Stokes, and Adam Przeworski. Cambridge: Cambridge University Press.

Fenno, Richard F. 1973. *Congressmen in committees.* Boston: Little, Brown.

———. 1978. *Homestyle: House members in their districts.* Boston: Little, Brown.

Ferguson, Andrew. 1996. The focus group fraud. *The Weekly Standard,* 14 October, 18–23.

Ferguson, Thomas. 1995. *Golden rule: The investment theory of party competition and the logic of money-driven political systems.* Chicago: University of Chicago Press.

Finnemore, Martha. 1996. *National society.* Ithaca: Cornell University Press.

Fiorina, Morris P. 1973. Electoral margins, constituency influence, and policy moderation: A critical assessment. *American Politics Quarterly* 1 (October): 479–98.

———. 1974. *Representatives, roll calls, and constituencies.* Lexington, Mass.: Lexington.

———. 1977. *Congress: Keystone of the Washington establishment.* New Haven: Yale University Press.

———. 1981. *Retrospective voting in American national elections.* New Haven: Yale University Press.

Fishel, Jeff. 1985. *Presidents and promises.* Washington, D.C.: CQ Press.

Fisher, Ian. 1995. Gingrich attacks Times-CBS poll, claiming bias against G.O.P. *New York Times,* 27 October.

Fishkin, James. 1991. *Democracy and deliberation: New directions for democratic reform.* New Haven: Yale University Press.

———. 1995. *The voice of the people.* New Haven: Yale University Press.

Fleisher, Richard. 1993. Explaining the change in roll-call voting behavior of Southern Democrats. *Journal of Politics* 55 (May): 327–41.

Fleisher, Richard, and Jon R. Bond. 1996. The President in a more partisan legislative arena. *Political Research Quarterly* 49 (December): 729–48.

Foster, H. Schuyler. 1983. *Activism replaces isolationism: U.S. public attitudes 1940–1975.* Washington, D.C.: Foxhall.

Frankovic, Kathleen A. 1998. Public opinion and polling. In *Politics of news, the news of politics,* edited by Doris A. Graber, Denis McQuail, and Pippa Norris, 150–70. Washington, D.C.: CQ Press.

Fraser, Nancy. 1992. Rethinking the public sphere: A contribution to the critique of actually existing democracy. In *Habermas and the public sphere,* edited by Craig Calhoun, 109–42. Cambridge: MIT Press.

Free, Lloyd A., Hadley Cantril. 1967. *The political beliefs of Americans: A study of public opinion.* New Brunswick, N.J.: Rutgers University Press.

Frisby, Michael K. 1996. Clinton seeks strategic edge with opinion polls. *Wall Street Journal,* 24 June, A16.

Gallup, George, and Saul Rae. 1940. *The pulse of democracy.* New York: Simon and Schuster.

Gamson, William A. 1992. *Talking politics.* Cambridge: Cambridge University Press.

Gans, Herbert. 1979. *Deciding what's news.* New York: Random House.

Geer, John G. 1996. *From tea leaves to opinion polls.* New York: Columbia University Press.

Gelman, Andrew, and Gary King. 1990. Estimating incumbency advantage without bias. *American Journal of Political Science* 34 (November): 1142–64.

Gerber, Elizabeth R., and John E. Jackson. 1993. Endogenous preferences and the study of institutions. *American Political Science Review* 87 (September): 639–56.

Gingrich, Newt. 1993. Health care: Time to get practical. *Washington Post,* 9 March.

Ginsberg, Benjamin. 1976. Elections and public policy. *American Political Science Review* 70 (March): 41–50.

———. 1986. *The captive public: How mass opinion promotes state power.* New York: Basic Books.

Glied, Sherry. 1997. *Chronic condition: Why health reform fails.* Cambridge: Harvard University Press.

Glynn, Carroll J., Susan Herbst, Garrett J. O'Keefe, and Robert Y. Shapiro. 1999. *Public opinion.* Boulder, Colo.: Westview.

Gormley, William. 1998. Witnesses for the revolution. *American Politics Quarterly* 26 (April): 174–95.

Graber, Doris A. 1984. *Processing the news: How people tame the information tide.* New York: Longman.

———. 1993a. *Mass media and American politics.* 4th ed. Washington, D.C.: CQ Press.

———. 1993b. Political communication: Scope, progress, promise. In *Political science: The state of the discipline II,* edited by Ada Finifter, 305–32. Washington, D.C.: American Political Science Association.

Greinstien, Fred I. 1988. *Leadership in the modern presidency.* Cambridge: Harvard University Press.

Greenblatt, Alan. 1998. Despite drop in partisan votes, bickering continued in 1997. *Congressional Quarterly Weekly Report,* 3 January, 18.

Greve, Frank. 1995. GOP's "contract" poll not adding up. *Knight-Tribune News Service,* 10 November.

Groseclose, Tim, and Nolan McCarty. 1996. Presidential vetoes: Bargaining, blame game, and gridlock. Unpublished manuscript, Department of Political Science, Ohio State University.

Gugliotta, Guy, and Juliet Eilperin. 1999. Managers put brave face on bitter loss. *Washington Post,* 13 February.

Gunn, J. A. W. 1995. "Public opinion" in modern political science. In *Political science in history: Research programs and political traditions,* edited by James Farr, John S. Dryzek, and Stephen T. Leonard, 99–122. New York: Cambridge University Press.

Habermas, Jurgen. 1989. *The structural transformation of the public sphere: An inquiry into a category of the public sphere.* Cambridge: MIT Press.

———. 1996. Three normative models of democracy. In *Democracy and difference: Contesting the boundaries of the political,* edited by Seyla Benhabib, 21–30. Princeton: Princeton University Press.

Hacker, Jacob. 1997. *The road to nowhere: The genesis of president Clinton's plan for health security.* Princeton: Princeton University Press.

Hagner, Paul R., and John Pierce. 1982. Correlative characteristics of levels of conceptualization in the American public: 1956–1976. *Journal of Politics* 44 (August): 779–809.

Hallin, Daniel C. 1992. Sound bite news: Television coverage of elections 1968–1988. *Journal of Communication* 42 (spring): 5–24.

Hamburger, Tom, Ted Marmor, and Jon Meacham. 1994. What the death of health reform teaches us about the press. *Washington Monthly.* November.

Hansen, Susan B. 1975. Participation, political structure and concurrence. *American Political Science Review* 69 (December): 1181–99.

Harris, Douglas B. 1998. The rise of the public speakership. *Political Science Quarterly* 113 (summer): 193–212.

Harris, John. 1997a. Morris's tactics still hold sway at White House. *Washington Post,* 27 January.

———. 1997b. Gone—but not forgotten. *Washington Post National Weekly Edition,* 3 February.

———. 1998. New Morris book highlights how polls, policy intersected. *Washington Post,* 22 December.

Harris, Louis, and Eric Pianin. 1995. Parties swap fire in fight on medicare: Details of plans remain hidden. *Washington Post,* 25 July.

Harris, Richard. 1966. *A sacred trust.* New York: Penguin.

Health Care Financing Review. 1992. Symposium on U.S. Bureau of the Census: Current Popular Survey 1980–91, 14 (fall).

Heclo, Hugh. 1978. Issue networks and the executive establishment. In *The new American political system,* edited by Anthony King, 87–124. Washington: D.C.: American Enterprise Institute.

———. 1995. The Clinton health plan: Historical perspective. *Health Affairs* 14 (spring): 86–98.

———. 1999. Hyperdemocracy. *Wilson Quarterly* 23 (winter): 62–71.

Heith, Diane. 1998. Staff the White House public opinion apparatus: 1969–1988. *Public Opinion Quarterly* 62 (summer): 165–89.

———. 2000. Presidential polling and the potential for leadership. In *Presidential power: Forging the presidency for the twenty-first century,* edited by Robert Y. Shapiro, Martha Joynt Komar, and Lawrence R. Jacobs. New York: Columbia University Press.

Held, David. 1987. *Models of democracy.* Stanford: Stanford University Press.

Heldman, Caroline E., and Richard Lau. 1997. Self-interest and attitudes toward health care reform. Presented at the annual meeting of the Midwest Political Science Association. Chicago, April 10–12.

Herbst, Susan. 1993. *Numbered voices: How opinion polling has shaped American politics.* Chicago: University of Chicago Press.

———. 1998. *Reading public opinion: How political actors view the democratic process.* Chicago: University of Chicago Press.

Hertzberg, Hendrik. 1998. Tap dance: The big, scary, hard-to-figure "American people." *New Yorker,* 20 April, 7–8.

Hess, Stephen. 1986. *The ultimate insiders: U.S. senators in the national media.* Washington, D.C.: Brookings Institution.

Hetherington, Mark. 1998. The political relevance of political trust. *American Political Science Review.* 92 (December): 791–807.

Hill, Kim Q., and Patricia A. Hurley. 1999. Dyadic representation reappraised. *American Journal of Political Science* 43 (January): 109–37.

Himelfarb, Richard. 1995. *Catastrophic politics: The rise and fall of the Medicare Catastophic Coverage Act of 1988.* University Park: Pennsylvania State University Press.

Hochschild, Jennifer. 1981. *What's fair: American beliefs about distributive justice.* Cambridge: Harvard University Press.

Hojnacki, Marie. 1997. Interest groups' decisions to join alliances or work alone. *American Journal of Political Science* 41 (January): 61–87.

Huckfeldt, Robert, and John Sprague. 1995. *Citizens, politics, and social communication: Information and influence in an election campaign.* New York: Cambridge University Press.

Huebner, Jeffrey, David P. Fan, and John Finnegan. 1996. Unpublished paper. Department of Genetics and Cell Biology, University of Minnesota.

Hula, Kevin. 1995. Rounding up the usual suspects: Forging interest group coalitions in Washington. In *Interest group politics,* edited by Alan Cigler and Burdett Loomis, 239–58. Washington, D.C.: CQ Press.

Huntington, Samuel P. 1950. A revised theory of American party politics. *American Political Science Review* 44 (September): 669–77.

———. 1975. The United States. In *The crisis of democracy: Report on the governability of democracies to the trilateral commission,* edited by Michel Crozier, Samuel Huntington, and Joji Watanuki, 59–118. New York: New York University Press.

Hurley, Patricia A. 1991. Partisan representation, realignment, and the Senate in the 1980s. *Journal of Politics* 53 (February): 3–33.

Hyde, Henry. 1999. Senate trial. *Congressional Record,* 23 January.

Immerwahr, John, and Jean Johnson. 1994. *Second opinions: Americans' changing views on health care reform.* New York: Public Agenda Foundation.

Immerwahr, John, Jean Johnson, and Adam Kernan-Schloss. 1992. *Faulty diagnosis: Public misconceptions about health care reform.* New York: Public Agenda Foundation.

Iverson, Torben. 1994. Political leadership and representation in western european democracies: A test of three models of voting. *American Journal of Political Science.* 38 (February): 45–74.

Iyengar, Shanto. 1991. *Is anyone responsible? How television frames political issues.* Chicago: University of Chicago Press.

Iyengar, Shanto, and Donald R. Kinder. 1985. Psychological accounts of agenda-setting. In *Mass media and political thought: An information-processing approach,* edited by Sidney Kraus, and Richard M. Perloff, 117–40. Beverly Hills, Calif.: Sage.

———. 1987. *News that matters: Television and American opinion.* Chicago: University of Chicago Press.

Iyengar, Shanto, Mark D. Peters, and Donald R. Kinder. 1982. Experimental demonstrations of the "not-so-minimal" consequences of television news programs. *American Political Science Review* 76 (December): 848–58.

Jacobs, Lawrence R., Ronald H. Hinckley, and Robert Y. Shapiro. 1999. Detached democracy: Americans see lobbyists and national interest as more influential than public opinion. Unpublished manuscript.

Jacobs, Lawrence R. 1992a. The recoil effect: Public opinion and policymaking in the U.S. and Britain. *Comparative Politics* 24 (January): 199–217.

———. 1992b. Institutions and culture: Health policy and public opinion in the U.S. and Britain. *World Politics* 44 (January): 179–209.

———. 1993. *The health of nations: Public opinion and the making of health policy in the U.S. and Britain.* Ithaca: Cornell University Press.

———. 1995. Politics of America's supply state: Health reform and technology. *Health Affairs.* 14 (summer): 143–57.

Jacobs, Lawrence R., Eric Lawrence, Robert Y. Shapiro, and Steven S. Smith. 1998. Congressional leadership of public opinion. *Political Science Quarterly.* 113 (spring): 21–42.

Jacobs, Lawrence R., and Robert Y. Shapiro. 1993. Leadership in a liberal democracy: Lyndon Johnson's private polls and public statements. Presented at the 1993 Annual Meeting of the American Political Science Association.

———. 1994a. Issues, candidate image and priming: The use of private polls in Kennedy's 1960 presidential campaign. *American Political Science Review* 88 (September): 527–40.

———. 1994b. Studying substantive democracy: Public opinion, institutions, and policymaking. *PS: Political Science and Politics* 27 (March): 9–16.

———. 1994c. Questioning the conventional wisdom on public opinion toward health reform. *PS: Political Science and Politics.* 27 (June): 208–14.

———. 1994d. Public opinion's tilt against private enterprise. *Health Affairs* 12 (spring I): 285–98.

———. 1995. The rise of presidential polling: The Nixon White House in historical perspective. *Public Opinion Quarterly* 59 (summer): 163–95.

———. 1996a. Presidential manipulation of public opinion: The Nixon administration and the public pollsters. *Political Science Quarterly* 110 (winter): 519–38.

———. 1996b. The Annenberg Public Policy Center poll watch: The 1996 presidential elections. Unpublished report, 4 November.

———. 1997a. The myth of the pandering politician. *The Public Perspective* 8 (April/May): 3–5.

———. 1997b. Pollwatch: The media's reporting and distorting of public opinion toward entitlements. Unpublished report, September.

———. 1998. The politicization of public opinion: The battle for the pulpit. In *The social divide: Political parties and the future of activist government,* edited by Margaret Weir, 83–125. Washington, D.C.: Brookings.

———. 1999. Pragmatic liberalism meets philosophical conservatism: Americans' reactions to managed care. *Journal of Health Policy, Politics and Law* 24 (fall): 5–16.

Jacobs, Lawrence R., Robert Y. Shapiro, and Lynn K. Harvey. 1998. The endogeneity of self-interest and collective interest in public opinion: The case of health care reform. Unpublished paper, Department of Political Science, University of Minnesota.

Jacobs, Lawrence R., Robert Y. Shapiro, and Eli Schulman. 1993. Poll trends: Medical care in the United States—an update. *Public Opinion Quarterly* 57 (fall): 394–427.

Jacobs, Lawrence R., Mark D. Watts, and Robert Y. Shapiro. 1995. Media coverage and public views of social security. *The Public Perspective* 6 (April/May): 9–10, 48–9.

Jacobson, Gary C. 1987. *The politics of congressional elections.* 2d ed. Glenview, Ill.: Scott, Foresman and Company.

Jamieson, Kathleen H. 1988. *Eloquence in an electronic age: The transformation of political speechmaking.* Oxford: Oxford University Press.

———. 1992. *Dirty politics.* New York: Oxford University Press.

Jamieson, Kathleen, and Joseph Cappella. 1995. Media in the middle: Fairness and accuracy in the 1994 health care reform debate. A report by the Annenberg Public Policy Center of the University of Pennsylvania for the Robert Wood Foundation, February.

———. 1998. The role of the press in the health care reform debate of 1993–1994. In *Politics of news, news of politics,* edited by Doris Graber, Denis McQuail, and Pippa Norris, 110–31. Washington, D.C.: CQ Press.

Johnson, Haynes, and David Broder. 1996. *The system: The American way of politics at the breaking point.* Boston: Little, Brown.

Just, Marion R., Ann N. Crigler, Dean E. Alger, Timothy E. Cook, Montague Kern, and Darrell M. West. 1996. *Crosstalk: Citizens, candidates and the media in a presidential campaign.* Chicago: University of Chicago Press.

Just, Marion R., Ann N. Crigler, and Tami Burr. 1999. Voice, substance, and cynicism in presidential campaign media. *Political Communication* 16 (January–March): 25–44.

Kahneman, Daniel, and Amos Tversky. 1984. Choices, values, and frames. *American Psychologist* 39 (April): 341–50.

Kalt, Joseph P., and Mark A. Zupan. 1984. Capture and ideology in the economic theory of politics. *American Economic Review* 74 (June): 279–300.

Katzenstein, Peter. 1996. *The culture of national security: Norms and identity in world politics.* New York: Columbia University Press.

Kau, James B., and Paul H. Rubin. 1979. Self-interest, ideology, and logrolling in congressional voting. *Journal of Law and Economics.* 22 (October): 365–84.

———. 1993. Ideology, voting, and shirking. *Public Choice* 76 (1–2): 151–72.

Kay, Alan. 1998. *Locating consensus for democracy: A ten-year experiment.* St. Augustine, Fla.: Americans Talk Issues Foundation.

Kay, Alan, Henry Henderson, Fred Steeper, and Celinda Lake. 1994. *Interviews with the public guide us . . . on the road to consensus.* St. Augustine, Florida: America Talks Issues Foundation.

Keeter, Scott, and Michael X. Delli Carpini. 1996. *What Americans know about politics and why it matters.* New Haven: Yale University Press.

Kelly, Michael. 1994. Clinton's escape clause. *New Yorker,* 24 October, 42–53.

Kernell, Samuel. 1986. *Going public: New strategies of presidential leadership.* Washington, D.C.: CQ Press.

Key, V. O. 1961. *Public opinion and American democracy.* New York: Knopf.

Kiewiet, D. Roderick, and Matthew D. McCubbins. 1991. *The logic of delegation.* Chicago: University of Chicago Press.

King, Anthony. 1997. Running scared. *Atlantic Monthly* 279 (January): 41–61.

King, David. 1997. The polarization of American parties and mistrust of government. In *Why people don't trust government,* edited by Joseph Nye, Philip Zelikow, and David King, 155–78. Cambridge: Harvard University Press.

Kingdon, John. 1989. *Congressmen's voting decisions.* 3d ed. Ann Arbor: University of Michigan Press.

Klapper, Joseph. 1960. *The effects of mass communications.* New York: Free Press.

Koch, Jeffrey. 1998. Political rhetoric and political persuasion: The changing structure of citizens' preferences on health insurance during policy debate. *Public
Opinion Quarterly* 62 (summer): 209–29.

Koetzle, William. 1998. The impact of constituency diversity upon the competitiveness of U.S. House elections 1962–96. *Legislative Studies Quarterly* 23 (November): 561–73.

Kollman, Ken. 1998. *Outside lobbying: Public opinion and interest group strategies.*
Princeton: Princeton University Press.

Kosterlitz, Julie. 1993. Dangerous diagnosis. *National Journal,* 16 January, 127–30.

———. 1994. Health focus—No room at the inn for reform? *National Journal,* 15
January, 144.

Kramer, Robert. 1999. Weaving the public into public administration. *Public Administration Review* 59 (January/February): 89–92.

Krashinsky, Michael, and William J. Milne. 1993. The effects of incumbency in
U.S. congressional elections, 1950–1988. *Legislative Studies Quarterly* 18 (August): 321–44.

Kraus, Clifford. 1993. Clinton's health plan: reaction. *New York Times,* 23 September.

Krehbiel, Keith. 1991. *Information and legislative organization.* Ann Arbor: University of Michigan Press.

Krosnick, Jon, and Donald Kinder. 1990. Research notes: Altering the foundations for support for the president through priming. *American Political Science
Review* 84 (June): 497–512.

Krukones, Michael. 1984. *Promises and performance: Presidential campaigns as
policy predictors.* Lanham, Md.: University Press of America.

Kuklinski, James H. 1977. District competitiveness and legislative roll-call behavior: A reassessment of the marginality hypothesis. *American Journal of Political
Science* 21 (August): 627–738.

———. 1978. Representativeness and elections: A policy analysis. *American Political Science Review* 72 (March): 165–77.

Kuklinski, James H., and Richard C. Elling. 1977. Representational role, constituency opinion and legislative roll-call behavior. *American Journal of Political Science* 21 (February): 135–47.

Kuklinski, James H., and Gary M. Segura. 1995. Endogeneity, exogeneity, time,
and space in political representation. *Legislative Studies Quarterly* 20 (February): 3–21.

Kull, Steven. 1999. Expecting more say: A study of American public attitudes on
the role of the public in government decisions. Report by Center on Policy Attitudes, Washington, D.C., 9 February.

Kull, Steven, and I. M. Destler. 1999. *Misreading the public: The myth of a new
isolationism.* Washington, D.C.: Brookings Institution.

Ladd, C. Everett. 1985. *The American polity: The people and their government.* New
York: W. W. Norton.

Lasswell, Harold D. 1948. The structure and function of communication in society.
In *The communication of ideas: A series of addresses,* edited by Lyman Bryson,
37–51. New York: Institute for Religious and Social Studies.

Lawrence, Regina G. 1998. Politicians, publics, and the game of politics: How the
news covered the welfare reform debate. Presented at the 1998 Annual Meeting
of the American Political Science Association.

Lavine, Harold, John Sullivan, Eugene Borgida, and Cynthia Thomsen. 1992. Still waltzing after all these years? Revisiting the issue salience-attitude accessibility hypothesis. Unpublished manuscript.

Lazarsfeld, Paul F., Bernard R. Berelson, and Hazel Gaudet. 1944. *The people's choice.* New York: Duell, Sloan and Pierce.

Lazarsfeld, Paul F., and Robert K. Merton. 1948. Mass communication, popular taste and organized social action. In *The communication of ideas: A series of addresses,* edited by Lyman Bryson, 95–118. New York: Institute for Religious and Social Studies.

Lebow, Richard N., andThomas R. Kappen, eds. 1995. *International relations theory and the end of the cold war.* New York: Columbia University Press.

Levitt, Steven D. 1996. How do senators vote? Disentangling the role of voter preferences, party affiliation, and senator ideology. *American Economic Review* 86 (June): 425–41.

Levitt, Steven D., and Catherine D. Wolfram. 1997. Decomposing the sources of incumbency advantage in the U.S. House. *Legislative Studies Quarterly* 22 (February): 45–60.

Lewis, Anthony. 1993. Not a rose garden. *New York Times,* 1 February.

Lipset, Seymour Martin, and William Schneider 1983. *The confidence gap: Business, labor, and government in the public mind.* New York: Free Press.

Litman, Theodore J., and Leonard S. Robins, ed. 1984. *Health politics and policy.* Albany: Delmar.

Lock, Shmuel, Robert Y. Shapiro, and Lawrence R. Jacobs. 1999. The impact of political debate on government trust: Reminding the public what the federal government does. *Political Behavior* 3 (September): 239–64.

Lott, John. R. Jr., and Stephen G. Bronars. 1993. Time series evidence on shirking in the U.S. House of Representatives. *Public Choice* 76 (1–2): 125–49.

Lott, John R. Jr., and Michael L. Davids. 1992. A critical review and an extension of the political shirking literature. *Public Choice* 74 (4): 461–85.

Lowi, Theodore. 1979. *The end of liberalism.* 2d ed. New York: Norton.

———. 1985. *The personal president: Power invested, promise unfulfilled.* Ithaca, N.Y.: Cornell University Press.

Luntz, Frank. 1995. Attention! All sales reps for the Contract with America. *New York Times,* 5 February.

Madison, James. 1966. *The Federalist papers.* New York: Doubleday.

Maltzman, Forrest, and Lee Sigelman. 1996. The politics of talk: Unconstrained floor time in the U.S. House of Representatives. *Journal of Politics* 58 (August): 819–30.

Manin, Bernard. 1997. *The principles of representative government.* New York: Cambridge University Press.

Maraniss, David, and Michael Weisskopf. 1996. *Tell Newt to shut up!* New York: Touchstone.

Marcus, Ruth, and Ann Devroy. 1993. Clinton stamps "urgent priority" on health plan. *Washington Post,* 23 September.

Margolis, Howard. 1996. Dealing with risk: *Why the public and the experts disagree on environmental issues.* Chicago: University of Chicago Press.

Marmor, Theodore. 1995. A summer of discontent: Press coverage of murder and medical care reform. *Journal of Health Policy, Politics, and Law* 20 (summer): 495–501.

Martin, Cathie J. 2000. *Stuck in neutral.* Princeton: Princeton University Press.

Mass, Arthur. 1983. *Congress and the common good.* New York: Basic Books.

Mayer, William G. 1993. *The changing American mind: How and why public opinion changed between 1960 and 1988.* Ann Arbor: University of Michigan Press.

Mayhew, David R. 1974a. *Congress: The electoral connection.* New Haven: Yale University Press.

——. 1974b. Congressional elections: The case of the vanishing marginals. *Polity* 6 (spring): 295–317.

——. 1991. *Divided we govern: Party control, lawmaking, and investigations 1946–1990.* New Haven: Yale University Press.

McCarty, Nolan, Keith Poole, and Howard Rosenthal. 1997. *Income redistribution and the realignment of American politics.* Washington, D.C.: American Enterprise Institute.

McCann, James. 1996. Presidential nomination activists and political representation: A view from the active minority studies. In *In pursuit of the White House: How we choose our presidential nominees,* edited by William Mayer, 72–104. Chathams, N.J.: Chatham House.

McChesney, Fred. 1997. *Money for nothing: Politicians, rent extraction, and political extortion.* Cambridge: Harvard University Press.

McClosky, Herbert, and John Zaller. 1984. *The American ethos: Public attitudes toward capitalism and democracy.* Cambridge: Harvard University Press.

McCombs, Maxwell E., and Donald L. Shaw. 1972. The agenda-setting function of mass media. *Public Opinion Quarterly* 36 (summer): 176–87.

——. 1993. The evolution of agenda-setting research: Twenty-five years in the marketplace of ideas. *Journal of Communication* 43 (spring): 58–67.

Merida, Kevin. 1994. GOP's fierce Armey takes no prisoners. *Washington Post,* 21 February.

Merkle, Daniel M. 1996. The national issues convention deliberative poll. *Public Opinion Quarterly* 60 (winter): 588–619.

Miller, Warren E., and Donald E. Stokes. 1963. Constituency influence in Congress. *American Political Science Review.* 57 (March): 45–56.

Miroff, Bruce. 1982. Monopolizing the public space: The president as a problem for democratic politics. In *Rethinking the presidency,* edited by Thomas E. Cronin, 218–32. Boston: Little, Brown.

Mitchell, Alison. 1996a. Despite his reversals, Clinton stays centered. *New York Times,* 28 July.

——. 1996b. Clinton campaign finds harmony after exit by Morris. *New York Times,* 15 October.

——. 1997. Clinton seems to keep running through the race is run and won. *New York Times,* 12 February.

Moe, Terry. 1985. The politicized presidency. In *New Directions in American Politics,* edited by John Chubb and Paul Peterson, 235–71. Washington, D.C.: Brookings Institution.

Monroe, Alan D. 1979. Consistency between public preferences and national policy decisions. *American Politics Quarterly* 7 (January): 3–19.

——. 1998. Public opinion and public policy 1980–1993. *Public Opinion Quarterly* 62 (spring): 6–28.

Morgan, Dan. 1996. A revolution is derailed. *Washington Post National Weekly Edition,* 28 October–3 November.

Morris, Dick. 1999. *Behind the Oval Office: Getting reelected against all odds.* Los Angeles: Renaissance.

Mutz, Diana C. 1998. *Impersonal influence: How perceptions of mass collectives affect political attitudes.* New York: Cambridge University Press.

Nacos, Brigitte L., Robert Y. Shapiro, John T. Young, David P. Fan, Torsten Kjellstrand, and Craig McCaa. 1991. Content analysis of news reports: Comparing human coding and a computer-assisted method. *Communication* 12 (2): 111–28.

National Journal. 1998. Assigning the vote ratings, 7 March.

Neijens, Peter. 1987. *The choice questionaire: Design and evaluation of an instrument for collecting informed opinions of a population.* Amsterdam: Free University Press.

Neijens, Peter, Jan A. De Ridder, and Willem E. Sarris. 1992. An instrument for collecting informed opinions. *Quality and Quantity* 26 (August): 245–58.

Nelson, Douglas, and Eugene Silberberg. 1987. Ideology and legislator shirking. *Economic Inquiry* 25 (January): 15–26.

Nelson, Thomas, Rosalie Clawson, and Zoe Oxley. 1997. Media framing of a civil liberties conflict and its effect on tolerance. *American Political Science Review* 91 (September): 567–83.

Neuman, W. Russell, Marion K. Just, and Ann N. Crigler. 1992. *Common knowledge: News and the construction of political meaning.* Chicago: University of Chicago Press.

Neustadt, Richard E. 1980. *Presidential power: The politics of leadership from FDR to Carter.* New York: Wiley.

Nitschke, Lori. 1998. Political trends come together to diminish coalition's clout. *Congressional Quarterly Weekly Report,* 3 January, 21.

Novak, Robert. 1994. GOP losing the health war. *Washington Post,* 24 March.

Nye, Joseph, Philip Zelikow, and David King, eds. 1997. *Why people don't trust government.* Cambridge: Harvard University Press.

Offe, Claus. 1992. Bindings, shackles, brakes: On self-limitation strategies. In *Cultural-political interventions in the unfinished project of enlightment,* edited by Axel Honneth, Thomas McCathery, Claus Offe, and Albrecht Wellmer, 95–120. Cambridge: MIT Press.

Oxford English dictionary. 2d ed. 1989. Oxford: Clarendon.

Oxley, Zoe M. 1998. Who led whom? The interaction of citizens, elites, and the media during the health care reform debate. Presented at the 1998 Annual Meeting of the Midwest Political Science Association.

Page, Benjamin I. 1978. *Choices and echoes in presidential elections: Rational man in electoral democracy.* Chicago: University of Chicago Press.

———. 1994. Democratic responsiveness? Untangling the links between public opinion and policy. *PS: Political Science and Politics* 27 (March) 25–28.

———. 1995. Who gets what from government. Paper prepared for the 1995 Richard S. and Nancy K. Hartigan Lecture on Politics and Government, Loyola University, Chicago.

———. 1996. *Who deliberates? Mass media in modern democracy.* Chicago: University of Chicago Press.

Page, Benjamin I., and Robert Y. Shapiro. 1983. Effects of public opinion on policy. *American Political Science Review* 77 (March): 175–90.

———. 1992. *The rational public.* Chicago: University of Chicago Press.

———. 1999. The rational public and beyond. In *Citizen competence and demo-*

cratic institutions, edited by Stephen L. Elkin and Carol E. Soltan, 93–113. University Park: Pennsylvania State University Press.

Page, Benjamin I., Robert Y. Shapiro, and Glenn R. Dempsey. 1987. What moves public opinion? *American Political Science Review* 81 (March): 23–43.

Page, Benjamin I., Robert Y. Shapiro, Paul W. Gronke, and Robert M. Rosenberg. 1984. Constituency, party, and representation in Congress. *Public Opinion Quarterly.* 48 (winter): 741–56.

Patterson, Thomas E. 1993. Trust politicians, not the press. *New York Times,* 15 December.

———. 1994. *Out of order.* New York: Knopf.

———. 1998. Political roles of the journalist. In *Politics of news, the news of politics,* edited by Doris Graber, Denis McQuail, and Pippa Norris, 17–32. Washington, D.C.: CQ Press.

Pear, Robert. 1996. Clinton to sign welfare bill that ends U.S. aid guarantee and gives states broad power. *New York Times,* 1 August.

Penny, Tim. 1994. Observations and reflections on leadership. *Extensions: A journal of the Carl Albert Congressional Research and Studies Center* (spring): 7–9.

Perry, James. 1994. Clinton relies heavily on White House pollster to take words right out of the public's mouth. *Wall Street Journal,* 24 March.

Peterson, Mark. A. 1990. *Legislating together: The White House and Capitol Hill from Eisenhower to Reagan.* Cambridge: Harvard University Press.

———. 1993. Political influence in the 1990s: From iron triangles to policy networks. *Journal of Health Politics, Policy and Law* 18 (summer): 395–438.

———. 1997. The limits of social learning: Translating analysis into action. *Journal of Health Policy, Politics and Law* 22 (August): 1077–1114.

Pew Research Center for the People and the Press. 1998. Public appetite for government misjudged: Washington leaders wary of public opinion. 17 April.

Pfetsch, Barbara. 1998. Government news management. In *Politics of news, the news of politics,* edited by Doris Graber, Denis McQuail, and Pippa Norris, 70–93. Washington, D.C.: CQ Press.

Pitkin, Hanna. 1967. *The concept of representation.* Berkeley, Calif.: University of California Press.

Polsby, Nelson W. 1980. *Consequences of party reform.* New York: Oxford University Press.

Polsby, Nelson W., and Aaron Wildavsky. 1996. *Presidential elections: Strategies and structures of American politics.* 9th ed. Chatham, N.J.: Chatman House.

Pomper, Gerald M., with Susan Lederman. 1976. *Elections in America.* New York: Dodd, Mead.

Poole, Keith T., and Thomas Romer. 1993. Ideology, "shirking," and representation. *Public Choice* 77 (1): 185–96.

Poole, Keith T., and Howard Rosenthal. 1984. The polarization of American politics. *Journal of Politics* 46 (November): 1061–79.

———. 1991. Patterns of congressional voting. *American Journal of Political Science* 35 (February): 228–78.

———. 1997. *Congress: A political-economic history of roll call voting.* New York: Oxford University Press.

Popkin, Samuel L. 1991. *The reasoning voter: Communication and persuasion in presidential campaigns.* Chicago: University of Chicago Press.

Poster, Mark. 1989. *Critical theory and poststructuralism: In search of a context.* Ithaca: Cornell University Press.

Price, Vincent, and Peter Neijens. 1998. Deliberative polls: Toward improved measures of "informed" public opinion? *International Journal of Public Opinion Research* 10 (2): 145–76.

Priest, Dana. 1993. Health care. *Washington Post,* 16 September.

Priest, Dana, and Dan Balz. 1994. Still seeking an alternative, GOP launches ads against Clinton health plan. *Washington Post,* 21 May.

Public Perspective. 1995. People, opinions and polls. *Public Perspective* 6 (February/March): 28–32.

———. 1996. The "deliberative opinion poll" comes to Texas—and to campaign '96—a Roper Center symposium. *Public Perspective* 7 (December/January): 1–20.

———. 1996b. Civic participation and American democracy. *Public Perspective* 7 (June/July): 1–55.

Purdum, Todd. 1996. Clinton recalls his promise, considers history, and signs. *New York Times,* 1 August.

Putnam, Robert D. 1995. Tuning in, tuning out: The strange disappearance of social capital in America. *PS: Political Science and Politics.* 28 (December): 664–83.

Quatrone, George A., and Amos Tversky. 1988. Contrasting rational and psychological analyses of political choice. *American Political Science Review* 82 (September): 719–36.

Quirk, Paul J., andJoseph Hinchliffe. 1998. The rising hegemony of mass opinion. *Journal of Policy History* 10(1): 19–50.

Quirk, Paul J., and Bruce Nemith. 1995. Divided government and policymaking: Negotiating the laws. In *The presidency and the political system,* 4th ed., edited by Michael Nelson, 531–54. Washington, D.C.: CQ Press.

Ragsdale, Lyn, and John Theis. 1997. The institutionalization of the American presidency 1924–92. *American Journal of Politics.* 41 (October): 1280–1319.

Rasmussen, Eric. 1989. *Games and information.* New York: Basil Blackwell.

Reese, Stephen, August Grant, and Lucig Danielian. 1994. The structure of news sources on television: A network analysis of "CBS News," "Nightline," "MacNeil/Leher," and "This Week with David Brinkley." *Journal of Communication* 44 (spring): 84–107.

Reich, Robert B. 1991. *The work of nations: Preparing ourselves for 21st century capitalism.* New York: A. A. Knopf.

Rich, Spencer. 1993. Who stands where on health care. *Washington Post,* 23 September.

Riker, William H. 1962. *The theory of political coalitions.* New Haven: Yale University Press.

Robbins, Bruce. 1993. *The phantom public sphere.* Minneapolis: University of Minnesota Press.

Rockman, Bert. 1984. *The leadership question: The presidency and the American system.* New York: Praeger.

Rogers, Everett M., and James W. Dearing. 1988. Agenda-setting research: Where has it been, where is it going? In *Communication yearbook 11,* edited by James A. Anderson, 555–94. Newbury Park, Calif.: Sage.

Rogers, Everett M., James W. Dearing, and Dorine Bregman. 1993. The anatomy of agenda-setting research. *Journal of Communication* 43 (spring): 68–84.

Rogers, Everett M., William B. Hart, and James W. Dearing. 1997. A paradigmatic history of agenda-setting research. In *Do the Media Govern?* edited by Shanto Iyengar and Richard Reeves. Thousand Oaks, Calif.: Sage.

Rohde, David. 1991. *Parties and leaders in the post-reform house.* Chicago: University of Chicago Press.

Rosen, Jay. 1994. Making things more public: On the political responsibility of the media intellectual. *Critical Studies in Mass Communication* 11 (December): 362–88.

Rosenbaum, David. 1998. Laws rule in inquiry, not polls, G.O.P. says. *New York Times,* 27 September.

Rosenstone, Steven J., and John M. Hansen. 1993. *Mobilization, participation, and democracy in America.* New York: Macmillan.

Rosenstone, Steven J., John M. Hansen, and Donald R. Kinder. 1986. Measuring change in personal economic well-being. *Public Opinion Quarterly* 50 (summer): 176–92.

Rubin, Alissa J. 1993. Clinton talk force all ears on the subject of overhaul. *Congressional Quarterly Weekly Report.* 22 May, 1293.

Rubin, Alissa J., and Cecil Connolly. 1993. Clinton deslivers health bill, all 1,342 pages of it. *Congressional Quarterly Weekly Report.* 30 October, 2968.

Safire, William. 1996. President vs. press. *New York Times,* 2 December.

Salisbury, Robert H. 1990. The paradox of interest groups in Washington—more groups, less clout. In *The new American political system,* 2d ed., edited by Anthony King, 203–29. Washington, D.C.: American Enterprise Institute.

Samuelson, Robert J. 1995. *The good life and its discontents: The American dream in the age of entitlement 1945–1995.* New York: Times Books.

Sartori, Giovanni. 1987. *The theory of democracy revisited: Part 1, the contemporary debate.* Chatham, N.J.: Chatham House.

Schattschneider, E. E. 1960a. *Party government.* New York: Holt, Reinhart and Winston.

———. 1960b. *The semi-sovereign people: A realist view of democracy in America.* New York: Reinhart and Winston.

Schlesinger, Arthur M. 1949. *The vital center: The politics of freedom.* Boston: Houghton Mifflin.

Schneider, William. 1995. Ka-Boom! It's another contract! *National Journal,* 22 April, 1010.

Schumpeter, Joseph A. 1950. *Capitalism, socialism, and democracy.* New York: Harper.

Sears, David, Richard Lau, Tom Tyler, and Harris Allen. 1980. Self-interest vs. symbolic politics in policy attitudes and presidential voting. *American Political Science Review* 74 (September): 670–84.

Sears, David, and Carolyn Funk. 1990. Self-interest in Americans' political opinions. In *Beyond self-interest,* edited by Jane Mansbridge. Chicago: University of Chicago Press.

Shapiro, Catherine R., David W. Brady, Richard A. Brody, and John A. Ferejohn. 1990. Linking constituency opinion and Senate voting scores: A hybrid explanation. *Legislative Studies Quarterly* 15 (November): 599–621.

Shapiro, Robert Y. 1982. *The dynamics of public opinion and public policy.* Ph.D. dissertation. University of Chicago.

———. 1998. Public opinion, elites, and democracy. *Critical Review* 12 (fall): 501–28.

Shapiro, Robert Y., and Lawrence R. Jacobs. 1988. The relationship between public opinion and public policy: A review. In *Political behavior annual vol. 2,* edited by Samuel Long, 149–79. Boulder, Colo.: Westview.

Shapiro, Robert Y., Lawrence R. Jacobs, and Lynn Harvey. 1994. Influences on public opinion toward health care policy: Self-interest and collective concern. Unpublished paper.

Shapiro, Robert Y., and John T. Young. 1986. The polls: Medical care in the United States. *Public Opinion Quarterly* 50 (fall): 418–28.

Shaw, Carolyn. 1998. President Clinton's first term: Matching campaign promises with presidential performance. *Congress and the Presidency* 25 (spring): 43–65.

Shaw, Greg, Robert Y. Shapiro, and Lawrence R. Jacobs. 1996. Searching presidential documents online: Advantages and limitations. *PS: Political Science and Politics* 29 (September): 501–4.

Shilts, Randy. 1987. *And the band played on.* New York: St. Martin's.

Sinclair, Barbara. 1982. *Congressional realignment 1925–1978.* Austin: University of Texas Press.

———. 1995. *Legislators, leaders, and lawmaking: The U.S. House of Representatives in the post-reform era.* Baltimore: Johns Hopkins Press.

Skocpol, Theda. 1992. *Protecting soldiers and mothers: The political origins of social policy in the United States.* Cambridge: Harvard University Press.

———. 1996. *Boomerang: Clinton's health security effort and the turn against government in U.S. politics.* New York: W. W. Norton.

Skowronek, Stephen. 1993. *The politics presidents make: Leadership from John Adams to George Bush.* Cambridge: Harvard University Press, Belknap Press.

Smith, Steven S., and Christopher J. Deering. 1990. *Committees in Congress.* Washington, D.C.: CQ Press.

Smith, Tom W. 1980. America's most important problem—a trend analysis 1946–1976. *Public Opinion Quarterly* 44 (summer): 164–80.

———. 1985a. The polls: America's most important problems, part 1: National and International. *Public Opinion Quarterly* 49 (summer): 264–74.

———. 1985b. The polls: America's most important problems, part 2: Regional, community, and personal. *Public Opinion Quarterly* 49 (fall): 403–10.

———. 1987. That which we call welfare by any other name would smell sweeter: An analysis of the impact of question wording on response patterns. *Public Opinion Quarterly* 51 (spring): 75–83.

Sobel, Richard. 1998. Portraying American public opinion toward the Bosnia crisis. *The Harvard International Journal of Press and Politics* 3 (spring): 16–33.

Solomon, Burt. 1995. Clinton—he's a Bush, not a Truman. *National Journal,* 14 October, 2551.

Sorauf, Frank. 1988. *Money in American elections.* Glenview, Ill.: Scott, Foresman.

Stanley, Harold W., and Richard G. Niemi. 1995. The demise of the New Deal coalition: Partisanship and group support 1952–92. In *Democracy's feast: Elections in America,* edited by Herbert Weisberg, 220–40. Chatham, N.J.: Chatham House.

Starr, Paul. 1994. *The logic of health care reform: Why and how the president's plan will work.* New York: Whittle.

———. 1995. What happened to health care reform? *American Prospect* 20 (winter): 20–31.

Statistical Abstract of the United States. Annual. Washington, D.C.: U.S. Government Printing Office.

Steele, Catherine, and Kevin Barnhurst. 1996. The journalism of opinion: Network news coverage of U.S. presidential campaigns, 1968–1988. *Critical Studies in Mass Communications* 13 (September): 187–209.

Steele, Janet E. 1990. Sound bite seeks expert. *Washington Journalism Review* 12 (September): 28–29.

Stein, Robert M., and Kenneth N. Bickers. 1995. *Perpetuating the pork barrel: Policy subsystems and American democracy.* Cambridge: Cambridge University Press.

Stengel, Richard, and Eric Pooley. 1996. The masters of the message: Inside the high-tech machine that set Clinton and Dole apart. *Time,* 18 November, 76–96.

Stimson, James A. 1991. *Public opinion in America: Moods, cycles, and swings.* Boulder, Colo.: Westview.

Stimson, James A., Michael B. MacKuen, and Robert S. Erikson. 1994. Opinion and policy: A global view. *PS: Political Science and Politics* 27 (March): 29–35.

———. 1995. Dynamic representation. *American Political Science Review* 89 (September): 543–65.

Stoker, Laura. 1994. A reconsideration of self-interest in American politics. Paper presented at the annual meeting of the Western Political Science Association, Albuquerque, N. M., 10–12 March.

Stolberg, Sheryl. 1993. "One-size-fits-all" plan chafes the GOP. *Los Angeles Times,* 23 September.

Stone, Walter J. 1982. Electoral change and policy representation in Congress: Domestic welfare issues, 1956–72. *British Journal of Political Science* 12 (January): 95–115.

Stout, Hilary. 1994. Many don't realize it's Clinton plan they like. *Wall Street Journal,* 10 March.

Sullivan, John, and Eric Uslaner. 1978. Congressional behavior and electoral marginality. *American Journal of Political Science* 22 (August): 536–53.

Thomas, John. 1999. Bringing the public into public administration: The struggle continues. *Public Administration Review* 59 (January/February): 83–88.

Thorpe, Kenneth. 1997. The rising number of uninsured workers. Unpublished paper prepared for the National Coalition on Health Care, October.

Times Mirror Center for the People and the Press, the Henry Kaiser Foundation, and the Columbia Journalism Review. 1995. Media coverage of the healthcare reform: A final report. *Columbia Journalism Review* (supplement to March/April Issue): 1–8.

Toner, Robin. 1993. Clinton's health plan: News analysis. *New York Times,* 23 September.

Truman, David. 1951. *The governmental process.* New York: Knopf.

Tuchman, Gaye. 1972. Objectivity as strategic ritual: An examination of newsmen's notion of objectivity. *Americal Journal of Sociology* 77 (January): 660–79.

Tufte, Edward R. 1975. Determinants of the outcomes of midterm congressional elections. *American Political Science Review* 69 (September): 812–26.

———. 1978. *Political control of the economy.* Princeton: Princeton University Press.

Tulis, Jeffrey. 1987. *The rhetorical presidency.* Princeton: Princeton University Press.

Underwood, Doug. 1993. *When MBAs rule the newsroom.* New York: Columbia University Press.

———. 1998. Market research and the audience for political news. In *Politics of news, the news of politics,* edited by Doris Graber, Denis McQuail, and Pippa Norris, 171–92. Washington, D.C.: CQ Press.

Verba, Sidney. 1996. The citizen as respondent: Sample surveys and American democracy. *American Political Science Review* 90 (March): 1–7.

Verba, Sidney, Kay Schlozman, and Henry Brady. 1995. *Voice and equality: Civic volunteerism in American politics.* Cambridge: Harvard University Press.

Wahlke, John C., Heinx Eulau, William Buchanan, and Leroy C. Ferguson. 1962. *The legislative system.* New York: Wiley.

Wainess, Flint J. 1999. The ways and means of national health care reform 1974 and beyond. *Journal of Health Politics, Policy and Law* 24 (April): 305–33.

Walker, Jack. 1991. *Mobilizing interest groups in America: Patrons, professions, and social movements.* Ann Arbor: University of Michigan Press.

Warren, Mark. 1996. Deliberative democracy and authority. *American Political Science Review.* 90 (March): 46–60.

Wayne, Stephen. 1997. *The road to the White House 1996.* New York: St. Martin's.

Weaver, R. Kent. 2000, forthcoming. *Ending welfare as we know it: Context and choice in policy toward low-income families.* Washington, D.C.: Brookings Institution.

Weaver, R. Kent, Robert Y. Shapiro, and Lawrence R. Jacobs. 1995a. The polls trends: Welfare. *Public Opinion Quarterly* 59 (winter): 606–27.

———. 1995b. Public opinion on welfare reform: A mandate for what? In *Looking before we leap: Social science and welfare reform,* edited by R. Kent Weaver and William T. Dickens, 109–28. Washington, D.C.: Brookings Institution.

Weber, Max. 1968. *Economy and society.* 3 vols. New York: Bedminster.

Weisberg, Herbert, Audrey Haynes, and Jon Krosnick. 1995. Social group polarization in 1992. *Democracy's feast: Elections in America,* edited by Herbert Weisberg, 241–59. Chatham, N.J.: Chatham House.

Weissberg, Robert. 1978. Collective vs. dynamic representation in Congress. *American Political Science Review* 72 (June): 535–47.

Weissert, Carol, and William Weissert. 1996. *Governing health: The politics of health policy.* Baltimore: Johns Hopkins University Press.

Weisskopf, Michael. 1994. Turning pique into power: Consultant molds voter anger to help GOP. *Washington Post,* 27 October.

Weisskopf, Michael, and David Maraniss. 1995. Republican leaders win battle by defining terms of combat. *Washington Post,* 29 October.

———. 1996. Behind the stage: Common problems. *Washington Post National Weekly Edition,* 5–11 February.

Weldes, Jutta. 1999. *Constructing the national interest: The United States and the Cuban missile crisis.* Minneapolis: University of Minnesota Press.

West, Darrell M., Diane Heith, and Chris Goodwin. 1996. Harry and Louise go to Washington: Political advertising and health care reform. *Journal of Health Politics, Policy and Law* 21 (spring): 35–68.

West, Darrell M., and Burdett A. Loomis. 1999. *The sound of money: How political interests get what they want.* New York: W. W. Norton.

Wilson, James Q. 1995. New politics, new elites, old publics. In *The new politics of public policy,* edited by Marc Landy and Martin Levin, 249–67. Baltimore: Johns Hopkins University Press.

Wilson, Woodrow. 1952. *Leaders of men,* edited by T. H. Vail Motter. Princeton: Princeton University Press.

Wittman, Donald. 1983. Candidate motivation: A synthesis of alternatives. *American Political Science Review* 77 (March): 142–57.

———. 1990. Spatial strategies when candidates have policy preferences. In *Advances in the spatial theory of voting,* edited by James M. Enelow and Melvin J. Hinich, 66–98. Cambridge: Cambridge University Press.

Wlezien, Christopher. 1995. The public as thermostat: Dynamics of preferences for spending. *American Journal of Political Science* 39 (November): 981–1000.

Wood, B. Dan, and Angela H. Andersson. 1998. The dynamics of senatorial representation 1952–1991. *Journal of Politics* 60 (August): 705–36.

Wood, Gordon. 1969. *The creation of the American republic.* Chapel Hill: University of North Carolina Press.

Woodward, Bob. 1994. *The agenda: Inside the Clinton White House.* New York: Simon & Shuster.

Wright, Matthew. B. 1993. Shirking and political support in the U.S. Senate. *Public Choice* 76 (1–2): 103–23.

Wright, Gerald C. 1989. Policy voting in the U.S. Senate: Who is represented? *Legislative Studies Quarterly* 14 (November): 465–86.

———. 1994. The meaning of "party" in congressional roll call voting. Paper delivered at the Annual Meeting of the Midwest Political Science Association, Chicago, 14–16 April.

Zaller, John R. 1992. *The nature and origins of mass opinion.* New York: Cambridge University Press.

———. 1998a. Coming to grips with V. O. Key's concept of latent opinion. Presented at symposium in honor of Philip Converse, Boston, 2 September.

———. 1998b. The rule of product substitution in presidential campaign news. *The Annals of the American Academy of Political and Social Science* 560 (November): 111–28.

———. 1999. Monica Lewinsky's contribution to political science. *PS: Political Science and Politics* 31 (June): 182–89.

Zaller, John R., and Dennis Chiu. 1996. Government's little helper: U.S. press coverage of foreign policy crises 1945–91. *Political Communication* 13:385–405.

Zinni, Frank P. Jr., and Robin Stanton. 1994. Thinking about the distribution of health care. Paper presented at the annual meeting of the American Political Science Association, New York, 1–4 September.

Index

priming approach: advantages of, 50–51;
changes in public opinion and, 222;
Clinton White House and, 106; impact
of, 290–91; overview of, xiv, 49–52; Republican Party and, 271–74; use of term,
369n. 68
print news outlets. *See* media; media coverage
proximity of elections, 42–44
public, perceptions of, 50, 62, 102, 295,
300–301
Public Agenda Foundation, 220, 336
public communications: deliberationists
and, 306–8; description of, 297; reform
of, 331–38
public opinion: ambivalence toward government, 222, 225–27, 230; anticipated future, 14, 69–70; assumptions of pandering to, 3–4; on Clinton health care plan,
228–29; on Clinton's behavior and impeachment, xi–xiii, 11, 316, 335–36;
Clinton White House and, 94–102, 112;
collective compared to self-interest in,
235–37, 240–42, 245, 247, 248, 250, 252–
53, 259–60; concept of, xix; economic
cycles and, 254–55, 314–15; explanations
for changes in, 219–23; formation of,
307; governing by, 126, 268; government
role in health care 1975–94, *226;* impact
of framing on, 232–35; individual and
group differences in, 244–49; media
coverage and, 65–66, 229–32, 335–37; media monitoring of, 334–35; multivariate
regression analysis of, 249–53; national
interest argument and, 305–6; as news
source, 208; perception of problem,
changes in, 223–24, 232; perceptions of
health care system, *224,* 232; personal
impact of reform and, 242–44; personal
satisfaction and, 237–40; policies that
failed to mirror, xii; policy decisions
and, xv–xvi; political cycle of, 61–64; as
political resource, 103; politicians' response to, xiv–xv; politicization of, 103–
5; politics, the media, and, *64;* quality
of, 298–99, 307–8, 325; spending on
health care, 227–28; stability of over time,
62–63; tax-financed national health insurance, *99;* thermostat hypothesis and,
256–58
public opinion polls. *See* polls
public sphere, 308–9

punishing politicians, xvii, 326–27
Putting People First, 80

racial policy and polarization of politics,
31–32
rapid response system, 131
Reagan, Ronald: anticipated future public
opinion and, 14; crusade to reduce taxes
and spending, 19–20, 167, 182; election
of, 256; health care and, 165, 205, 206;
media coverage of, 199; Medicare and,
168–69, 183, 190, 193; as minority president, 42
Reeves, Christopher, 285
reform issues in health care: description of,
353; framing of, 180–82, 185–86; issue
negativity in media and, 192–94; media
coverage of, 163–64
reform issues in politics: debate regarding
responsiveness, 337–38; democratic processes, 333–37; political parties, 330–31;
public communication of private citizens,
331–33
regulation and New Democratic creed, 81,
84
Reich, Robert, 282–83
reliability of content coding, 355–57
representation: Burke on, 299, 300; policy-
specific approach to study of, 341–44
reproductive issues, 162–63, 169, 170
Republican National Committee (RNC),
273, 274
Republican Party: balanced budget and,
274–75, 276, 288–89; bipartisanship on
health care reform and, 143; Contract
with America, 265, 273, 292; crafted talk
and, 271–74, 293–94, 328–29; criticism of
by Clinton, 286–87; deceptive practices
of, 321–23; declining responsiveness of,
5; elections of November 1994, 263–64;
environmental protection and, 266–67,
292; erosion in confidence in, 289–90;
impeachment of Clinton and, xi–xiii, 11,
335–36; Medicare and, 259, 275–77, 289;
muted responsiveness and, 15; as news
source, 200–201; as opponents of health
care reform, 126–27, 130–33, 138, 142–44;
policy goals of, xiii, 265–69; polls and,
129–30, 267, 272–73; potential to break
ranks over health care reform, 132–33;
presidential-type calculations of, 270–71;
pursuit of centrist opinion by, 291–93;